Carpentry and Joinery
for Advanced Craft Students:
Site Practice

by the same author

Carpentry and Joinery for Building Craft Students 1
Carpentry and Joinery for Building Craft Students 2
Carpentry and Joinery for Advanced Craft Students:
    Purpose-made Joinery
Mutiple Choice Questions in Carpentry and Joinery
    for Building Craft Students
Industrial Studies: a workbook for building craft
    students
Site Carpentry and Joinery NVQ2

Carpentry and Joinery for Advanced Craft Students: Site Practice

Peter Brett

Brooklyn College, Birmingham

Stanley Thornes (Publishers) Ltd

First published in 1985 by:
Hutchinson Education

Reprinted in 1989 by:
Stanley Thornes (Publishers) Ltd
Delta Place
27 Bath Road
CHELTENHAM
GL53 7TH
United Kingdom

04 05 06 / 15 14 13 12

A catalogue record for this book is available from the British Library

ISBN 0 7487 0270 9

Printed in Great Britain by Ashford Colour Press

Contents

Seasoning of timber – Protection of seasoned timber and joinery components – Decay of timber – Preservation of timber – Adhesives – Mechanics – Glue-laminated timber – Mechanical fasteners for structural work – Self-assessment questions

Preface

This book is designed to cover the City and Guilds of London Institute Carpentry and Joinery 585 Advanced Craft Certificate course. The course is aimed at students who, having obtained their craft certificate, wish to develop their knowledge and understanding of craft processes, technology and associated subjects, and the interrelationship of their craft activities with the industry as a whole. This will enable them to become fully skilled in their craft and also to form a foundation for further study and possible career progression.

At the advanced craft stage students are required to specialize in a particular aspect of their craft. The two specialist options that are available for study in most colleges are:

Site practice
Purpose-made joinery.

In addition there are core topics which are common to all carpentry and joinery advanced craft students irrespective of the chosen option. These core topics consist of a study of general carpentry and joinery processes. Each course is divided into ten equal units which are allocated to the following sections:

Core topics	3 units
Specialist option	3 units
Practical activities	4 units.

The core topics and one specialist option are covered in this book. In addition, a brief revision of certain craft-level topics and associated studies have been included where required as an aid to a fuller understanding of the subjects.

Each of the following chapters begins with a list of learning objectives and ends with a series of short-answer self-assessment questions, the answers to which are contained within the text. This will enable students to evaluate their understanding of the relevant chapter and to check their progress through the course. The last section of the book deals with examination and study techniques.

The City and Guilds of London Institute examination at advanced craft level consists of a college assessment of practical work and two written papers, one covering the specialist option and the other the core topics. Examples of each examination paper have been included in the examination and study techniques section.

Acknowledgements

The author wishes to thank the following for supplying technical information and photographs for inclusion in this book:

Agrément Board
American Plywood Association
Brick Development Association
British Industrial Fastenings Ltd
British Standards Institution
British Woodworking Federation
Building Centre
Building Research Establishment
Cement and Concrete Association
Chipboard Promotion Association
Copper Development Association
Council of the Forest Industries of British
   Columbia
Cuprinol
Elu Machinery Ltd
Erskine Systems Ltd
Fibre Building Board Development Organiz-
   ation
Finnish Plywood International
Fosroc Ltd Timber Treatments Division
Lawtons Ltd
Lead Development Association
Norton Construction Products
Protimeter plc
Sachs Dolmar (UK) Ltd
Swedish and Finnish Timber Council
Timber Research and Development Association
Wadkin plc

The forms shown in Figures 6, 7, 8, 9, 10, 11, 12 are reproduced with permission of The Controller of Her Majesty's Stationery Office who reserve Crown Copyright.

Specimen examination papers are reproduced with the kind permission of the City and Guilds of London Institute. Any worked examples or typical answers given in this book are the author's own and cannot be attributed to the Institute.

My sincere thanks go to my colleagues for their assistance and encouragement, in particular Derek Crafts.

Finally I would like to dedicate this book to my wife Christine and two children James and Sarah, without whose help, patience and encouragement, little would have been achieved.

chapter 1

Sources of technical information

After reading this chapter the student should be able to:

1 Define the need for up-to-date technical information.
2 Identify the most appropriate source or sources of information relevant to a given task.
3 Define the main function of given organizations.
4 Define the main purpose of given documents.

It is not possible to absorb and remember all the information required for a particular job; even if it were, it is essential that this information is regularly updated to take account of changes in legislation and technology.

Throughout your working life from apprentice-student to various levels in industry, you will have to make decisions and solve problems. To do this effectively, various sources of information will have to be consulted. Specialist information may be obtained from the following sources as well as from textbooks. Copies of the publications produced by the various information sources listed are normally available for student reference in most college libraries.

1 Building Regulations
2 British Standards Institution
   British Standard Specifications and Codes of Practice
3 Building Research Establishment
   BRE Digests, information papers and current papers
4 Research, manufacturers and trade development associations:

   Agrément Board
   American Plywood Association
   Brick Development Association
   British Woodworking Federation
   Building Centre
   Cement and Concrete Association
   Chipboard Promotion Association
   Copper Development Association
   Council of the Forest Industries of British Columbia
   Fibre Building Board Development Organization
   Finnish Plywood International
   Forestry Commission
   Lead Development Association
   Swedish and Finnish Timber Council
   Timber Research and Development Association
   etc.

Building regulations

The system of Building Regulations as we know them today stems from the Industrial Revolution. Development at this time was taking place rapidly, although as it was largely unplanned and uncontrolled by local authorities, it resulted in appalling housing conditions.

The Public Health Act of 1875 allowed local authorities to make local by-laws to control the planning and construction of buildings. As these were local there were many anomalies, what might be permitted in one authority could be prohibited in another. Therefore the Minister of Housing and Local Government was given under the 1961 Public Health Act powers to prepare a national system of building regulations. The Building Regulations 1965 replaced the local by-laws and were applicable to work in England and Wales, with the exception of work in Inner London which was controlled by the London Building Acts 1930 to 1978.

In 1984 a new building act was approved by Parliament. The Building Regulations 1985 which were made under this act apply to all building work carried out in England and Wales, including inner London. (Similar controls and regulations exist for building work in Scotland and Northern Ireland.)

The main purpose of the regulations is to provide safe and healthy buildings/accommodation for the public and to conserve energy. They do this by laying down minimum acceptable standards of building work and materials.

Copies of the Building Regulations 1985 and their supporting approved documents can be obtained from Her Majesty's Stationery Office (HMSO), Publications Centre, PO Box 276, London SW8 5DT.

British Standards Institution (BSI)

The BSI was granted a Royal Charter in 1929, its main purpose being to produce voluntary standards in consultation with all interested parties and to promote their use. The scope of these standards include:

Glossary of terms
Definitions and symbols
Methods of testing
Methods of assembly or construction
Specifications for quality, safety, performance or dimensions

The BSI publishes over 7000 publications of which around 1500 are related to the construction industry. The majority of these publications take the form of a British Standard Specification (BS) or a Code of Practice (CP)

Basically, British Standard Specifications deal with materials and components and Codes of Practice cover the design and workmanship of a whole process. Other publications include Drafts for Development (DD), Published Documents (PD) and Promotional Publications (PP).

A kitemark approval scheme is operated by the BSI. The presence of a BSI kitemark indicates that the BSI is satisfied that the product has been made in accordance with the relevant British Standard Specification.

Up-to-date details of BSI publications can be obtained from their year-book or sectional lists, which are available for reference in many libraries, or from: British Standards Institution, 2 Park Street, London W1A 2BS.

Building Research Establishment (BRE)

Founded in 1921 to carry out research and development for the government and construction industry. The BRE is a group of four laboratories within the Department of Environment. These four laboratories are:

The Building Research Station, Hertfordshire
The Fire Research Station, Hertfordshire
The Princes Risborough Laboratory (timber and wood-based materials). Buckinghamshire
The Scottish Laboratory (research relevant to Scotland), Glasgow

Note: The Scottish laboratory is concerned with research relevant to Scotland. This is because different solutions to problems are often required to cope with the effect on building materials of the climate.

The main activities of the BRE include:

Research into current practical problems facing the construction industry, covering environmental design, structural design, materials, production and development
Advice with the preparation of BS, CP, and Building Regulations
Investigation of new building products
Answering technical enquiries

The BRE present the results of their research in various forms:
BRE News
BRE Digests
Current papers
Information papers
Films and educational packages

Details of current publications, films and services, many of which are free of charge, are contained in an information directory which is published annually by the BRE and can be obtained from the following address: Distribution Unit, Building Research Establishment, Bucknalls Lane, Garston, Watford, Hertfordshire WD2 7JR.

Research, manufacturers and trade development associations

The objectives of these associations will be individual to each organization, but in general they will include:

Research and development of materials and construction techniques
Prevention of waste
Safety
Source of technical information
Technical advisory service
Means of communication between members, industry and the general public

Note: Details of free and priced publications can be obtained from the relevant association.

Agrément Board
Founded in 1966, the Agrément Board is sponsored by the Department of Environment. It is principally concerned with the testing, assessment and certification of normally new or innovatory products for the construction industry. An Agrément Certificate gives an independent opinion of the performance in use of a product, component, material or system, when used and installed in the specified manner. This facilitates their acceptance by architects, specifiers, local authorities, building contractors and consumers. Information can be obtained from: The Agrément Board, PO Box 195, Bucknalls Lane, Garston, Watford, Hertfordshire WD2 7NG.

American Plywood Association (APA)
The American Plywood Association is a nonprofit trade association that represents the softwood plywood manufacturers of America. The Association carries out research and development, offers technical advice and publishes product guides and brochures. Information can be obtained from: American Plywood Association, Index House, Ascot, Berkshire SL5 7EU.

Brick Development Association (BDA)
A trade association formed in 1945 to promote all aspects of the brick industry, including research and development, manufacture, sale and use. All areas of bricks and brickwork are catered for in the wide range of technical publications produced by the BDA. Its address is: Brick Development Association, Woodside House, Winkfield, Windsor, Berkshire SL4 2DP.

British Woodworking Federation (BWF)
A trade association formed by the amalgamation of two associations in 1976. Through its six specialist sections, which are:

Architectural and general joinery
Kitchen furniture
Doors and doorsets
Timber frame construction
Laminated structures and timber engineering
Windows

It represents and promotes the interests of manufacturers of timber components for the building industry. The British Woodworking Federation produce on their members' behalf a wide range of technical and promotional literature which can be obtained from: British Woodworking Federation, 82 New Cavendish Street, London W1M 8AD.

Building Centre
The Building Centre, established in 1931, is part of the Building Centre Group, which in addition to the London centre includes regional centres in Bristol, Cambridge, Durham, Glasgow, Manchester and Southampton. They display building materials and components and provide a product and technical information service for the building industry and the consumer. In addition the centres in London, Manchester, Bristol and Cambridge house branches of the Building Bookshop which stock a vast range of building and architectural books, pamphlets, BSI and HMSO publications. The London address is: Building Centre, 26 Store Street, London WC1E 7BT.

Cement and Concrete Association (C&CA)
An association financed by Portland Cement producers and founded in 1935. It provides

technical information to cement users and promotes high standards of concrete design and construction. The Cement and Concrete Association produces a wide range of technical publications, films and slide sets, details of which are contained in their catalogue. Its address is: Cement and Concrete Association, 52 Grosvenor Gardens, London SW1W 0AQ.

Chipboard Promotion Association (CPA)

The Chipboard Promotion Association is a manufacturers' association which provides technical information on the correct use and potential of wood chipboard to specifiers and users of the material. Its publications include technical notes, data sheets and general advisory brochures, and can be obtained from: Chipboard Promotion Association Limited, 7a Church Street, Esher, Surrey.

Copper Development Association (CDA)

A non-trading organization founded in 1933. It is sponsored by the world's copper producers to encourage the use of copper and to promote its correct application. The Copper Development Association services include the publication of information sheets and priced technical notes, and these can be obtained from: Copper Development Association, Orchard House, Mutton Lane, Potters Bar, Hertfordshire EN6 3AP.

Council of Forest Industries of British Columbia (COFI)

The Council of Forest Industries is an organization which was set up by the major timber and plywood producers of British Columbia. Their objective is to promote and extend the use of their members' products in both Canada and other export markets around the world. They operate a technical advisory service, a film and video library and publish product and application literature. Information can be obtained from: Council of Forest Industries of British Columbia, Tileman House, 131–133 Upper Richmond Road, London, SW15 2TR.

Fibre Building Board Development Organization (FIDOR)

This is a non-trading information body that promotes and develops the use of fibre building boards in the UK. FIDOR operates a technical advisory service and publishes a range of data sheets, technical bulletins and sitework recommendations applicable to the building industry, and can be obtained from: Fibre Building Board Development Organization Limited, 6 Buckingham Street, London WC2N 6BZ.

Finnish Plywood International

Finnish Plywood International is concerned with the development of unsurfaced and surfaced Finnish plywood, blockboard and laminboard for applications in building and construction. It provides technical information on the use of its materials in the building industry. Copies of publications can be obtained free of charge. The organization also provides technical advice. Its address is: Finnish Plywood International, PO Box 99, Welwyn Garden City, Hertfordshire AL6 0HS.

Forestry Commission

The Forestry Commission set up in 1919, promotes the development of forestry and also carries out research of forestry in order to ensure the best use of the country's forest resources. A range of leaflets, guides and information pamphlets (details of these are contained in their catalogue of publications) are available from: Forestry Commission, 25 Saville Row, London W1X 2AY.

Lead Development Association (LDA)

Set up in 1953, the LDA is a non-trading body supported by leading producers and manufacturers of lead products. The Association provides authoritative information on every aspect of lead to users and potential users worldwide. A number of publications aimed at the building industry are available from: Lead Development Association, 34 Berkeley Square, London W1X 6AJ.

Swedish Finnish Timber Council

This is a technical organization which promotes the use mainly in the construction industry of Swedish and Finnish timber. Details of the Council's various publications are contained in the technical publications list, and can be obtained from: The Swedish Finnish Timber Council, 21/25 Carolgate, Retford, Notts. DN22 6BZ.

Timber Research and Development Association (TRADA)

TRADA, established in 1934 as the Timber Development Association (TDA), is an independent research and development organization. It is jointly financed by firms and individuals in the timber trade, professions and industry and grant aided by the Department of the Environment. It employs architects, engineers and technicians all working in the interests of timber users and specifiers. Research and development carried out by the Association has made important contributions to the use of timber in housing and building, timber engineering, industrial applications, fire research, timber drying, stress grading and the testing of structures, components and finishes. The results of TRADA's work are made available through its advisory service and its many publications including technical brochures, leaflets, teaching aids and information sheets. These can be obtained from: Timber Research and Development Association, Stocking Lane, Hughenden Valley, High Wycombe, Buckinghamshire HP14 4ND.

Other information sources

Much useful information can be obtained through reading various trade periodicals, for example, *Building Trades Journal*, *What's New in Building* etc. In addition many trade periodicals operate a reader's enquiry service whereby technical brochures and information can be obtained from various manufacturers and suppliers.

Self-assessment questions

1 Explain the purpose of the following
(a) British Standards
(b) Building Regulations
(c) Codes of Practice

2 Define the main function of the following
(a) Timber Research and Development Association
(b) Building Research Establishment
(c) Agrément Board

3 Technical information concerning the use of plywood is required. List *three* possible sources of reference.

4 Identify the various organizations from the following list of abbreviations

(a) TRADA
(b) CPA
(c) C&CA
(d) BWF
(e) HMSO

5 Briefly explain why it is necessary to regularly update technical information.

chapter 2

Building control

After reading this chapter the student should be able to:

1 Define the main areas of building control and state their purpose.

2 State the procedures involved when applying for planning permission or Building Regulations approval.

3 Explain the role of the Health and Safety Executive.

4 Define the main duties under the Health and Safety at Work etc. Act 1974 of:
   (a) Employers
   (b) Employees
   (c) Self-employed
   (d) Designers, manufacturers, suppliers

5 Name the relevant statutory safety regulations applicable to a given situation.

There are three main areas of building control, these are illustrated in Figure 1.

Planning permission
Building Regulations
Health and safety controls

In brief, planning controls restrict the type and position of a building or development in relation to the environment, whereas the Building Regulations state how a building should be constructed to ensure safe and healthy accommodation and the conservation of energy. Both of these forms of control are administered by the relevant local authorities, to whom an application must be made and permission received before work is started. Health and safety controls, on the other hand, are concerned with the health and safety of building site workers, visitors and the general public. These controls are administered by the Health and Safety Executive under the Health and Safety at Work etc. Act 1974.

Planning permission

All development is controlled by planning laws, which exist to control the use and development of land in order to obtain the greatest possible environmental advantages with the least inconvenience, both for the individual and society as a whole. The submission of a planning application provides the local authority and the general public with an opportunity to consider the development and decide whether or not it is in the general interest of the locality. The key word in planning is development. This means all building work, other operations such as the construction of a driveway, and a change of land or building use, such as running a business from your home. Certain developments are known as 'permitted developments' where no planning approval is required. These permitted developments include limited extensions to buildings and the erection of boundary fences and walls within certain height limits. The two main types of application are:

Outline planning permission
Full planning permission

Outline planning permission
This enables the owner or prospective owner to obtain approval of the proposed development in principle without having to incur the costs involved with the preparation of full working

TOWN AND COUNTRY PLANNING ACT 1971 APPLICATION FOR PERMISSION TO DEVELOP LAND	BRACKENDOWNS BOROUGH COUNCIL

Building Control Dept
Council Buildings
Brackendowns
Bedfordshire
BR1 4AC

For office use only

Borough ref. _____

Registered no. _____

Date received _____

1 APPLICANT

Name _____

Address _____

_____

_____ Tel. no. _____

AGENT (if any) to whom correspondence should be sent

Name _____

Address _____

_____

_____ Tel. no. _____

2 PARTICULARS OF PROPOSED DEVELOPMENT

(a) Full address or location of the land to which this application relates and site area (if known).

(b) Brief particulars of proposed development including the purpose(s) for which the land and/or buildings are to be used.

(c) State whether applicant owns or controls any adjoining land and if so, give its location.

(d) State whether the proposal involves:

State Yes or No

(i) New building(s) _____

If 'Yes' state gross floor area of proposed building(s).   m^2/sq ft*

If residential development, state number of dwelling units proposed and type if known, e.g. houses, bungalows, flats.

(ii) Alterations _____

(iii) Change of use _____

If 'Yes' state gross area of land or building(s) affected by proposed change of use (if more than one use involved state gross area of each use).

(iv) Construction of a new access to a highway } vehicular ___ pedestrian ___

(v) Alteration of an existing access to a highway } vehicular ___ pedestrian ___

hectares/acres/m^2/sq ft*

*Please delete whichever inapplicable

3 PARTICULARS OF APPLICATION

State whether this application is for:

State Yes or No

(i) Outline planning permission _____

(ii) Full planning permission _____

If 'Yes' delete any of the following which are not reserved for subsequent approval

1 siting   3 external appearance
2 design   4 means of access

(iii) Renewal of a temporary permission or permission for retention of building or continuance of use without complying with a condition subject to which planning permission has been granted _____

If 'Yes' state the date and number of previous permission and identify the particular condition (see General Notes)

Date

Number

The condition

(iv) Consideration under Section 72 only (Industry) _____

Figure 2 *Planning application form*

BRACKENDOWNS BOROUGH COUNCIL
BUILDING CONTROL DEPARTMENT

The Building Act 1984
The Building Regulations 1985
The Building (Prescribed Fees) Regulations

FULL PLANS NOTICE

PART 1.   TO BE COMPLETED IN ALL CASES

a)   Name and Address of Owner   a)   MR. W.H. WHITEMAN, WHITEMAN ENTERPRISES, ENGINEERING HOUSE, BEDFORD.

Telephone No. 0641293

b)   Name and Address of Agent, if any   b)   B.B.S. DESIGN, SARBIE HOUSE, BRACKENDOWNS, BEDS.

Telephone No. 0581 423

c)   Address or location of the building to   c)   PLOT 3, HILLTOP ROAD, BRACKENDOWNS, which this notice relates.   BEDS.

d)   Description of the building work   d)   NEW DETACHED HOUSE AND GARAGE

e)   Present use of building   e)   NOT APPLICABLE

f)   Proposed use of building   f)   PRIVATE DWELLING

g)   Do you agree to the plans being passed   g)   YES / NO
     subject to conditions?

h)   Is a new crossing over a footway required?   h)   YES / NO

PART 2.   TO BE COMPLETED IF AN UNVENTED HOT WATER STORAGE SYSTEM IS TO BE INSTALLED

a)   Name and Type of System   a)   NOT APPLICABLE

b)   Agreement Certificate Number   b)

c)   Name and Address of Installer   c)

PART 3.   BUILDING (PRESCRIBED FEES) REGULATIONS – COMPLETE 'a', 'b' or 'c' and 'd'

a)	New Dwellings:– (enter number)	i)	Number of dwellings to which this notice relates	ONE
		ii)	Number of dwellings with floor area over 64m^2	ONE
		iii)	Total number of dwellings in 'multiple work scheme'	
b)	Garage, Carport, or Domestic Extensions:– (tick as appropriate)	i)	Detached garage/carport with floor area under 40m^2	
		ii)	One or more rooms in roof space	
		iii)	Domestic extension with floor area less than 20m^2	
		iv)	Domestic extension with floor area 20–40m^2	
c)	All other building work or Material Changes of Use:–	i)	Total estimated cost of work to which notice relates	£.
		ii)	Aggregate total estimated cost of all buildings in 'multiple work scheme'	£.
d)	Plan Fee calculated in accordance with the current Building (Prescribed Fees) Regulations:–	i)	Plan Fee	£. 39
		ii)	Plus VAT at current rate	£. 5·85p
		iii)	Total Enclosed	£. 44·85p

PART 4.   DECLARATION

This notice and duplicate copies of the relevant plans and particulars in relation to the above mentioned building work, are deposited in accordance with Building Regulation 11(i)(b).

The Plan Fee shown above is enclosed and I acknowledge that the relevant Inspection Fee will, upon demand after the first inspection, be payable to the Council by the person by whom, or on whose behalf, the work is being carried out.

Date   2nd MARCH 1986   Signed   R.D. Paull.   Agent
                                                                                   P.T.O.

Figure 3   *Building application form*

**BRACKENDOWNS
BOROUGH COUNCIL**

BUILDING INSPECTION NOTICE

Plan no. B _____ Date _____

Nature of works _____

Address of works _____

The undermentioned works will be ready for inspection on _____

_____ Signature of builder

_____ Address of builder

1 Commencement	5 Oversite Concrete
2 Foundation Excavations	6 Drains under Test
3 Concrete Foundations	7 Back filling of Drain Trenches
4 Damp Proof Course	8 Completion

Note (a) Strike out words not applicable.

Figure 4 *Building inspection notice*

Where an application is refused or the applicant and the local authority are in dispute, there is an appeal procedure to the Secretary of State for the Environment.

Note: The local authority has the power to relax or dispense with certain requirements of the Building Regulations.

Building Notice

Application using the Building Notice method can be made by depositing a Building Notice and limited accompanying information (e.g. specification, block plan, site plan and general location plans). In addition the local authority may request further information as the work proceeds, in order to show compliance to specific items which cannot be inspected on site (e.g. structural calculations, material specifications, etc.).

Note: You cannot use the Building Notice method when erecting shops or offices.

Approved inspector

Application using the Approved Inspector method can be made by you and the inspector jointly, by depositing an initial notice, limited plans and evidence of their insurance cover to the local authority. The local authority must accept or reject this initial notice within ten working days. Once accepted, their powers to enforce the Regulations are suspended and the Approved Inspector will carry out the building control function and issue a final certificate to you and the local authority when the work has been satisfactorily completed.

Inspection of building work

When either the full plans method or the Building Notice method has been adopted the local authority's Building Control Officer will inspect the work as it proceeds. The builder must give the local authority written notice of the following building stages (this notice need not be in writing if the local authority agrees) (see Figure 4 for a typical Building Inspection Notice):

At least 48 hours before the commencement of work

At least 24 hours before the covering up of any excavation for a foundation, any foundation, any damp proof course or any concrete or other material laid over a site

At least 24 hours before haunching or covering up any drain

Not more than seven days after laying, concreting or back filling a drain

Not more than seven days after completion of building work

Where a builder fails to notify the local authority of any stage as required, the local authority has the power to require them to 'open up' or 'pull down' part of the work at a later date to enable inspection. After inspection by the Building Control Officer, the local authority may require modifications or additional work to be carried out in order to comply with the Regulations.

Where an Approved Inspector has been appointed she or he will be responsible for inspecting the work as it proceeds. They may also require the builder to notify them of commencement and/or particular stages of building work.

The local authority will charge a set fee for considering an application and inspecting the work as it proceeds. If an Approved Inspector is appointed she or he will negotiate their fee with you.

Note: In addition to planning permission and Building Regulations approval an application must also be made to the local authority (highways officer) for permission to deposit a rubbish skip or erect a hoarding or scaffold on or partly on the highway (road, footpath or verge).

Health and safety controls

In 1974 the Health and Safety at Work Act (HASAWA) was introduced. This Act became the main statutory legislation completely covering the health and safety of all persons at their place of work and protecting other people from risks occurring through work activities. All of the existing health and safety requirements operate in parallel with the HASAWA until they are gradually replaced by new regulations and codes of practice etc. made under the Act. The main health and safety legislation applicable to building sites and workshops is indicated in Table 1.

The four main objectives of the HASAWA are:

1 To secure the health, safety and welfare of all persons at work.
2 To protect the general public from risks to health and safety arising out of work activities.
3 To control the use, handling, storage and transportation of explosives and highly flammable substances.
4 To control the release of noxious or offensive substances into the atmosphere.

These objectives can only be achieved by involving everyone in health and safety matters.

Table 1   **Health and safety legislation**

Acts of Parliament	Regulations
Control of Pollution Act 1974	
Explosives Act 1875 and 1923	
Factories Act 1961	Abrasive Wheels Regulations 1970
	Asbestos Regulations 1969
	Construction (General Provision) Regulations 1961
	Construction (Lifting Operations) Regulations 1961
	Construction (Health and Welfare) Regulations 1966
	Construction (Working Places) Regulations 1966
	Construction (Head Protection) Regulations 1989
	Diving Operations Special Regulations 1960
	Electricity (Factories Act) Special Regulations 1908 and 1944
	Highly Flammable Liquids and Liquified Petroleum Gases Regulations 1972
	Lead Paint Regulations 1927
	Protection of Eyes Regulations 1974
	Woodworking Machines Regulations 1974
	Work in Compressed Air Special Regulations 1958 and 1960
Fire Precautions Act 1971	Fire Certificates (Special Premises) Regulations 1976
Food and Drugs Act 1955	Food Hygiene (General) Regulations 1970
Health and Safety at Work etc. Act 1974	Hazardous Substances (Labelling of Road Tankers) Regulations 1978
	Control of Lead at Work Regulations 1980
	Safety Signs Regulations 1980
	Health and Safety (First Aid) Regulations 1981
	Control of Asbestos at Work Regulations 1987
	Control of Substances Hazardous to Health Regulations 1988 (COSHH)
	Reporting of Injuries, Diseases and Dangerous Occurences Regulations 1985 (RIDDOR)
Mines and Quarries Act 1954	
Offices, Shops and Railway Premises Act 1963	

This includes:

Employers and management
Employees
Self-employed
Designers, manufacturers and suppliers of equipment and materials

Employers' and management's duties

Employers have a general duty to ensure the health and safety of their employees, visitors and the general public. This means that the employer must:

1 Provide and maintain a safe working environment.
2 Ensure safe access to and from the workplace.
3 Provide and maintain safe machinery, equipment and methods of work.
4 Ensure the safe handling, transport and storage of all machinery, equipment and materials.
5 Provide their employees with the necessary information, instruction, training and supervision to ensure safe working.
6 Prepare, issue to employees and update as required a written statement of the firm's safety policy.
7 Involve trade union safety representatives (where appointed) with all matters concerning the development, promotion and maintenance of health and safety requirements.

Note: An employer is not allowed to charge an employee for anything done or equipment provided to comply with any health and safety requirements.

Employees' duties

An employee is an individual who offers his or her skill and experience etc. to his or her employer in return for a monetary payment. It is the duty of every employee while at work to:

1 Take care at all times and ensure that his or her actions do not put at 'risk' himself or herself, workmates or any other person.
2 Co-operate with his or her employer to

enable them to fulfil the employer's health and safety duties.
3 Use the equipment and safeguards provided by employers.
4 Never misuse or interfere with anything provided for health and safety.

Self-employed duties

The self-employed person can be thought of as both his or her employer and employee; therefore the duties under the Act are a combination of those of the employer and employee.

Designers', manufacturers' and suppliers' duties

Under the Act, designers, manufacturers and suppliers as well as importers and hirers of equipment, machinery and materials for use at work have a duty to:

1 Ensure that the equipment machinery or material is designed, manufactured and tested so that when it is used correctly no hazard to health and safety is created.
2 Provide information or operating instructions as to the correct use, without risk, of their equipment, machinery or material.

Note: Employers should ensure this information is passed on to their employees.

3 Carry out research so that any risk to health and safety is eliminated or minimized as far as possible.

Enforcement

Under the HASAWA a system of control was established, aimed at reducing death, injury and ill-health. This system of control is represented by Figure 5. It consists of the Health and Safety Commission which controls the work of the Health and Safety Executive (HSE). The Executive is divided into a number of specialist inspectorates or sections which operate from local offices situated throughout the country. From the local offices, inspectors visit the individual workplaces.

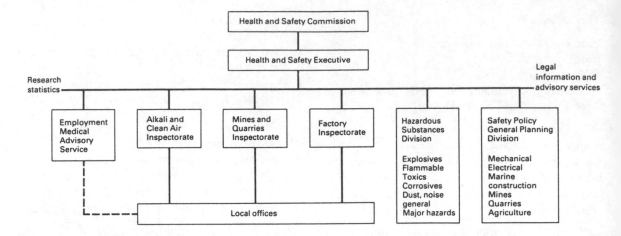

Figure 5   *Health and safety control*

Note: The section with the main responsibility for the building and construction industry is the factory inspectorate.

The health and safety inspectors have been given wide powers of entry, examination and investigation in order to assist them in the enforcement of the HASAWA and earlier safety legislation. In addition to giving employers advice and information on health and safety matters, an inspector can:

1   *Enter premises*   In order to carry out investigations including the taking of measurements, photographs, recordings and samples. The inspector may require the premises to be left undisturbed while the investigations are taking place.
2   *Take statements*   An inspector can ask anyone questions relevant to the investigation and also require them to sign a declaration as to the truth of the answers.
3   *Check records*   All books, records and documents required by legislation must be made available for inspection and copying.
4   *Give information*   An inspector has a duty to give employees or their safety representative information about the safety of their workplace and details of any action he proposes to take. This information must also be given to the employer.

5   *Demand*   The inspector can demand the seizure, dismantling, neutralizing or destruction of any machinery, equipment, material or substance that is likely to cause immediate serious personal injury.
6   *Issue an improvement notice*   (Figure 6)   This requires the responsible person (employer or manufacturer etc.) to put right within a specified period of time any minor hazard or infringement of legislation.
7   *Issue a prohibition notice* (Figure 7)   This requires the responsible person to immediately stop any activities which are likely to result in serious personal injury. This ban on activities continues until the situation is corrected. An appeal against an improvement or prohibition notice may be made to an industrial tribunal.
8   *Prosecute*   All persons, including employers, employees, the self-employed, designers, manufacturers and suppliers who fail to comply with their safety duty may be prosecuted in a magistrates court or in certain circumstances in the higher court system. Conviction can lead to unlimited fines, or a prison sentence, or both.

Safety documentation
In order to comply with the various safety legislation an employer is required to:

HEALTH AND SAFETY EXECUTIVE
Health and Safety at Work etc. Act 1974, Sections 21, 23, and 24

IMPROVEMENT NOTICE

Serial No. I

Name and address (See Section 46) To..

(a) Delete as necessary (a) Trading as ....

(b) Inspector's full name I (b) .... one of (c) ....

(c) Inspector's official designation of (d) ....

(d) Official address .... Tel. no. ....

hereby give you notice that I am of the opinion that at

(e) Location of premises or place and activity (e) ....

you, as (a) an employer/a self employed person/a person wholly or partly in control of the premises.

(f) Other specified capacity (f) .... (a) are contravening/have contravened in circumstances that make it likely that the contravention will continue or be repeated

....

The reasons for my said opinion are:—

....

and I hereby require you to remedy the said contraventions or, as the case may be, the matters occasioning them by

(g) Provisions contravened (g) ....

(h) Date (h) .... Date ....

(a) in the manner stated in the attached schedule which forms part of the notice.

Signature .... Date ....

Being an inspector appointed by an instrument in writing made pursuant to Section 19 of the said Act and entitled to issue this notice.

(a) An improvement notice is also being served on

LP 1 of .... related to the matters contained in this notice.

Dd 347139 5000 Pads 2/75 COH

NOTES

1 Failure to comply with an Improvement Notice is an offence as provided by Section 33 of this Act and renders the offender liable to a fine not exceeding £400 on summary conviction or to an unlimited fine on conviction on indictment and a further fine of not exceeding £50 per day if the offence is continued.

2 An inspector has power to withdraw a notice or to extend the period specified in the notice, before the end of the period specified in it. You should apply to the inspector who has issued the notice if you wish him to consider this, but you must do so before the end of the period given in it. *(Such an application is not an appeal against this notice.)*

3 The issue of this notice does not relieve you of any legal liability resting upon you for failure to comply with any provision of this or any other enactment, before or after the issue of this notice.

4 Your attention is drawn to the provision for appeal against this notice to an Industrial Tribunal. Details of the method of making an appeal are given below *(see also Section 24 of the Health and Safety at Work etc. Act 1974)*.

(a) Appeal can be entered against this notice to an Industrial Tribunal. The appeal should be sent to —

(for England and Wales) The Secretary of the Tribunals
Central Office of the Industrial Tribunals
93 Ebury Bridge Road LONDON SW1W 8RE

(for Scotland) The Secretary of the Tribunals
Central Office of the Industrial Tribunals
Saint Andrew House
141 West Nile Street GLASGOW G1 2RU

(b) The appeal must be commenced by sending in writing to the Secretary of the Tribunals a notice containing the following particulars:—

(1) The name of the appellant and his address for the service of documents;

(2) The date of the notice or notices appealed against; and the address of the premises or place concerned;

(3) The name and address *(as shown on the notice)* of the respondent;

(4) Particulars of the requirements or directions appealed against;

(5) The grounds of the appeal.

and

A form which may be used for appeal is attached.

(c) Time limit for appeal

A notice of appeal must be sent to the Secretary of the Tribunals within 21 days from the date of service on the appellant of the notice or notices appealed against, or within such further period as the tribunal considers reasonable in a case where it is satisfied that it was not reasonably practicable for the notice of appeal to be presented within the period of 21 days. If posted, the appeal should be sent by recorded delivery.

(d) The entering of an appeal suspends the Improvement Notice until the appeal has been determined, but does not automatically alter the date given in this notice by which the matters contained in it must be remedied.

(e) The rules for the hearing of an appeal are given in:

The Industrial Tribunals (Improvement and Prohibition Notices Appeals) (S1 1974 No. 1925) for England and Wales.

and

The Industrial Tribunals (Improvement and Prohibition Notices Appeals) (S1 1974 No. 1926) for Scotland.

SPECIMEN

Figure 6 *Improvement notice*

Health and Safety Executive
Health and Safety at Work etc Act 1974
Reporting of Injuries, Diseases and Dangerous Occurrences Regulations 1985

Spaces below
are for office
use only

Report of an injury or dangerous occurrence

- Full notes to help you complete this form are attached.
- This form is to be used to make a report to the enforcing authority under the requirements of Regulations 3 or 6.
- Completing and signing this form does not constitute an admission of liability of any kind, either by the person making the report or any other person.
- If more than one person was injured as a result of an accident, please complete a separate form for each person.

A   Subject of report *(tick appropriate box or boxes) — see note 2*

Fatality	□	Specified major injury or condition	□	"Over three day" injury	□	Dangerous occurrence	□	Flammable gas incident (fatality or major injury or condition)	□	Dangerous gas fitting	□
	1		2		3		4		5		6

B   Person or organisation making report (ie person obliged to report under the Regulations) *— see note 3*

Name and address —

Nature of trade, business or undertaking —

If in construction industry, state the total number of your employees —

and indicate the role of your company on site *(tick box)* —

Post code —

Main site contractor	□ 7	Sub contractor	□ 8	Other	□ 9

Name and telephone no. of person to contact —

If in farming, are you reporting an injury to a member of your family? *(tick box)*   □ □
                                                                          Yes No

C   Date, time and place of accident, dangerous occurrence or flammable gas incident *— see note 4*

Date | 19 | Time —
day   month   year

Give the name and address if different from above —

ENV

Where on the premises or site —
and
Normal activity carried on there

Complete the following sections D, E, F & H if you have ticked boxes, 1, 2, 3 or 5 in Section A. Otherwise go straight to Sections G and H.

D   The injured person *— see note 5*

Full name and address —

Age		Sex		Status *(tick box)* —	Employee	□ 10	Self employed	□ 11	Trainee (YTS)	□ 12
		(M or F)			Trainee (other)	□ 13	Any other person			□ 14

Trade, occupation or job title —

Nature of injury or condition and the part of the body affected —

F2508 (rev 1/86)   *continued overleaf*

Figure 9   *Report of accident*

E Kind of accident - *see note 6*

Indicate what kind of accident led to the injury or condition (*tick one box*) —

Contact with moving machinery or material being machined ☐ 1	Injured whilst handling lifting or carrying ☐ 5	Trapped by something collapsing or overturning ☐ 8	Exposure to an explosion ☐ 12
Struck by moving, including flying or falling, object. ☐ 2	Slip, trip or fall on same level ☐ 6	Drowning or asphyxiation ☐ 9	Contact with electricity or an electrical discharge ☐ 13
Struck by moving vehicle ☐ 3	Fall from a height* ☐ 7	Exposure to or contact with a harmful substance ☐ 10	Injured by an animal ☐ 14
Struck against something fixed or stationary ☐ 4	*Distance through which person fell ☐ (metres)	Exposure to fire ☐ 11	Other kind of accident (give details in Section H) ☐ 15

Spaces below are for office use only.

☐

F Agent(s) involved — *see note 7*

Indicate which, if any, of the categories of agent or factor below were involved (*tick one or more of the boxes*) —

Machinery/equipment for lifting and conveying ☐ 1	Process plant, pipework or bulk storage ☐ 5	Live animal ☐ 9	Ladder or scaffolding ☐ 13
Portable power or hand tools ☐ 2	Any material, substance or product being handled, used or stored. ☐ 6	Moveable container or package of any kind ☐ 10	Construction formwork, shuttering and falsework ☐ 14
Any vehicle or associated equipment/ machinery ☐ 3	Gas, vapour, dust, fume or oxygen deficient atmosphere ☐ 7	Floor, ground, stairs or any working surface ☐ 11	Electricity supply cable, wiring, apparatus or equipment ☐ 15
Other machinery ☐ 4	Pathogen or infected material ☐ 8	Building, engineering structure or excavation/underground working ☐ 12	Entertainment or sporting facilities or equipment ☐ 16
			Any other agent ☐ 17

Describe briefly the agents or factors you have indicated —

☐

G Dangerous occurrence or dangerous gas fitting — *see notes 8 and 9*

Reference number of dangerous occurrence ☐   Reference number of dangerous gas fitting ☐

H Account of accident, dangerous occurrence or flammable gas incident - *see note 10*

Describe what happened and how. In the case of an accident state what the injured person was doing at the time —

☐

☐

☐

Signature of person making report ☐   Date ☐

PART 2

Appointment of persons to mount abrasive wheels (regulation 9)

	APPOINTMENT			REVOCATION	
Name of person appointed	Class or description of abrasive wheels for which appointment is made (*See Note* 7)	Date of appointment	Signature of occupier or his agent	Date of revocation of appointment (*See Note* 5)	Signature of occupier or his agent
(1)	(2)	(3)	(4)	(5)	(6)

3

Figure 11 *Abrasive wheel register*

weekly, monthly or other periodic tests and examinations required by the construction regulations, as follows:

>   Cranes (form F96)
>   Hoists (form F75)
>   Other lifting appliances (form F80)
>   Wire ropes (form F87)
>   Chain slings and lifting gear (form F97)

Safety signs

Formerly there were many vastly different safety signs in use. BS 5378: Part 1: 1980: *Safety Signs and Colours* introduced a standard system for giving health and safety information with a minimum use of words. Its purpose is to establish an internationally understood system of safety signs and safety colours which draw attention to objects and situations that do or could affect health and safety. Details of these signs and typical examples of use are given in Table 2.

Accident prevention

It should be the aim of everyone to prevent accidents. Ask yourself the following questions and 'if in doubt find out'. Remember, you are required by law to be aware and fulfil your duties under the Health and Safety at Work etc. Act.

1   Do I know what safety legislation is relevant to my job?
2   Have I received, read and understood my employer's safety policy?

Name or title of employer or contractor ______________

Factories Act 1961

Address of site ______________

Construction (Working Places) Regulations 1966

SECTION A

Work commenced—Date ______________

SCAFFOLD INSPECTIONS

Reports of results of inspections under Regulations 22 of scaffolds, including boatswain's chairs, cages, skips and similar plant or equipment (and plant or equipment used for the purposes thereof)

Location and description of scaffold, etc. and other plant or equipment inspected (1)	Date of inspection (2)	Result of inspection State whether in good order (3)	Signature (or, in case where signature is not legally required, name) of person who made the inspection (4)

NOTES TO SECTION A

(1) ***Short check list—at each inspection check that your scaffolding does not have these faults:***

		Week 1	2	3	4
FOOTINGS	Soft and uneven No base plates No sole boards Undermined				
STANDARDS	Not plumb Joined at same height Wrong spacing Damaged				
LEDGERS	Not level Joint in same bays Loose Damaged				

		Week 1	2	3	4
BRACING 'Facade and ledger'	Some missing Loose Wrong fittings				
PUTLOGS and TRANSOMS	Wrongly spaced Loose Wrongly supported				
COUPLINGS	Wrong fitting Loose Damaged No check couplers				
BRIDLES	Wrong spacing Wrong couplings Weak support				

		Week 1	2	3	4
TIES	Some missing Loose				
BOARDING	Bad boards Trap boards Incomplete Insufficient supports				
GUARD RAILS & TOE BOARDS	Wrong height Loose Some missing				
LADDERS	Damaged Insufficient length Not tied				

(2) *This check list is not part of the report required by Regulation 22: see also para 5 of Notes and Regulation 22 on page (ii) of cover and Notes on page 13.*

Figure 12 *Scaffold form*

3 Have I been given all the training and information required to do my job safely?
4 Am I aware of the hazards involved in my particular job?
5 Am I aware of the hazards involved with using particular materials?
6 Do I know what protective equipment is required for a particular operation? Have I been issued with it and do I wear it?
7 Do I understand the meaning of the safety signs that I come into contact with?
8 Do I always work in the safest possible way?

Self-assessment questions

1 What information must be recorded in the general register?

2 List the main powers of the health and safety inspector.

3 Explain the meaning of:
(i) Outline planning permission
(ii) Full planning permission

4 Briefly define the need for planning controls.

5 List *four* building stages when the builder must forward inspection notices to the local authority.

6 Give examples of *two* situations where Building Regulations approval will be required.

Table 2 **Safety signs**

Purpose	Sign	Definition	Examples of use
Prohibition	white — red	A sign prohibiting certain behaviour	No smoking / Smoking and naked flames prohibited / Do not extinguish with water / Not drinking water / Pedestrians prohibited
Caution	yellow — black	A sign giving warning of certain hazards	Caution, risk of fire / Caution, toxic hazard / Caution, corrosive substance / General warning caution, risk of danger / Caution, risk of electric shock / Perimeter of hazard
Safe condition	green	A sign providing information about safe conditions	First aid / Indication of direction / Indication of direction

Mandatory

blue

A sign indicating that a special course of action is required

Head protection must be worn

Eye protection must be worn

Hearing protection must be worn

Hand protection must be worn

Foot protection must be worn

Respiratory protection must be worn

Supplementary

white or colour of sign it is supporting

A sign with text. Can be used in conjunction with a safety sign to provide additional information.

IMPORTANT REPORT ALL ACCIDENTS IMMEDIATELY

SCAFFOLDING INCOMPLETE

SAFETY HELMETS ARE PROVIDED FOR YOUR SAFETY AND MUST BE WORN

PETROLEUM MIXTURE HIGHLY FLAMMABLE NO SMOKING OR NAKED LIGHTS

WARNING HIGH VOLTAGE CABLES OVERHEAD

EYE WASH BOTTLE

7 Describe the purpose of a prohibition notice.

8 List *two* duties under the Health and Safety at Work etc. Act of each of the following:
   (a) Employers
   (b) Employees

9 Explain briefly what is meant by a notifiable dangerous occurrence and state to whom it should be reported.

10 Name the statutory document applicable to each of the following:
   (a) Provision of site accommodation
   (b) Machinery in a joiner's shop
   (c) Scaffolding
   (d) First-aid requirements

chapter 3

Building administration

After reading this chapter the student should be able to:

1 Specify the necessary procedures both prior to and during building operations.

2 Name, state the purpose of, and interpret various contract documents.

3 State the purpose of and describe the preparation of various site records and reports.

4 Outline the main employment conditions applicable to the industry.

Contract procedures

The first step in building projects is for a prospective building client to appoint an architect to act for him in the construction or alteration of a building. On being appointed the architect will obtain from the client a brief, consisting of full details of his requirements and the proposed site. Having inspected the site and assessed the feasibility of the client's requirements, the architect will prepare sketch designs and submit them to the client for approval and apply for outline planning permission.

When approval is obtained, a design team consisting of the architect, a structural engineer, a services engineer and a quantity surveyor is formed. This team will consider the brief and sketch designs and come up with proposals that will form the basis of the structure. Location drawings, outline specifications and preliminary details of costs are then produced and are submitted to the client for approval. If these details are acceptable, applications will be made for full planning permission and Building Regulations approval. When these approvals have been obtained, contract documents will be prepared and sent to a number of building contractors for them to produce and submit tenders. The returned tenders will be considered by the quantity surveyor who will advise the architect and client of the most suitable contractor. The client and contractor will then sign the contract.

Contract documents

These documents will vary depending on the nature of the work, but will normally consist of:

Working drawings
Specification
Schedules
Bill of quantities
Conditions of contract

Working drawings

These are scale drawings showing the plans, elevations, sections, details and locality of the proposed construction. These drawings can be divided into a number of main types:

Location drawings (Figure 13)
Block plans, scale 1:2500, 1:1250, identify the proposed site in relation to the surrounding area.
Site plans, scale 1:500, 1:200, give the position of the proposed building and the general layout of roads, services and drainage etc. on the site.
General location plans (Figure 14), scale 1:200, 1:100, 1:50, show the position occupied by the various areas within the building and identify the location of the principal elements and components.

Component drawings
Range drawings (Figure 15), scale 1:100, 1:50, 1:20, show the basic sizes and reference system of a standard range of components.

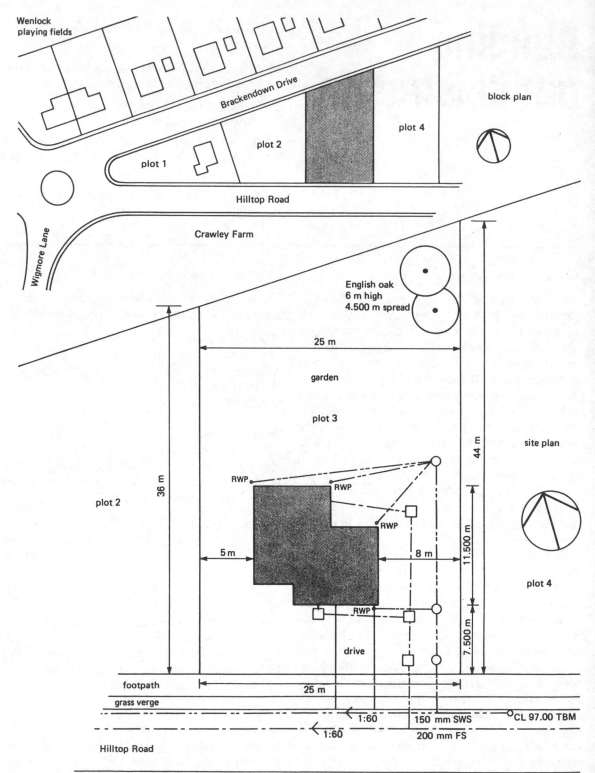

Figure 13   *Location drawings*

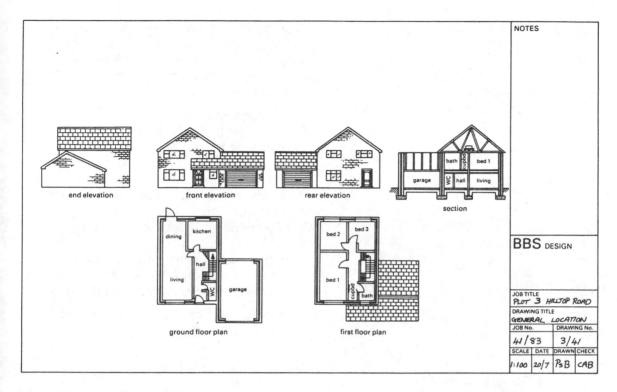

Figure 14   *General location plans*

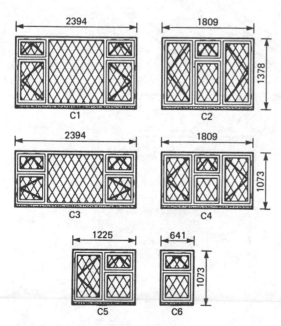

Figure 15   *Component range drawing*

Detail drawings (Figure 16), scale 1:10, 1:5, 1:1, show all the information that is required in order to manufacture a particular component.

Assembly drawings

Assembly details (Figure 17), scale 1:20, 1:10, 1:5, show in detail the junctions in and between the various elements and components of a building.

Note: All working drawings should be produced in accordance with the recommendations contained in BS 1192: *Construction Drawing Practice*.

Specification

Except in the case of very small building works the drawings cannot contain all the information required by the builder, particularly concerning the required standards of materials and workmanship. For this purpose the architect will prepare a document, called the specification, to supplement the working drawings. The speci-

Figure 16 *Component detail drawing*

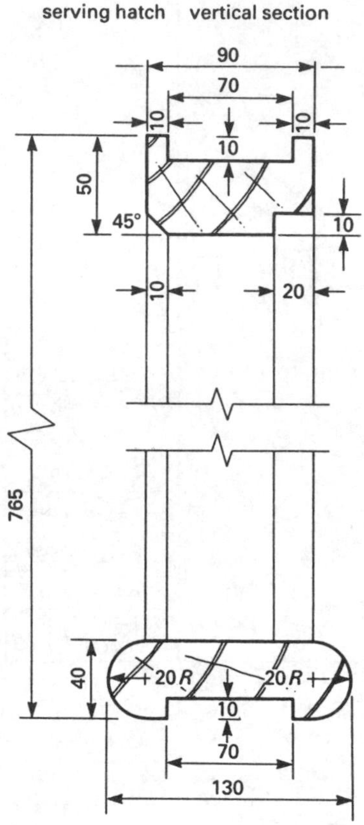

serving hatch   vertical section

fication is a precise description of all the essential information and job requirements that will affect the price of the work but cannot be shown on the drawings. Typical items included in specifications are:

1 Site description
2 Restrictions (limited access and working hours etc.)
3 Availability of services (water, electricity, gas, telephone)
4 Description of materials, quality, size, tolerance and finish
5 Description of workmanship, quality, fixing and jointing
6 Other requirements: site clearance, making good on completion, nominated suppliers and subcontractors, who passes the work etc.

Various clauses of a typical specification are shown in Figure 18.

Figure 17 *Assembly details*

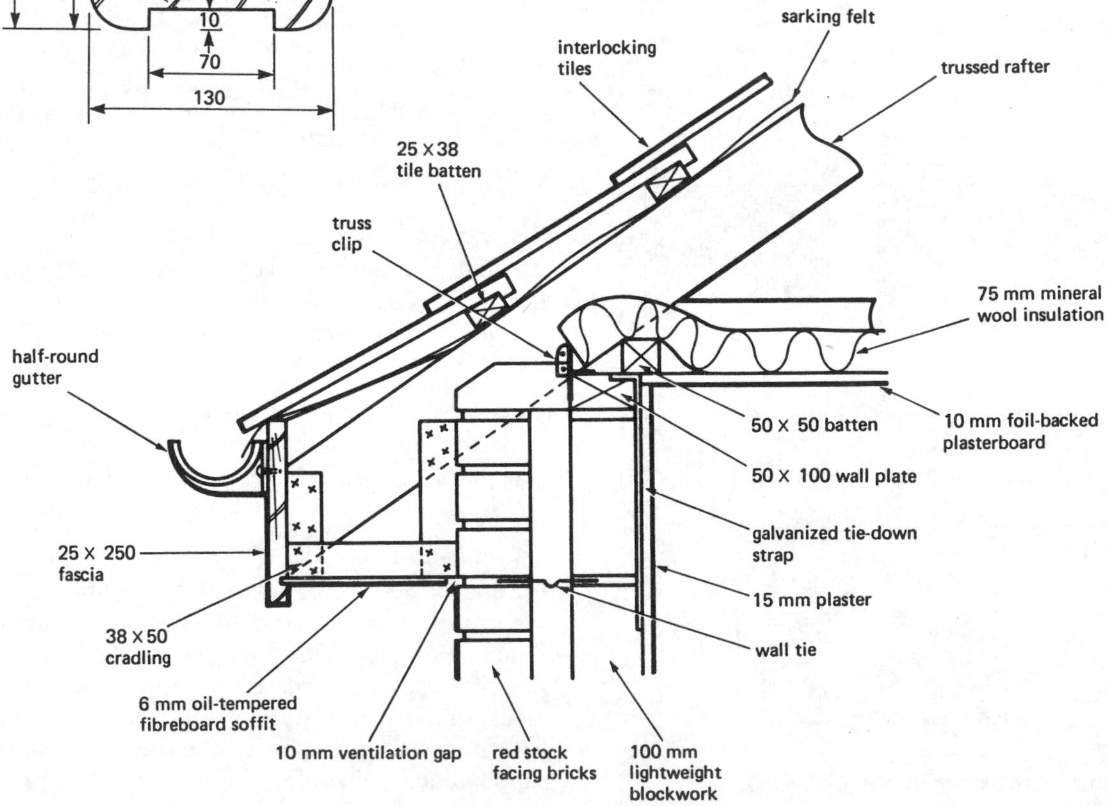

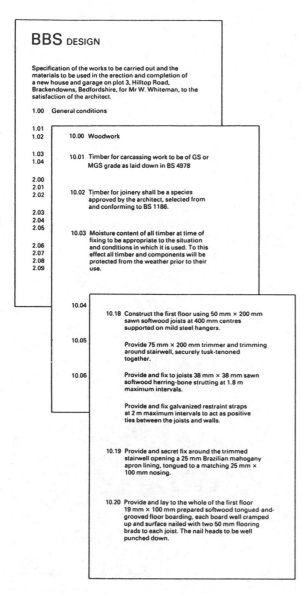

BBS DESIGN

Specification of the works to be carried out and the materials to be used in the erection and completion of a new house and garage on plot 3, Hilltop Road, Brackendowns, Bedfordshire, for Mr W. Whiteman, to the satisfaction of the architect.

1.00 General conditions

1.01
1.02

1.03
1.04

2.00
2.01
2.02

2.03
2.04
2.05

2.06
2.07
2.08
2.09

10.00 Woodwork

10.01 Timber for carcassing work to be of GS or MGS grade as laid down in BS 4978

10.02 Timber for joinery shall be a species approved by the architect, selected from and conforming to BS 1186.

10.03 Moisture content of all timber at time of fixing to be appropriate to the situation and conditions in which it is used. To this effect all timber and components will be protected from the weather prior to their use.

10.04

10.05

10.06

10.18 Construct the first floor using 50 mm × 200 mm sawn softwood joists at 400 mm centres supported on mild steel hangers.

Provide 75 mm × 200 mm trimmer and trimming around stairwell, securely tusk-tenoned together.

Provide and fix to joists 38 mm × 38 mm sawn softwood herring-bone strutting at 1.8 m maximum intervals.

Provide and fix galvanized restraint straps at 2 m maximum intervals to act as positive ties between the joists and walls.

10.19 Provide and secret fix around the trimmed stairwell opening a 25 mm Brazilian mahogany apron lining, tongued to a matching 25 mm × 100 mm nosing.

10.20 Provide and lay to the whole of the first floor 19 mm × 100 mm prepared softwood tongued-and-grooved floor boarding, each board well cramped up and surface nailed with two 50 mm flooring brads to each joist. The nail heads to be well punched down.

Figure 18   *Extracts from a specification*

Schedules

These are used to record repetitive design information about a range of similar components. The main areas where schedules are used includes:

1 Doors, frames, linings
2 Windows
3 Ironmongery
4 Joinery fitments
5 Sanitary ware, drainage
6 Heating units, radiators
7 Finishes, floor, wall, ceiling
8 Lintels
9 Steel reinforcement

The information that schedules contain is essential when preparing estimates and tenders. In addition, schedules are also extremely useful when measuring quantities, locating work and checking deliveries of materials and components.

Obtaining information from a schedule about any particular item is fairly straightforward. For example, the range drawing, floor plans and door schedules shown in Figures 19, 20 and 21 are consulted. Details relevant to a particular door opening are indicated in the schedules by a dot or cross; a figure is also included where more than one item is required. The following information concerning the WC door D2 has been extracted or 'taken off' from the schedules:

One polished plywood internal flush door type B2 762 mm × 1981 mm × 35 mm hung on 38 mm × 125 mm softwood lining with planted stops, transom and 6 mm obscure tempered safety glass fanlight infill, including the following ironmongery:

One pair of 75 mm brass butts
One mortise lock/latch
One brass mortise lock/latch furniture and
Two brass coat hooks

Bill of quantities

The bill of quantities (BoQ) is prepared by the quantity surveyor. This document gives a complete description and measure of the quantities of labour, material and other items required to carry out the work, based on drawings, specification and schedules. Its use ensures that all estimators prepare their tender on the same information. An added advantage is that as each individual item is priced in the tender they can be used for valuing the work in progress and also form the basis for valuing any variation to the contract.

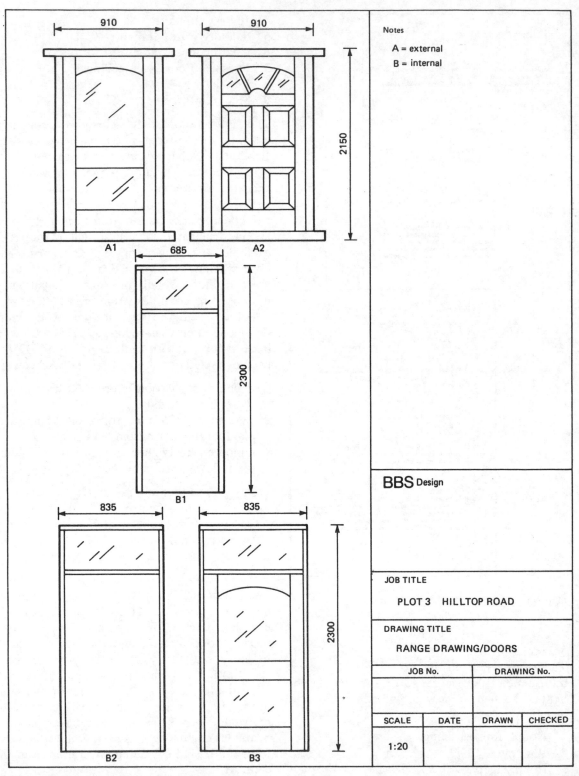

Figure 19   *Door range drawing*

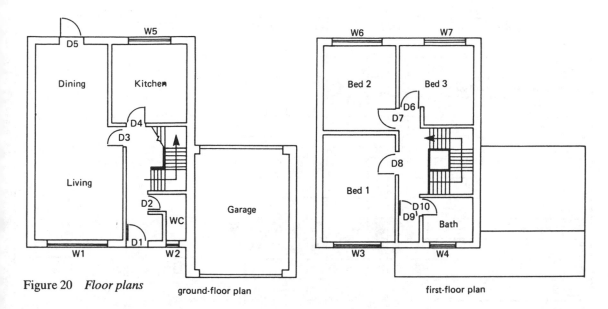

Figure 20   *Floor plans*

ground-floor plan   first-floor plan

Description	D1	D2	D3	D4	D5	D6	D7	D8	D9	D10		
Type (see range)												
External glazed A1					●							
External panelled A2	●											
Internal flush B1									●			
Internal flush B2		●				●	●	●		●		
Internal glazed B3			●	●								
Size												
813 mm × 2032 mm × 44 mm	●				●							
762 mm × 1981 mm × 35 mm		●	●	●		●	●	●		●		
610 mm × 1981 mm × 35 mm									●			
Material												
Hardwood	●											
Softwood			●	●	●							
Plywood/polished		●										
plywood/painted						●	●	●	●	●		
Infill												
6 mm tempered safety glass												
clear			●	●	●							
obscured	●											

NOTES

BBS DESIGN

JOB TITLE
   PLOT 3 Hilltop Road

DRAWING TITLE
   Door Schedule/doors

JOB NO.   DRAWING NO.

SCALE   DATE   DRAWN   CHECKED

Figure 21   *Door schedules*

continued over page

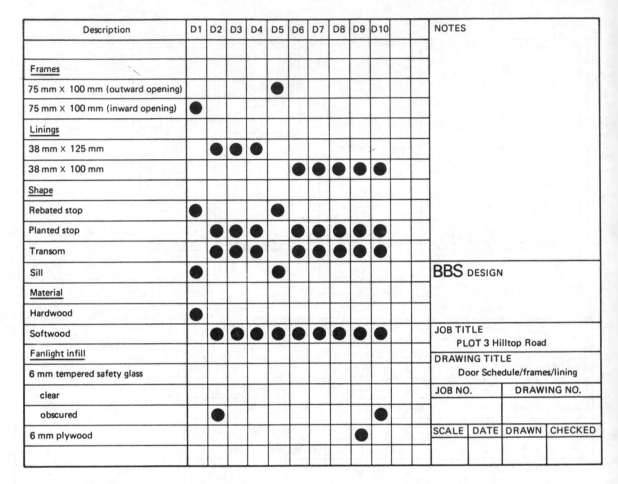

Description	D1	D2	D3	D4	D5	D6	D7	D8	D9	D10			NOTES
Frames													
75 mm × 100 mm (outward opening)					●								
75 mm × 100 mm (inward opening)	●												
Linings													
38 mm × 125 mm		●	●	●									
38 mm × 100 mm						●	●	●	●	●			
Shape													
Rebated stop	●				●								
Planted stop		●	●	●		●	●	●	●	●			
Transom		●	●	●		●	●	●	●	●			
Sill	●				●								BBS DESIGN
Material													
Hardwood	●												
Softwood		●	●	●	●	●	●	●	●	●			JOB TITLE PLOT 3 Hilltop Road
Fanlight infill													DRAWING TITLE Door Schedule/frames/lining
6 mm tempered safety glass													JOB NO. DRAWING NO.
clear													
obscured		●							●				
6 mm plywood								●					SCALE DATE DRAWN CHECKED

Figure 21   *Door schedules — continued*

All bills of quantities will contain the following information:

Preliminaries   These deal with the general particulars of the work, such as the names of the parties involved, details of the works, description of the site and conditions of the contract etc.

Preambles   These are introductory clauses to each trade covering descriptions of the material and workmanship similar to those stated in the specifications.

Measured quantities   A description and measurement of an item of work, the measurement being given in metres run, metres square, kilograms etc. or just enumerated as appropriate.

Provisional quantities   Where an item cannot be accurately measured, an approximate quantity to be allowed for can be stated. Adjustments will be made when the full extent of the work is known.

Prime cost sum (PC sum)   This is an amount of money to be included in the tender for work services or materials provided by a nominated subcontractor, supplier or statutory body.

Provisional sum   A sum of money to be included in the tender for work which has not yet been finally detailed or for a 'contingency sum' to cover the cost of any unforeseen work.

Extracts from a typical bill of quantities are shown in Figure 22.

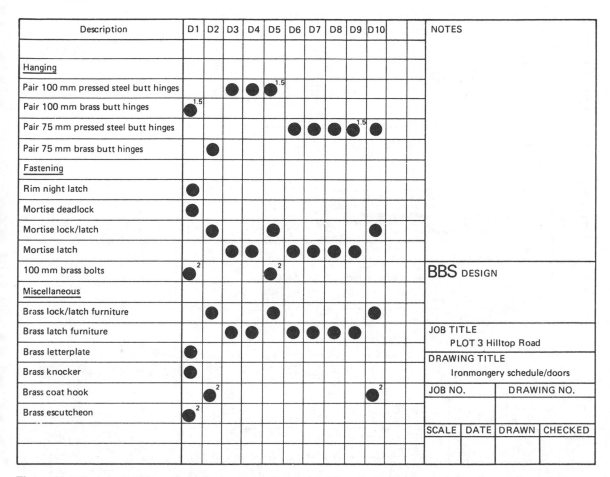

Description	D1	D2	D3	D4	D5	D6	D7	D8	D9	D10			NOTES
Hanging													
Pair 100 mm pressed steel butt hinges			●	●	●¹·⁵								
Pair 100 mm brass butt hinges	●¹·⁵												
Pair 75 mm pressed steel butt hinges						●	●	●	●¹·⁵	●			
Pair 75 mm brass butt hinges		●											
Fastening													
Rim night latch	●												
Mortise deadlock	●												
Mortise lock/latch		●			●				●				
Mortise latch			●	●		●	●	●	●				
100 mm brass bolts	●²				●²								BBS DESIGN
Miscellaneous													
Brass lock/latch furniture		●			●				●				
Brass latch furniture			●	●		●	●	●	●				JOB TITLE PLOT 3 Hilltop Road
Brass letterplate	●												DRAWING TITLE Ironmongery schedule/doors
Brass knocker	●												
Brass coat hook		●²								●²			JOB NO. DRAWING NO.
Brass escutcheon	●²												
													SCALE DATE DRAWN CHECKED

Figure 21 *Door schedules – continued*

Standard method of measurement

In order to ensure that the bill of quantities is readily understood and interpreted in a consistent manner by all concerned, the various items should be described and measured in accordance with the latest edition of the *Standard Method of Measurement of Building Works* (SMM). This document, prepared by The Royal Institution of Chartered Surveyors and the Building Employers' Confederation, provides a uniform basis for measuring building work and it embodies the essentials of good practice.

The main requirements of the SMM as far as the carpenter and joiner is concerned are as follows:

Carcassing All carcassing timber, for example, joists, plates, studs, rafters and firrings etc. shall be given in metres run, stating the cross-section dimensions.

First fixing Boarding, sheeting and cladding shall be described, stating width, thickness, the method of jointing and fixing and given in square metres. Studs, plates and grounds etc. shall be given in metres run stating the cross-section dimensions.

Second fixing Unframed second-fixing items such as skirting, picture rails, dado rails, architraves, cover fillets, stops, glazing beads, window boards, shelves, worktops and handrails shall be given in metres run, stating the cross-section dimensions.

Composite items This means all items which

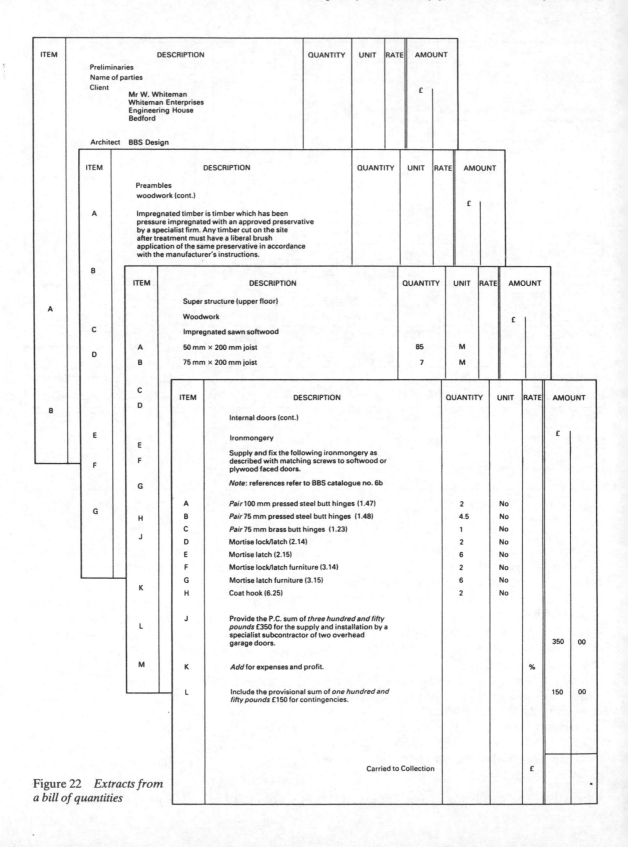

ITEM	DESCRIPTION	QUANTITY	UNIT	RATE	AMOUNT
	Preliminaries Name of parties Client				£
	Mr W. Whiteman Whiteman Enterprises Engineering House Bedford				
	Architect BBS Design				

ITEM	DESCRIPTION	QUANTITY	UNIT	RATE	AMOUNT
	Preambles woodwork (cont.)				£
A	Impregnated timber is timber which has been pressure impregnated with an approved preservative by a specialist firm. Any timber cut on the site after treatment must have a liberal brush application of the same preservative in accordance with the manufacturer's instructions.				
B					

ITEM	DESCRIPTION	QUANTITY	UNIT	RATE	AMOUNT
	Super structure (upper floor)				£
	Woodwork				
	Impregnated sawn softwood				
A	50 mm × 200 mm joist	85	M		
B	75 mm × 200 mm joist	7	M		
C					
D					

ITEM	DESCRIPTION	QUANTITY	UNIT	RATE	AMOUNT
	Internal doors (cont.)				£
	Ironmongery				
	Supply and fix the following ironmongery as described with matching screws to softwood or plywood faced doors.				
	Note: references refer to BBS catalogue no. 6b				
A	*Pair* 100 mm pressed steel butt hinges (1.47)	2	No		
B	*Pair* 75 mm pressed steel butt hinges (1.48)	4.5	No		
C	*Pair* 75 mm brass butt hinges (1.23)	1	No		
D	Mortise lock/latch (2.14)	2	No		
E	Mortise latch (2.15)	6	No		
F	Mortise lock/latch furniture (3.14)	2	No		
G	Mortise latch furniture (3.15)	6	No		
H	Coat hook (6.25)	2	No		
J	Provide the P.C. sum of *three hundred and fifty pounds* £350 for the supply and installation by a specialist subcontractor of two overhead garage doors.			350	00
K	*Add* for expenses and profit.			%	
L	Include the provisional sum of *one hundred and fifty pounds* £150 for contingencies.			150	00
	Carried to Collection			£	

(Left stack item column reads:) A, B / A, C, D, E, F, G / C, D, E, F, G, H, J, K, L, M

Figure 22   *Extracts from a bill of quantities*

are fabricated or partly fabricated off-site. Where an item requires assembly or other works on-site this should be included in its description.

Trussed rafters and roof trusses These should be described, enumerated and accompanied by component details.

Doors Doors shall be described and enumerated, double or multileave doors being counted according to the number of leaves.

Door frames and linings Group these together, stating the number required. Numbers of jambs, heads, sills, mullions and transoms should be stated along with their description, metres run and cross-section dimensions.

Windows These should be described, enumerated and accompanied by component details.

Staircases and balustrades These should be described, enumerated and accompanied by component details.

Fittings Fittings should be described, enumerated and accompanied by component details.

Ironmongery Each unit or set should be enumerated separately. In all cases particulars of the following must be given:

Kind and quality
Surface finish
Constituent parts of a unit or set
Material to which item is to be fixed
Constraints in respect of fixing

Sundries All other items not mentioned should be described and enumerated and, where applicable, given in square metres or metres run and cross-section dimensions etc.

Conditions of contract

Most building work is carried out under a 'standard form of contract' such as the Joint Contractors Tribunal (JCT) forms of contract or the Building Employers' Confederation (BEC) form of contract. The actual standard form of contract used will depend on the following:

Type of client (local authority, public limited company or private individual)
Size and type of work (subcontract, small or major project, package deal)

Contract documents (with or without quantities or approximate quantities).

A building contract is basically a legal agreement between the parties involved in which the contractor agrees to carry out the building work and the client agrees to pay a sum of money for the work. The contract should also include the rights and obligations of all parties and details of procedures for variations, interim payments retention and the defects liability period.

These terms can be defined as follows:

Variations A modification of the specification by the client or architect. The contractor must be issued with a written variation order or architect's instruction. Any cost adjustment as a result of the variation must be agreed between the quantity surveyor and the contractor.

Interim payment A monthly or periodic payment made to the contractor by the client. It is based on the quantity surveyor's interim valuation of the work done and the materials purchased by the contractor. On agreeing the interim valuation the architect will issue an interim certificate which authorizes the client to make the payment.

Final account Final payment on completion. The architect will issue a certificate of practical completion when the building work is finished. The quantity surveyor and the contractor will then agree the final account less the retention.

Retention A sum of money which is retained by the client until the end of an agreed defects liability period.

Defects liability period A period of normally six months after practical completion to allow any defects to become apparent. The contractor will be entitled to the retention after any defects have been rectified to the architect's satisfaction.

Work programming

On obtaining a contract for a building project a contractor will prepare a programme which shows the sequence of work activities. In some cases an architect may stipulate that a programme of work is submitted by the contractor at the time of tendering; this gives the architect a measure of the contractor's organizing ability.

A programme will show the interrelationship between the different tasks and also when and for what duration resources such as materials, equipment and workforce are required. Once under way the progress of the actual work can be compared with the target times contained in a programme. If the target times are realistic, a programme can be a source of motivation for the site management who will make every effort to stick to the programme and retrieve lost ground when required. There are a number of factors, some outside the management's control, which could lead to a programme modification. These factors include: bad weather; labour shortages; strikes; late material deliveries; variations to contract; lack of specialist information; bad planning and bad site management etc. Therefore when determining the length of a contract the contractor will normally make an addition of about 10 per cent to the target completion date to allow for such eventualities.

Note: Contracts that run over the completion date involve extra costs, loss of profit and often time penalty payments.

There are a number of different ways in which a programme can be produced and displayed. These include:

Bar charts
Line of balance charts
Critical path diagrams
Procedure diagrams

The most widely used and popular as far as the building contractor is concerned are the bar or Gantt charts. These charts are probably the most simple to use and understand.

They are drawn up with the individual tasks listed in a vertical column on the left-hand side of the sheet and a horizontal time scale along the top. The target times of the individual tasks are shown by a horizontal bar. A second horizontal bar is shaded in to show the work progress and the actual time taken for each task. Plant and labour requirements are often included along the bottom of the sheet. A typical bar/Gantt chart is shown in Figure 23. In addition to their use as an overall contract programme, bar charts can be used for short-term, weekly and monthly plans.

Site layout

A building site can be seen as a temporary workshop and store from which the building contractor will erect the building. Site layouts can be planned on a pinboard using cardboard cutouts held with map pins to represent the various requirements. The cutouts can then be moved around until a satisfactory layout is achieved. See Figure 24 for a typical layout. A satisfactory layout is one which minimizes the movement of operatives, materials and plant during the course of construction while at the same time providing protection and security for materials.

Points to bear in mind when planning the layout are as follows:

1 Site accommodation must comply with the requirements of the HASAWA Construction Regulations (health and welfare) and the National Working Rules for the building industry.
2 Materials storage areas should be convenient to the site access and the building itself. Different materials have differing requirements. For example, timber in general should be stacked in 'stick' clear of the ground and covered with a tarpaulin; kiln-dried timber should be in a heated store; cement in a dry store; frames, pipes and drains etc. in a locked compound; and ironmongery, copper pipe, plumbing and electrical fittings in a locked secure store.
3 Consider phased deliveries of materials. It is often impossible to store on site the complete stock required. Delay delivery of joinery fitments etc. Use can be made of the new building for storage.
4 On larger sites, provide work areas for formwork, reinforcement and pipework fabrication etc.; provide through routes for material deliveries, to avoid any reversing of lorries and traffic congestion; locate site

NOTES

target
actual

GL	general labourer
DL	drain layer
BL	bricklayer
CJ	carpenter and joiner
S/C	sub-contractor

BBS CONSTRUCTION

JOB TITLE — PLOT 3 Hilltop Road

DRAWING TITLE — Programme

JOB NO.	DRAWING NO.

SCALE	DATE	DRAWN	CHECKED

Contract completion date 15 June

Task	Week comm.	21 Mar	28 Mar	4 Apr	11 Apr	18 Apr	25 Apr	2 May	9 May	16 May	23 May	30 May	6 Jun	13 Jun	20 Jun
	Week no.	1	2	3	4	5	6	7	8	9	10	11	12	13	14
Site preparation															
Setting out															
Excavate foundations and drains															
Concrete foundations lay drains (readymix conc.)															
Brickwork to DPC															
Hardcore/concrete to ground floor (readymix conc.)															
Brickwork to first floor															
First-floor joists															
Brickwork to eaves															
Roof structure															
Roof tile	S/C														
Internal blockwork partitions															
Carpentry and joinery						1st fix		2nd fix							
Plumbing	S/C						1st fix		2nd fix						
Electrical	S/C							1st fix	2nd fix						
Services water, electric, gas, telecom	S/C														
Plastering	S/C														
Decoration and glazing	S/C				Glazing					Decorations					
Internal finishing															
External finishing															
Labour requirements	GL / DL	3	2 / 2	3	1	1	1	1	1	1	2	2			
	BL		2	4/2L	4/2L		2/1L								
	CJ					2	2	2	2	2		1			
Plant requirements	JCB mix														
	scaff.														

Figure 23 *Bar/Gantt chart*

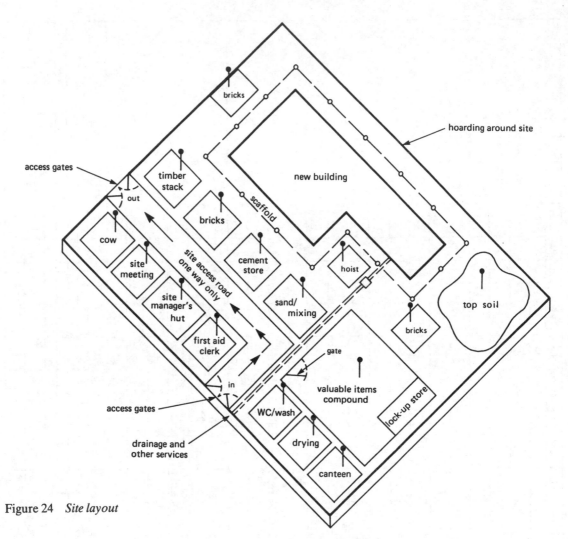

Figure 24   *Site layout*

management's accommodation away from the noise of the main building works; consider use of crane or hoist; consider use of security lighting and patrols.

General site paperwork

No building site could function effectively without a certain amount of day-to-day paperwork and form filling. Those more likely to be encountered include:

Time sheets (Figure 25)
These are completed by each employee on a weekly basis, on which they give details of their hours worked and a description of the job or jobs carried out. Time sheets are used by the employer to determine wages and expenditure, gauge the accuracy of target programmes, provide information for future estimates and form the basis for claiming daywork payments. These sheets are sometimes completed by the foreman and timekeeper, especially on larger sites where a time clock is used.

Daywork sheets (Figure 26)
A common misconception is that daywork sheets are the same as time sheets; they are not. Daywork is work which is carried out without an estimate. This may range from emergency or

BBS CONSTRUCTION
WEEKLY TIME SHEET

Name _____

Craft _____

Week commencing _____

Registered office

	Job title	Description of work	Time: start/finish	total
MON				
TUE				
WED				
THUR				
FRI				
SAT				
SUN				

Details of expenses
(attach receipts)

Authorized by _____ Position _____

For office use only

Standard hours _____ at _____ = _____
Overtime hours _____ at _____ = _____
Overtime hours _____ at _____ = _____
Overtime hours _____ at _____ = _____

TOTAL = _____

Figure 25 *Time sheet*

BBS CONSTRUCTION
DAYWORK SHEET

Registered office

Sheet no. _____

Job title _____

Week commencing _____

Description of work

Labour	Name	Craft	Hours	Gross rate	Total	
			—			
			Total labour			
Materials		**Quantity**	**Rate**	**% Addition**		
			Total materials			
Plant		**Hours**	**Rate**	**% Addition**		
			Total plant			

Note Gross labour rates include a percentage for overheads and profit as set out in the contract conditions.	Sub total		
	VAT (where applicable) _____ %		
	Total claim		

Site manager/foreman _____

Architect _____

Figure 26 *Daywork sheet*

repair work carried out by a jobbing builder to work that was unforeseen at the start of a major contract, for example, repairs, replacements, demolition, extra ground work, late alterations etc. Daywork sheets should be completed by the contractor, authorized by the clerk of works or architect and finally passed on to the quantity surveyor for inclusion in the next interim payment. This payment is made from the provisional contingency sum included in the bill of quantities for any unforeseen work. Details of daywork procedures should be included in the contract conditions. A written architect's instruction is normally required before any work commences.

Confirmation notice (Figure 27)

Where architects issue verbal instructions for daywork or variations, written confirmation of these instructions should be sought by the contractor from the architect before any work is carried out. This does away with any misunderstanding and prevents disputes over payment at a later date.

Note: Although clerk of works's instructions are of an advisory or informative nature and do not normally involve extra payment, written confirmation of these should be received from the architect.

Daily report/site diary (Figure 28)

This is used to convey information back to head office and also to provide a source for future reference, especially should a problem or dispute arise later in the contract regarding verbal instructions, telephone promises, site visitors, delays or stoppages due to late deliveries, late starts by subcontractors or bad weather conditions. Like all reports its purpose is to disclose or record facts; it should therefore be brief and to the point. Many contractors use a duplicate book for the combined daily report and site diary. After filling in, the top copy is sent to head office, the carbon copy being retained on site. Some firms use two separate documents to fulfil the same function.

Orders/requisitions (Figure 29)

The majority of building materials are obtained through the firm's buyer, who at the estimating stage would have sought quotes from the various suppliers or manufacturers in order to compare prices, qualities and discounts. It is the buyer's responsibility to order and arrange phased deliveries of the required materials to coincide with the contract programme. Each job would be issued with a duplicate order/requisition book for obtaining sundry items from the firm's central stores or, in the case of a smaller builder, direct from the supplier. Items of plant would be requisitioned from the plant manager or plant hirers using a similar order/requisition book.

Delivery notes (Figure 30)

When materials and plant are delivered to the site, the foreman is required to sign the driver's delivery note. A careful check should be made to ensure all the materials are there and undamaged. Any missing or damaged goods must be clearly indicated on the delivery note and followed up by a letter to the supplier. Many suppliers send out an advice note prior to delivery which states details of the materials and the expected delivery date. This enables the site management to make provision for its unloading and storage.

Delivery records (Figure 31)

This forms a complete record of all the materials received on site and should be filled in and sent to head office along with the delivery notes on a weekly basis. This record is used to check deliveries before paying suppliers' invoices and also when determining the interim valuation.

Memorandum (memo) (Figure 32)

This is a printed form on which internal communications can be carried out. It is normally a brief note about the requirements of a particular job or details of an incoming inquiry (representative/telephone call) while a person was unavailable.

BBS CONSTRUCTION
CONFIRMATION NOTICE

No._____ Date _____

Job title _____

From _____

To _____

Registered office

I confirm that today I have been issued with * verbal/written instructions from _____

Position _____

to carry out the following * daywork/variation to the contract

Additions

Omissions

Please issue your official * confirmation/variation order

Copies to head office   Signed _____

_____

_____   Position _____

* Delete as appropriate

Figure 27   *Confirmation notice*

BBS CONSTRUCTION
DAILY REPORT/SITE DIARY

Registered office

No._____ Date _____

Job title _____

Labour force on site		Labour force required	
Our employ	Subcontract	Our employ	Subcontract

Materials	Information
Received (state delivery no.) Required by (state requisition no.)	Received Required by

Plant	Drawings
Received (state delivery no.) Required by (state requisition no.)	Received Required by

Telephone calls To From	Site visitors
Accidents	Stoppages
Weather conditions	Temperature a.m. p.m.

Brief report of progress and other items of importance

Site manager/foreman _____

Note Send top copy daily to head office and retain carbon copy as an on-site record.

Figure 28   *Daily report/site diary*

BBS CONSTRUCTION
ORDER/REQUISITION

Registered office

No. _____

Date _____

To _____   From_____

Address   Site address

_____   _____

_____   _____

Please supply or order for delivery to the above site the following:

Description	Quantity	Rate	Date required by

Site manager/foreman _____

Note Please advise site within 24 hours of request if order cannot be fulfilled by the date required

Figure 29   *Order/requisition*

BBS SUPPLIES
DELIVERY NOTE

Registered office

No. _____

Date _____

Delivered to

_____

_____

_____

Invoice to

_____

_____

_____

Please receive in good condition the undermentioned goods

Received by _____

Remarks _____

Note Claims for shortages and damage will not be considered unless recorded on this sheet.

Figure 30   *Delivery note*

BBS CONSTRUCTION
DELIVERIES RECORD

Registered office

Week no. _____ Date _____

Job title _____

Delivery note no.	Date	Supplier	Description of delivery	For office use only		
				Rate	Value	
				Total		

Site manager/foreman _____

Note Send weekly to head office with delivery notes

Figure 31 *Deliveries record*

```
┌─────────────────────────────────────────────────────────────────┐
│  BBS CONSTRUCTION           MEMO                                  │
│                                                                   │
│  From _____    To _____ │
│                                                                   │
│  Subject _____    Date _____ │
│  ┌─────────────────────────────────────────────────────────────┐ │
│  │ Message                                                      │ │
│  │                                                              │ │
│  │                                                              │ │
│  │                                                              │ │
│  │                                                              │ │
│  │                                                              │ │
│  │                                                              │ │
│  │                                                              │ │
│  │                                                              │ │
│  └─────────────────────────────────────────────────────────────┘ │
└─────────────────────────────────────────────────────────────────┘
```

Figure 32   *Memorandum*

Employment conditions

The employment of any person is controlled by various Acts of Parliament. The main ones are:

Employment Protection (Consolidation) Act 1978

Sex Discrimination Act 1975 (this embodies the Equal Pay Act 1970)

Race Relations Act 1976

On engagement an employee record card as shown in Figure 33 should be completed and signed by the employee. This card should be kept up to date during the employment to form a permanent record. The employee should be given a copy of the company's safety policy and a statement of the company's terms of employment. In addition many companies issue their employees with a handbook containing details of general policy and procedures, safety policy and disciplinary rules.

Terms of employment

These terms of employment, a typical copy of which is shown in Figure 34, include details of commencement date; job title; hours of work; rates of pay; overtime; pay-day; holiday entitlement and pay; sick pay; pension scheme; disciplinary procedures; termination of employment; disputes procedure.

Disciplinary rules

This is a written statement outlining the company's disciplinary rules and dismissal procedures. It should be issued to all employees to ensure they are fully aware of the rules and procedures involved. They normally provide for verbal warnings of unsatisfactory conduct – for example, bad attendance, timekeeping or production, and the failure to comply with working instructions or safety rules – followed by a final written warning. Where this written warning is not heeded, dismissal may follow. Figure 35 shows a typical written final warning.

Note: Verbal and written warnings are not required in cases of gross misconduct where instant dismissal can result. These cases are defined as: theft from the company; falsification of records for personal gain; and acts placing persons or property in danger.

BBS CONSTRUCTION
EMPLOYEES
RECORD CARD

Registered office

Surname _____   Forenames _____

Permanent address _____   Temporary address _____

_____   _____

_____   _____

National Insurance number _____   Date of birth _____

Title of job _____

Commencement date _____

Other relevant details _____

_____

_____

_____

Documents received

P45 yes/no _____

Holiday card   yes/no   if yes state number and value of stamps

_____

_____

Documents issued

Statement of terms of employment   yes/no

The Company handbook   yes/no

(i) general policy and procedures
(ii) safety policy
(iii) disciplinary rules

I certify that the above details are correct and that I have been issued with the documents indicated.

Employees signature _____   Date _____

Personnel/training manager _____   Date _____

chapter 4

Applied calculations

After reading this chapter the student should be able to:

1 Identify the SI units of measurement.

2 Perform calculations using the basic processes.

3 Perform calculations on an electronic calculator.

4 Apply mathematical processes to solve work measurement and costing problems.

Calculations at advanced level consist mainly of applying the previously learned basic processes to the solution of more advanced practical problems. Although many readers will have mastered the main basic processes, they are briefly covered in this chapter to provide a source of reference and revision where required.

Units of measurement

The system of measurement employed by much of the world is the Système International d'Unités (SI) or metric system. For each quantity of measurement (length, mass, capacity etc.) there is a base unit, a multiple unit and a submultiple unit. The base unit of length is the metre (m). Its multiple unit the kilometre (km) is a thousand times larger: m × 1000 = km. The submultiple unit of the metre is the millimetre (mm), which is a thousand times smaller: m ÷ 1000 = mm. The units used most frequently by the carpenter and joiner are shown in Table 3.

Basic processes

Addition
It is most important that the decimal points in all numbers to be added are directly underneath one another.

Example
11.38 + 6.57 + 0.124

$$
\begin{array}{r}
11.38 \\
6.57 \\
0.124 \\
\hline
\end{array}
$$

Answer 18.074   18.074

Subtraction
When subtracting one number from another it is also very important that the decimal points are underneath one another, as they were for addition.

Example
16.697 − 8.565

$$
\begin{array}{r}
16.697 \\
8.565 \\
\hline
8.132
\end{array}
$$

Answer 8.132

Multiplication
When multiplying, the decimal points can be forgotten until the two sets of numbers have been multiplyed together. The position of the decimal point can then be located by the following rule:

The number of figures to the right of the decimal point in the answer will always equal the number of figures to the right of the decimal point in the problem.

Example 11.6 × 4.5
                (1)   (2)

Two figures to the right of the decimal point

$$
\begin{array}{r}
116 \times \\
45 \\
\hline
580 \\
4640 \\
\hline
5220 \\
\hline
\end{array}
$$
                                              ↑ ↑
                                            (2)(1)
Two figures to the right of the decimal point

Answer 52.20

Table 3   **Units for carpenters and joiners**

Quantity	*Base unit*	*Multiple*	*Submultiple*	*Equivalents*
Length				
	metre m	kilometre km m × 1000	millimetres mm m ÷ 1000	1 km = 1,000,000 mm
Area				
	square metre m^2	square kilometre km^2 m × 1,000,000 or hectare ha m × 10,000	square millimetres mm^2 m ÷ 1,000,000	
Volume				
	cubic metre m^3		cubic millimetres mm^3 m ÷ 1,000,000	1 m^3 = 1,000,000,000 mm^3
Capacity				
	litre (no symbol)		millilitre ml litre ÷ 1000	1 m^3 = 1000 litres
Mass				
	kilogram kg	tonne (no symbol) kg × 1000	gram g kg ÷ 1000	1 litre water = 1 kg

Quantity	Base unit	Multiple	Submultiple	Equivalents
Density mass ÷ volume	kilograms per cubic metre kg/m^3			water = 1000 kg/m^3
Force mass + pull of gravity	newton N	kilonewton kN N × 1000		1 kg = 9.81 N
Pressure	bar 1000 kN/m^2 (no symbol)		millibar mb bar ÷ 1000 or pascal P mb ÷ 100	1 bar = atmospheric pressure (approximately)
Temperature	degree Celsius (centigrade) °C			100 °C = boiling point of water 0 °C = freezing point of water
Time	second s			60 s = 1 minute 1 hour = 60 minutes

continued

Table 3 continued

Quantity	Base unit	Multiple	Submultiple	Equivalents
Heat	joule J	kilojoule kJ J × 1000		
Heat flow J/s	watt W	kilowatt kW W × 1000		

Division

When dividing we need to make the number we are dividing by a whole number. If it is not we can move its decimal point a number of places to the right until it is a whole number, but to compensate we must also move the decimal point in the number to be divided by the same number of places.

Example

164.6 ÷ 0.2   164 $\overset{\curvearrowright}{6}$. ÷ 0 $\overset{\curvearrowright}{2}$.

Move point to make the number you are dividing by a whole number

$$\begin{array}{r} 823 \\ 2\overline{)1646} \end{array}$$ *Answer* $\underline{823}$

Approximate answers

Common causes of incorrect answers to calculation problems are incomplete working out and incorrectly placed decimal points. Rough checks of the expected size of an answer and the position of the decimal point would overcome this problem. These rough checks can be carried out quickly using approximate numbers.

Example

$$\frac{4.65 \times 2.05}{3.85}$$

For a rough check, say

$$\frac{5 \times 2}{4} = \underline{2.5}$$

Correct answer $\underline{2.476}$

The rough checks and the correct answer are of the same order. This confirms that the answer is 2.476 and not 0.2476 or 24.76 etc.

Rough checks will be nearer to the correct answer if, when choosing approximate numbers, some are increased and some are decreased. In cases where the rough check and the correct answer are not of the same order the calculation should be reworked to find the cause of the error.

Note: This process of approximating answers should be carried out even when using an electronic calculator, as wrong answers are often the result of miskeying, even a slight hesitation on a key can cause a number to be entered twice.

Fractions

Parts of a whole number are represented in the metric system by decimals. The imperial system uses fractions. Where fractions are encountered they may be converted into decimals by dividing the bottom number into the top number.

Example
⅞ as a decimal

$$\begin{array}{r} 0.875 \\ 8\overline{)7.000} \\ 6\ 4 \\ \hline 60 \\ 56 \\ \hline 40 \\ 40 \\ \hline 00 \end{array}$$

Answer 0.875

Ratio and proportion
Ratios and proportions are ways of comparing or stating the relationship between two like quantities.

Example
If £72 is to be shared by two people in a ratio of 5:3, what will each receive?

number of shares = 5 + 3 = 8
one share = 72 ÷ 8 = £9
five shares = 5 × 9 = £45
three shares = 3 × 9 = £27

Answer £45 and £27

Example
A 1:3 pitched roof has a span of 3.600 m: what is its rise?
This means that for every 3 m span the roof will rise 1 m or the rise is ⅓ of the span:

rise = $\dfrac{1.200}{3\overline{)3.600}}$ *Answer* 1.200 m

Percentages
This is another way of representing part of a quantity. Percentage means per hundred.
When finding a certain percentage of a given quantity, the first step is to turn the percentage into a decimal. This is done by dividing the percentage by 100. This can be done quickly by placing an imaginary point behind the percentage and then moving two places forward.

Example
10% becomes   0.10

There are three circumstances where percentages are used:

1 *Where a straightforward percentage of a number is required*

Turn percentage into decimal and multiply by it.

Example
12% of 55

$$\begin{array}{r} 55 \\ \times\ .12 \\ \hline 110 \\ 550 \\ \hline 660 \end{array}$$

Answer 6.6

2 *Where a number plus a certain percentage (increase) is required*
Turn percentage into decimal, place a one in front of it (to include the original quantity) and multiply by it.

Example
55 plus 12%

$$\begin{array}{r} 55 \\ 1.12 \\ \hline 110 \\ 550 \\ 5500 \\ \hline 6160 \end{array}$$

Answer 61.6

3 *Where a number minus a certain percentage (decrease) is required*
Take away percentage from 100, place a point in front and then multiply by it.

Example
55 minus 12%

$$\begin{array}{r} 55 \\ .88 \\ \hline 440 \\ 4400 \\ \hline 4840 \end{array}$$

Answer 48.4

Averages
An average is the mean value of several quantities. It is found by adding the quantities and dividing by the number of quantities.

Example
Find the average mark obtained for a number of college assessments.

48, 27, 49, 75, 84, 44, 65,
Total marks = 392.

divide by number of marks $7\overline{)392}$ = 56

Answer Average mark 56

Powers and roots

A simple way of writing repeated factors (multiplication) is to raise the number to a power or index.

Example

$$10 \times 10 \qquad\qquad = \quad 100 \text{ or } 10^2$$
$$10 \times 10 \times 10 \qquad = \quad 1000 \text{ or } 10^3$$
$$10 \times 10 \times 10 \times 10 = 10000 \text{ or } 10^4$$

and so on.

Large numbers can be written in a standard form by the use of an index.

Example

$$30000 = 3 \quad \times 10000 \text{ or } 3 \quad \times 10^4$$
$$6600 = 6.6 \times \quad 1000 \text{ or } 6.6 \times 10^3$$
$$990 = 9.9 \times \quad 100 \text{ or } 9.9 \times 10^2$$

The index is the number of places that the decimal point will have to be moved to the right if the number is written in full.

Standard form can also be used for numbers less than one, by using a negative index.

Example

$$0.036 \quad = 3.6 \times 10^{-2} \text{ or } 36 \times 10^{-3}$$
$$0.0099 = 9.9 \times 10^{-3} \text{ or } 99 \times 10^{-4}$$
$$0.00012 = 1.2 \times 10^{-4} \text{ or } 12 \times 10^{-5}$$

The negative index is the number of places that the decimal point will have to be moved to the left if the number is written in full.

It is sometimes necessary to find a particular root of a number. The square root is a number multiplied by itself to give the number in question.

Example

The square root of 25 is 5, since $5 \times 5 = 25$. The common way of writing this is to use the square root sign.

$$\sqrt{25} = 5$$

The cube root is a number multiplied by itself twice to give the number in question.

Example

The cube root of 125 is 5, since $5 \times 5 \times 5 = 125$. The common way of writing this is to use the root sign and an index.

$$\sqrt[3]{125} = 5$$

From this it can be seen that there is a connection between powers and roots, in fact they are opposite processes.

Example

$$10^2 = \quad 100 \quad \sqrt{100} = 10$$
$$10^3 = 1000 \quad \sqrt[3]{100} = 10$$

Electronic calculators

All of the basic calculators will look similar. They consist of:

Ten numbered keys $\boxed{0}\boxed{1}\boxed{2}\boxed{3}\boxed{4}\boxed{5}\boxed{6}\boxed{7}\boxed{8}\boxed{9}$

Four operation keys $\boxed{+}$ $\boxed{-}$ $\boxed{\div}$ $\boxed{\times}$

An equals key $\boxed{=}$

A decimal point key $\boxed{\cdot}$

A square root key $\boxed{\sqrt{}}$

A percentage key $\boxed{\%}$

A $\boxed{C}$ key which clears everything in the machine and a $\boxed{CI}$ or $\boxed{CE}$ key to clear the last key pressed. This enables you to clear a wrongly pressed key without clearing the whole calculation.

The operation of your calculator will vary depending on the model; therefore consult the booklet supplied with it before use. After some practice you should be able to operate your calculator quickly and accurately.

Example

$55.335 \times 2.1 \div 3.52$

Press these keys

switch on	Display
$\boxed{C}$	0.
$\boxed{5}\,\boxed{5}\,\boxed{\cdot}\,\boxed{3}\,\boxed{3}\,\boxed{5}$	55.335
$\boxed{\times}$	55.335
$\boxed{2}\,\boxed{\cdot}\,\boxed{1}$	2.1
$\boxed{\div}$	116.2035
$\boxed{3}\,\boxed{\cdot}\,\boxed{5}\,\boxed{2}$	3.52
$\boxed{=}$	33.012357

Answer   33.012357

For most purposes calculations which show three decimal figures are considered accurate. These can therefore be rounded off to three decimal places. This entails looking at the fourth decimal figure; if it is a five or above add one to the third decimal figure. Where it is below five ignore it. For example:

| 33.012357 | becomes | 33.012 |
| 2.747642 | becomes | 2.748 |

Example
Twelve doors costing £15.55 each are to be purchased. What would be the total amount payable if a 10 per cent discount is allowed.

This means 12 × £15.55 − 10%

| *Press these keys* | *Display* |
| switch on | |

C		0.
1 2		12.
×		12.
1 5 · 5 5		15.55
−		186.6
1 0		10.
%		167.94
=		167.94

Answer Total cost £167.94

Note: A decimal point is used to separate pounds and pence.

Formulae

Formulae are normally stated in algebraic terms. Algebra uses letters and symbols instead of numbers to simplify statements and enable general relations to be worked out.

Example
The area of a triangle can be found by using the formula:

Area = Base × Height ÷ 2

If we say A = area, B = base and H = height, then

$$A = B \times H \div 2$$

In algebra we can abbreviate by missing out the multiplication sign (×) and expressing a division in its fractional form:

$$A = \frac{BH}{2} \text{ means } A = B \times H \div 2$$

Plus and minus (+, −) signs cannot be abbreviated and must always be shown.

In general, multiplication and division must be done before addition and subtraction, except in formulae that contain brackets. These are used to show that the work inside the brackets must be done first.

Example
The perimeter of a rectangle can be found by using the formulae $P = 2(L + B)$. To obtain the correct answer L must be added to B before multiplying by 2.

Transposition of formulae
When solving a problem, sometimes formulae have to be rearranged in order to change the subject of the formulae before the calculation is carried out. Basically anything can be moved from one side of the equals sign to the other by changing its symbol. This means that on crossing the equals sign, plus changes to minus, multiplication changes to division, powers change to roots and vice versa.

Example
The formula for the perimeter or circumference of a circle is:

circumference = π × diameter

Suppose we were given the circumference as 7.855 m and asked to find the diameter:

$$C = \pi \times D$$
$$C \div \pi = D$$
$$7.855 \div 3.142 = D$$
$$2.5 = D$$

Answer The diameter is 2.500 m.

Alternatively, where the multiplication and division signs have been abbreviated out of a formula, we can cross-multiply. This means that on crossing the equals sign anything on the top line moves to the bottom line, and conversely anything on the bottom line moves to the top line.

Example
If the area and base of a triangle were known, but we wanted to find out its height, the formula could be rearranged to make the height the subject. For example, to find the height if area = 4.500 m, base = 1.500 m:

$$\text{area} = \frac{\text{base} \times \text{height}}{2}$$

$$A = \frac{BH}{2}$$

$$2A = BH$$

$$\frac{2A}{B} = H$$

$$\frac{2 \times 4.5}{1.5} = H$$

$$\frac{9}{1.5} = H$$

$$6 = H$$

Answer   The height is 6 m.

Areas and perimeters

The areas and perimeters of common figures can be found by using the formulae given in Table 4. The area of a figure is the extent of its surface (square measurement, given in square metres (m^2)). The perimeter of a figure is the distance or length around its boundary (linear measurement, given in metres run).

Complex areas can be calculated by breaking them into a number of recognizable areas and solving each one in turn.

Example
The area of the room shown in Figure 36 is equal to area *A* plus area *B* minus area *C*. What is the area of the room?

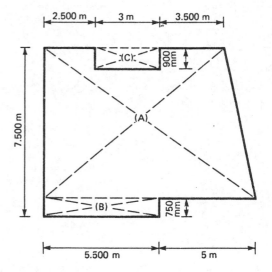

Figure 36

Table 4   **Areas and perimeter**

Name	Figure	Area equals	Perimeter equals
Square		*A A*	*4 A*

Name	Figure	Area equals	Perimeter equals
Rectangle		LB	$2(L+B)$
Parallelogram		BH	$2(A+B)$
Triangle		$\dfrac{BH}{2}$ or $\sqrt{S(S-A)(S-B)(S-C)}$ where $S = \dfrac{A+B+C}{2}$	$A+B+C$
Trapezium		$\dfrac{A+B}{2}H$	$A+B+C+D$
Circle		πR^2	πD or $2\pi R$
Ellipse		πAB	$\pi(A+B)$
Sector		$\dfrac{\sigma°}{360}\pi R_2$	(arc only) $\dfrac{\sigma°}{360}2\pi R$

Note: π is the same for any circle. It is the number of times the diameter will divide into the circumference, circumference/diameter and is taken to be 3.142.

$$\text{area } A = \frac{9 + 10.5}{2} \times 6.75$$

$$= 65.813 \text{ m}^2$$
$$\text{area } B = 0.75 \times 5.5$$
$$= 4.125 \text{ m}^2$$
$$\text{area } C = 0.9 \times 3$$
$$= 2.7 \text{ m}^2$$
$$\text{total area} = 65.813 + 4.125 - 2.7$$
$$= 67.238 \text{ m}^2$$

Answer   The area of the room is 67.238 m².

Note: We can only multiply like terms. Where metres and millimetres are contained in the same problem, first convert the millimetres into a decimal part of a metre by dividing by 1000. Move the imaginary point behind the number three places forward.

Example
50 mm becomes 0.050 m

Volumes

The volume of an object can be defined as the space it takes up (cubic measurement, given in cubic metres (m³)).

Many solids have a uniform cross-section and parallel edges. The volume of these can be found by multiplying their base area by their height:

volume = base area × height

Example
A house contains forty-eight 50 mm × 225 mm softwood joists, 4.50 m long. How many cubic metres of timber are required?

$$\text{volume} = 48 \times 0.05 \times 0.225 \times 4.5$$
$$= 2.43 \text{ m}^3$$

Answer   2.43 m³ are required.

The lateral surface area of a solid with a uniform cross-section is found by multiplying its base perimeter by their height.

lateral surface area = base perimeter × height

The formulae for calculating the volume and lateral surface area of frequently used common

solids are given in Table 5. It can be seen from the table that the volume of any pyramid or cone will always be equal to one-third of its equivalent prism or cylinder.

Complex volumes are found by breaking them up into a number of recognizable volumes and solving for each one in turn. This is the same as the method used when solving for complex areas.

Example
The horizontal cross-section of a 2.400 m high concrete column is shown in Figure 37. What volume of concrete would be required to cast it?

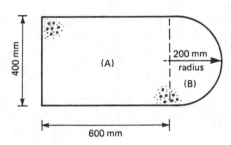

Figure 37

The column can be considered as a rectangular prism (*A*) and half a cylinder (*B*).

$$\text{volume } A = 0.4 \times 0.6 \times 2.4$$
$$= 0.576 \text{ m}^3$$
$$\text{volume } B = \frac{3.142 \times 0.2 \times 0.2 \times 2.4}{2}$$
$$= 0.151$$
$$\text{total volume} = 0.576 + 0.151$$
$$= 0.727 \text{ m}^3$$

Answer   0.727 m³ of concrete is required.

Where a solid tapers, its volume can be found by multiplying its average cross-section by its height.

volume = average cross-section × height

Example
How many cubic metres of concrete are required to cast the 4.500 m high tapered column shown in Figure 38?

Table 5 **Volume and surface areas of common solids**

Name	Solid	Volume	Lateral surface area
Rectangular prism		LBH	$2(L + B)H$
Rectangular pyramid		$\dfrac{LBH}{3}$	$S(L + B)$
Cylinder		$\pi R^2/H$	πDH
Cone		$\dfrac{\pi R^2 H}{3}$	πRL
Sphere		$\dfrac{4\pi R^3}{3}$	$4\pi R^2$

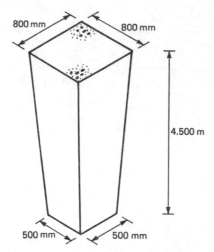

Figure 38

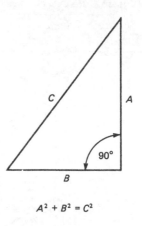

Figure 39   *Pythagoras's Theorem*

$$\text{volume} = \frac{(0.8 \times 0.8) + (0.5 \times 0.5)}{2} \times 4.5$$

$$= \frac{0.64 + 0.25}{2} \times 4.5$$

$$= 2.003 \text{ m}^3$$

Answer $\underline{2.003 \text{ m}^3}$ of concrete are required.

Pythagoras's Theorem

The lengths of the sides in a right-angled triangle can be found using Pythagoras's Theorem. According to this theorem, in any right-angled triangle the square of the hypotenuse is equal to the sum of the square of the other two sides. This is illustrated in Figure 39.

A simple version of this is the 3:4:5 rule shown in Figure 40. This is often used for setting out and checking right angles, since a triangle whose sides equal 3 units, 4 units and 5 units must be a right-angled triangle because $5^2 = 3^2 + 4^2$. If we known the lengths of two sides of a right-angled triangle we can use Pythagoras's Theorem to find the length of the third side. In fact this theorem forms the basis of pitched roof calculations.

Example
Figure 41 represents a line diagram of a pitch roof section. Calculate the length of the common rafter.

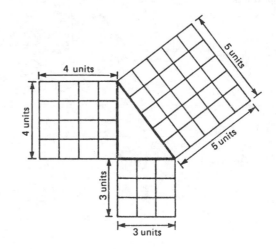

Figure 40   *3:4:5 rule*

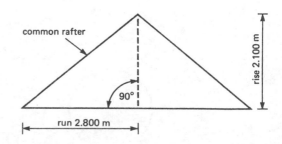

Figure 41

A = rise 2.100 m
B = run 2.800 m
C = common rafter
$C^2 = A^2 + B^2$
$C^2 = 2.1^2 + 2.8^2$
$C^2 = 4.41 + 7.84$
$C^2 = 12.25$
$C = \sqrt{12.25}$
$C = 3.5$ m

Answer The common rafter is <u>3.500 m</u> long.

Intersecting chords' rule

Where two chords intersect in a circle, the product (result of multiplication) of the two parts of one chord will always be equal to the product of the two parts of the other chord. This rule is shown in Figure 42. It is very useful for finding radius lengths.

Example
What radius would be used to set out the turning piece shown in Figure 43?

A = 0.600 m, B = 0.600 m, C = 0.100 m, D = ?

$$A \times B = C \times D$$
$$\frac{A \times B}{C} = D$$
$$\frac{0.6 \times 0.6}{0.1} = D$$
$$\frac{0.36}{0.1} = D$$
$$3.6 = D$$

Since $C + D$ is the chord representing the diameter, the radius must be half of this:

$$\text{radius} = \frac{C + D}{2}$$
$$R = \frac{0.1 + 3.6}{2}$$
$$R = 1.850 \text{ m}$$

Answer The radius would be <u>1.850 m</u>.

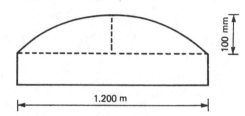

$A \times B = C \times D$

Figure 42 *Intersecting chords' rule*

Figure 43

Problem solving

You should tackle any problem in a simple straightforward manner. Marks are awarded for each part of a calculation, not just for the final answer: therefore it is very important that you write down what you are doing at each stage, even when using a calculator.

Example
The following materials are required for a refurbishing contract:

Softwood
Sawn softwood at £158.50 per m³

Item	Number	Size
Joists	16	50 × 225 × 3600
Strutting	10	50 × 50 × 4200
Studwork	84	50 × 100 × 2400
Battening	50	25 × 50 × 4800

Flooring
18 mm flooring grade chipboard at £49 per 10 m²: 30 sheets 600 × 2400 mm

Calculate the total cost including an allowance of 10 per cent for cutting and wastage and 15 per cent for VAT.

Typical answer

Softwood
Joists $16 \times 0.05 \times 0.225 \times 3.600 = 0.648$ m³
Strutting $10 \times 0.05 \times 0.05 \times 4.200 = 0.105$ m³
Studwork $84 \times 0.05 \times 0.1 \times 2.400 = 1.008$ m³
Battening $50 \times 0.025 \times 0.05 \times 4.800 = 0.003$ m³

volume	2.061
+ 10 per cent cutting allowance	0.2061
total	2.2671 m³

Cost of softwood $2.2671 \times 158.5 = £359.33½$

Flooring
18 mm chipboard $30 \times 0.6 \times 2.4 = 43.200$ m²
+ 10 per cent cutting allowance   4.320

                                              47.520 m²

Cost of flooring $\dfrac{47.520 \times 49}{10} = £232.85$

Total cost $359.33½ + 232.85 = £592.18½$
             + 15 per cent VAT   £ 88.83

                                 £ 681.01½

The total cost is £681.01½ inclusive.

Self-assessment questions

1   Calculate: $36.432 + 827.4 + 0.14 + 51.002 + 22.22$.

2   Calculate: $46.215 - 24.307$.

3   Calculate: 3.72×81.12.

4   Calculate: $35.948 - 1.75$.

5   Calculate: $\dfrac{55.335 \times 2.1}{3.52}$

6   What radius is required to set out a centre for a segmental arch having a rise of 550 mm and a span of 4.500 m?

7   What is the diameter of a circular rostrum if its perimeter measures 12 m?

8   A rectangular room 4.200 m $\times$ 6 m is to be floored using hardwood boarding costing £9.55 per square metre.
(a) Allowing 12½ per cent for cutting and wastage, how many square metres are required?
(b) What would be the total cost including 15 per cent VAT?

9   The hipped-end roof shown in Figure 44 has a pitch of 45°. Calculate:
(a) Length of common rafter
(b) Length of hip rafter

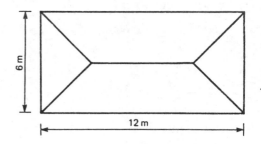

Figure 44

10   The roof shown in Figure 44 has 50 mm $\times$ 100 mm common rafters spaced at 400 mm c/c. Calculate:
(a) Volume in m³ of the common rafters, including two crown rafters, allowing 20 per cent for eaves and cutting
(b) Total cost of common rafters if 1 m³ of carcassing softwood is £123.50

chapter 5

Timber technology and design

After reading this chapter the student should be able to:

1 Identify commercial timbers and timber-based materials.

2 Describe the procedures involved in timber marketing.

3 Describe the various methods of grading timber and plywood.

4 Describe the various methods of timber conversion.

5 Describe the various methods and purpose of timber seasoning.

6 Describe the main causes of timber decay and procedures to be followed for their prevention and eradication.

7 State the various types and methods of application of timber preservatives.

8 List and state the main characteristics of woodworking adhesives.

9 State and use the mechanical principles of structural timber design.

Available forms of timber

The word 'timber' was traditionally taken to mean sawn or planed wood in its natural state. Today timber is available in many diverse forms, from the felled log right through to a wide range of timber panel products and reconstituted wood. Details of the main forms of timber available and their uses are given in Table 6.

Commercial timbers

All commercial timbers are botanically divided into two classes, softwoods and hardwoods. Softwoods (gymnosperms) are produced by coniferous trees which are in the main evergreen. Hardwoods (angiosperms) come from broadleaf trees. The temperate hardwoods are mostly deciduous whereas many tropical hardwoods are evergreen.

This classification has little to do with the relative hardness of the timber concerned, as the division is based on the cellular structure of the trees. Softwoods have a simple structure with only two types of cell, tracheids and parenchyma. Hardwoods have a more complex structure consisting of three types of cell, fibres, vessels or pores, and parenchyma.

Tracheids have a dual function. The thin-walled spring growth of cells (early wood) conduct raw sap up the tree from the roots to the leaves, and the thicker-walled summer growth of cells (late wood) provide most of the tree's mechanical strength.

In hardwoods the tracheids' dual function is carried out by two different cells. Fibres are the structural tissue giving the tree most of its mechanical strength, and the vessels or pores are the sap-conducting cells.

Parenchyma cells in both softwoods and hardwoods are food storage tissue.

Table 6   **Timber forms and uses**

Form	Main uses
Log	Hardwoods are often shipped in this form for conversion in United Kingdom sawmills Poles or posts for agricultural, garden, dock and harbour work
Baulk	Reconversion into smaller section Dock and harbour work, shoring hoarding, beams and posts in heavy structural work
Waney edge (*utskott*)	Slash sawn timber mainly hardwoods Reconversion into smaller section Cladding and rustic garden furniture
Sawn or planed sections	For general use in construction and joinery
Premachined sections	Floorboarding, cladding, skirting, architraves, cover mouldings, sash stock and other premachined mouldings
Glue-laminated timber	Structural use especially where large sections, long spans, shapes are required, for example, arches, columns, beams, portals etc. Furniture, shelving, counter and work tops

Form		Main uses
Plywoods These consist of an odd number of thin layers of timber with their grains alternating across and along the panel or sheet. They are then glued together to form a strong board which will retain its shape and not have a tendency to shrink, expand or distort	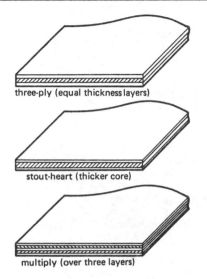 three-ply (equal thickness layers) stout-heart (thicker core) multiply (over three layers)	Stressed skin panels, flooring, decking, cladding, panelling, sheathing and formwork Furniture, shelving and cabinet construction
Laminated boards These consist of strips of wood which are laminated together and sandwiched between two veneers. The width of the strips varies with each type of board. Laminboard has strips which are up to 8 mm in width; in blockboard these are up to 25 mm and battenboard, which is now rarely available, has strips up to 75 mm	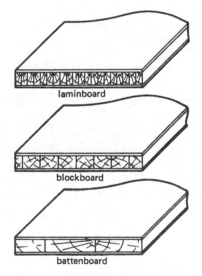 laminboard blockboard battenboard	Flooring, panelling, partitions, door blanks Furniture, shelving and cabinet construction
Chipboard (particle board) This is manufactured mostly from softwood forest thinnings and timber waste from sawmills or manufacturing processes.	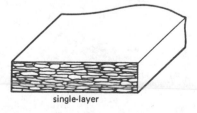 single-layer	Flooring, decking, cladding, panelling, sheathing, formwork, ceilings, partitions Furniture, shelving and cabinet construction Extruded boards are thicker for partitioning and door blanks. Also used as core stock for veneering

continued

Table 6 *continued*

Form	Main uses

(Chipboard continued)

It is made up of a mixture of wood chips and wood flakes which are impregnated with resin. They are then pressed to form a flat, smooth-surfaced board. In general its strength increases with its density

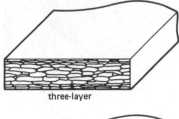
three-layer

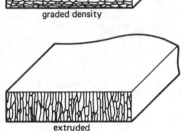
graded density

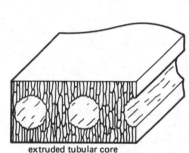
extruded tubular core

extruded

Fibreboards

These are manufactured from pulped wood or other vegetable fibre, which is mixed with an adhesive and pressed into sheets to the required thickness. Use tempered hardboard where extra strength or moisture resistance is required.
Bitumen-impregnated insulating board is also used where moisture resistance is required and for expansion strips to support mastic sealer

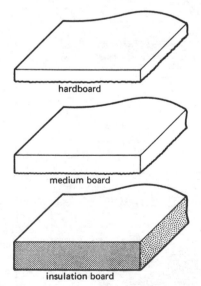
hardboard

medium board

insulation board

Stressed skin panels
Floor, wall, ceiling and formwork linings
Cladding, sheathing, insulation, display boards expansion strips

Form		Main uses
Woodwool slabs These are manufactured from long wood shavings, coated with a cement slurry and pressed into slabs between 25 mm and 100 mm thick	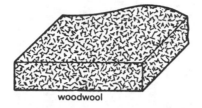 woodwool	Permanent formwork, roof decks, insulation, ceiling and wall linings
Decorative paper laminates (plastic laminate) These are thin synthetic plastic sheets, manufactured from about ten layers of kraft paper bonded and impregnated with a resin. A printed pattern paper is used for the top layer which is coated with a clear coat of melamine formaldehyde to provide a matt, satin or gloss finished surface	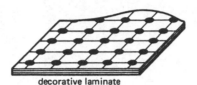 decorative laminate	Decorative, hygienic, hardwearing finish Applied to board material for use both on horizontal and vertical surfaces

Note: In addition to the boards mentioned there is also a wide range of composite boards and panels manufactured for certain specific purposes, but these are far too varied and numerous to be considered in this table.

Source of supply

Hundreds of different spieces of timber are used in Britain. Very few of these are in fact British grown; the vast majority have to be imported from various sources worldwide.

Table 7 gives the main sources of supply for a number of timbers that are most frequently used.

Properties of timber

The properties of different species of timber vary widely. There can even be a distinct difference between the same species of timber grown in different parts of the world.

The selection of a particular species of timber for a specific end use depends on a number of factors:

Availability (often varies widely from merchant to merchant)
Suitability
Density
Durability
Impregnability
Moisture movement
Price

As an aid to selection a summary of these factors is given in Table 7. The timbers are listed in descending colour order from light to dark and are listed under their common name; where a timber is also known by an alternative name this is indicated. Often different species of timber but with similar properties are grouped together and given one commercial name. Their geographical origin is sometimes given for further

Table 7 Properties of commercial timbers

Common name	Country of origin	Hardwood or softwood	Structural	Cladding	Flooring	External joinery	Internal joinery	Fitments/furniture	Density, kg/m³	Durability	Impregnability	Moisture movement	Price range	Remarks
Sycamore (plane)	Europe UK	Hardwood					*	*	625	P	P	M	££	Good turning properties
Birch European (silver birch white birch)	Europe UK	Hardwood			*		*	*	670	P	P	L	£	Works fairly easily
Whitewood (Norway spruce white deal)	N.Europe UK	Softwood	*		*		*		470	ND	R	S	£	Also suitable for external joinery if preservative treated
Maple (rock or hard)	Canada E. USA	Hardwood			*			*	740	ND	MR	M	££	Hard-wearing but can be difficult to work
Beech	Europe UK	Hardwood			*		*	*	740	P	P	L	££	Often steamed to produce a light pink colour
Jelutong	Malaysia Indonesia	Hardwood					*	*	470	MD	P	S	££	Also used for pattern-making
Redwood European (Scots pine, yellow deal, red pine)	N. Europe	Softwood	*	*	*	*	*	*	515	ND	MR	M	£	Should be preservative treated when used externally
Oak European	Europe UK	Hardwood	*	*	*	*	*	*	720	D	VR	M	£££	Hard-wearing; avoid damp contact with iron
Idigbo (emeri, framiré)	W. Africa	Hardwood		*	*	*	*	*	560	D	VR	S	££	Avoid damp contact with iron
Obeche	W. Africa	Hardwood					*	*	390	ND	R	S	£	Very stable. Often used as core stock for plywood
Ash	Europe UK	Hardwood	*					*	710	P	MR	M	££	Has good bending properties; also used for plywood and decorative veneer

Name	Source	Type				Properties	Price	Notes
Ramin (ramin telur, malawis)	Sarawak Malaysia	Hardwood	*	*	*	670 P P L	££	Ideal for mouldings
Douglas fir (Columbian pine, Oregon pine, British Columbian pine)	Canada USA, UK	Softwood	*	*	*	*	530 MD R S	££	Avoid damp contact with iron
Western red cedar (red cedar, British Columbian red cedar)	Canada USA, UK	Softwood	*	*	*	390 D R S	££	Ideal cladding, weathers to silver-grey. Avoid damp contact with iron
Meranti	Malaysia	Hardwood	*	*	*	550/D VR S 710	££	Wide variation in properties. Varies in colour from light to dark red
Oak (red oak)	E. Canada USA	Hardwood	*	*	790 ND R M	£££	Good bending properties
Mahogany African	W. Africa E. Africa Central Africa	Hardwood	*	*	*	480/MD VR S 720	££	Variations in character, particularly in density
Keruing (gurjun, yang)	E. Asia, India, Burma, Thailand, Philippines	Hardwood	*	*	*	740 MD MR L	£	Often extrudes resin
Yew	Europe UK	Softwood	*	*	670 D R	£££	Can be difficult to work
Elm English	England Europe	Hardwood	*	560 ND MR M	££	Often used for boat construction
Parana pine	Brazil	Softwood	*	*	545 ND MR M	££	Straight grained, works easily and has attractive variations in colour
Afrormosia (kokrodua assamela)	W. Africa	Hardwood	*	*	*	710 VD VR S	£££	Avoid damp contact with ferrous metals. Often used as an alternative to teak
Mahogany American	Central America	Hardwood	*	*	560 D VR S	£££	Easy to work and finish. Often used in high-class furniture and cabinet-making
Hemlock Western (Pacific hemlock, British Columbian hem-)	Canada USA	Softwood	*	*	500 ND R S	££	Requires preservative treatment for external use

Table 7 continued

Common name	Country of origin	Hardwood or softwood	Structural	Cladding	Flooring	External joinery	Internal joinery	Fitments/furniture	Density, kg/m³	Durability	Impregnability	Moisture movement	Price range	
Greenheart	Guyana	Hardwood	*						1040	VD	VR	M	££	Mostly used for external construction and marine work
Agba (Tola)	W. Africa	Hardwood		*	*	*	*	*	510	D	R	S	££	A tendency to extrude resin
Walnut African	W. Africa	Hardwood		*	*	*	*	*	560	MD	VR	S	£££	Works well and produces a fine finish
Oak Japanese	Japan	Hardwood			*	*	*	*	670	MD	VR	M	£££	Lighter in colour than European oak
Lauan	Philippines	Hardwood	*		*	*	*	*	630	MD	R		££	Widely used for veneer
Utile	E. Africa W. Africa	Hardwood	*	*	*	*	*	*	660	D	VR	M	£££	Works well but tends to blunt cutting edges
Iroko	W. Africa E. Africa	Hardwood	*	*	*	*	*	*	660	VD	VR	S	££	Used as an alternative to teak
Teak	India, Burma Thailand	Hardwood	*	*	*	*	*	*	660	VD	VR	S	£££	Produces a good finish if the cutting edges are kept sharp. Extremely resistant to chemicals
Makore	W. Africa	Hardwood	*	*	*	*	*	*	640	VD	VR	S	££	Requires tipped tools and dust extraction
Sapele	E. Africa W. Africa	Hardwood	*	*	*	*	*	*	640	MD	R	M	££	Has a tendency to distort
Rosewood	India S. America	Hardwood						*	870	VD		S	£££	Can be difficult to work, blunts cutting edges easily, can be oily but highly decorative
Ekki (eba)	W. Africa	Hardwood	*		*				1070	VD	VR	L	££	Can be very difficult to work but ideal for heavy construction

Note: See text for explanation of table

identification, for example, European oak, Japanese oak and American oak. To enable formal scientific identification every plant also has a botanical Latin name consisting of two parts, the first indicating its genus and the second its species. In addition trees with similar genera are grouped into families and related families are put together in orders. The botanical classification of trees is shown in Figure 47.

Note: Only a few examples of family, genus and species are shown although there are, of course, many more. In some cases it is not possible to give a commercial timber an individual botanical name because it can consist of more than one species. In these cases the generic name is followed by 'SPP', for example, oak in general can be referred to as *quercus SPP*.

The columns in Table 7 contain the following information:

Country of origin
This column lists the main areas of supply in the world for the most commonly used commercial timbers.

Suitability
This often depends on the timber's natural appearance, strength and durability etc. A general guide to the typical uses of each timber is given but the list is not comprehensive as many timbers, given the right conditions or treatment, are suitable for other uses; for example, European redwood requires preservative treatment when used in external joinery.

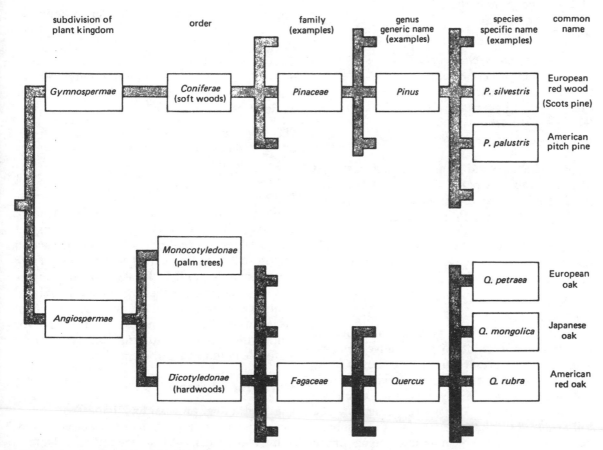

Figure 47 *Botanical classification of trees*

Density

Average density in kilograms per cubic metre (kg/m³) is given for timbers with a moisture content of 15 per cent, although in many cases the density can vary by as much as 20 per cent or more.

Durability

This is the natural durability of the timber and refers to its resistance to fungal decay in use. Each timber is given a grade of durability based on the approximate life of a 50 mm × 50 mm heartwood section stake in contact with the ground.

	Grade
VD	very durable
D	durable
MD	moderately durable
ND	non-durable
P	perishable

	Life in ground contact
VD	more than 25 years
D	15–25 years
MD	10–15 years
ND	5–10 years
P	less than 5 years

Note: The sapwood of most timbers is graded as non-durable or perishable. External timbers not in contact with the ground can be expected to have a longer life than indicated.

The durability of timbers that are not naturally durable can be increased by treating with an appropriate preservative.

Impregnability

This is a measure of the permeability or treatability in relation to preservative penetration. Complete preservative penetration is easily obtained in permeable timbers, whereas it is difficult to achieve little more than a surface coating with timbers that are very resistant. The following grades are given for the timber's heartwood, sapwood normally being more permeable.

VR	very resistant
R	resistant
MR	moderately resistant
P	permeable

Moisture movement This refers to the dimensional changes that occur when seasoned timbers are exposed to changes in atmospheric conditions. All timbers are classified into one of three groups, according to the sum of their average radial and tangential percentage change in dimension occurring as a result of a 30 per cent change in the relative humidity of the atmosphere. In general radial shrinkage is about half that of tangential shrinkage.

L	more than 4.5 per cent
M	3.0 per cent to 4.5 per cent
S	less than 3.0 per cent

This proportion varies from timber to timber.

Price range

The price of timber is dependent on world market conditions, the method of purchase and the grade of timber required, but as a general guide prices are indicated as:

£££	high
££	medium
£	low

Colour

A description of colour is not given in the table as most timbers vary in colour to some extent and nearly all become either lighter or darker on exposure to the weather and also when finishing treatments are applied. Printed colour samples are available, at a small charge to non-members, from the Timber Research and Development Association. These samples can be used for comparing and identifying many readily available commercial timbers.

Marketing of timber

The marketing process for timber can be a complicated one. Most timber is purchased in its country of origin and shipped to the United Kingdom by an importer. Timber importers sell their supplies to timber merchants and major users (large joinery works). The larger timber merchants may also be importers and sometimes major users are both importers and merchants.

Imported timbers may be purchased at any stage of its travel from the forest to the port of entry in the United Kingdom. Typical methods of purchase are FAS, FOB and CIF.

FAS

When a buyer contracts to purchase timber FAS the purchase price will include the actual cost of the timber and its delivery alongside the vessel at the port of departure. FAS means 'free along side' or inclusive of all costs alongside the vessel. The buyer is responsible for chartering the ship, loading the timber and arranging insurance cover for the passage.

FOB

This is a similar method to FAS but in addition the purchase price includes the cost of loading the timber on the ship. FOB therefore means 'free on board' or inclusive of all costs on board the vessel. The buyer is still responsible for chartering the ship and arranging insurance cover.

CIF

This stands for 'cost, insurance, freight'. This means that the contract price includes the actual cost of the timber, the insurance cover and all transport, handling and shipping charges from the forest to its destination in the United Kingdom.

Grading of timber

Most imported timber and plywood is graded for quality at its source of origin by the exporting sawmill. Quality varies from country to country but in all cases it is the higher grades, which are practically defect free, that command the higher prices.

Shipping marks

The exporting mill marks every piece of timber with its own private trade or shipping mark. This

identifies its origin and quality. It may be stamped, stencilled or hammer branded on the end of each piece; different combinations of letters, symbols and colours are used for each grade. A typical shipping mark is illustrated in Figure 48.

As many hundreds of marks are in use they are of little significance to the end user, but details of the timber may be obtained by consulting a directory of timber shipping marks.

Softwood grading

A number of countries, using different gradings, export timber to the United Kingdom. Only a small percentage is British grown. Most softwoods are graded using a defects system which specifies the maximum amount or size of defect permissable for each grade of timber.

The North European countries – Sweden, Finland etc. – have a unified grading system. Their mill grading rules describe six basic qualities of redwood and whitewood, numbered I, II, III, IV, V, and VI (first, second, third, fourth, fifth and sixth). Figure 49 shows typical examples of 100 mm wide sawn boards graded to these rules.

Figure 48 *Typical shipping mark*

Figure 49 *Softwood grading*

Table 8   **Approximate comparison of softwood qualities**

Northern Europe and Eastern Canada	Russia	Canada and North America	Brazil	Common end use
		All clear qualities	No. 1 No. 2	Joinery and high-class work
I II III IV U/S (unsorted)	I II III U/S (unsorted)	Selected merchantable No. 1 merchantable		
V	IV	No. 2 merchantable		General construction and carcassing
VI	V	No. 3 common		Utility grade mainly for packaging

The basic qualities I, II, III, IV are rarely obtainable separately. The normal procedure employed by most sawmills is to group these together and sell them as one grade known as unsorted (U/S). This is also known as joinery quality.

The V quality is available separately and is used for general construction and carcassing work. The VI quality is a low-grade timber used mainly for packaging. It is available separately and often known as *utskott*, a term used to describe any edge boards.

Other parcels of timber may be described as saw felling quality. This is a mixed batch of qualities I to V sold without further sorting, but will consist mainly of IV and V qualities, percentages of I, II and III qualities being very limited. Saw felling quality is termed by some sawmills as V and better.

East Canadian timber for export to Europe is often graded using these Northern Europe qualities.

The Russian grading system is similar, but uses only five basic qualities; I – III are exported as unsorted, and this is approximately the same as the North European unsorted. The Russians basic qualities IV and V are similar or slightly better than the Swedish/Finnish V and VI.

Canadian and North American timber is often grown and marketed in mixed species groups such as hem/fir (Western hemlock and Amabilis fir) and spruce/pine/fir. The main grades are:

Selected merchantable and No. 1 merchantable; these are similar to the Swedish/Finnish unsorted qualities

No. 2 merchantable is general carcassing quality

No. 3 common is a utility grade, used mainly for packaging timber

Clear grades of virtually knot-free timber are available for high-quality work:

No. 2 clear and better (B and better) is the top grade of clear timber normally free of all imperfections

No. 3 clear (C clear) and No. 4 clear (D clear) are slightly lower qualities containing a number of imperfections.

Door stock and remanufacturing grades are also produced.

Parana pine from Brazil is graded into four basic qualities, but only No. 1 and No. 2 qualities are normally exported to Europe. Table 8 gives an approximate comparison of softwoods together with their stated common end uses.

British-grown softwood was previously graded to a British Standard which described five basic qualities: I clear, I, II, III and IV. This standard was rarely used. The common practice in most British sawmills is to produce what is known as 'run of the mill'; this is normally sorted into joinery and carcassing qualities by the timber merchants.

Hardwood grading

Hardwoods are obtained from a far wider range of sources than softwoods. This results in more varied grading systems. Often a grading system is not applied and the timber is sold for a specific end use, by mutual agreement between the buyer and seller.

Most hardwood grading is based on a 'cutting system' which estimates the percentage of clear defect-free timber, or timber with minimal acceptable defects that can be obtained from each plank.

The main system which is used by North America and West Africa contains five main export grades: first, seconds, selects, No. 1 common and No. 2 common. The top two qualities are often grouped together and sold as FAS quality ('first and seconds'). This quality consists of clear defect-free timber and is used for high-quality joinery work. Selects and No. 1 common qualities will contain minor defects. The No. 2 common quality often contains a high percentage of timber that is not suitable for joinery.

Round logs are also exported from West Africa and may be described as FAQ (fair average quality).

The Malaysian grading rules consist of four basic qualities: prime, select, standard, and serviceable. The serviceable grade is not exported.

British-grown hardwoods can be graded into four basic qualities: 1, 2, 3 and 4 under the cutting system, or A, B, C, and D qualities under the defects system. However, as for British-grown softwood, this grading system is rarely applied; most home-grown timbers are sold for a specific end use.

Timber for joinery work, both softwoods and hardwoods, may be specified in accordance with BS 1186 Part 1, *Quality of Timber*. This standard lists timbers that are suitable for joinery work and defines four classes for the exposed surfaces of joinery timber: class 1S, class 1, class 2, and class 3. Class 1S must be defect-free timber and is intended for clear finishings. The other classes can contain a limited number of permitted defects.

Plywood grading

Plywood is graded according to the appearance of its outer faces, each face being assessed separately. In common with timber, the grading rules for plywood vary widely from country to country. There are three basic qualities of face veneers from which plywood is manufactured:

Clear veneer quality This is the best-quality face veneer and is intended for clear finishing. Therefore it should be virtually blemish free. No manufacturing or natural defects are permitted and any permitted knots are restricted in both number and size. Where joints occur in the face veneer this must be grain and colour matched.

Repaired veneer quality Repaired or 'solid' veneer is a lower quality and will have a number of visible defects. These will be repaired by patching unsound knots and making good shakes either with shims or filler to present a flush, solid face. Mismatching and discolouration of veneer is to be expected.

Unrepaired veneer quality As its name suggests, no attempt is made to repair the veneer in this quality. A large number of manufacturing and natural defects is to be expected. Therefore unrepaired veneer is mainly used as a backing veneer or for industrial or structural uses where its visual appearance is not important.

Most plywood manufacturers base their grading rules on these three basic qualities, but it is normal to further subdivide them into five or six different board grades. Typical examples of the grades available are as follows:

Northern Europe/Russia

Grade mark	Permitted defects
A	practically defect free
B	a few small knots and minor defects
BB	several knots and well-made plugs
C or WG	all defects allowed, only guaranteed to be well glued

It is rarely necessary for the face and back veneer to be of the same grade; most manufacturers offer a wide combination of face and back veneer grades: A/B A/C B/BB B/C etc.

Canada/America

Plywood from these sources is available in the following grades, which are approximately equivalent to the Northern Europe and Russian grades shown.

Grade mark		Equivalent to
G2S	(good two sides)	A/A
G/S	(good one side/solid reverse)	A/B
G1S	(good one side)	A/C
Solid 2S	(solid two sides)	B/B
Solid 1S	(solid one side)	B/C
Sheathing		C/C

Note: In some cases the grade marks are followed by the letter X. This indicates boards of exterior quality.

Common abbreviations

On reading the previous sections and looking through timber price lists and catalogues it will be apparent that there is a vast selection of abbreviations used in the timber trade. Many of these are defined in Table 9.

Stress grading

The strength properties of timber vary widely between species and even between different pieces cut from the same tree. To be used as a structural material some method must be used to classify the stronger from the weaker pieces.

Stress or strength grading classifies timber for structural purposes and provides architects and structural designers with material of a known minimum strength. Stress grading is based upon

Table 9   **Common abbreviations**

a.d.	air dried	p.a.r.	planed all round
avge	average	p.e.	plain edged
bd	board	p.h.n.d.	pin-holes no defect (a grading term
bdl	bundle		indicating that pin-holes are not
Com. & Sels	common and selects		considered to be a defect)
Clr & Btr	clear and better	p.s.e.	planed and square edged
Com.	common	p.s.j.	planed and square jointed
d.b.b.	deals, battens, boards (sizes of	p.t.g.	planed, tongued and grooved
	timber)	qtd	quartered
FAS	first and seconds	sap	sapwood
f.s.p.	fibre saturation point	S/E	square edged
hdwd	hardwood	sftwd	softwood
h.g. or B.g.	home grown	sels	selects
k.d.	kiln dried	s.n.d.	sapwood no defect (a grading term
lgth	length		indicating that sapwood is not
m.c.	moisture content		considered to be a defect)
Merch.	merchantable	t. & g.	tongued and grooved
P1E or S1E	planed or surfaced one edge	t. & t.	through and through
P2E or S2E	planed or surfaced two edges	t.g.b.	tongued, grooved and beaded
P1S or S1S	planed or surfaced one side	t.g.v.	tongued, grooved and V-jointed
P2S or S2S	planed or surfaced two sides	U/E	unedged
P1S1E or	planed or surfaced one side and one	U/S	unsorted
S1S1E	edge	v.j.m.	V-jointed matching
P2S1E or	planed or surfaced two sides and one	W/E	waney edged
S2S1E	edge	w.h.n.d.	worm-holes no defect (a grading
P1S2E or	planed or surfaced one side and two		term indicating that worm-holes are
S1S2E	edges		not considered to be a defect)
P4S	planed four sides	wt	weight

the strength of clear defect-free timber. This strength, or basic stress as it is known, is the stress which can be permanently and safely sustained by a piece of timber. The basic stress does not make allowance for the inevitable inclusion in practice of strength-reducing defects (knots, rate of growth, slope of grain and distortions etc.). By measuring these defects it is possible to select timber that has a strength equal to a certain percentage of clear defect-free timber.

BS Code of Practice 112: Part 2: 1971, *The Structural Use of Timber*, defined four main grades, 40, 50, 65 and 75, meaning that the timbers were equivalent to 40, 50, 65 and 75 per cent, respectively, of the basic stress. The numbered grade system has been superseded by a visual grading method based on knot/area ratio (KAR), and a machine grading method which measures the amount of deflection or stiffness of the timber.

This method, introduced by BS 4978: 1973: *Timber Grades For Structural Use*, defined the following grades:

Visually graded: general structural (GS)
                   special structural (SS)
Mechanically graded: machine general structural (MGS)
                   machine special structural (MSS)

There is no direct relationship between the numbered grades and the grades defined in BS 4978, as the grading rules differ. However, in general the following are acceptable approximations:

GS = 30–35 per cent of basic stress
SS = 50–60 per cent of basic stress

The machine grades have the same grade stresses as the visual grades, thus allowing interchangeability:

MGS = GS
MSS = SS

In addition, numbered mechanical grades are available. Grading machines can be set to select timber of any strength up to the maximum basic stress for a particular species. Although in principle it is possible to obtain any numbered mechanical grades, the two almost exclusively specified are M50 and M75, having grade stresses of 50 per cent and 75 per cent. Therefore there is a range of six commercially available stress grades which in descending strength order are M75, MSS/SS, M50, MGS/GS.

The grading of tropical hardwoods for structural use is catered for by BS 5756: 1979: Graded Tropical Hardwoods for Structural Use. This specifies the visual characteristics of a single tropical hardwood, Structural Grade HS.

BS 5268: Part 2: 1984 Structural Use of Timber (which replaced CP 112) uses the grades defined in BS 4978 and BS 5756 and further classifies them by grade and species into new strength classes.

Grading rules

Visual
British Standard 4978 limits the size of permitted defects for visual grades in respect of knots, wane, slope of grain, rate of growth, fissures and other defects. A summary of these defects is given in Table 10.

Knots
These are measured by the knot/area ratio (KAR) at the worst cross-section. A distinction being made between knots near the edge (margin knots) and knots near the centre: the reason for this is that margin knots affect strength to a far greater extent than knots in the relatively unstressed central cross-section. No distinction is made betwen knot holes, live knots or dead knots. Knots less than 5 mm in diameter can be ignored.

The following definitions apply to knot assessment:

KAR This is the ratio of the sum of projected cross-sectional areas of all knots at any particular cross-section to the cross-sectional area of the piece being considered.

Margin area This is the area of a cross-section which adjoins an edge and occupies a quarter of the total cross-section; the top and bottom quarters of a piece, as shown in Figure 50.

Table 10 Stress grading rules

Defects	GS	MGS	SS	MSS	M50	M75
Knots — Maximum permitted value of ratio projected area of knots total area of section	If margin condition applies 1/3; If no margin condition 1/2	No limit other than that automatically imposed by the machine as a result of reduction in strength	If margin condition applies 1/5; If no margin condition 1/3	No limit other than that automatically imposed by the machine as a result of reduction in strength		
Wane	1/3 except that not nearer the end than 300 mm wane may be up to 1/2 within one continuous length not exceeding 300 mm	1/3	1/4	1/4	1/4	1/8
Slope of grain — Slope of grain must not be greater than	1 in 6	No limit	1 in 10	No limit		
Rate of growth	Not less than 4 annual rings per 25 mm	No limit	Not less than 4 annual rings per 25 mm	No limit other than that automatically imposed by the machine as a result of reduction in strength		
Fissures — Resin pockets are measured as fissures	If the size of the defect is less than or equal to 1/2 the thickness of the piece, then the fissures may be unlimited in number wherever they occur in the piece. If the size of the defect is greater than 1/2 the thickness of the piece, but less than the thickness of the piece, then the length of the fissures shall not exceed 900 mm or 1/4 the length of the piece, whichever is the lesser. If the size of the defect is equal to the thickness of the piece, then the length of the fissures shall not exceed 600 mm: if the fissures occur at the end of the piece their length shall not exceed 1½ times the width of the piece		If the size of the defect is less than or equal to 1/2 the thickness of the piece, then the fissures may be unlimited in number wherever they occur in the piece. If the size of the defect is greater than 1/2 the thickness of the piece, but less than the thickness of the piece, then the length of the fissures shall not exceed 600 mm or 1/4 the length of the piece, whichever is the lesser. If the size of the defect is equal to the thickness of the piece, then the fissures shall be permitted only if they occur at the ends of the piece and their length shall not exceed the width of the piece		For defects less than, or equal to 1/2 the thickness of the piece, the length of the fissure shall not exceed 600 mm or 1/4 the length of the piece whichever is the lesser. For defects greater than 1/2 the thickness of the piece, the fissures shall be permitted only if they occur at the ends of the piece and their length shall not exceed the width of the ...

Sap stain	Sap stain is not a structural defect and may be permitted to a limited extent
Worm-holes	Pin-holes and worm-holes are permitted to a slight extent in a small number of pieces provided there is no active infestation of the material. Wood wasp-holes are not permitted
Distortion	Any piece which is bowed, twisted, cupped or sprung to an excessive extent, having regard to the end use, shall be rejected BS4978 does not give precise limits for distortion but, for guidance, states that the following limits of bow, spring, twist and cup may be applied to parcels of graded timber: Bow should not exceed ½ of the thickness in any 3 m length Spring should not exceed 15 mm in any 3 m length Twist should not exceed 1 mm per 25 mm of width in any 3 m length Cup should not exceed 1/25 of the width
Abnormal defects	All pieces showing fungal decay, brittle heart and other abnormal defects affecting strength shall be excluded Pieces may be accepted, however, where the reduction in strength caused by the abnormal defect is obviously less than that caused by the defects admitted by the grade of timber, subject to the provision that these abnormal defects are of a type which will not progress after conversion and seasoning (for example, white pocket rot derived from the standing tree)

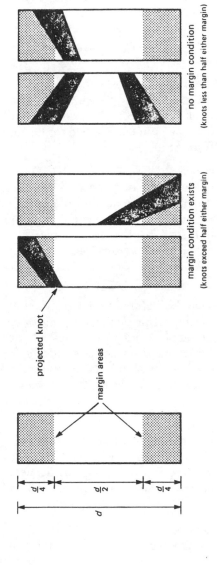

Figure 50 *Margin areas and margin condition*

Margin condition This exists when more than half of either margin area is occupied by the projected area of knots. Figure 50 shows the method used to determine whether or not a margin condition exists.

Wane

The amount of wane in proportion to the face or edge of a piece is limited to one-third when within 300 mm of either end or up to one-half when further away and not exceeding 300 mm in any one continuous length. Figure 51 shows how to measure the proportion of wane.

Slope of grain

Surface checks when present can give an indication of the slope of the grain. A slope to the edge of up to 1 in 6 is allowed for GS and up to 1 in 10 for SS.

Rate of growth

This is measured on one end of a piece and is taken to be the average number of growth rings per 25 mm on a 75 mm line normal to the curve. On smaller sections the average per 25 mm should be measured over the longest normal line possible.

Fissures

A fissure can be defined as a separation of the wood tissue appearing on the face, side or end of a piece of timber, and so includes all checks, shakes, splits and resin pockets etc. Figure 52 shows how fissures should be measured; adjacent fissures on opposite faces should be measured as one.

Other defects

Distortions, sap stain and worm-holes are all permitted to a limited extent, but pieces of timber showing fungal decay, brittle heart or other abnormal strength reducing defects will be rejected.

Machine grading

Mechanical grading is based on the relationship between the timber's stiffness and its breaking strength. Each piece of timber is passed through the grading machine where a constant load is applied by rollers. A small computer measures the amount of deflection and quickly determines

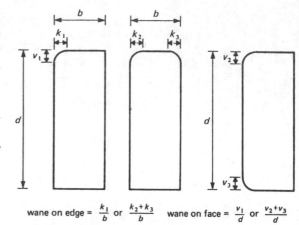

wane on edge = $\frac{k_1}{b}$ or $\frac{k_2+k_3}{b}$ wane on face = $\frac{v_1}{d}$ or $\frac{v_2+v_3}{d}$

Figure 51   *Measurement of wane*

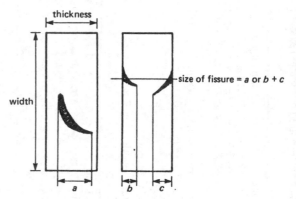

size of fissure = a or $b + c$

Figure 52   *Measurement of fissures*

the grade, which it marks on the timber in the same operation by splashes of coloured dyes towards one end of the piece or at intervals throughout its length. The standard colour coding recommended for the machine stress grades is:

M75	red
MSS	purple
M50	blue
MGS	green

Although machine-graded timber is not inspected for knots, slope of grain or rate of growth, it does have to comply with the other limitations set out for the visual grades. See Table 10 for details.

Marking

In accordance with BS 4978 each piece of

visually stress-graded timber or component must be clearly marked at least once on one face, edge or end, with:

1   Its grade mark GS or SS
2   A mark to indicate the grader or the company responsible for the grading.

The timber may also be stamped with the TRADA mark. This means that the grader and the company supplying the timber are members of TRADA's quality assurance scheme for visually stress-graded softwood (see Figure 53).

Machine-graded timber must be marked at least once on each piece, normally on its face, with:

1   The licence number of the grading machine
2   The grade mark MGS, M50, MSS or M75
3   The British Standards Institution kitemark
4   The British Standard number BS 4978
5   The species of timber (required by the British Standards Institution quality assurance scheme)

A typical machine stress-grading mark is illustrated in Figure 54. In addition the timber may also be marked with the relevant splashes of coloured dye.

Remarking

Where a company removes the grade mark during processing (regularizing or planing) it should remark the timber with its original grade and their own identification mark. The original grade mark should be prefixed by the letter R to denote that the timber has been remarked. The resawing of timber into smaller sections invalidates its original grade. Each resulting piece requires regrading and marking.

Overseas stress grading

Timber may be imported not stress graded, ready for grading in the United Kingdom, or it may have been stress graded at source.

Stress-graded timber that is imported from Europe can be visually or mechanically graded at source in accordance with British Standard 4978, and is marked in the same way. It will also contain a mark to identify its country of origin,

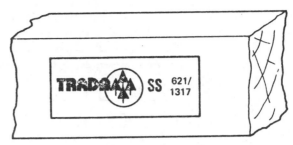

Figure 53   *Visual stress-grading mark*

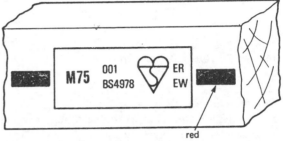

red

Figure 54   *Machine stress-grading mark*

for example, S for Sweden, the axe outline ∇ for Finland and L 'eagle' P for Poland.

Timber imported from Canada is stress graded under the NLGA (National Lumber Grades Authority) rules. The timber is grouped into sizes according to its end use. Three basic end-use groups are mainly imported to the United Kingdom. These basic groups are subdivided into a number of grades and marked accordingly, as follows:

Size group	Grade
Light framing	
38 mm thick by 38 mm to 100 mm wide	Construction standard utility
Stud	
38 mm to 89 mm thick by 38 mm to 140 mm wide	One grade only, not subdivided
Structural joists and planks	
38 mm to 100 mm thick by 114 mm and wider	Select structural
	No. 1 structural
	No. 2 structural
	No. 3 structural

Often the grades within each end-use groups are shipped in mixed packages, the higher grades being selected in the United Kingdom for more critical structural applications before use.

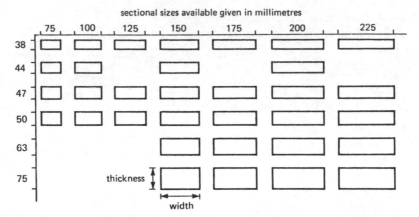

Figure 55 *Common sawn stress-graded sizes*

Commercial sizes

Stress-graded timber is available either sawn or processed. The basic range of sawn sizes commonly available is shown in Figure 55. Other sizes may be made available by special arrangement with the grading company. Any sawn size may be processed by regularizing or planing.

Regularizing of structural timber ensures a uniform width, which is most useful for floor joists and wall studs. It may be carried out by machining one or both edges. A reduction in width of 3 mm is allowed for timbers up to 150 mm and 5 mm over this width, for example, 50 mm × 200 mm joist may be regularized to 50 mm × 195 mm.

Planed all round (PAR) structural timber is easier to handle and has the advantage of being uniform in width. Certain sawmills, notably the Canadian ones, often supply PAR structural timber with its four arrises eased or pencil rounded. The normal reductions from the basic sawn size, for planing two opposite faces or edges is 3 mm for dimensions up to 100 mm, 5 mm for dimensions between 100 mm and 150 mm, and 6 mm for dimensions over 150 mm.

Size tolerance

It is recognized that the moisture content of timber affects its actual size. The basic sizes refer to timber with a 20 per cent moisture content. Certain size tolerances are permissible, but any minus tolerances are restricted to not more than 10 per cent of the pieces in any one parcel of sawn softwood.

For sawn wood, a tolerance of minus 1 mm plus 3 mm for dimensions up to 100 mm is allowed, and for dimensions over 100 mm it is increased to minus 2 mm plus 6 mm. For regularized, a tolerance on the width of plus or minus 1 mm is given and for PAR a tolerance of plus or minus 0.5 mm.

Standard lengths start at 1.800 m and rise by 300 mm increments. European timber is rarely available over 5.700 m but lengths of up to 12 m are available from Canadian sources. Longer lengths can be obtained from most sources by using structurally finger-jointed timber.

Strength Class A comparison of the various grades is made possible through BS 5268: Part 2: 1984 Structural Use of Timber. This classifies different species and stress grades of timber into one of the nine strength classes as shown on p. 97.

Conversion of timber

The conversion of timber is the sawing up or breaking down of the tree trunk into variously sized pieces of timber for a specific purpose. Theoretically a tree trunk can be sawn to the required size in one of two ways: by sawing in a tangential direction (see Figure 56); and by sawing in a radial direction.

Species	Strength class (SC) and grade								
	1	2	3	4	5	6	7	8	9
Imported softwood									
Parana Pine			GS	SS					
Redwood			GS/M50	SS	M75				
Whitewood			GS/M50	SS	M75				
Western Red Cedar	GS	SS							
Douglas Fir	No.3		GS	SS					
			No.1 No.2	Sels					
Hem-Fir	No.3		GS/M50	SS	M75				
			No.1 No.2	Sels					
Spruce-Pine-Fir	No.3		GS/M50	SS/M75					
			No.1 No.2	Sels					
British grown softwood									
Douglas Fir		GS	M50/SS		M75				
Larch			GS	SS					
Scots Pine			GS/M50	SS	M75				
Spruce	GS	M50/SS	M75						
Tropical hardwood									
Ekki								HS	
Greenheart									HS
Iroko				HS					
Keruing							HS		
Teak				HS					

The terms 'radial' and 'tangential' refer to the cut surfaces of the timber in relation to the growth rings of the tree. Both methods have their advantages and disadvantages. In practice very little timber is cut either truly tangentially or truly radially because there would be too much wastage in both timber and manpower.

To be classified as either a tangential or a radial cut, the timber must conform to the following standards:

Tangential Timber converted so that the annual rings meet the wider surface of the timber over at least half its width, at an angle of less than 45°. See Figure 57.

Radial Timber converted so that the annual rings meet the wider surface of the timber throughout its width at an angle of 45° or more. See Figure 58.

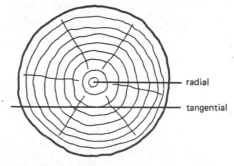

Figure 56　*Timber conversion*

Figure 57　*Tangential cut, annual rings at less than 45°*

Figure 58　*Radial cut, annual rings at 45° or more*

There are four main methods of conversion to produce timber to these standards:

Through and through
Tangential
Quarter
Boxed heart

Through and through (Figure 59)

This method is also known as slash or slab sawing. It is the simplest and cheapest way to convert timber, with very little wastage.

Note: Approximately two-thirds of the boards will be tangential and one-third (the middle boards) will be radial.

The majority of boards produced in this way are prone to a large amount of shrinkage and distortion.

Tangential (Figure 60)

This method is used when converting timber for floor joists and beams, since it produces the strongest timber. It is also used for decorative purposes on timbers which have distinctive annual rings, for example, pitch pine and Douglas fir, because it produces 'flame figuring' or 'fiery grain'.

Quarter (Figure 61)

This is the most expensive method of conversion, although it produces the best quality timber which is ideal for joinery purposes. This is because the boards have very little tendency to shrink or distort. In timber where the medullary rays are prominent, the boards will have a figured finish, for example, figured or silver-grained oak. See Figure 62.

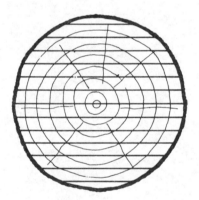

Figure 59   *Through-and-through conversion*

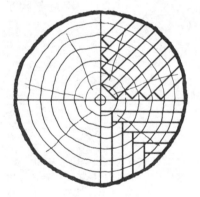

Figure 61   *Quarter conversion*

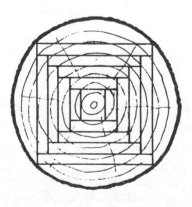

Figure 60   *Tangential conversion*

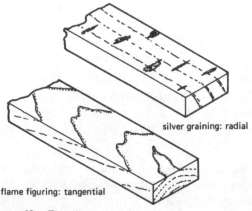

silver graining: radial

flame figuring: tangential

Figure 62   *Figuring*

Boxed heart (Figure 63)

This is a type of radial sawing and is done when the heart of a tree is rotten or badly shaken. It is also known as floorboard sawing as the boards produced are ideal for this purpose because they wear well and do not distort. The waste pieces of timber are of an inferior quality but are often used for fencing etc.

Types of machine

There are three main types of machine used to convert round tree trunks into square-section timber.

The circular sawmill

This is also known as a rack saw bench. It consists of a circular saw blade of up to 2.1 m in diameter and a travelling table on to which the tree trunk is fastened.

The log band mill

This can be of either horizontal or vertical type. Both types consist of a continuous band saw blade, up to 250 mm in width, mounted on two large-diameter pulleys and a travelling carriage on to which the tree trunk is fastened. The carriage runs on a track and feeds the tree trunk through the saw.

The log frame saw

This consists of a number of vertically mounted saw blades which move up and down in a frame. The tree trunk is fed through the saw by large feed rollers.

Moisture and movement

Moisture occurs in the timber in two forms:

As free water in the cell cavities
As bound water in the cell walls

When all of the free water in the cell cavities has been removed, the fibre saturation point is reached. At this point the timber normally has a moisture content of between 25 and 30 per cent. It is only when the moisture content of the timber is reduced below the fibre saturation point that shrinkage occurs. The amount of

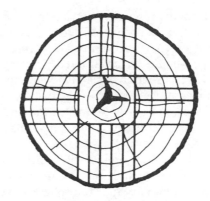

Figure 63   *Boxed heart conversion*

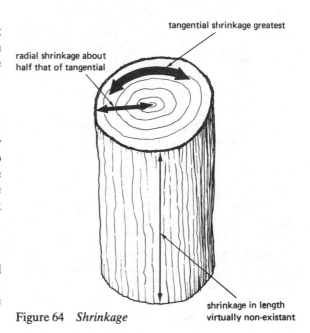

Figure 64   *Shrinkage*

shrinkage is not the same in all directions. The majority of shrinkage takes place tangentially, that is, in the direction of the annual rings. Radial shrinkage is approximately half that of tangential shrinkage, while shrinkage in length is virtually non-existent and can be disregarded (see Figure 64). This differential shrinkage causes distortion to take place in the timber. If it is remembered that in effect a shortening of the annual rings takes place, then the likely results of shrinkage can be predicted. Figure 65 gives typical results of shrinkage for different sections.

Timber is a hygroscopic material; this is to say that it will readily absorb or give off moisture depending on the surrounding environment. The timber should be dried out to a moisture content which is approximately equal to the surrounding atmosphere in which it will be used. This moisture content is known as the equilibrium moisture content and, providing the moisture content and temperature of the air remains constant, the timber will remain stable and not shrink or expand. But in most situations the moisture content of the atmosphere will vary to some extent and sometimes this variation can be quite considerable.

Timber fixed in a moist atmosphere will absorb moisture and expand. If it was then fixed in a dry atmosphere the bound moisture in the cells of the timber would dry out and the timber would start to shrink.

The moisture content of the atmosphere is known as its relative humidity. It is expressed as a percentage and can be measured with a hygrometer or wet-and-dry bulb thermometers. Saturated air is said to have a relative humidity of 100 per cent and air that is half saturated will have a relative humidity of 50 per cent. If the temperature of the air is increased its relative humidity will fall; this is because warm air has a greater capacity than cold air for absorbing and holding moisture. The equilibrium moisture content of the timber is therefore dependent on the relative humidity of the air. Externally, equilibrium will be reached at about 18–20 per cent moisture content. Internally, the relative humidity of the air is generally much lower, particularly near sources of heat, where equilibrium might be reached as low as 7–10 per cent moisture content.

The moisture content of timber is expressed as a percentage. This refers to the weight of the water in the timber compared to the dry weight of the timber. In order to determine the average moisture content of a stack of timber, select a board from the centre of the stack, cut off the end 300 mm and discard it, as this will normally be dryer than sections nearer the centre. Cut off a further 25 mm sample and immediately weigh it. This is the wet weight of the sample. Place

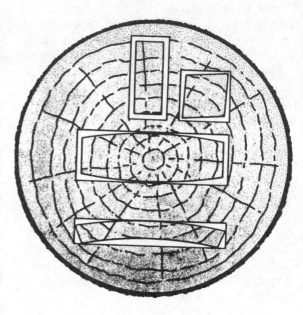

Figure 65   *Results of shrinkage*

this sample in a small drying oven and remove it periodically to check its weight. When no further loss of weight is recorded, assume this to be the dry weight of the sample.

The moisture content of a piece of timber can now be found by using the following formula:

$$\text{moisture content (per cent)} = \frac{\text{wet weight} - \text{dry weight}}{\text{dry weight}} \times 100$$

Example
Wet weight of sample 50 g
Dry weight of sample 40 g

$$\text{moisture content} = \frac{50 - 40}{40} \times 100 = 25 \text{ per cent}$$

An alternative way of finding the moisture content of timber is to use an electric moisture meter. Although not as accurate, it has the advantage of giving an on-the-spot reading and it can even be used for determining the moisture content of timber already fixed in position. The moisture meter measures the electrical resistance between the two points of a twin electrode which is pushed into the surface of the timber.

Figure 66   *Moisture meter*

Its moisture content can then easily be read off a calibrated dial (see Figure 66).

Figure 67 consists of two charts that show the average range of relative humidity that will be encountered both internally and externally throughout the year. From these charts the relationship between relative humidity of the air and moisture content of timber can be seen. These moisture contents must be taken as average values. This is because different species of timber have different hygroscopic values which cause them to achieve equilibrium at slightly higher or lower moisture contents.

As it is almost impossible to maintain a constant relative humidity, timber is all the time absorbing and giving off moisture in an attempt to maintain equilibrium. This inevitably causes a certain amount of moisture movement that the carpenter and joiner must make allowances for. The following are typical points of consideration.

Figure 67   *Relative humidity and moisture content*

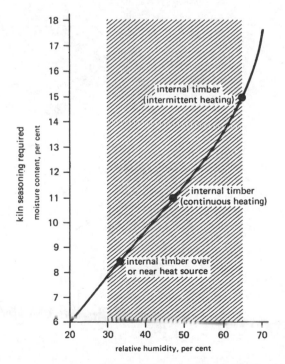

average range of relative humidity (internal)

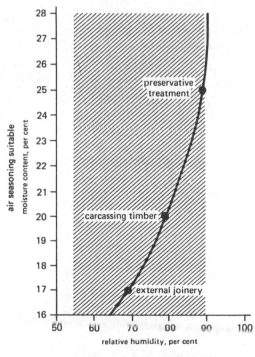

average range of relative humidity (external)

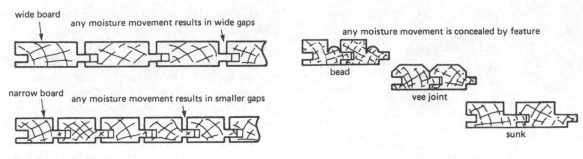

Figure 68   *Moisture movement*

Figure 69   *Use of features*

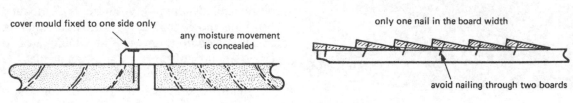

Figure 70   *Use of cover mould*

Figure 71   *Nailing*

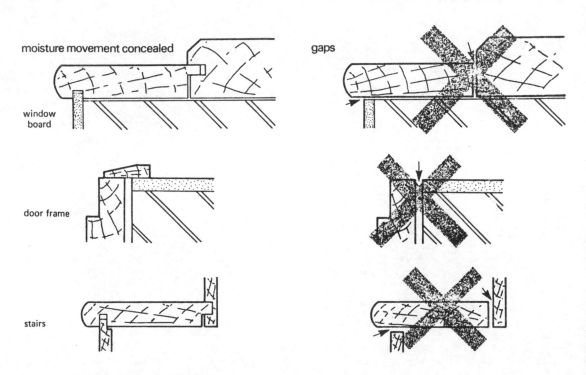

Figure 72   *Concealing effects of movement*

Figure 68 illustrates that wide boards show a bigger open joint as a result of moisture movement than do narrow boards. This open joint might be acceptable for floorboards etc. but for panelling and cladding etc. it is preferable to incorporate a decorative feature that conceals the movement. Typical examples are shown in Figure 69.

Figure 70 shows how a cover mould can be used to conceal movement.

Note: It is only fixed to one side; this prevents it splitting.

Care must be taken when fixing fencing and cladding not to double nail in the board width as this would restrict movement and result in the board splitting. This is shown in Figure 71.

Tongued joints and cover moulds are often used to mask the effects of moisture movement. Typical details are illustrated in Figure 72.

Wide tangentially sawn boards always cup away from the heart. Greater stability can be achieved by using narrower boards or ripping wider boards and joining up with alternative heart side up, heart side down, as shown in Figure 73.

Made-up wide boards, such as solid table and countertops, act as one board, with any movement taking place over the total width. The use of slot-screwed battens on the underside is desirable to prevent distortion while still allowing movement. Slotted steel washers may be used in conjunction with the battens (see Figure 74). When fixing solid timber tops, differential

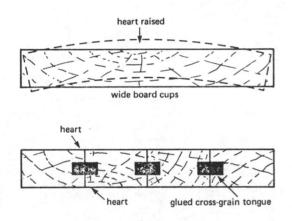

Figure 73   *Greater stability with narrow board*

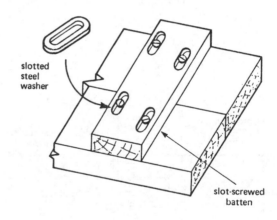

Figure 74   *Slot-screwed batten*

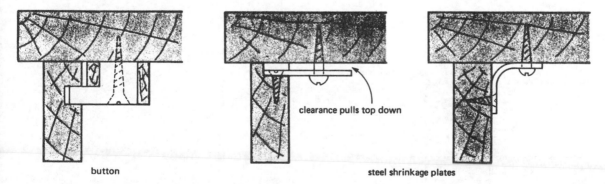

Figure 75   *Allowing for movement*

Figure 76   *Cabinet construction*

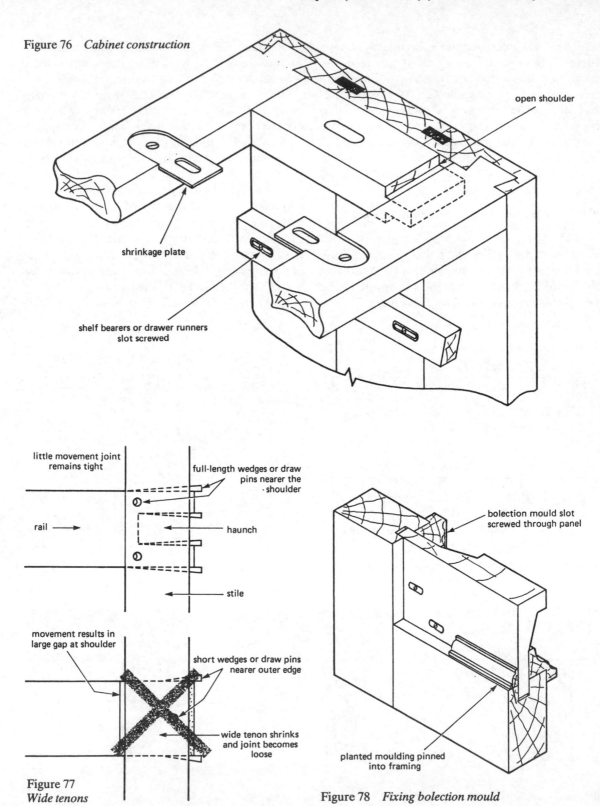

open shoulder

shrinkage plate

shelf bearers or drawer runners
slot screwed

little movement joint
remains tight

full-length wedges or draw
pins nearer the
· shoulder

rail →

haunch

stile

movement results in
large gap at shoulder

short wedges or draw pins
nearer outer edge

wide tenon shrinks
and joint becomes
loose

Figure 77
Wide tenons

bolection mould slot
screwed through panel

planted moulding pinned
into framing

Figure 78   *Fixing bolection mould*

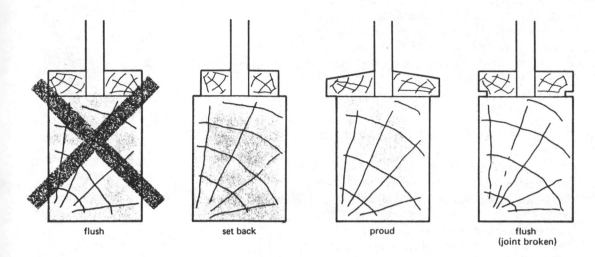

flush   set back   proud   flush (joint broken)

Figure 79   *Planted mouldings*

movement between the top and frame or carcass is allowed for by using buttons or shrinkage plates as shown in Figure 75.

Cabinet construction in solid timber involves a number of considerations. These are illustrated in Figure 76.

The width of tenons in framed joinery should be restricted to a maximum of five times their thickness. Wide tenons should be avoided as these are prone to a large amount of movement. The use of a haunch reduces their effective width, thus minimizing movement. Movement at shoulders is avoided by using full-length wedges or draw pinning near the shoulder. See Figure 77.

Figure 78 shows how bolection mouldings should be slot screwed through the panel in order to prevent the panel splitting. The planted moulding used to cover the screw holes should be fixed to the framing and not the panel. When planted mouldings are used such as glazing or panel beads they should never finish flush with the framing as an unsightly gap will result. Always either set them back, make them proud or break the joint by incorporating a decorative feature. See Figure 79.

Seasoning of timber

The term seasoning refers to the controlled drying by natural or artificial means of converted timber. There are many reasons why seasoning is necessary, the main ones being:

To ensure the moisture content of the timber is below the dry rot safety line of 20 per cent

To ensure that any shrinkage takes place before the timber is used

Dry timber is easier to work with than wet timber

Using seasoned timber, the finished article will be more reliable and less likely to split or distort (in general, dry timber is stronger and stiffer than wet timber)

Wet timber will not readily accept glue, paint or polish

Timber may be seasoned in one of two ways:

By natural means (air seasoning)
By artificial means (kiln seasoning)

Air seasoning

In this method the timber is stacked in open-sided covered sheds which protect the timber from rain while still allowing a free circulation of air. In Britain a moisture content of between 18 per cent and 20 per cent can be achieved in a period of two to twelve months, depending on the size and type of timber. Figure 80 shows an ideal timber stack for the air seasoning of softwoods. The following points should be noted:

1 Brick piers and timber joists keep the bottom of the stack well clear of the ground and ensure good air circulation underneath.
2 The boards are laid horizontally, largest at the bottom, smallest at the top, one piece above the other. This reduces the risk of the timber distorting as it dries out.
3 The boards on each layer are spaced approximately 25 mm apart.
4 Piling sticks or stickers are introduced between each layer of timber at approximately 600 mm distances, to support the boards and allow a free air circulation around them.

   Note: The piling sticks should be the same type of timber as that being seasoned otherwise staining may occur.

5 The ends of the boards should be painted or covered with strips of timber to prevent them from drying out too quickly and splitting.

Hardwood can be seasoned in the same air seasoning sheds, but when the boards have been converted using the through-and-through method they should be stacked in the same order as they were cut from the log. Figure 81 shows a slash sawn hardwood log stacked in stick, air seasoning prior to kilning.

Kiln seasoning
Most timber for internal use is kiln seasoned as this method, if carried out correctly, is able to safely reduce the moisture content of timber to any required level without any danger of degrading (causing defects). Although timber can be completely kiln seasoned, sometimes when a sawmill has a low kiln capacity the timber is air seasoned before being placed in the kiln for final seasoning. The length of time the

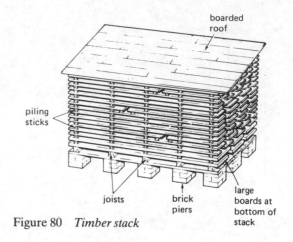

Figure 80　*Timber stack*

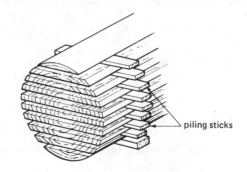

Figure 81　*Hardwood stacked for seasoning*

timber needs to stay in the kiln normally varies between two days and six weeks according to the type and size of timber being seasoned.

There are two main types of kiln in general use:

Compartment kiln
Progressive kiln

Compartment kiln
This is normally a brick or concrete building in which the timber is stacked. The timber will remain stationary during the drying process, while the conditions of the air are adjusted to the correct levels as the drying progresses.

Note: The timber should be stacked in the same way as that used for air seasoning. Figure 82 shows a battery of 20 kilns installed by a large timber merchant. Each kiln has a capacity ranging from 28 m^3 to 56 m^3 per load.

Figure 82   *Compartment kiln battery*

Figure 83 shows a section through a compartment kiln, in which the drying of the timber depends on three factors:

1 Air circulation, which is supplied by fans
2 Heat, which is normally supplied by heating coils through which steam flows
3 Humidity (moisture content of the air). Steam sprays are used for raising the humidity

Progressive kiln
This can be thought of as a tunnel full of open trucks containing timber which are progressively moved forward from the loading end to the discharge end. The drying conditions in the kiln become progressively more severe so that loads at different distances from the loading end are at different stages of drying.

Progressive kilns are mainly used in situations

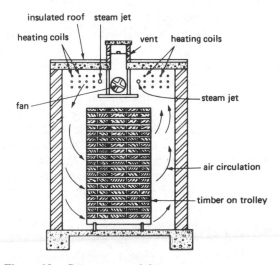

Figure 83   *Compartment kiln*

where there is a need for a continuous supply of timber which is of the same species and dimensions.

Drying schedules

These are available for the kiln drying of different types of timbers. They set out the drying conditions required for a given size and type of timber. Although all types of timber require different conditions for varying lengths of time, the drying process in general involves three stages:

1 Wet timber inserted; controls set to high steam, low heat
2 Timber drying; controls set to reduce steam, increase heat
3 Timber almost dry; controls set to low steam, high heat. The seasoned timber can then be removed from the kiln.

Developments in seasoning

Other innovatory methods of seasoning are in limited use or are being developed. These include the following.

In chemical or salt seasoning the timber is treated with hygroscopic salts before air or kiln seasoning. This encourages the moisture in the inner core to move outward while at the same time preventing the surface layers drying prematurely.

Press drying has been used for the rapid seasoning of very permeable timber. It involves pressing the timber between two metal plates across which an electric potential is applied. This raises the temperature of the moisture up to boiling, when it escapes as steam.

Microwave energy has ben used to season timber. The centre core of the timber is excited by the microwave energy; at the same time cool air is circulated over its surface. This creates a temperature difference which causes the moisture in the warmer centre core to move to the cooler surfaces.

Seasoning has been carried out in kilns using dehumidifying equipment. Basically this involves forcing completely dried air through timber stacked in a drying chamber. This absorbs a great deal of moisture from the timber. The wet air is then dehumidified by a refrigeration and heating technique before being recirculated through the chamber. This process is repeated until the required moisture content is achieved.

Second seasoning

This is rarely carried out nowadays, but refers to a further drying of high-class joinery work after it has been machined and loosely framed up but not glued or wedged. The framed joinery is stacked in a store which has a similar moisture content to the building where it will be finally fixed. Should any defects occur during this second seasoning, which can last up to three months, the defective component can easily be replaced.

Water seasoning

This is not seasoning as we understand it at all. It refers to timber logs which are kept under water before conversion in order to protect them from timber decay. This process is also sometimes used to wash out the sap of some hardwoods that are particularly susceptible to attack by the Lyctus beetle.

Conditioning

This is a form of reverse seasoning. It refers to the practice of brushing up to one litre of water on the back of hardboard twenty-four to forty-eight hours before fixing. This is so that the board will tighten on its fixings as it dries out and shrinks. If this were not done, expansion could take place which would result in the board bowing or buckling.

Seasoning defects

Incorrect or haphazard seasoning can be very costly as it causes a number of defects in timber which may lead to the excessive waste of material. Some defects, if undetected, can present a potential source of danger to the woodworking machinist.

Distortions (Figure 84)

These may be the result of an inherent weakness

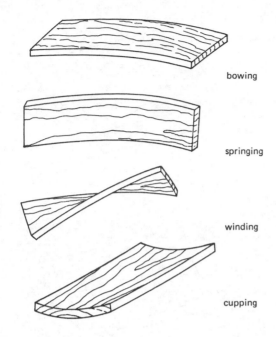

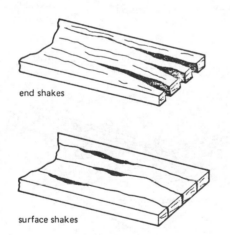

Figure 84 *Distortions*

bowing

springing

winding

cupping

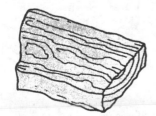

end shakes

surface shakes

Figure 85 *Shaking*

in the timber or bad conversion, but often they develop during seasoning through poor stacking or uneven air circulation. Returning the timber to the kiln and subjecting it to a high humidity followed by restacking, placing heavy weights on top of the load and then reseasoning to a suitable drying schedule may straighten the timber out. Often the results of this reversal are of a temporary nature, the distortion soon returning.

Shaking (Figure 85)

These are splits or checks which develop along the grain of a piece of timber, particularly at its ends. They are the result of the surface or ends of the timber drying out too fast during seasoning, or possibly the result of high-humidity reversal treatment. Small surface checks often close up or, if shallow may be removed completely by planing.

Collapse (Figure 86)

This is also known as wash boarding and is caused by the cells collapsing through being kiln dried too rapidly. This can rarely be reversed but in certain circumstances prolonged high-humidity treatment is successful.

Case hardening (Figure 87)

This is also the result of too rapid kiln drying. In this case the outside of the board is dry but moisture is trapped in the centre cells of the timber. This defect is not apparent until the board is resawn, when it will tend to twist and distort. The kerf will close in and bind on the saw. See Figure 88. Case hardening can be remedied if the timber is quickly returned to the

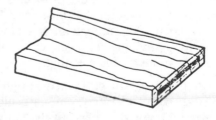

Figure 86 *Collapse*

Figure 87 *Case hardening*

kiln and given a high-humidity treatment followed by reseasoning.

Honeycombing (Figure 89)
This is internal shaking or splitting and may occur when the inner core of case-hardened timber subsequently dries out. No reversal of this defect is possible.

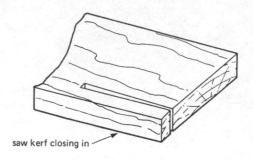

saw kerf closing in

Figure 88   *Result of case hardening*

Protection of seasoned timber and joinery components

The seasoning of timber is a reversible process. As stated previously, timber will readily absorb or lose moisture in order to achieve an equilibrium moisture content. Care must therefore be taken to ensure the stability of the required moisture content during transit and storage.

Conditions during transit and storage are rarely perfect, but by observing the points in the following checklist, materials wastage, damage and subsequent drying-out defects can be reduced to a minimum.

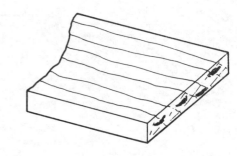

Figure 89   *Honeycombing*

Transit and storage checklist
1   *Plan all deliveries* of timber and joinery to coincide with the work programme, in order to prevent unnecessarily long periods of site storage.
2   *Prepare suitable storage areas in advance of deliveries* Carcassing timber and external joinery should be stacked on bearers clear of the ground using piling sticks between each layer or item, and covered with waterproof tarpaulins as shown in Figure 90.

Note: The stack is covered to provide protection from rainwater, snow and direct sunlight etc. Care must be taken to allow a free air circulation through the stack thereby preventing problems from condensation that would form under the covering.

Trussed rafters can be racked upright and covered with a waterproof tarpaulin as shown in Figure 91. Alternatively they could be laid flat on bearers.

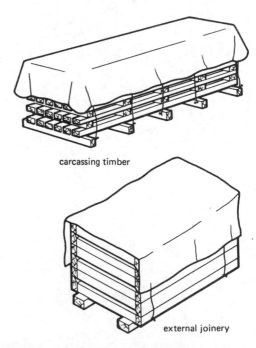

carcassing timber

external joinery

Figure 90   *Storage of carcassing timber and external joinery*

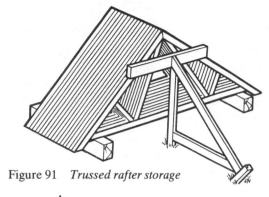

Figure 91   *Trussed rafter storage*

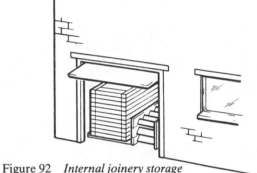

Figure 92   *Internal joinery storage*

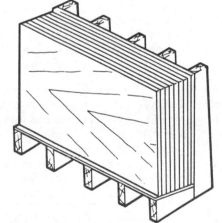

Figure 93   *Board material storage*

Figure 94   *Bad handling*

Internal joinery items are stacked in a dry, preferably heated, store using piling sticks where required (Figure 92).

Note: As far as practically possible the conditions in the store (humidity, tempera-ture etc.) should be equal to those in which the material is to be used.

Where the materials are stored in the building under construction it should be fully glazed, heated and ventilated. The ventila-tion of the building is essential to prevent the build-up of high humidities, which could increase the moisture content of the timber.

All types of board material must be kept flat and dry. Ideally they should be stacked flat, in conditions similar to internal joinery. Piling sticks can be used to provide air circulation between each sheet. Alternative-ly where space is limited board material can be racked on edge (see Figure 93).

3 *Ensure timber and joinery items are protected during transit* The supplier should make deliveries in closed or tarpaulin-covered lorries. Priming or sealing should preferably be carried out before delivery to the site or, where this is not possible, promptly there-after. Many joinery suppliers now protect their products by vacuum sealing them in plastic coverings directly after manufacture.

4 *Build to the work programme* Do not allow carcassing work to stand exposed to the weather for any longer than necessary. Ensure glazing and roof tiling is complete before laying the flooring.

Note: It is advisable to protect the floor after laying by completely covering with polythene sheet or building paper.

Prevent moisture absorption from 'wet trades' by drying out the building before introducing kiln-dried timber and joinery components.

5 *Handle with care* Careless or unnecessary, repeated handling can cause extra costs through damaged material and even personal injury. Both can be avoided by a little planning and care. (See Figure 94).

Decay of timber

In general, decay in building timbers can be attributed to two main causes or a combination of both. These are:

An attack by wood-destroying fungi
An attack by wood-boring insects

Wood-destroying fungi (Table 11)

Dry rot
The most common type of wood-destroying fungus is *Merulius lacrymans*. Its common name is dry rot or weeping fungus. As well as being the most common, it is also more serious and more difficult to eradicate than any other fungus.

Dry rot attacks the cellulose found mainly in sapwood and causes the affected timber to:

Lose strength and weight
Develop cracks, both with and across the grain
Become so dry and powdery that it can be easily crumbled in the hand

The appearance of a piece of timber after an attack of dry rot is shown in Figure 95. Note the deep cracking of the timber into a brick-shaped pattern.

Two initial factors for an attack of dry rot in timber are:

1   Damp timber (i.e. timber with a moisture content above 20 per cent)

Note: 20 per cent is known as the dry rot safety line.

Table 11   **Wood-destroying fungi**

Type	Location and timber attacked	External appearance	Fruit bodies	Effect on wood
Dry rot *Merulius lacrymans*	Houses and buildings internally Attacks mainly softwoods but occasionally hardwoods	White mat of cotton-wool-like threads later turning to a matted grey skin often tinged yellow or lilac	Large fleshy pancake with a white border and a red-brown centre	Rotted wood shrinks becomes dry and powdery. Develops cracks in a brick like pattern
Wet rot Cellar rot *Coniophora-cerebella*	Very damp buildings External joinery, fences and sheds Attacks both softwood and hardwoods	Very often no external signs of growth. When apparent the fine yellowish thread-like strands quickly turn dark brown or black	Rarely found in buildings, but are thin, irregular, plate shaped, olive-green in colour with a pimpled surface	Darkened and brittle with longitudinal cracks and often cubical cracking below a thin skin of sound timber
Mine rot *Poria vaillantii* and other *poria*	Very damp buildings Attacks mainly softwoods	Fan shaped spread of white branching strings forming into white or cream sheets	Flat, white, plate shaped covered with fine pores	Similar to dry rot but cracking is less severe
Polystictus versicolor	Timber in ground contact External joinery Attacks mainly hardwoods but sometimes painted softwoods	Rarely shows any external growth, sometimes forms a whitish sheet	Rarely seen, when apparent are thin brackets grey and brown on top with a cream pore surface underneath	Rotted wood turns light in colour and becomes much weaker

Figure 95 *Timber after dry rot attack*

Figure 96 *Dry rot attack stage 1: spores land on damp timber and send out hyphae*

Figure 97 *Dry rot attack stage 2: hyphae branch out and form mycelium, and a fruiting body starts to grow*

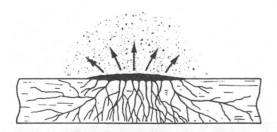

Figure 98 *Dry rot attack stage 3: fruiting body ripens and starts to eject millions of spores into the air*

2 Bad or non-existent ventilation (for example, no circulation of air)

Given these two conditions and a temperature above freezing, an attack by dry rot is practically certain.

Stages of attack

An attack of dry rot occurs in three stages:

Stage 1 The microscopic spores (seeds) of the fungus are blown about in the wind and are already present in most timbers. Given the right conditions, these spores will germinate and send out hyphae (fine hair-like rootlets) which bore into the timber surface. See Figure 96.

Stage 2 The hyphae branch out and spread through and over the surface of the timber forming a mat of cotton-wool-like threads called mycelium. It is at this stage that the hyphae can start to penetrate plaster and brickwork in search of new timber to attack. The hyphae are also able to conduct water and this enables them to adjust the water content of the new timber to the required level for their continued growth. Once the mycelium becomes sufficiently prolific a fruiting body will start to form. See Figure 97.

Stage 3 The fruiting body, which is like a large

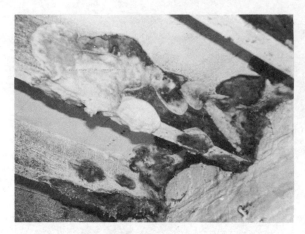

Figure 99   *Advanced dry rot*

fleshy pancake, with a white border and an orange-brown centre, starts to ripen. When fully ripe, the fruiting body starts to discharge into the air millions of rust-red spores which begin the process elsewhere (see Figure 98). Figure 99 shows an attack of dry rot in an advanced stage. The hanging sheets of mycelium can be clearly seen.

Prevention

As the two main factors for the growth of dry rot are damp timber and bad ventilation, by paying attention to the following points an attack of dry rot can be prevented:

Always keep all timber dry (even before fixing into the building)
Always ensure good ventilation

Note: All constructional timbers should be placed so as to allow a free circulation of air around them.

Always use well-seasoned timber
Always use preservative-treated timbers in unfavourable or vulnerable positions.

Recognition

Very often in the early stages there is little evidence of a dry rot attack on the surface of the timber. It is not until panelling, skirting boards or floorboards, etc. are removed that the full effect of an attack is realized.

When dry rot is suspected a simple test is to probe the surface of the timber with a small penknife blade. If there is little resistance when the blade is inserted there is a good possibility that dry rot is present. In addition to the other results of dry rot previously mentioned, a damp musty smell can also be taken as an indication of the presence of some form of fungal attack.

Eradication

By following the stages in the order given, an attack of dry rot can be successfully eradicated:

Stage 1   Increase the ventilation and cure the cause of the dampness which may be one or a combination of any of the following:

Cracked or missing tiles
Defective flashings to parapet walls and chimneys etc.
Defective drains and gulleys
Defective, bridged or non-existent damp-proof course
Defective plumbing, including leaking gutters, downpipes, radiators, sinks, basins or WC etc.
Blocked, or an insufficient number of, air bricks

Stage 2   Remove all traces of the rot. This involves cutting away all the infected timber and at least 600 mm of apparently sound wood beyond the last signs of attack, since this may also have been penetrated by the hyphae.

Stage 3   Burn immediately, on site, all the infected timber, and all materials which are likely to contain traces of the fungus, including dust, dirt, old shavings, sawdust and insulating material etc.

Stage 4   Strip the plaster from the walls at least 600 mm beyond the last signs of hyphae growth.

Stage 5   Clean off all brickwork with a wire brush and sterilize the walls by playing a blowlamp flame over them until the bricks are too hot to touch. While still warm brush or spray the walls with a dry rot fungicide. Apply a second coat when the first is dry.

Stage 6   Treat all existing sound timber with three coats of a dry rot preservative. This can be applied with brush or spray.

Stage 7   Replace all timber which has been taken out with properly seasoned timber, which has also been treated with three coats of dry rot preservative, or timber which has been pressure impregnated with a preservative.

Note: All fresh surfaces which have been exposed by cutting or drilling must also be treated with a preservative.

Wet rot
This is another common type of wood-destroying fungus which is also known as cellar rot. Its name is *Coniophora cerebella*.

Wet rot is mainly found in wet rather than damp conditions such as:

Cellars
Neglected external joinery
Ends of rafters
Under leaking sinks or baths
Under impervious (waterproof) floor coverings

Note: *Coniophora cerebella* is the main wet rot but others are listed in Table 11.

Recognition
The timber becomes considerably darker in colour and has longitudinal cracks (along the grain). Very often the timber decays internally with a fairly thin skin of apparently sound timber remaining on the surface. The hyphae of wet rot, when apparent, are yellowish but quickly turn to dark brown or black. Fruiting bodies, which are rarely found, are thin, irregular in shape and olive-green in colour. The spores are also olive-green. Figure 100 shows the results of wet rot in the rafters of a roof.

Identification
The chart shown in Table 11 gives a concise list of the main wood-destroying fungi stating their principal characteristics and the location and type of timber likely to be attacked.

Eradication
Wet rot does not normally involve such drastic treatment as dry rot, as wet rot does not spread to adjoining dry timber. All that is normally required to eradicate an attack of wet rot is to cure the source of wetness. Where the decay has become extensive, or where structural timber is affected, some replacement will be necessary.

Figure 100   *Wet rot in rafters*

Weathering
In addition, exterior timber is subject to the effects of the weather (weathering). Exposure to sunlight can cause bleaching, colour fading and movement. Exposure to rainwater will cause swelling and distortion. Exposure to freezing causes moisture in the timber to expand, thus assisting in the break-up of the surface layers. Weathering results in repeated swelling and shrinkage of the timber or joinery item, often causing distortion, surface splitting and joint movement, leading to a breakdown in the paint or other finish. Water will penetrate into the splits and open joints. As the main paint finish is intact there will be little ventilation to the actual surface of the timber to evaporate this moisture: the timber will therefore remain damp, almost inevitably leading to an attack by a wet rot fungi.

Wood-boring insects (Table 12)
The majority of damage done to building timber in the British Isles can be attributed to five

Table 12   **Characteristics of wood-boring insects**

Species	Actual size	Bore dust	Location and timber attacked
Furniture beetle (*Anobium punctatum*) This is the most common wood-boring insect in the British Isles. Its life cycle is usually 2–3 years, with adult beetles emerging during the period between May and September. After mating the females usually lay between 20 and 40 eggs each	beetle flight holes	Small gritty pellets which are egg shaped under magnification	Attacks both hardwoods and softwoods, although heartwood is often immune. Commonly causes a considerable amount of damage in structural timber floorboards, joists, rafters and furniture
Death-watch beetle (*Xestobium rufovillosum*) Rarely found in modern houses, its attack being mainly restricted to old damp buildings, normally of several hundred years old, e.g. old churches and historic buildings. Named the death-watch because of its association with churches and its characteristic hammering noise that the adults make by hitting their heads against the timber. This hammering is in fact the adults' mating call. Its life cycle is between 4 and 10 years with adult beetles emerging during the period between March and June. Females normally lay between 40 and 70 eggs each		Coarse gritty bun-shaped pellets	Attacks old oak and other hardwoods. Can occasionally be found in softwoods near infested hardwoods. Mainly found in large-sectioned structural timber in association with a fungal attack.
Lyctus or powder-dust beetle In the British Isles there are four beetles in this species which attack timber. The most common is: *Lyctus brunneus* This species is rarely found in buildings, as it attacks mainly recently felled timber before it has been seasoned. Therefore it is only usually found in timber yards and storage sheds. Its life cycle is between 1 and 2 years, but is often less in hot surroundings. Adult beetles emerge during the period between May and September. Females normally lay between 70 and 220 eggs each		Very fine and powdery	Attacks the sapwood of certain hardwoods, oak, ash, elm, walnut etc., normally before seasoning, but has been known to attack recently seasoned timber. An attack is considered unlikely in timber over 10–15 years old

Species	Actual size	Bore dust	Location and timber attacked
House longhorn beetle (*Hylotrupes bajulus*) This is by far the largest wood-boring insect found in the British Isles. It is also known as the Camberley beetle, for its attacks are mainly concentrated around Camberley and the surrounding Surrey and Hampshire areas. Its life cycle is normally between 3 and 10 years, but can be longer. The adult beetles emerge during the period between July and September, with females laying up to 200 eggs each.		Barrel-shaped pellets mixed with fine dust	Attacks the sapwood of softwood, mainly in the roof spaces e.g. rafters, joists and wall plates etc. Owing to its size and long life cycle, very often complete collapse is the first sign of an attack by this species. Therefore complete replacement of timber is normally required
Weevils (*Euophryum confine and Pentarthrum huttoni*) These are mainly found in timber which is damp or subjected to a fungal attack. Unlike other wood-boring insects the adult weevils as well as the larvae bore into the timber and cause damage. Its life cycle is very short, between 6 and 9 months. Two life cycles in one year are not uncommon. Adult beetles can be seen for most of the year. Females lay about 25 eggs each		Small gritty egg-shaped pellets. Similar to bore dust of furniture beetle but smaller	Attacks both damp or decayed hardwoods and softwoods. Often found around sinks, baths, WCs and in cellars.

species of insect or woodworm, as they are commonly called. See Figure 101.

In addition to these five main types of wood-boring insects, several other species such as the bark borer, the pinhole borer and the wharf borer may occasionally be found in forests or timber yards and, in the case of the wharf borer, in waterlogged timber.

Recognition

It is easy to distinguish an attack of wood-boring insects and other forms of timber decay by the presence of their characteristic flight holes which appear on the surface. Also, when a thorough inspection is made below the surface of the timber, the tunnels or galleries bored by the

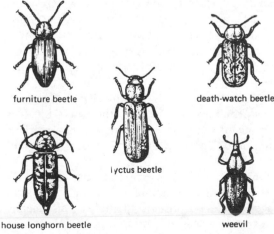

furniture beetle

death-watch beetle

lyctus beetle

house longhorn beetle

weevil

Figure 101　*Common species of wood-boring insects*

larvae will be found. The adult beetles of the different species can be readily identified but, as these only live for a short period in the summer, the identification of the species is generally carried out by a diagnosis of the flight holes, bore dust and the type and location of the timber attacked.

Life cycle
The life cycle of all the wood-boring insects is a fairly complex process, but it can be divided up into four distinct stages:

Stage 1: Eggs (Figure 102)   The female insect lays eggs during the summer months, usually on the end grain or in the cracks and shakes of the timber which afford the eggs a certain amount of protection until they hatch.

Stage 2: Larvae (Figure 103)   The eggs hatch into larvae, or woodworm, between two and eight weeks after being laid. It is at this stage that damage to the timber is done. The larvae immediately start to bore into and eat the timber. The insects, while boring, digest the wood and excrete it in variously shaped pellets or bore dust, which is often used to identify the particular species of insect that is attacking the timber. The destructive stage can last between six months and ten years, according to the species.

Stage 3: Pupae (Figure 104)   During the early spring, the larva hollows out a pupal chamber near the surface of the timber, in which it can change into a pupa or chrysalis. The pupa remains inactive for a short period of time in a mummified state. It is during this period that it undergoes the transformation into an adult insect.

Stage 4: Adult insects (Figure 105)   Once the transformation is complete, the insect bites its way out of the timber, leaving its characteristic flight hole. This is often the first external sign of an attack.

Once the insect has emerged from the timber, it is an adult and capable of flying. The adult insect's sole purpose is to mate. This usually takes place within twenty-four hours. Very soon after mating, the male insect will die, while the

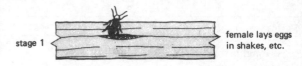

stage 1   female lays eggs in shakes, etc.

Figure 102   *Eggs*

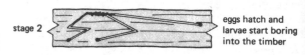

stage 2   eggs hatch and larvae start boring into the timber

Figure 103   *Larvae*

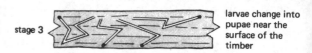

stage 3   larvae change into pupae near the surface of the timber

Figure 104   *Pupae*

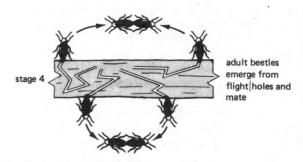

stage 4   adult beetles emerge from flight holes and mate

Figure 105   *Adult insects*

Figure 106   *Adult furniture beetles*

female will search for a suitable place in which to lay her eggs, thus completing one life cycle and starting another. The female insect will also die, normally within fourteen days.

Figure 106 shows adult furniture beetles on the surface of the timber after emerging from the flight holes.

Identification
The chart shown in Table 12 outlines the main identifying characteristics of the various species of wood-boring insects and also gives the location and type of timber mainly attacked.

Prevention
The wood-boring insects feed on the cellulose and starch which is contained in all timber, both heartwood and sapwood, although sapwood is usually more susceptible to insect attacks. The only sure way of preventing an attack is to poison the food supply by pressure-treating the timber, before it is installed in the building, with a suitable preservative.

Eradication
By following the stages in the order given, an attack of wood-boring insects can be successfully eradicated:

Stage 1 Open up affected area, for example, take up floorboards or remove panelling. Carefully examine all structural timber.

Stage 2 Remove and burn all badly affected timber.

Stage 3 Strip off any surface coating or finish on the timber, for example, paint, polish or varnish.

Note: This is because the fluid used to eradicate the woodworm will not penetrate the surface coating.

Stage 4 Thoroughly brush the timber in order to remove from its surface all dirt and dust.

Stage 5 Replace all timber which has been taken out with properly seasoned timber that has been treated with two or three coats of woodworm preservative or, alternatively, with timber that has been pressure-impregnated with a preservative.

Note: All fresh surfaces which have been exposed by cutting or drilling must also be treated with a preservative.

Stage 6 Apply a proprietary woodworm killer, by brush or spray, to all timber, even that which is apparently unaffected. Pay particular attention to joints, end grain and flight holes. Apply a second coat of the fluid as soon as the first has been absorbed.

Note: Floorboards must be taken up at intervals to allow thorough coverage of the joists and the underside of the floorboards. Care must be taken to avoid the staining of plaster, particularly when treating the ceiling joists and rafters in the loft.

Stage 7 In most cases it is possible to completely eradicate an attack by one thorough treatment as outlined in stages 1 to 6, but to be completely sure inspections for fresh flight holes should be made for several successive summers. If fresh holes are found, retreat timber with a woodworm killer.

Large-section timber
To eradicate an attack of wood-boring insects in large-section structural timber, deeper preservative penetration is required. A timber injection system is available. This involves drilling holes into the timber at intervals, inserting a nozzle and then pumping preservative under pressure into the timber. This method is also suitable for the *in situ* treatment of external joinery etc.

Alternatively, a paste preservative can be used for structural timbers. The paste, like thick creamy butter, is spread on all the exposed surfaces of the affected timber. Over a period of time the paste releases toxic chemicals which penetrate deep into the timber.

Note: Neither of these methods impart structural strength to timber, therefore replacement of badly affected timbers is still required.

Furniture
When timbers inside a building have been attacked by a wood-boring insect, it is almost certain that the furniture will also be affected. Therefore, to successfully eradicate the attack,

the furniture must also be treated. This can be done by following the stages in the order given.

Stage 1   Remove all dirt and dust, then inject a proprietary woodworm killer into the flight holes. A special aerosol can with tube, or nozzled injector bottles, are available for this purpose.

Stage 2   Apply two coats of a proprietary woodworm killer to all unfinished surfaces, that is, all surfaces which are not painted, polished or varnished.

Stage 3   Make inspections for fresh flight holes for several successive summers. Repeat if required.

Preservation of timber

All timbers, especially their sapwood, contain food on which fungi and insects live. The idea behind timber preservation is to poison the food supply by applying a toxic liquid to the timber. The ideal requirements of a timber preservative are as follows:

It must be toxic to the fungi and insects, but safe to animals and humans.
It should be permanent and not liable to be bleached out by sunshine or leached out by rain.
It should be economical and easy to obtain.
It should not corrode or affect metal in any way.
It should be easy to handle and apply.
It should, as far as possible, be odourless.
It should not affect the subsequent finishing of the timber, for example, painting or polishing.
It should be non-flammable.

Note: Although these are the ideal requirements of a preservative, bear in mind that most preservatives will not embody all these points. Care should be taken therefore to select the best type of preservative for the work in hand.

There are three main types of timber preservative available:

Tar oils
Water-soluble preservatives
Organic solvent preservatives

Tar oils

These are derived from coal and are dark brown or black in colour. They are fairly permanent, cheap, effective and easy to apply. However, they should not be used internally, as they are flammable and possess a strong lingering odour. They should never be used near foodstuffs as the odour will contaminate the food. The timber, once treated, will not accept any further finish; that is, it cannot be painted. Its main uses are for the treatment of external timber such as fences, sheds, telegraph poles etc.

Water-soluble preservatives

These are toxic chemicals which are mixed with water. They are suitable for use in both internal and external situations. The wood can be painted subsequently. They are odourless and non-flammable.

Note: As the toxic chemicals are water soluble, some of the types available are prone to leaching out when used in wet or damp conditions.

Organic solvent preservatives

These consist of toxic chemicals which are mixed with a spirit that evaporates after the preservative has been applied. This is an advantage because the moisture content of the timber is not increased. The use and characteristics of these types of preservatives are similar to those of water-soluble preservatives, but with certain exceptions. Some of the solvents used are flammable, so care must be taken when applying or storing them. Some types also have a strong odour. In general, organic solvent preservatives are the most expensive type to use but are normally considered to be superior because of their excellent preservation properties.

Methods of application

To a large extent it is the method of application rather than the preservative that governs the degree of protection obtained. This is because each method of application gives a different depth of preservative penetration. The greater the depth of penetration the higher the degree of protection. Preservatives can be applied using a number of methods but all of these can be classed in two groups:

Non-pressure treatment, for example, brushing, spraying, dipping and steeping

Pressure treatment, for example, empty-cell process and full-cell process

Non-pressure treatment

Brushing

In this method the preservative is brushed on. It can be used for all types but the effect is very limited as only a surface coating is achieved (very little penetration of the preservative into the timber).

Spraying

The preservative is sprayed on, but the effect is similar to brushing, that is, little penetration is achieved.

Dipping

In this method the timber is immersed in a container full of preservative. After a certain length of time the timber is taken out and allowed to drain. The depth of penetration depends upon the length of time that the timber is immersed. Although better than brushing or spraying, penetration may still be very limited.

Steeping

This is known as the hot and cold method. The timber is immersed in large tanks containing the preservative. The preservative is then heated for about two hours, the heat is then removed and the preservative allowed to cool. As the preservative is heated, the air in the cells of the timber expands and escapes as bubbles to the surface. On cooling the preservative is sucked into the spaces left by the air. Fairly good penetration can be achieved, making this by far the best non-pressure method.

Pressure treatment

This is the most effective form of timber preservation, as almost full penetration of the cells can be achieved.

Empty-cell process

The timber is placed in a sealed cylinder. The air in the cylinder is then subjected to pressure which causes the air in the timber cells to compress. At this stage preservative is run into the cylinder and the pressure increased further. This forces the preservative into the timber. The pressure is maintained at this high level until the required amount of penetration is achieved. The pressure is then released and the surplus preservative is pumped back into a storage container. As the air pressure is reduced, the compressed air in the cells expands and forces out most of the preservative, leaving only the cell walls coated.

Full-cell process

The timber is placed into the sealed cylinder as before but this time, instead of compressing the air, it is drawn out. This creates a vacuum in the cylinder, as well as a partial one in the cells of the timber. At this stage the preservative is introduced into the cylinder. When the cylinder is full, the vacuum is released and the preservative is sucked into the timber cells by their partial vacuum. This method is ideal for timbers which are to be used in wet locations, for example, marine work, docks, piers, jetties, etc. as water cannot penetrate into the timbers cells because they are already full of preservative.

A variation of these pressure treatments which is often used is the double-vacuum method. The timber is placed in a sealed cylinder as before and a vacuum is applied. An organic solvent preservative is introduced into the cylinder. With the cylinder full the vacuum is released and a positive air pressure applied. This causes the preservative to be sucked and forced into the timber. Finally the vacuum is once again applied to remove the excess preservative. No further seasoning or drying of the timber is required before use. See Figure 107.

Diffusion

This method of application can only be used with green unseasoned timber and is mainly carried out in the country of origin before being shipped. Immediately after conversion a water-soluble preservative is applied to the timber, preferably by dipping. The timber is then close

Figure 107   *Double-vacuum pressure treatment*

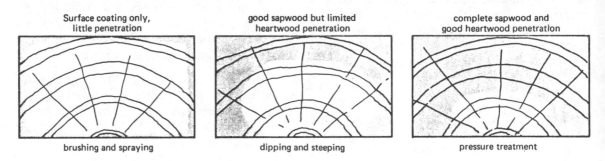

Figure 108   *Preservative penetration*

stacked and covered for several weeks to prevent drying. After this time the preservative will have diffused through the timber, giving fairly deep penetration even in timbers which prove difficult to treat by other methods. The main disadvantage of this method is that it is prone to leaching.

Preservative penetration
The depth of preservative penetration will depend on the permeability of the timber concerned, the method of application and the amount of heartwood present. Figure 108 shows typical depths of preservative penetration when using different methods of application.

Note: In each case sapwood penetration is greater than heartwood penetration.

Preservative safety
Preservatives contain chemicals which can be harmful to your health. They must therefore always be handled and used with care.

1 Always follow the manufacturer's instructions with regard to use and storage.
2 Avoid contact with skin, eyes or clothing.
3 Avoid breathing in the fumes, particularly when spraying.
4 Keep away from foodstuffs, to avoid contamination.
5 Always wear protective clothing:
   (a) · Barrier cream or disposable protective gloves
   (b) A respirator when spraying.
6 Do not smoke or use near a source of ignition.
7 Ensure adequate ventilation when used internally.
8 Thoroughly wash your hands before eating and after work with soap and water or an appropriate hand cleanser.
9 In the case of accidental inhalation, swallowing or contact with the eyes, medical advice should be sought immediately.

Adhesives

Primarily an adhesive must be capable of sticking or adhering to timber. Adhesion results from the formation of a large number of very small chemical bonds between the adhesive and the timber when these are brought into contact. In addition, for the formation of a strong glued joint, it is essential that the adhesive penetrates the timber surface and keys into the porous layers below. This is known as mechanical adhesion. The most important factors affecting the depth of penetration when gluing are as follows:

The amount of pressure applied to the joint (this forces the adhesive into the timber surface)
The viscosity (thickness) of the adhesive (thinner adhesives penetrate more easily than thicker adhesives)

Apart from penetrating and adhering to the timber an adhesive must also have strength within itself (cohesion). Only solids have a high cohesive strength; therefore every adhesive after application must be able to change from its liquid state to a solid state. This change takes place during the setting and curing of the adhesive in one of the following ways:

By loss of solvent This takes place either by the evaporation of the solvent as with contact adhesives or by its absorption into the timber, as with emulsion adhesives.
By cooling Some adhesives are applied in a molten condition and subsequently solidify on cooling. This method has the advantage that a very fast set is achieved, as with animal and hot melt.
By chemical reaction This is brought about by the addition of a hardener or catalyst or by the application of heat, as with synthetic resin adhesives.

Note: Many adhesives set by using a combination of the previous processes.

Factors affecting strength

Timber preparation
The timber should be seasoned, preferably to the equilibrium moisture content it will obtain in use. The timber should be planed to a smooth even surface and all dust must be removed before gluing. The gluability of a timber surface deteriorates with exposure; therefore the time between preparation and gluing should be as short as possible.

Adhesive preparation
Adhesives that consist of two or more components must be mixed accurately in accordance with the manufacturer's instructions. It is normally advisable to batch the component parts by weight rather than volume.

Application of adhesive
Adhesives may be applied either by brush, roller, spray, spatula or mechanical spreader. For maximum strength a uniform thickness of adhesive should be applied to both sides of the joint. Adhesives that set by chemical reaction begin to react as soon as the components are mixed. This reaction rate is dependent mainly on the temperatures of the adhesive, the timber and the surrounding room or workshop. These

factors must be taken into account to ensure that the pot life of the adhesive is not exceeded, otherwise the strength of the joint will be affected.

Assembly time
This is the elapsed time between the application of the adhesive and the application of pressure. Some adhesives benefit in strength if they are allowed to partly set before the surfaces are brought into contact (open assembly time). Other adhesives require a period to thicken while the surfaces are in contact but before pressure is applied (closed assembly time). These times will be specified by the manufacturer and must be carefully controlled to ensure that the adhesive is not too thick to spread out into a uniform layer or too thin that all the adhesive is squeezed out when the pressure is applied.

Pressure
Pressure should be applied to the glued joint in order to:

1 Spread the adhesive uniformly
2 Squeeze out excess adhesive and pockets of air
3 Ensure close contact between the two adjoining surfaces

This pressure must be sustained until the joint has developed sufficient strength (cramping period). The application of heat will speed the development of strength and therefore reduce the cramping period.

Curing
This is the process that leads to the development of full strength and resistance to moisture. It starts during the cramping period and is completed while the components are in storage prior to use (conditioning period). Curing is also dependent on temperature and can be speeded up by heating.

Radiofrequency heating
In order to gain the maximum possible output from jigs, cramps and presses etc., cramping periods should be kept to a minimum. A shorter cramping period can be achieved by raising the temperature of the glue line. There are two main ways of doing this:

By applying heat externally However, because of timber's low thermal conductivity the outside has to be raised to a much higher temperature than the centre and the heat is required for a long period of time.

By generating heat internally using radio or high-frequency heating This involves sandwiching the timber component between two metal plates (electrodes) that are connected to a source of radiofrequency (RF) energy. When a positive voltage is applied to one electrode and a negative voltage to the other the timber molecules (minute particles) which all have a positive and negative end will tend to turn so that their charged ends face their like-charged electrodes. On reversing the voltage the molecules will tend to turn back immediately, causing internal friction and thus heat. The amount of heat is dependent on the frequency of the voltage reversals.

quicker reversals = higher temperatures

Glue lines can be cured in a matter of minutes or even seconds using this process.

Classification of adhesives
Timber adhesives are made from either naturally occurring animal or vegetable products or from synthetic resins.

Adhesives made from synthetic resins fall into two classes:

1 *Thermoplastic* This class of adhesive sets by either loss of solvent or cooling and will soften again if solvent is added or it is reheated.
2 *Thermosetting* This class of adhesive undergoes a chemical reaction which causes the adhesive to solidify and set. This is an irreversible change, and the adhesive cannot be melted or dissolved.

Adhesives that will set at room temperature are known as cold setting. Those that require heating to a temperature of around 100 °C are known as hot setting. In addition some adhesives require heating between these two ranges and are called intermediate temperature setting adhesives.

The durability of an adhesive is important as it must retain its strength under the conditions it will be subjected to during its service. Durability can be tested by exposure tests over long periods, or by quick tests made over a few days, that subject the adhesive to heating, soaking, boiling and micro-organisms. Timber adhesives can be classified into one of the following durability classes.

Weather and boil-proof (WBP) These adhesives have a very high resistance to all weather conditions. They are also highly resistant to cold and boiling water, steam and dry heat, and micro-organisms.

Boil resistant (BR) These adhesives have a good resistance to boiling water and a fairly good resistance to weather conditions, and are highly resistant to cold water and micro-organisms, but they will fail on prolonged exposure to the weather.

Moisture resistant (MR) These adhesives are moderately weather resistant and will withstand prolonged exposure to cold water but very little to hot water. They are also resistant to micro-organisms.

Internal (INT) These adhesives are only suitable for use in dry internal locations. They will fail on exposure to weather or in damp conditions, and are not normally resistant to micro-organisms.

Types of adhesive

Animal glue (INT)
Animal glue is made from the bones and hides of animals. It is light brown in colour and sold in solid form which has to be dissolved before application. It sets by cooling as well as by the loss of water and will resoften on exposure to moisture. Although it was used extensively in the past in cabinet-making and joinery, it has now been largely replaced by synthetic adhesives.

Casein (INT)
Casein is derived from soured, skimmed milk curds which are dried and crushed into a powder. An alkali and certain fillers are added to the powder to make it soluble in water and give it its gap-filling properties. Its main use is for general joinery although it is inclined to stain some hardwoods, particularly oak. Little preparation is required as the powder is simply mixed in a non-metal container with a measured quantity of cold water and stirred until a smooth creamy consistency is achieved. It sets by a chemical reaction accompanied by the loss of water. Prolonged exposure will soften casein, causing a loss in strength.

Polyvinyl acetate (INT)
This is a thermoplastic adhesive supplied as a white ready-mixed creamy emulsion which sets by the loss of water to form a clear glue line. It requires no preparation and sets rapidly at room temperature, although it will resoften on exposure to high temperature or moisture.

Contact adhesives (INT)
These consist of a rubber solution in a volatile solvent ready for use. When the adhesive has been applied to both surfaces, a ten to thirty minute open assembly time must elapse to enable the solvent to evaporate. After this the two surfaces can be brought together, forming an immediate contact bond. Little or no adjustment is possible except with the thixotropic types which have a certain amount of manoeuvrability. Care must be taken to use contact adhesives in a well-ventilated area, where no smoking or naked lights are allowed.

Hot melts (INT)
These are made from ethylene vinyl acetate and are obtained in a solid form. They become molten at very high temperatures and set immediately on cooling. Small hand-held electric glue guns and automatic edging machines normally use this type of adhesive.

Phenol formaldehyde (WBP)
Phenol formaldehyde resin is a dark brown

thermosetting adhesive that sets at either high temperatures or upon the addition of an acid catalyst.

Resorcinol formaldehyde (WBP)

Resorcinol formaldehyde resin is a dark purplish-brown thermosetting adhesive that is classified as cold setting and sets by the addition of a hardener. As the resorcinol is very expensive it is often mixed with the cheaper phenol, making a phenol/resorcinol formaldehyde adhesive. This has the same properties as the pure resorcinol adhesive, although a higher setting temperature is required.

Melamine formaldehyde (BR)

Melamine formaldehyde resin is a colourless thermosetting adhesive that sets at high temperatures and is suitable for use where the dark colour of the phenol and resorcinol adhesives are unacceptable.

Urea formaldehyde (MR)

Urea formaldehyde is also a colourless thermosetting adhesive that will set at either high or low temperatures. Urea is often mixed with the more expensive melamine or resorcinol resin to form a fortified urea formaldehyde adhesive that has an increased (BR) durability.

General characteristics

A summary of the main characteristics, properties and uses of woodworking adhesives is given in Table 13.

Adhesive safety

Adhesives can be harmful to your health. Many adhesives have an irritant effect on contact with the skin and may result in dermatitis. Some are poisonous if swallowed, while others can result in narcosis if the vapour or powder is inhaled. These and other harmful effects can be avoided if proper precautions are taken:

1 Always follow the manufacturer's instructions
2 Always use a barrier cream or disposable protective gloves.

3 Do not use those with a flammable vapour near sources of ignition.
4 Always provide adequate ventilation.
5 Avoid inhaling any toxic fumes or powders.
6 Thoroughly wash your hands, before eating or smoking and after work, with soap and water or an appropriate hand cleanser.
7 In the case of accidental inhalation, swallowing or contact with eyes, medical advice should be sought immediately.

Mechanics

Mechanics can be defined as the study of the effect of forces on materials. Remember forces are measured in newtons (N); owing to the earth's gravitational pull, every mass will exert a force. The force will vary slightly from place to place on the earth's surface, but on average the force of gravity on a mass of 1 kg is 9.81 N; therefore the 'weight' of 1 kg is 9.81 N. For most practical purposes it is sufficiently accurate to take the weight of 1 kg to be 10 N, thus simplifying any calculations and at the same time erring on the safe side.

A 50 kg box of nails placed on the ground will exert a force of almost 500 N; the earth in turn will push back with an equal and opposite reaction of 500 N (see Figure 109).

The force that supports a force is called a reaction. Where no movement is taking place as a result of these forces, they are said to be in equilibrium or balanced. A force that is not in direct line with its reaction will have a turning

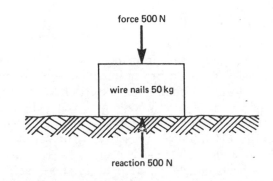

Figure 109   *Force and reaction*

Table 13   Characteristics of woodworking adhesives

Type of adhesive	Suitable service conditions						Classification				Gap filling — Capable of filling 1.3 mm without loss of strength		Available form — one part			Available form — two parts		Life expectancy in fully exposed external conditions
	Fully exposed external use	Protected external use	Internal or external use in chemically polluted areas	Internal use in high-heat or high-humidity areas	Internal use in dry normal heat conditions	Internal use in dry normal heat conditions. Non-structural	INT	WBP	BR	MR	Yes	No	Solid	Powder	Liquid	Powder/liquid	Liquid/liquid	
Animal glue						*	*				*		*					3–4 months
Casein					*	*	*				*			*				1–2 years
Polyvinyl acetate						*	*					*			*			—
Contact adhesive		*			*	*	*					*			*			—
Hot melts					*	*	*				*		*					—
Phenol formaldehyde	*	*	*	*	*	*		*				*				*		25 + years
Resorcinol formaldehyde	*	*	*	*	*	*		*			*					*	*	25 + years
Melamine formaldehyde				*	*	*			*		* can be					*	*	5–10 + years
Urea formaldehyde					*	*				*	* can be			*		*	*	2–5 + years

effect. This turning effect is known as the moment of a force. It is equal to the product of the force and its distance from the point of support or fulcrum:

moment = force × distance

Consider the see-saw arrangement shown in Figure 110. This consists of a beam loaded at either end, the reaction being provided by the fulcrum (pivot point). The two forces can be seen as having either a clockwise or an anticlockwise moment. For the beam to be in equilibrium (balanced), force A multiplied by distance A must be equal to force B multiplied by distance B:

$$F_A \times D_A = F_B \times D_B$$

This can be summed up by the statement known as the *principle of moments*. For a body to exist in a state of equilibrium the sum of the anticlockwise moments must equal the sum of the clockwise moments:

anticlockwise moments (ACWM)
           = clockwise moments (CWM)

Example
The see-saw arrangement shown in Figure 111 balances when the three forces are placed in the positions illustrated. Find distance Z.

Taking moments about the fulcrum:

$$\begin{aligned} \text{ACWM} &= \text{CWM} \\ 3 \times 500 + 1 \times 250 &= Z \times 350 \\ 1750 &= Z \times 350 \\ \frac{1750}{350} &= Z \\ 5 &= Z \end{aligned}$$

Answer   Distance Z must be 5 m.

Levers
A lever is a simple machine that can turn about a pivot. It operates on the principle of moments. When using a lever a force (effort) is applied at one position on the lever to overcome a resisting force (load) acting at another position on the lever. The positions of the effort and load will

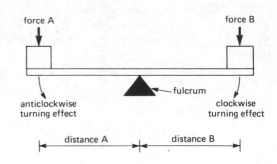

Figure 110   *Moments*

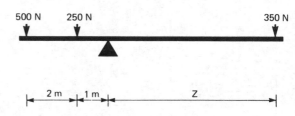

Figure 111   *Moments*

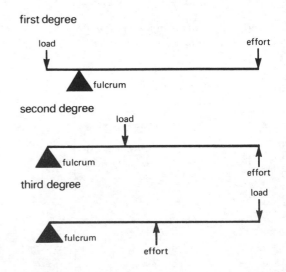

Figure 112   *Levers*

vary depending on which of the three orders or degrees of lever is being used. These three degrees of lever are illustrated in Figure 112. In the first-degree lever the distance between the load and the fulcrum is normally less than the distance between the effort and the fulcrum. This in effect magnifies the effort, enabling a bigger load to be moved than the effort applied, but the effort has to move further than the load. This magnification of the effort is called the mechanical advantage of the machine and can be expressed as:

$$\text{mechanical advantage} = \frac{\text{load}}{\text{effort}}$$

The second-degree lever has a similar mechanical advantage in that the effort is less than the load. In the third-degree lever, where the effort is positioned between the load and the fulcrum, the effort will always be greater than the load, but the load will move further than the effort. Typical examples of levers in use are shown in Figure 113. These can be seen in daily use on any building site.

To find the effort required in each of these examples involves a simple calculation.

Example
What effort is required at Z to lift the load of 100 N shown in Figure 114? What is the mechanical advantage of the arrangement?

Taking moments about the fulcrum:

$$ACWM = CWM$$

$$0.750 \times 100 = 3 \times Z$$

$$75 = 3 \times Z$$

$$\frac{75}{3} = Z$$

$$25 = Z$$

Answer Effort just greater than 25 N.

Note: With an effort of 25 N the forces will be in equilibrium; therefore an effort just greater than this will be required to lift the load.

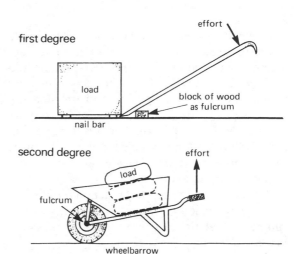

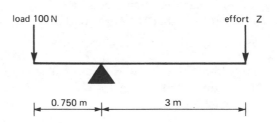

Figure 113 *Levers in use*

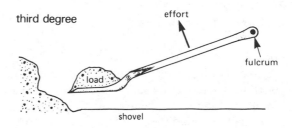

Figure 114 *Levers*

The mechanical advantage (MA) of the set-up shown in Figure 114 is

$$MA = \frac{\text{load}}{\text{effort}}$$

$$MA = \frac{100}{25}$$

$$MA = 4$$

Answer The mechanical advantage is 4.

Beam reactions

A beam is the general name given to a wide range of structural members within a building. These include lintels, joists, binders, rafters and purlins etc. They all have the same purpose, which is to span an opening and transfer any loads imposed upon them back to the supports (wall columns etc.). If the beam is to remain in equilibrium, and in a building it obviously must, these supports must provide an equal and opposite reaction.

To determine the support reaction required to bear a known load system normally involves a simple calculation. There are two ways of loading a beam:

Point loads
Uniformly distributed loads

Point loads

If a load is placed in the centre of a beam the reaction at each support will be half the load. When the load is not central or where there is more than one load the reactions will have to be calculated. This means taking moments about each end in turn. An easy way of doing this is to consider the beam to be a second-degree lever, one of the reactions being considered as the fulcrum and the other the effort required.

Example

A simply supported beam with a point load of 16 kN is illustrated in Figure 115. Find both support reactions.

Taking moments about R_L:

$$ACWM = CWM$$
$$8 \times R_R = 3 \times 16$$
$$8 \times R_R = 48$$
$$R_R = \frac{48}{8}$$
$$R_R = 6 \text{ kN}$$

If R_R is 6 kN then R_L must be 10 kN since the sum of the reactions must be equal to the total applied load. But the calculation should always be checked by taking moments about the other reaction.

Taking moments about R_R:

$$ACWM = CWM$$
$$5 \times 16 = 8 \times R_L$$
$$80 = 8 \times R_L$$
$$\frac{80}{8} = R_L$$
$$10 \text{ kN} = R_L$$

Answer

Left-hand reaction equals 10 kN.
Right-hand reaction equals 6 kN.

Example

Where there is more than one point load, as in the beam shown in Figure 116, the method used to find the support reactions will be similar.

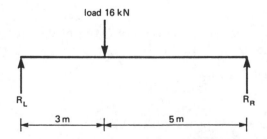

Figure 115   *Beam reactions, one point load*

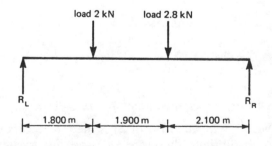

Figure 116   *Beam reactions, two point loads*

Taking moments about R_L:

ACWM = CWM
$5.8 \times R_R$ = $1.8 \times 2 + 3.7 \times 2.8$
$5.8 \times R_R$ = $3.6 + 10.26$
R_R = $\dfrac{13.96}{5.8}$
R_R = 2.407 kN

Therefore R_L must be 2.393 kN since $4.8 - 2.407 = 2.393$.

Check by taking moments about R_R.

ACWM = CWM
$2.1 \times 2.8 + 4 \times 2$ = $5.8 \times R_L$
$5.88 + 8$ = $5.8 \times R_L$
13.88 = $5.8 \times R_L$
$\dfrac{13.88}{5.8}$ = R_L
2.393 kN = R_L

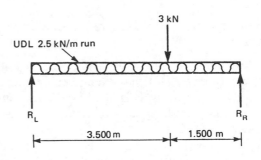

Figure 117   *UDL and one point load*

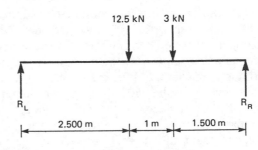

Figure 118

Answer
Left-hand reaction equals 2.393 kN.
Right-hand reaction equals 2.407 kN.

Uniformly distributed loads
When a load is evenly dispersed along the whole or part of a beam it is said to be a uniformly distributed load (UDL). The self-weight of a beam is a uniformly distributed load and must be taken into account when it forms a significant proportion of the total load.

The total UDL on a beam must be calculated and it can then be considered as a point load acting through its centre of gravity.

Example
The beam shown in Figure 117 has a UDL of 2.5 kN/m run and a point load of 3 kN. Determine the support reactions.

total UDL = span × load/m run
= 5×2.5
= 12.5 kN

This UDL is now considered as a point load acting through the centre of gravity (centre of the UDL). The beam diagram now has two point loads as shown in Figure 118. The support reactions can now be calculated using the same procedure as before. In the case of a floor or roof a UDL or imposed load will be stated in kN/m^2 and not as the load carried by one joist or rafter. It will be necessary to find the load carried by one member before the support reactions can be determined.

Example
Floor joists spanning 3.500 m and spaced at 400 mm centres carry a UDL of kN/m^2. Find the load carried by one joist.

load on one joist = span × load/m^2 × c/c
                     spacing
= $3.5 \times 4 \times 0.4$
= 5.6 kN

Answer   Load on each joist is 5.6 kN.

Design of timber members

Stress
When a body is subjected to a force it is said to

be in a state of stress. There are three types of stress:

Tensile stress (Figure 119)   This tends to pull or stretch a material; it has a lengthening effect.
Compressive stress (Figure 120)   This causes squeezing, pushing and crushing; it has a shortening effect.
Shear stress (Figure 121)   This occurs when one part of a member tends to slip or slide over another part; it has a slicing effect.

When a beam is subjected to a load, bending occurs, causing an internal combination of these stresses (see Figure 122). The centre line of the beam is subjected to neither compression or tension and is known as the neutral stress line, although maximum horizontal shear occurs along this line as the two halves of the beam tend to slide over each other. The amount of compression or tension increases with the distance from the neutral stress line. This is represented in the section by the shaded areas. The maximum stresses therefore occur at the top and bottom edges of the beam, the upper part being in a state of compression and the lower part in a state of tension. This stress along the beam varies and is related to the amount of bending. The larger the bending the larger the stress. In the case of a centre point load the maximum bending and therefore the maximum stress will occur at the centre of the beam. This will diminish towards the supports where vertical shear occurs. When a beam has an additional central support the position of the stresses in this area will be reversed (see Figure 123).

Strength tests
The strength of timber varies according to the type of stress and whether it is applied with or at right angles to the grain (see Figure 124). Strength tests on timber form the basis for determining permissible stress values used in structural timber design calculations. Various types of stress are now considered.

Ultimate stress
Small clear defect-free samples of timber are tested to destruction to obtain their breaking or ultimate stress value.

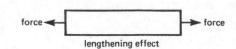

Figure 119   *Tensile stress*

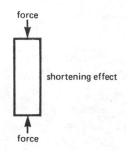

Figure 120   *Compressive stress*

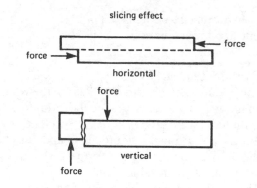

Figure 121   *Shear stress*

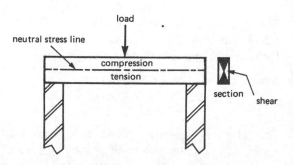

Figure 122   *Beam under stress*

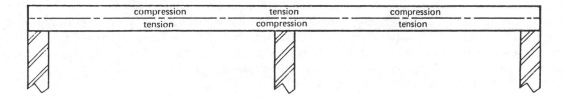

Figure 123   *Stress reversal in centrally supported beam*

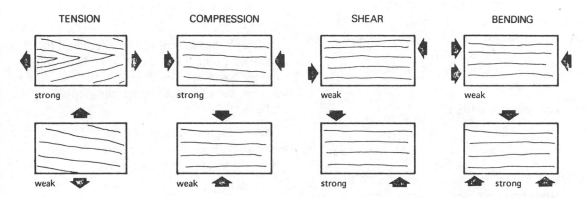

Figure 124   *Relative strength of timber*

Characteristic stress

The ultimate stress value will vary between different samples of the species. Therefore a characteristic stress value is determined and is normally defined as the stress below which only 1 per cent of the samples will fail.

Basic stress

The characteristic stress makes no allowance for accidental overloading of the timber in use; therefore it must be divided by an appropriate factor of safety to obtain the basic stress. This is defined as the stress that can be safely and permanently sustained by clear defect-free timber.

Grade stress

As the basic stress is for clear defect-free timber a modification must be made for the inclusion of strength-reducing defects. This is the grade stress, and can be defined as the stress that can be safely and permanently sustained by a particular grade of timber.

Permissible stress

Grade stresses are used for conditions where the timber may have to support a load throughout its useful life, which could be in excess of 50 to 60 years. This is known as long-term loading conditions. Clearly some adjustment can be made where the loading is for a short period. In addition grade stresses are for dry timber (below 18 per cent moisture content (MC)); where green timber (above 18 per cent (MC)) is used another adjustment must be made.

The stress value after making these adjustments is known as the permissible stress, and is defined as the stress that can be safely sustained after allowing for the duration of load and moisture content.

Beam design

In general the strength of a beam varies in direct proportion to changes in its breadth and in proportion to the square of its depth. For example, doubling the breadth of a section doubles its strength, whereas doubling the depth of the section increases its strength by four times. Thus less material is required for the same strength when the greatest dimension of a beam is placed vertically rather than horizontally.

The size of a timber beam depends on its loading, span and spacing. It is most important that these factors are taken into consideration when determining what sectional size to use. The Building Regulations Approved Documents (AD) A Tables B contains various tables of suitable sectional sizes for use in different situations, although some situations do not fall within the scope of these tables.

Sectional sizes can be determined by the rule of thumb method:

$$\frac{\text{span of joists in millimetres}}{20} + 20$$

$$= \text{depth of 50 mm wide joist}$$

While this may be suitable for a one-off situation it is not very accurate or cost effective as it usually results in sectional sizes far bigger than is really necessary. It is therefore desirable that a carpenter and joiner has a basic understanding of the principles of beam design.

A beam has to be designed so that the permissible bending and shear stresses for the grade of timber being used are not exceeded. At this level beam design is restricted to simply supported beams with centre point or uniformly distributed loads.

Bending

The equation that is used for determining the sectional size is:

maximum bending moment (BM_{max}) = moment of resistance (MR)

Maximum bending moment

This is the total sum of forces acting on the beam which are tending to bend or even break it. Although the maximum bending moment will vary according to the beam's loading and support, Table 14 contains the formulae for use in standard situations.

Moment of resistance

This is the resistance to bending offered by the beam section. For timber beams of a rectangular section the moment of resistance is given by the following formula:

$$MR = \frac{fbd^2}{6}$$

where f is the permissible bending stress (N/mm^2), b is the breadth of the beam (mm), and d is the depth of the beam (mm).

Example

A timber beam spanning 3 m is required to carry a centre point load of 4 kN. Determine a suitable commercially available section, assuming that the permissible bending stress of the timber is 8 N/mm^2.

Note: All measurements must be stated in the same units; for example, change m to mm and kN to N by multiplying by 1000.

$$BM_{max} = MR$$
$$\frac{WL}{4} = \frac{fbd^2}{6}$$

transpose formula to get bd^2 on its own:

$$\frac{WL6}{4f} = bd^2$$
$$\frac{4000 \times 3000}{4 \times 8} \times = bd^2$$
$$\frac{72,000,000}{32} = bd^2$$
$$2,250,000 = bd^2$$

say $b = 75$: therefore

$$\frac{2,250,000}{75} = d^2$$
$$\sqrt{\left(\frac{2,250,000}{75}\right)} = d$$
$$173 = d$$

Answer Nearest commercial size (NCS) is 75 mm × 175 mm.

As an alternative to this section we could say $b = 50$ mm; therefore

Table 14 Beam design formulae

System	Diagram	Bending moment BM_{max}	Shear S_{max}
Simply supported beam with a centre point load		$\dfrac{WL}{4}$	$\dfrac{3\,W}{4\,bd}$
Simply supported beam with a uniformly distributed load		$\dfrac{WL}{8}$	$\dfrac{3\,W}{4\,bd}$

W = weight (load) L = length (span) b = breadth of beam d = depth of beam

$$\sqrt{\left(\frac{2,250,000}{50}\right)} = d$$

$$212 = d$$

In this case the NCS would be 50 mm × 225 mm.

Example
Floor joists spanning 3.500 m and spaced at 450 mm centres carry a uniformly distributed load of 2.5 kN/m^2. Using the formula $WL/8 = fbd^2/6$, calculate the depth of a 50 mm wide joist when $f = 6.8$ N/mm^2.

$$\text{total load per joist} = 3.5 \times 2.5 \times 0.45$$
$$= 3.938 \text{ kN}$$
$$BM_{max} = MR$$
$$\frac{WL}{8} = \frac{fbd^2}{6}$$
$$\frac{WL6}{f8} = bd^2$$
$$\frac{3938 \times 3500 \times 6}{8 \times 6.8} = bd^2$$
$$\frac{82,698,000}{54.4} = bd^2$$
$$1,520,183.8 = bd^2$$

$b = 50$ mm; therefore

$$\frac{1,520,183.8}{50} = d^2$$

$$\sqrt{\left(\frac{1,615,195.3}{50}\right)} = d$$

$$174.366 = d$$

Answer NCS is 50 mm × 175 mm.

Shear
In general a timber beam that is designed to resist bending stresses will be more than strong enough to resist shear, but it can be checked by using the formulae shown in Table 14.

Example
Calculate the maximum shear stress for a 50 mm × 200 mm simply supported timber beam carrying a centre point load of 4.8 kN.

Answer

$$\text{maximum shear}\quad S(\text{max}) = \frac{3W}{4bd}$$

$$S(\text{max}) = \frac{3 \times 4800}{4 \times 50 \times 200}$$

$$S(\text{max}) = \frac{14,400}{40,000}$$

$$S(\text{max}) = 0.36 \text{ N/mm}^2$$

This is less than the typical value of 0.86 N/mm² for structural softwood and is therefore satisfactory for shear strength.

Note: In addition to the previous calculations a structural engineer will also check the following:

The minimum amount of end bearing required to avoid crushing

The amount of deflection or sag under load; deflection is normally limited to 0.003 of the span or 3 mm in every metre.

These calculations are not within the scope of your course.

Note: Tables of permissible stress values for bending and shear of various species, grades and strength classes are given in BS 5268.

Glue-laminated timber

Structural timber members which are of a large cross-section, long in length, or shaped, can be fabricated by the process of glue lamination (glulam). Examples of this are shown in Figure 125.

A glulam member comprises boards of small cross-section, glued and layered up either horizontally or vertically. The boards are layered with a parallel grain direction and cramped up in special jigs which are set up to provide the straight or curved profile of the finished member. Specifications for glulam members are given in BS 4169: *Glue-Laminated Timber for Structural Members*.

A reduction in sectional size or greater span over solid beams of the same section is possible when using glue-laminated sections. This is because higher stress values may be used in design calculations. There are a number· of reasons for this, in addition to the grade of timber used, the main ones being:

1   The strength of timber is variable, but by joining a number of timbers together to act as one beam, the average strength of each layer (laminate) will be greater than the strength of the weakest laminate.
2   Strength-reducing defects, such as large knots or shakes, are restricted in size to the thickness of one laminate.

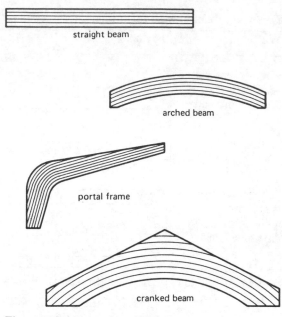

Figure 125   *Examples of glulam*

3   Higher-quality timber can be used in critical areas.
4   Members can be precambered to offset any deflection under loaded conditions.
5   Because of the relatively small cross-section of each laminate, a tightly controlled moisture content can be achieved, resulting in a dimensionally stable finished member.

Laminate thickness

In straight glulam members the thickness of each laminate is dependent upon the depth of the member, although no laminate should be in excess of 50 mm thick. When curved members are laminated the timber must be flexible enough to enable it to be bent easily without breaking. The timber must be bent in a dry state, as steam treatment or soaking of the laminate prior to bending is not permissible. The maximum thickness of the laminations that can be used will therefore depend on the radius of the curve, but in any case this should not exceed 50 mm. For practical purposes the following maximum laminate thicknesses may be used:

When bending softwood: radius (mm)/100

When bending hardwood: radius (mm)/150.

Example

What would be the maximum laminate thickness for a softwood arched beam having a radius of 2 m?

$$\text{maximum laminate thickness} = \frac{\text{radius}}{100}$$

$$= \frac{2000}{100}$$

Answer Maximum laminate thickness would be 20 mm.

Timber grade

In use, structural glulam members in common with other beams will be subjected to stress – the outer laminates to tension and compression and the middle ones to shear.

A glulam member may be manufactured using one grade of timber, but to reduce costs it is usual to employ a lower grade in the middle layers of a member. BS 4978 specifies three grades for laminating based on the knot/area ratio. These are LA, LB and LC, and are based on grade stresses of approximately 95, 75 and 50 per cent, respectively, of the basic stress of clear defect-free timber. A typical beam cross-section, shown in Figure 126, might consist of LA or LB timber in the outer layers and LB or LC in the middle layers. This lower-grade centre section, comprising one-third to one-half of the total depth, is possible because the shear strength of timber is not significantly affected by the drop in grade.

Jointing

Laminates can be jointed in various ways to produce full-length or -width laminations. End jointing is normally carried out using a scarf joint; ideally, for maximum strength, these should have a slope of 1:6 for laminates in the compression area and 1:12 for laminates in the tension area (see Figure 127). Scarfs with a slope outside this range will have an adverse affect on strength.

As an alternative, structural finger joints may be used (see Figure 128). These may vary in length but 50 mm is common in the United Kingdom. Finger joints are more economical in

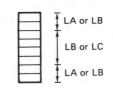

Figure 126   *Timber grades*

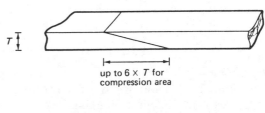
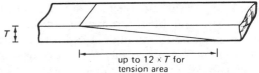

Figure 127   *Scarf joints*

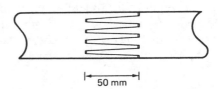

Figure 128   *Finger joints*

Figure 129   *Edge joints*

terms of timber wastage than scarf joints. The end joints of laminates should preferably be glued, preassembled, cured and flushed off before final assembly of the member, particularly where curved sections are involved. During final assembly all end joints should be evenly distributed throughout the member so that grouping in any one section is avoided.

Edge jointing of inside laminates to form the full width of a member is possible, but should be separated in adjacent laminates by about 25 mm or the thickness of the laminate if this is greater (see Figure 129).

Preparation of laminates

Each individual laminate must be carefully prepared to fine tolerances. Planing should be carried out within forty-eight hours prior to gluing. The use of sharp· planer knives and suitable pressure is essential in order to ensure that the timber is cut cleanly without compressing or damaging the timber in any way.

At the time of gluing the moisture content of the timber should be either 12 per cent to 15 per cent or within plus or minus 3 per cent of its expected equilibrium. In addition the surface of each laminate must be free from oil, dust, excessive natural resin or any other substance likely to affect the strength of the glue line.

Assembly

Before gluing and cramping the laminates should be assembled dry (dry assembly) to determine the position of the different grades of laminate and stagger the end joints. Any laminates that show cupping, outside the permitted range shown in Table 15, at this stage must be rejected.

Wet assembly of the member follows. To achieve a controlled spread of glue, each laminate is passed in turn through a mechanical glue spreader. They are then placed into the cramping jig in their previously determined positions. The type of jig used will vary widely depending on the nature of the work in hand and the type of firm, from the occasional assembly of small glulam members in a joiner's shop to large-scale specialist timber engineering plants using complex machinery. A small cramping jig suitable for a limited number of members is shown in Figure 130.

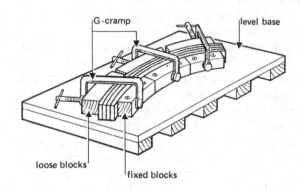

Figure 130   *Small cramping jig*

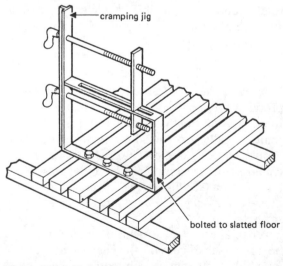

Figure 131   *Cramping frame*

Table 15   **Maximum permitted depth of cupping**

Laminate thickness	For laminate widths	
	up to 150 mm	over 150 mm
Up to 16 mm	1.5 mm	1.5 mm
17 mm to 29 mm	1 mm	1.5 mm
30 mm to 47 mm	0.5 mm	1.0 mm

Figure 132   *Cramping set-up for curved member*

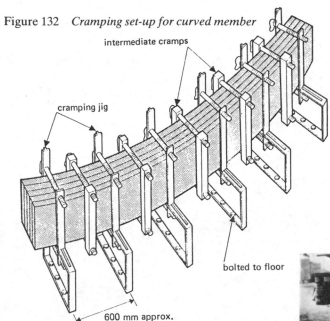

Where glulam assembly is carried out fairly frequently or large numbers of members are required, the vertical cramping frame shown in Figure 131 is often used. A number of these are bolted to a grillage or slots in the floor, so that the vertical uprights conform to the shape of the finished member. For most curved shapes this is achieved by setting up the jigs to the required shape, with the aid of a template. Figure 132 shows the cramping set-up for a curved member. Although the cramping jigs incorporate cramps, additional intermediate cramps and caulboards (outer pressure-distributing boards) are required to ensure the continuity of pressure necessary to achieve a thin uniform glue line. Cramps are spaced at up to 400 mm centres for straight work, but on curved work this must be reduced in some cases to 100 mm centres. The centre cramps are tightened first, gradually working outwards to the ends. Precise uniform clamp pressure over the whole length and width of the glue line is required initially. This is to be not less than 0.7 N/mm^2, and should be rechecked after fifteen minutes to ensure there has been no reduction. This precision is achieved with the use of a torque wrench, although in many cases calibrated hydraulic or pneumatic cramps are used.

Figure 133   *Finishing glulam member using wide-panel planer*

The type of adhesive used will depend on the intended use of the member. Casein or urea formaldehyde is specified for use in low-heat, low-humidity, internal conditions. Phenol and/or resorcinol formaldehyde is specified for use in any other conditions where there is no restriction on temperature or humidity levels.

Finish

After curing and conditioning, the member is finished to the required standard by planing,

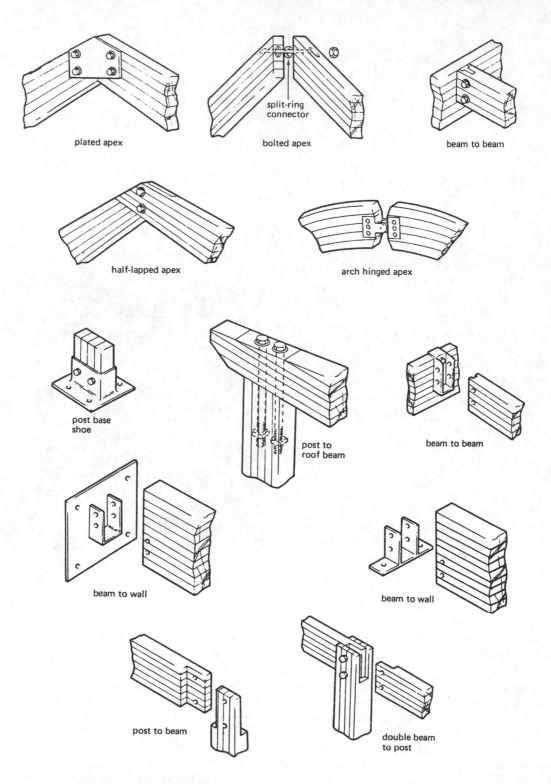

plated apex

bolted apex

split-ring
connector

beam to beam

half-lapped apex

arch hinged apex

post base
shoe

post to
roof beam

beam to beam

beam to wall

beam to wall

post to beam

double beam
to post

Figure 134   *Glulam joint and fixing details*

sanding, patching and filling. Figure 133 shows a large glulam member being finished using a wide-panel planer. Glulam members are normally finished to one of the following surface grades:

Regularized This must be at least 50 per cent sawn or planed to remove protruding laminations, mainly for industrial use where its surface is concealed or its appearance is not of prime importance.

Planed This has a fully planed surface free from glue stains; any significant defects (knot holes and fissures) will have to be filled or patched. Suitable for most applications except where a varnish or other clear finish is required.

Sanded This has a fully planed and sanded surface, any significant defects being filled or patched. End joints in the laminates or patching will, as far as possible, be matched for grain direction and colour. Suitable for all applications where a high-quality clear finish is required.

Marking

On completion each glulam member should be marked with the following information:

The manufacturer's name or trade mark
The type of adhesive used
The British Standard number BS 4169.

Protection and treatment

Glulam members, in common with other timber components, must be suitably protected during treatment, transit, storage and erection. Where preservative or fire-retardant treatments are used, these must be compatible with both the timber and the adhesive. It is preferable to carry out these treatments on the finished member, although in some cases treatment before lamination may be required, in which case water-repellent preservatives must be avoided.

Site erection

Glulam members are often delivered on site shrink-wrapped in a plastic or waterproof covering. This should be left in place after erection to protect the member from the effects of weather and subsequent wet and finishing trades. Where members are to be jointed or fitted into metal shoes etc. the protective covering can be temporarily pulled back.

The site work for glulam members normally involves jointing, erection, plumbing and fixing. In order to prevent accidental collapse, temporary ties and braces must be used until the structure is stable. Care must be taken to avoid distortions when lifting the members. For large structures manufacturers will provide or specify lifting points in certain positions, to ensure that any stresses in erection do not exceed the permissible stresses in any member.

A range of typical joint and fixing details are illustrated in Figure 134. The main method of securing a member is with bolts and metal plates. The feet of arched or portable frames and posts are fixed to the base by the use of a metal shoe. This method has the added advantage of preventing moisture rising up the timber.

Mechanical fasteners for structural work

This section covers some of the common types of mechanical fasteners that are used for structural work. Table 16 summarizes their main characteristics.

Nailed and screwed joints

Most nailed joints have good resistance to lateral or sideways movement, but little resistance when loaded in tension (withdrawal). See Figure 136.

Care must be taken when spacing the nails to avoid splitting the timber. In general this is related to the diameter of the nail. The minimum spacing distances for 2.5 mm diameter wire nails are shown in Table 17 and illustrated in Figure 137. These distances may be reduced if the timber being fixed is pre-bored or the points of the nails are blunted.

When compared to plain wire nails, screws have a better resistance to withdrawal but a reduced lateral resistance. The minimum spacing distances for screws is similar to those used for nailing.

***Table 16*   Mechanical Fasteners**

Type			Material and finish	Notes
Nails				
Round plain wire			Mild steel with either bright galvanized or sherardized finishes	Used for the securing of all structural timbers
Lost-head wire				Machine driven nails are packed in strips or coils for use in various forms of pneumatic gun
Clout nail				
Machine driven nails			Copper and aluminium also available	
				Duplex nails have a double head, the lower one being driven home for maximum holding power while the upper head projects enabling easy withdrawal
Duplex nail				
Improved nails				
Twisted-shank nail			Mild steel with either a bright galvanized or sherardized finish	Used for all construction work where extra holding power is required. Especially good for fixing sheet materials and attaching proprietary metal nail plates, joist hangers and framing anchors
Annular ring shanked nail				
Staples			Steel coated in either zinc or resin	Used as an alternative to pneumatically driven nails for fixing plywood, fibreboard and insulation etc., particularly in the factory assembly of timber frame housing units
Screws				
Countersunk head			Steel with either a bright zinc sherardized enamelled or plated finish Stainless steel, brass and aluminium also available	Limited use in structural work because of their increased cost and assembly time when compared with nails
Round head				
Raised countersunk head				
Recessed head				
Coach screws			Steel usually finished in black, sometimes zinc	Used in heavy-duty constructional work for both timber to timber or metal to timber joints

Type	Material and finish	Notes
Bolts		
Hexagonal head	Steel usually finished in black	Used in heavy-duty constructional work for both timber to timber or metal to timber joints. Used in conjunction with connectors where extra strength is required
Square head		
Coach bolts		
Cartridge fasteners		
Nail	Zinc-plated steel	Available in a varied range for fixings to brickwork concrete and structural steel
Stud		
Eyelet		
Connectors		
Double-toothed plate	Steel, either zinc plated or galvanized	Used to increase the resistance to shear of bolted joints. Double and split-ring connectors are used for timber to timber joints, whereas single and shear-plate connectors are used for timber to metal, timber to other components or demountable timber to timber joints using two connectors back to back. Split-ring and shear-plate connectors are for heavy-duty structural joints; they require the use of special grooving and housing tools before assembly (see Figure 135). The teeth of the double- and single-toothed plate connectors are embedded into the timber by using a special high-tensile threaded steel rod, nuts and a ballbearing washer to draw up the joint prior to inserting the ordinary bolt
Single-toothed plate		
Split ring		
Shear plate		

continued

Table 16 *continued*

Type	Material and finish	Notes
Nail plates.	Steel, either zinc plated or galvanized	Used for the manufacture of trussed rafters, trussed purlins and beams Punched plates are only suitable for factory installation where specialist machinery is available Gusset plates are suitable for on-site fabrication using hand or pneumatic driven nails
Punched plate		
Gusset plate		
Joist hangers	Steel with a galvanized finish	Available in a wide range for either timber to timber or timber to wall connections
Framing anchors	Steel with a galvanized finish	Suitable for a wide range of applications including studwork, rafter to wall plate connections, and other uses where timbers run at right angles to one another

Type		Material and finish	Notes
Truss clip	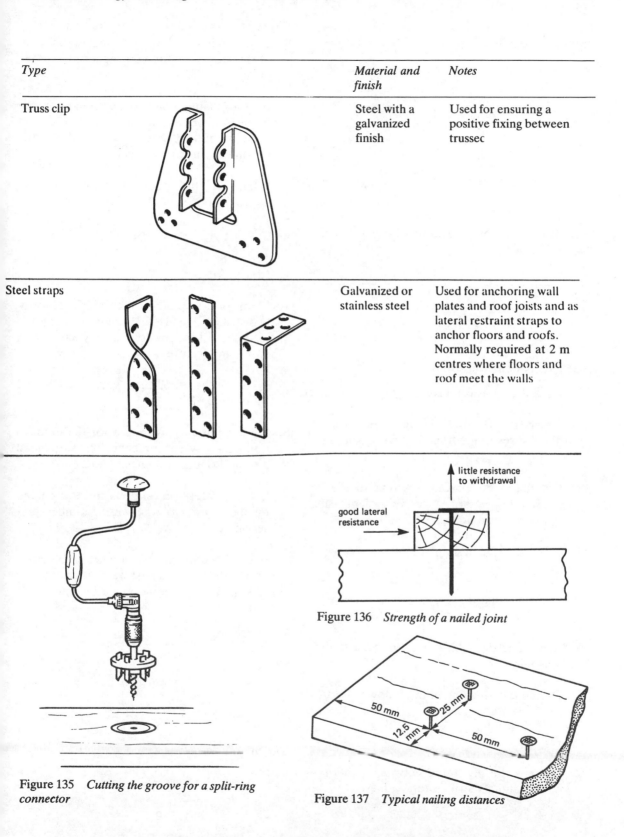	Steel with a galvanized finish	Used for ensuring a positive fixing between trussec
Steel straps		Galvanized or stainless steel	Used for anchoring wall plates and roof joists and as lateral restraint straps to anchor floors and roofs. Normally required at 2 m centres where floors and roof meet the walls

little resistance to withdrawal

good lateral resistance

Figure 136 *Strength of a nailed joint*

Figure 135 *Cutting the groove for a split-ring connector*

50 mm

25 mm

12.5 mm

50 mm

Figure 137 *Typical nailing distances*

Table 17   **Nailing distances**

Minimum spacing for	End distance	Edge distance	Side spacing between nails	Spacing between adjacent nails along the grain
Normal nailing	50 mm	1.25 mm	25 mm	50 mm
Nailing in pre-bored holes or nails with blunted points	25 mm	12.5 mm	7.5 mm	25 mm

Self-assessment questions

1 Describe what is meant by stress grading.

2 Describe with the aid of sketches *four* defects resulting from incorrect kiln seasoning.

3 List the safety precautions that should be observed by the operative when using synthetic resin adhesives.

4 Write a brief description of the following sheet materials:
(a) Plywood
(b) Chipboard
(c) Plastic laminate

5 Name and describe *two* methods of timber seasoning.

6 Define the meaning of the following terms:
(a) Compression
(b) Tension
(c) Shear

7 What is the difference between a thermoplastic and a thermosetting adhesive?

8 Briefly describe how the moisture content of timber can be found using a small drying oven.

9 In the manufacture of a glulam portal frame, softwood laminates have to be bent a radius of 1200 mm. What would be the maximum thickness of each laminate?

10 What do the following timber grading abbreviations mean?
(a) FAS
(b) FAQ
(c) US
(d) KAR

11 Floor joists spanning 4.8 m carry a uniformly distributed load of 2.1 kN/m^2. What is the load carried by one joist if they are spaced at 400 mm centres?

12 What is the difference between GS and MGS timber?

13 State a suitable procedure for the eradication of a dry rot attack in the suspended ground floor of a domestic house.

14 List the safety precautions to be observed by the operative when using timber preservatives.

15 Explain the precautions that must be taken during the transit and storage prior to fixing of kiln seasoned joinery components.

chapter 6

Principles of insulation

After reading this chapter the student should be able to:

1 State the principles involved in the following:
   (a) Fire-resistant construction
   (b) Thermal insulation
   (c) Sound insulation.

2 Prepare sketches to show insulation details suitable to a given situation.

3 State the Building Regulations that are applicable to fire, thermal and sound insulation.

Fire-resistant construction

In order to have an understanding of fire-resistant construction it is necessary to have a knowledge of the nature of fire and its related terminology.

Fire or combustion is burning. This is a chemical reaction between a substance and oxygen, during which heat is produced and the original form of the substance is destroyed. All substances or materials both solid and liquid can be classified into the two following groups:

Those that are capable of burning: solid materials are known as combustible and liquids as flammable.

Those that are incapable of burning: solid materials are known as non-combustible and liquids as non-flammable.

It is not the actual combustible or flammable material that combines with the oxygen when they burn. In both cases it is the vapour that they give off when they are heated that actually burns. The lowest temperature at which a material will give off a flammable vapour is known as the ignition temperature of combustible materials and the flashpoint of flammable materials. This ignition temperature or flashpoint of materials will vary widely. Combustible solids require preheating to fairly high temperatures before their flammable vapours are given off, for example, timber to about 300 °C, whereas many flammable liquids give off a flammable vapour at well below normal room

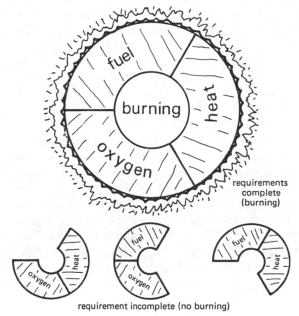

Figure 138 *Requirements for burning*

temperatures, for example, petroleum spirit at −43 °C.

Figure 138 shows the essential requirements for burning. These are:

Fuel A combustible or flammable material to burn.
Oxygen Normally from the air to combine with the flammable vapour given off by the material.
Heat Initial heat to bring a material up to its ignition temperature or flashpoint.

Burning takes place when all of the requirements are met. If one of the requirements is removed or is not available then burning cannot occur.

Growth of a building fire

Most building fires are started from a relatively small source of heat, for example, a lighted match, a cigarette end or an overloaded electric circuit. Any of these can supply the initial heat required to ignite a small fuel source, such as an armchair or waste paper in a rubbish bin etc. These heat sources in turn preheat other materials. This cycle of events will continue to escalate, with more flammable vapours being given off as each different material in a room is heated above its ignition temperature. It is at this point that a 'flashover' will occur. The term 'flashover' is used to describe the simultaneous ignition of the flammable vapours, causing an intense fire involving all the contents of a room or building.

The rate of burning depends upon the supply of oxygen. It is possible for a fire in a room or small building to burn itself out owing to the depletion of the oxygen supply. However, if the hot gases produced as a result of the fire are allowed to escape, then a fresh oxygen supply will be drawn in causing a rapid fire growth. The transference of heat in a fire takes place by one or a combination of the following processes.

Conduction
Convection
Radiation

Conduction

This is the transfer of heat within a material from hotter to cooler areas. Non-combustible materials such as brickwork and steel have been known to conduct heat sufficient to cause temperatures high enough to ignite combustible materials such as timber etc. in locations remote from the fire.

Convection

This is the transfer of heat within liquids and gases. The heated particles expand and become less dense; this causes them to rise, and their place is taken by colder and therefore denser particles. Convection currents can cause a rapid spread of fire within a building, especially in vertical shafts, for example, lift shafts, stairwells, cavities and ventilation ducts etc. Hot gases from a ground-floor fire can travel rapidly up a stairwell causing ignition in the upper floors and roof structure.

Radiation

Heat rays are given off by any hot object. This is known as radiated heat. These heat rays are transmitted through the air or even a vacuum in the same way as we receive heat from the sun. When the rays come into contact with a material most of them are absorbed, causing the material's temperature to rise. The remainder of the rays will be reflected. Radiant heat can raise the temperature of materials at great distances from the fire itself. Fire can even spread to adjacent buildings by this process.

Surface spread of flame

Some materials will ignite more readily and burn faster than others. In general the speed at which a flame will travel across the surface of a combustible material depends upon its density and the amount of surface exposed to the air. Low density means rapid flame spread. Porous materials burn quickly because of the oxygen supply inside them. Large surface area means rapid flame spread. A solid piece of timber will take longer to burn than the same piece of timber cut into a number of thin strips. This is because the thin strips expose a larger surface area to the fire.

Note: Wood dust and other fine combustible dusts expose a very large surface area. These are therefore highly combustible, and even a small spark can cause them to explode.

BS 476: Part 7: 1971: *Surface Spread of Flame Tests for Materials* sets out a method of test to establish the behaviour of the surface of a material during the early stages of a fire. The test equipment is illustrated in Figure 139. The results of this test grade combustible materials into the following four classes according to how rapidly the flame spreads across their surface:

Class 1 surfaces of very low flame spread
Class 2 surfaces of low flame spread
Class 3 surfaces of medium flame spread
Class 4 surfaces of rapid flame spread

The Building Regulations (surface spread of flame)

The Building Regulations AD: B Fire Spread, which exerts control over the types of material that can be used in various situations, introduces an additional class 0 surface. This is non-combustible material or class 1 material with a surface that has spread of flame characteristics similar to non-combustible material. Table 18 gives typical surface spread of flame classifications for a number of common materials used as wall and ceiling linings.

Table 18 Surface spread of flame classification

Material	Class of surface (untreated)
Brickwork	0
Blockwork	0
Concrete	0
Ceramic tiles	0
Asbestos boards and other proprietary non-asbestos substitutes	0
Plasterboard	0
Woodwool slabs	0
Hardboard	3
Particle board	3
Plywood	3
Timber	3

Note: Timber and other timber based materials with a density below 400 kg/m³ have a class 4 surface. Those with a class 3 surface may be brought up to class 1 with proprietary treatments.

The Building Regulations AD: B also classifies building into two main divisions, those with sleeping accommodation are called residential and those without are called non-residential. These divisions are further sub-divided into nine purpose groups according to the building's or com-

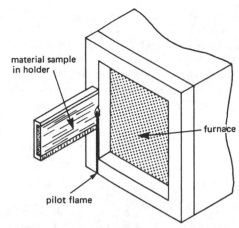

Figure 139 *Surface spread of flame test equipment*

partment's intended purpose. These are shown in Table 19.

The internal surfaces of walls and ceilings are controlled by the regulations and, apart from certain exceptions, the materials used to line walls and ceilings must have the minimum surface spread of flame classification shown in Table 20.

Table 19 Purpose groups

Main category	Purpose groups	Intended use
Residential		
	Dwelling house	Private dwelling house (not a flat or maisonette)
	Flat (including a maisonette)	Self-contained dwelling not being a house
	Institutional	Hospitals, schools and homes used as living accommodation for persons suffering from disabilities due to illness, old age, physical or mental disorders and those under five years old, where these persons sleep on the premises
	Other residential	Residential accommodation not included in previous groups, e.g. hotels, boarding houses, and hostels, etc.

Table 19 **Purpose groups** – *cont*

Main category	Purpose groups	Intended use
Non-residential		
	Assembly	Public building or assembly building where people meet for social, recreational, or business activities (not office, shop or industrial)
	Office	All premises used for administration procedures, e.g. clerical, drawing, publishing and banking, etc.
	Shop	All premises used for the retail sale of goods or services, including restaurants, public houses, cafes, hairdressers and hire or repair outlets
	Industrial	All premises defined as a factory in section 175 of the factories act 1961, not including slaughter houses, etc.
	Other non-residential	All places used for the deposit or storage of goods, the parking of vehicles and other premises not covered in the previous non-residential groups

Any part of the wall surface in rooms may be of a lower class provided it is not less than class 3 and does not exceed:

half the floor area of the room, 20 m² in any residential building.

60 m² in any non-residential building.

Note: fire surrounds, fitted furniture, frames, architraves, skirting, other trim and unglazed parts of doors are excluded from the surface spread of flame requirements

Small room A totally enclosed room with a floor area not exceeding 4 m² for residential buildings and 30 m² in non-residential ones.

Circulation spaces A hall, corridor, landing or lobby etc. used as an access between rooms or protected shafts, or as an access between rooms or protected shafts and an exist.

Protected shafts A stairway, lift shaft, escalator or service duct opening that permits the passage of items and/or persons from one compartment to another.

Fire resistance

Unlike surface spread of flame, fire resistance is a property of an element of building construction (walls, floors and roofs etc.) and not an individual material. Fire resistance is defined as the ability of an element of building construction to satisfy stated criteria, when subjected to a standard fire test as defined in BS 476 Part 8. The fire resistance of an element can be defined by reference to the following criteria:

Stability The ability of an element to resist collapse.

Integrity The ability of an element to resist the passage of flames or hot gases, from its exposed to its unexposed face.

Insulation The ability of an element to resist the passage of heat which would increase the surface temperature of the unexposed face to an unacceptable level.

Note: The unexposed face means the side of an element remote from the fire.

The results of a typical test might be expressed as 30/20/15, which means that the insulation of the element failed after 15 minutes, the integrity after 20 minutes and the stability either failed after 30 minutes or the test was terminated at this time.

Building Regulations (fire resistance)

The Building Regulations AD: B set out the periods of stability, integrity and insulation that are required for an element of building construction. These periods vary up to four hours depending on the buildings, purpose group, height, floor area, cubic capacity and its position in relation to the site boundary. The Approved Document contains a table of common construction giving notional periods of fire resistance for them. These constructions will be accepted as satisfying

Table 20 **Surface spread of flame requirements**

Purpose group	Location of surface	small room (max. 4 m²)	other room	circulation spaces and protected shaft
Dwelling house				
1 or 2 storey	Walls	3	1	1
(not counting basements)	Ceiling	3	3	3
3 or more storeys	Walls	3	1	0
	Ceiling	3	1	0
Flat	Walls	3	1	0
	Ceiling	3	1	0
Institutional	Walls	1	0	0
	Ceiling	1	1	0
Other residential	Walls	3	1	0
	Ceilings	3	1	0
Assembly		(max 30 m²)		
	Walls	3	1	0
	Ceilings	3	1	0
Offices	Walls	3	1	0
Shops	Ceilings	3	1	0
Industrial				
Other non-residential				

the relevant requirements of the regulations without the need of further proof or test.

Fire resistance of structural timber

The main purpose of structural fire precautions is public health and safety. A building should be constructed so that in the event of a fire it will in the early stages retain most of structural strength, thus enabling the safe evacuation of its occupants and the safe working of fire-fighting teams, without the fear of structural collapse.

Timber, although a combustible material, has a number of qualities that give an advantage over some structural materials:

High insulation
Low conductivity
Low thermal expansion

Known rate of charring
Charred layer provides further insulation
Mechanical strength not affected by high temperatures
Difficult to ignite
High spontaneous ignition temperature

Timber fire resistance will also depend on its density, sectional size and moisture content.

Timber in fire

On exposure to a flame or heat source, timber will not burn until the moisture in the outer layers has evaporated. This will temporarily hold the temperature at about 100 °C, thus causing a check to the fire. Little chemical change takes place until the temperature reaches about 300 °C, when the exposed surface layers of timber begin to disintegrate and flammable vapours are released which can ignite if there is a flame present. Where there is a heat source but no flame, timber will not spontaneously ignite until it reaches a temperature of about 500 °C.

Note: At these temperatures aluminium and steel are rapidly losing their strength.

The process of heating and drying out the timber has little effect on its dimensions. The very minimal expansion on heating is balanced out by the slight shrinkage due to a reduction of its moisture content. As timber burns the disintegrating outer layers form into charcoal; this insulates the inner core from the effects of the fire, by preventing heat build-up and restricting the oxygen supply. The effect of this insulation is illustrated in Figure 140(a), which shows a temperature plot through a structural timber beam that has been subjected to a furnace temperature of almost 1000 °C. The unaffected

edges of the core at a temperature of around 200 °C are still well below their ignition temperature, while the centre of the beam is still less than 100 °C. The insulating charcoal layer will not burn below 500 °C; above this temperature a glowing combustion starts, gradually consuming the outer layers of charcoal as the charring area advances into the unburnt timber core at a steady rate. See Figure 140(b).

Note: During fire exposure the arrises will become progressively rounded; their radius of rounding will be equal to the total depth of charring.

The steady rate of charring varies with the type and density of the timber. Table 21 shows the charring rates for common structural timbers. Research has proved that the charring rate is little affected by the intensity of the fire, thus enabling the strength carrying capacity of a structural timber member to be calculated after a known period of exposure to a fire. Structural timber members can be designed oversize with a

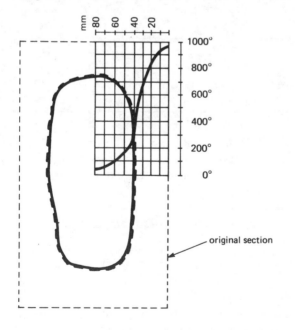

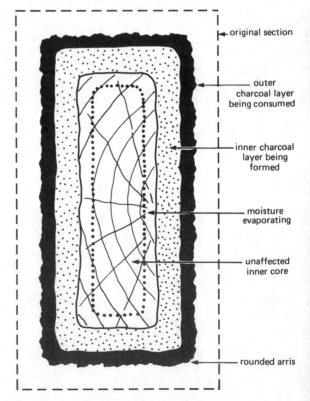

Figure 140 (a) *Temperature plot*
(b) *Timber burning*

layer of (sacrificial) timber to allow for the expected loss in dimensions after a particular period of fire.

When a timber member is exposed on all four faces it is normal to multiply the depth of charr by 1.25. This allows for the more rapid temperature rise experienced under such conditions. Glue-laminated members (glulam) can be considered to charr in a manner similar to solid timber providing that thermo-setting, resorcinol, phenol or urea formaldehyde adhesive has been used.

Where bolts, nails or screws are not totally enclosed in the unaffected core, rapid conduction of heat will cause localized charring around the fastener leading to a loss of anchorage.

Note: Where other adhesives are used for glulam members or mechanical fasteners are not fully enclosed within the unaffected core, charring must be assumed on all four faces of each laminate of the component to the depth shown in Table 21.

Fire treatments and seals

No amount of treatment can make timber completely fireproof, but treatment can be given to increase the timber's resistance to ignition and, to a large extent, stop its active participation in a fire. This treatment is known as a fire-resisting or fire-retarding treatment. It consists of treating the timber with a fire-resisting chemical. The main fire-resisting chemicals are: diammonium phosphate; monammonium phosphate; or a mixture of one of these with ammonium sulphate; ammonium chloride; zinc chloride; and boric acid. They work by giving off a vapour that will not burn. Alternatively there are intumescent paints available that when heated bubble and expand forming an insulating layer that cuts off the fire's oxygen supply. Intumescent material is also used for fire strips around door openings etc. (see Figure 141). These strips are activated by heat. In the early stages of a fire they will expand to up to 50 times their original thickness, thus efficiently sealing the gap around the door and prolonging its integrity.

Table 21 Rate of charring

Timber	Depth of charring after 30 minutes	Depth of charring after 60 minutes
Western red cedar and other timbers with a density below 420 kg/m³	25 mm	50 mm
European redwood, douglas fir, Western hemlock, parana pine, spruce, larch, mahogany, ash and beech	20 mm	40 mm
Oak, utile, keruing, teak, green heart and jarrah	15 mm	30 mm

Note: Charring depths for periods betwen 15 minutes and 90 minutes can be found from this table, for example European redwood – charring depth after 15 minutes 10 mm, 90 minutes 60 mm.

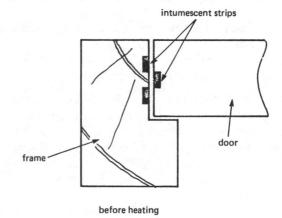

Figure 141 *Intumescent seals*

Thermal insulation

Thermal insulation can be seen as an attempt to isolate heat within a building. No thermal insulation system can be 100 per cent effective, because there is no known material that will completely isolate heat. Providing there is a difference in the temperature between the two sides of the material or structure, heat will transfer through the material from the warm to the cold side. Therefore the purpose of thermal insulation is to restrict heat transfer, thus preventing heat loss from the building in cold weather conditions and heat gain by the building in warm weather conditions.

Heat transfer

Remember there are three processes by which heat may be transferred:

Conduction   The transfer of heat within a material from hotter to cooler areas
Convection   The transfer of heat within liquids and gases
Radiation   The transfer of heat from one object to another in the form of heat rays.

Heat is transferred through an element of construction by a combination of all three processes. This is shown in Figure 142. Warmth from the inside is conducted through the structure. The heated structure then radiates heat which is dispersed into the air with the assistance of convection currents.

The three main factors that influence the rate of heat transfer are:

Type of material
Temperature difference
Rate of air change

Type of material

Heat travels through a material by conduction. A material that is a poor conductor will therefore be a good insulator. Still air is a very good insulator as it is a poor conductor. In fact the majority of thermal insulators available are basically air traps.

Note: In order to be effective, thermal insula-

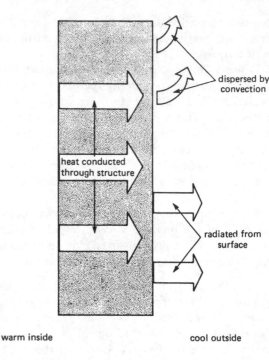

warm inside   cool outside

Figure 142   *Heat transfer through element of construction*

tors must be kept dry. This is because if they are allowed to become saturated, water, which is a better conductor, takes the place of the air.

Temperature difference

The rate of heat transfer from the warm to the cold side of the structure is dependent on the temperature difference. A small difference in temperature will result in a low rate of heat transfer, whereas a large difference in temperature will result in a high rate of heat transfer. For example, an unheated house in cold weather conditions will have almost no heat transfer as the inside and outside temperatures will be approximately equal, but when heat is switched on the rate of heat transfer will rise rapidly.

Rate of air change

This is the rate at which the warm air on one side of the structure is displaced by the cold air from the other side. Many buildings, especially those with badly fitting doors and windows, open fires and air vents, can have three to four complete air changes every hour. A rate of air change of between one-half and one every hour is considered suitable for most purposes. Much can be done to restrict this unwanted ventilation by the use of weather seals around door and window openings.

Note: Although ventilation increases the rate of air change and heat transfer, it is a necessary requirement for the physical comfort of the occupants of a building. Also, condensation can be attributed to poor ventilation.

k, R and U values (Figure 143)

k values
Some building materials are better for thermal insulation purposes than others. By looking at their *k* value (thermal conductivity) a comparison can be made between various options available. Thermal conductivity *k* value is a measure of a material's ability to conduct heat. It is expressed as the flow of heat, in watts, through a square metre of material, 1 metre thick, with a temperature difference of 1 °C or K (Kelvin 1 K = 1 °C) between its inside and outside surfaces:

The *k* value of many common building materials is given in Table 22. The *k* value for specific building materials can be obtained from the relevant manufacturer.

R value
Building materials are not of course used in 1 metre thicknesses; therefore their *R* value (thermal resistance) is required. The *R* value is a measure of a material's resistance to the flow of heat per square metre for any given thickness. It can be found by dividing the material's thickness in metres by its *k* value:

$$R = \frac{\text{material thickness in metres}}{k}$$

U value
The structure of a building is rarely a single material; it is commonly a combination of materials, possibly with cavities (air spaces) between them. To compare the thermal insulation values of various composite structures the *U* value (thermal transmittance) is used. Thermal transmittance is the rate of heat flow through an element of building construction. The *U* value is the reciprocal of the sum of the resistances of the component parts of the structure; the internal and external surfaces, and any cavity within the structure:

$$U = \frac{1}{\text{sum of resistances}} \qquad U \text{ has units W/m}^2\text{K}$$

Note: The internal and external surfaces of a structure have a certain resistance to heat flow owing to the thin layer of air clinging to the surface.

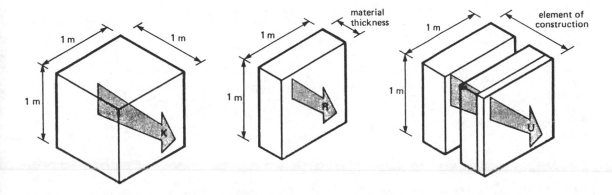

Figure 143   *Definition of terms*

Table 22   **Thermal conductivity (*k* values) of common materials**

Material	Density (kg/m²)	Thermal conductivity (k value)
Walls		
Asbestos cement sheet	700	0.35
Asbestos cement decking	1500	0.36
Brickwork (outer leaf)	1700	0.84
Brickwork (inner leaf)	1700	0.62
Cast concrete (dense)	2100	1.40
Cast concrete (lightweight)	1200	0.38
Blockwork (heavyweight)	2300	1.63
Blockwork (medium weight)	1400	0.51
Blockwork (lightweight)	600	0.19
Surface finishes		
External rendering	1300	0.50
Plaster (dense)	1300	0.50
Plaster (lightweight)	600	0.16
Fibreboard	300	0.06
Plasterboard	950	0.16
Tile hanging	1900	0.84
Roofs		
Aerated concrete slabs	500	0.16
Asphalt	1700	0.50
Felt bitumen layers	1700	0.50
Screed	1200	0.41
Steel sheeting	7800	50.00
Stone chippings	1800	0.96
Tile	1900	0.84
Wood woolslab	500	0.10
Floors		
Cast concrete	2000	1.13
Screed	1200	0.41
Timber flooring	650	0.14
Wood blocks	650	0.14
Insulation		
Expanded polystyrene slab	25	0.035
Fibre glass quilt	12	0.040
Fibre glass slab	25	0.035
Mineral fibre (Rockwool) slab	30	0.035
Phenolic foam	30	0.040
Polyurethane board	30	0.025
Urea formaldehyde foam	10	0.040

Note: The *k* value of brickwork and concrete will vary according to their density and whether they are in an exposed or protected situation.

The surface resistances of a structure will vary according to the type of material used and the height, location and exposure of the building. For comparison of the thermal insulation values of alternative materials and structures, the standard values given in Table 23 can be used.

Table 24 gives standard values for air spaces in the construction.

U value calculation

When calculating the *U* value of a particular element of construction, the following basic procedure can be adopted using Tables 22, 23 and 24 for *k* values and resistances:

•1 Using a *U* value worksheet, shown in Figure 144, sketch in column 1 the element of construction being considered.
2 List in column 2 the materials and cavities that form each layer of the construction.
3 Select the *k* value for each material and enter in column 3.
4 Enter in column 4 the thickness in metres of each material (*t*).
5 Divide in turn each material's *t* by *k* to find resistance and enter in column 5.

Table 23   **Surface resistances**

Surface	Internal resistance	External resistance
Exposed walls	0.12	0.06
Roofs	0.10	0.04
Exposed floors	0.14	0.04

Table 24   **Air space resistances**

Air space	Resistance
Wall cavity	0.18
Roof space	
pitched	0.18
flat	0.16

Note: The surface and cavity values stated are for most normal building materials, but for corrugated materials these values are decreased and for shiny metallic surfaces they are increased.

U value worksheet no.		Job title			Date	Ref.
1		2		3	4	5
Element of construction		Component		Conductivity k value	Thickness t metres	Resistance $R = \dfrac{t}{k}$
		External surface resistance				
		Internal surface resistance				
BBS DESIGN				Total resistance		
				U value $\dfrac{1}{R}$		

Figure 144   *U value worksheet*

6 Select the internal, external and cavity resistances and enter in column 5.

7 Add up column 5 and enter the total resistance.

8 Divide total resistance into 1 to find the U value; enter this in the space provided.

An example of a U value calculation is given in Figure 145, which shows a completed U value worksheet for a typical cavity wall construction.

Building Regulations (thermal insulation)

The need to conserve heat within buildings is becoming increasingly more important. This has been brought about by the so-called 'energy crisis' resulting in the constant acceleration in fuel prices and the improved levels of comfort that people expect. These two points stress the need for buildings to be effectively insulated against heat loss.

The Building Regulations Part L lay down minimum standards of thermal insulation for the main enclosing elements (roof, walls, exposed floors and ground floors) of building construction. These regulations state the maximum U values permitted for each purpose group. These maximum U values are given in Table 25.

The area of glazing in windows and rooflights is also controlled by Part L. Table 26 gives the maximum area of single glazing permitted for each purpose group. For dwellings this is a percentage of the total floor area.

U value worksheet no.		Job title			Date	Ref.
1		2		3	4	5
Element of construction		Component		Conductivity k value	Thickness t metres	Resistance $R = \frac{t}{k}$
fibreglass insulation　　dense plaster brickwork　　blockwork		External surface resistance				0·06
		BRICKWORK (OUTER LEAF)		0·84	0·105	0·125
		FIBREGLASS		0·04	0·075	1·875
		BLOCKWORK (LIGHTWEIGHT)		0·19	0·100	0·526
		PLASTER (DENSE)		0·50	0·015	0·03
		Internal surface resistance				0·12
BBS DESIGN				Total resistance		2·736
				U value $\frac{1}{R}$		0·365

Figure 144　*U value worksheet*

Table 25　Maximum U values

	Dwellings	All other buildings
Exposed walls Exposed floors Ground floors	0.45	0.45
Roofs	0.25	0.45
Semi exposed walls and floors	0.6	0.6

Exposed elements are in contact with outside air whilst semi exposed elements separate a heated space from an unheated space.

Table 26　Maximum area of single glazing

Building type	Windows	Rooflights
Dwellings	15% of total floor area for both combined	
Other residential institutional	25% of exposed wall area	20% of roof area
Assembly, offices and shops	35% of exposed wall area	20% of roof area
Industrial and storage	15% of exposed wall area	20% of roof area

Note: This requirement does not include display windows in shops.

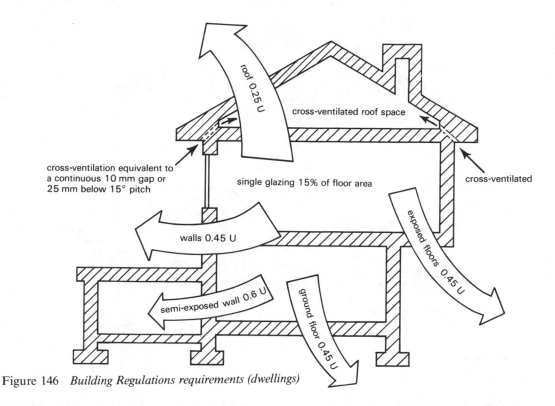

Figure 146   *Building Regulations requirements (dwellings)*

Whilst for other purpose groups it is a percentage of the exposed wall area. The areas of walls, roofs and floors should be measured between the internal finished faces of the building. Roof areas should be measured in the plane of its insulation.

Windows and roof lights which are double glazed may be up to twice the size of single glazed ones; whereas those which are triple glazed or are double glazed and have a low emissivity coating (low ability to radiate energy) may be up to three times the size of single glazing.

The Regulations allows a flexible approach for limiting heat loss, they permit a trade off in U values between different building elements, providing the total heat loss for the building is not increased. For example:

1 The exposed walls could have a U value of 0.6 if half the windows in the building were double glazed.
2 The exposed walls could have a U value of 0.6, the roof a U value of 0.35 and the floor left uninsulated if all the windows were double glazed.
3 The roof could have a U value of 0.35 if the ground floor is also insulated to 0.35.

Thermal insulation of existing buildings

Prior to 1974 only very modest standards of thermal insulation were required for new buildings; consequently houses built before 1974 have a very high rate of heat transfer. Approximately 75 per cent of the heat input in an uninsulated building can be lost to the outside. Improved thermal insulation in these buildings will reduce the rate of heat transfer and reduce the amount of energy used and/or increase the standards of comfort for the occupants.

Figure 147 shows the percentage of heat lost from the various elements of an uninsulated building.

When carrying out thermal insulation improvements the aim is to achieve the greatest benefit from the start with the least cost. The

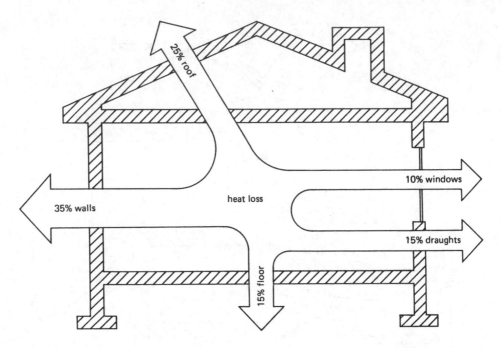

Figure 147   *Heat loss*

suggested order for carrying out these improvements is:

1   Weather seals around doors and windows; Figure 148 illustrates typical details.
2   Roof insulation, normally in the form of mineral/fibreglass between the ceiling joists.
3   Wall insulation, normally either by an injection of cavity wall foam/fibre or in the case of solid walls the external or internal application of an insulating material.
4   Double or triple glazing, preferably sealed units and not in the form of secondary glazing, as convection currents can be set up when the air space increases in width above about 25 mm.

Condensation

The atmosphere contains a certain amount of water vapour in the form of a invisible gas. The amount of water vapour that the air can hold is dependent on the air temperature. Warm air can hold more water vapour than cold air. The maximum amount of water vapour that the air can hold is known as its saturation point; the temperature at this point is known as its dew point. If air at its saturation point is cooled it can no longer hold all of its water vapour, and the excess will revert to water. This process is known as condensation. There are two main condensation problems:

Surface condensation (Figure 149)
Whenever warm moist air meets a cool surface, condensation will occur, possibly causing structural damage, mould growth and damp unhealthy living conditions.

Interstitial condensation (Figure 150)
This means condensation within a structure. Warm air has a higher vapour pressure than cool air; water vapour is therefore driven through most building materials. As this water vapour cools on its passage through the structure condensation can occur, even where there is no surface condensation, causing in many cases severe structural damage.

Over the last twenty years there have been a number of changes in new and modernized

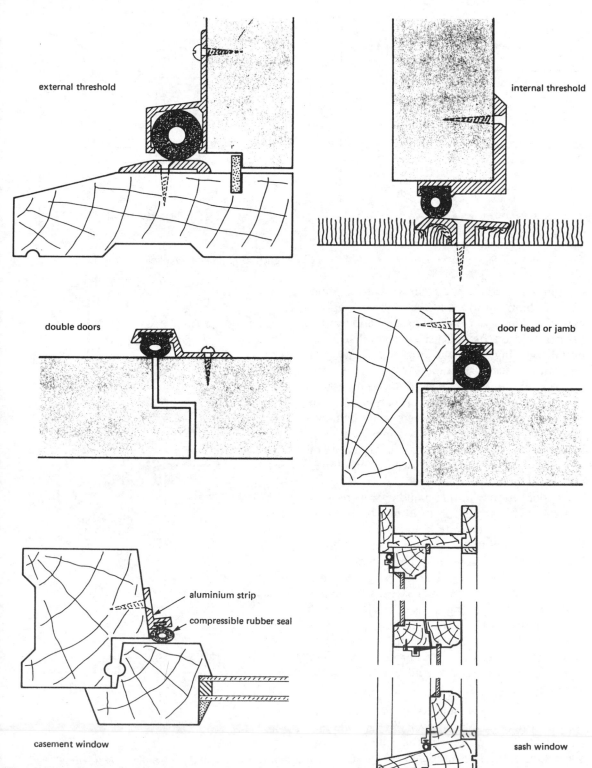

Figure 148   *Door and window seals*

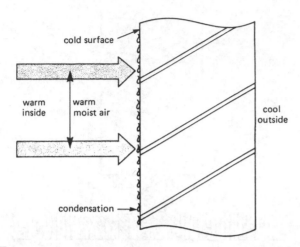

Figure 149   *Surface condensation*

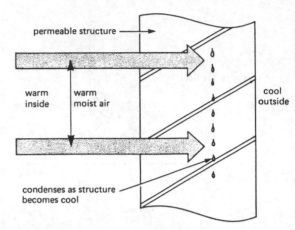

Figure 150   *Interstitial condensation*

buildings to reduce their energy consumption. The air temperature and therefore its vapour-carrying capacity within domestic buildings has been increased by the use of central heating, double glazing, draught-proofing, cavity wall and roof space insulation. At the same time, natural ventilation has been reduced by double glazing, draught-proofing, insulation and the virtual elimination of fireplaces and chimneys. Also the production of water vapour has been increased by the wider use of flueless gas and oil heaters, baths, showers, washing machines, dishwashers and tumble dryers.

Condensation within a building can only be controlled by achieving a proper balance between heating, ventilation and insulation. The two main vapour producing areas within a building are kitchens and bathrooms. These should be well ventilated, possibly by mechanical means, in order to prevent excessive spread of moisture into the living areas of the building. A small amount of natural ventilation in living rooms can make a big difference. This can be easily achieved using various proprietary adjustable window ventilators, one type of which is shown in Figure 151.

The risk of surface condensation can be reduced by the use of insulating wall lining materials. Interstitial condensation can be dealt with in two ways. One is to use a vapour check or barrier on the inside of a building, for example, polythene

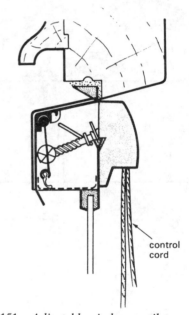

Figure 151   *Adjustable window ventilator*

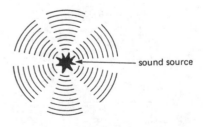

Figure 152   *Sound wave moving outwards from source*

sheet or foil-backed plasterboard etc. In the second, where the structure contains a ventilated cavity, the vapour can be allowed to enter the cavity where it will be dispersed by the ventilation.

Note: As it is almost impossible to provide a perfect vapour barrier because of leaks at joints and fixings etc., a combination of these methods is often used.

Building Regulations (condensation)

In order to limit the risk of condensation in roof spaces above insulated ceilings, the Building Regulations Part F states that a reasonable provision shall be made to prevent excessive condensation in the roof space of dwellings. AD: F sets out the conditions to satisfy the requirements. Roof spaces should have ventilation openings in opposite eaves or at the eaves and opposite high level in the case of a lean-to roof. The area of the opening along each side should be equivalent to a continuous gap of 10 mm for pitched roofs or 25 mm for flat roofs and those of less than 15 degrees pitch (see Figure 146). The AD allows these to be either continuous or distributed along the length of the roof. In addition it also suggests that provision should be made to ensure that the insulation does not obstruct the air flow where the insulation and roof slope meet.

Sound insulation

Nature of sound

Sound is a vibration. The sound we hear is a vibration of the air, which causes a sensation in the ear mechanism, which in turn sends a message to the brain where it is interpreted as sound. Anything that vibrates, normally causes a sound. Vibrations from a source of sound cause the air to move, resulting in a series of waves or ripples moving spherically outwards from the original source (see Figure 152), much like the ripple produced when a stone is thrown in a pond. The sound energy – its intensity or loudness – is progressively spread as the waves move outwards from the sound source until eventually the motion stops and the sound dies away. In addition to travelling through the air,

Table 27 **Common sound levels**

Sound source	Sound level dB(A)
Jet engine	140
Pneumatic drill	110
Machine shop	100
Busy traffic	80
Shouting	80
Car	70
Conversation	60
A whisper	30
Quiet house	20

sound waves can also travel through other media such as liquids and solids. When sound waves meet a hard surface most of their energy is reflected, much like light rays in a mirror. Soft surfaces reflect very little of the energy as most of it is absorbed. The number of vibrations or waves that occur in one second is known as the frequency. Something vibrating 200 times a second will produce a sound that has a frequency of 200 cycles per second or 200 Hz (hertz). It is the frequency of sound that determines its pitch; sound sources of high frequency produce high-pitch notes and sound sources of low frequency produce low-pitch notes.

Human hearing responds to a wide range of frequencies; anything between 20 and 20,000 Hz produces an audible sound. Decibels (dB) are the units which are used to define the loudness of a sound. The decibel scale ranges from 0 dB (threshold of hearing), which is virtually silence, to about 130 dB (threshold of feeling), which is painful sound. The approximate sound levels of common sources are given in Table 27.

Note: The suffix A after dB is a weighted decibel in which simple meter measurements can be made.

Sound control

In the building design process, architects and planners will consider sound control. In general the three essential considerations are:

1 To keep noisy areas and quiet areas as far apart as possible or erect a screen between

them to reflect or absorb the sound waves. See Figure 153.

2 Structural design, to reduce sound penetration and avoid sound transfer through the structure (sound insulation).

3 The acoustics of a room (sound absorption).

Sound insulation and sound absorption are two terms often taken to mean the same thing. To be specific, sound insulation is concerned with the transfer of sound energy through barriers from one area or space to another, whereas sound absorption is concerned with the reflection or absorption of sound energy by the surfaces within the area or space.

Sound insulation
There are two main types of sound insulation: airborne sound insulation and impact sound insulation.

Airborne sound
The transmission of airborne sound through the walls, roof, and floors of a building is dependent on their mass. Transmission occurs when a sound wave meets a building element, causing it to vibrate, which in turn sets up a new sound wave on the other side. Sound transmission through the building element is known as direct transmission. The vibrating building element will also cause its adjoining elements to vibrate, resulting in indirect or flanking transmission. Figure 154 illustrates the transmission of sound from one room to another.

Clearly, the greater the mass of the building elements the harder it is to set them into vibration, and therefore the better their sound insulation value. This value can be severely reduced by a lack of uniform resistance to sound, lightweight construction or air passages such as partially filled mortar joints, gaps around windows, doors and keyholes etc.

Impact sound
This results from an impact or vibration communicated directly to the building element, such as footsteps or vibrating machinery. Mass is of little advantage; the solution is to isolate

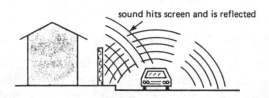

Figure 153   *Position of building in relation to sound source*

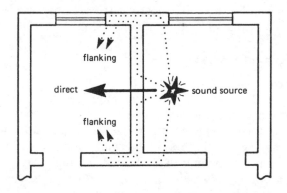

Figure 154   *Direct and flanking sound transmission*

elements or create a discontinuous structure so that vibrations are not allowed to pass through. Soft finishes such as thick carpet, rubber underlay and cork can significantly reduce the amount of vibrations generated.

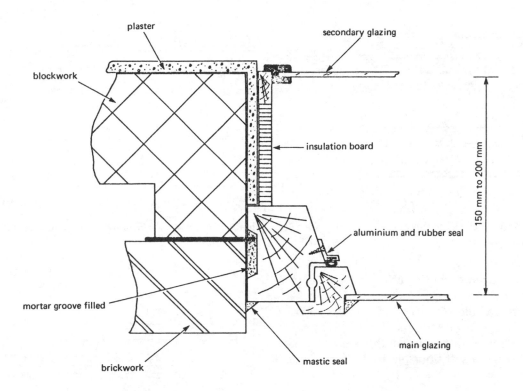

Figure 155 *Secondary double glazing*

Sound absorption

Sound within a room is made up of two parts: direct sound, which travels straight from its source to the ear, and reverberant sound, which is the sum of all the sound reflected back from the room surfaces. Much of this reverberant sound is absorbed by the soft furnishings, carpets and curtains within a room. In factories and offices sound absorption materials can be used to line walls and ceilings. Noisy sound sources, can be enclosed with free-standing sound absorption screens or panels hanging from the ceiling. The most commonly used absorbent materials are fibre insulation boards or mineral/glassfibre faced with perforated metal or hardboard. Basically, all soft materials and lightweight porous materials are good sound absorbers. They work by soaking up the sound and reflecting it to and fro between their particles or fibres until all the sound energy has been used up.

Practical sound insulation

Windows

The most effective form of sound insulation for windows is secondary double glazing. Air tightness of the existing window is extremely important. A typical detail is shown in Figure 155.

Note: Sealed unit double glazing with an air space of up to 20 mm is for thermal insulation. It gives only a minimal reduction in sound.

Floors

The need for sound insulation in the floors of a domestic house occupied by one family is fairly limited, but it is considered essential for buildings in multiple occupancy.

Figure 156 illustrates typical details for suspended timber floors. Detail A would be effective against airborne sound, but detail B incorporates a floating floor and would be

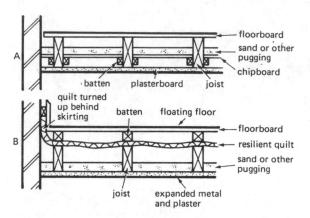

Figure 156   *Suspended floor details to reduce sound transmission*

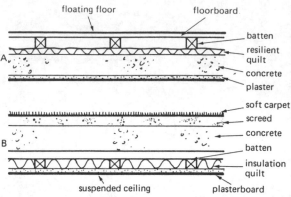

Figure 157   *Concrete floor details to reduce sound transmission*

effective against both airborne and impact sound.

Figure 157 illustrates typical sound insulation details for concrete floors. Detail A shows a floating timber raft on top of the concrete floor. Detail B has a soft floor finish and a suspended ceiling.

Partition walls

Stud partition walls can be given a reasonable amount of airborne sound insulation by filling the spaces between the studs and noggins with mineral/fibreglass quilt. For a greater degree of insulation, especially from impact sound, some form of separation is required. Details A and B illustrated in Figure 158 show alternative horizontal sections through discontinuous partitions. Strips of insulation board are fixed to the back of the head, sole and wall studs to isolate the partition from any vibrations in the structure. The backs of any door linings should also receive the same treatment. Door openings or borrowed lights in a partition are often the weak link. Insulation of doors can be improved by the use of a solid-core door, proprietary sealing strips and thresholds. In extreme cases two doors are used, one on each face of the partition.

Borrowed lights in sound insulating partitions should be double glazed. A typical detail is shown in Figure 159. A packet of silica gel can be placed in the air space to keep it dry and prevent condensation.

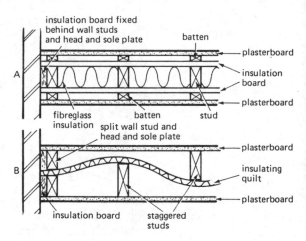

Figure 158   *Partition details to reduce sound transmission*

Building Regulations (sound insulation)

The Building Regulations Part E states that walls which separate one dwelling from another or that separate a dwelling from another part of a building used for a different purpose must have a reasonable resistance to the passage of airborne sound; whereas floors which separate one dwelling from another, or from another part of the same building used for a different purpose, must have a reasonable resistance to both airborne and impact sound.

AD: E gives details of typical constructions that satisfy these requirements.

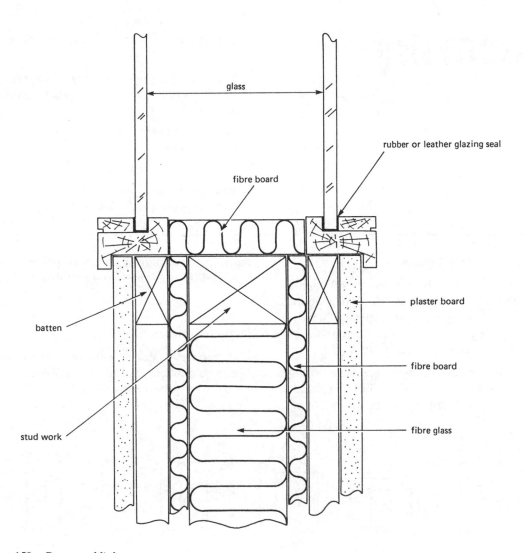

Figure 159 *Borrowed light*

Self-assessment questions

1 Briefly explain the process by which timber burns.

2 State the *three* requirements needed for burning.

3 Define what is meant by k, R and U values.

4 Briefly name the *three* processes by which heat may be transferred.

5 Describe the difference between sound insulation and sound absorption.

6 Briefly explain the principles of insulating against
(a) Airborne sound
(b) Impact sound

7 Explain why thermal insulation materials must be kept dry.

chapter 7

Geometry

After reading this chapter the student should be able to:

1 Produce drawings to show true sections, developments and interpenetrations of geometrical solids.

2 Apply geometrical principles to solve practical problems.

3 Recognize various plane figures.

4 Recognize and define the properties of various geometric solids.

Plane geometric figures

A plane is a flat surface; it has both length and breadth but no thickness. A plane figure is therefore a two-dimensional surface having an area bounded by one or more lines. A range of plane figures is illustrated in Table 28.

Note: When the bounding lines are all straight, the plane figure is said to be rectilineal or rectilinear. Regular polygons have sides of equal length and equal angles. Irregular polygons have sides of differing length and unequal angles.

Geometric solids

Solid geometry deals with three-dimensional objects having length, breadth and thickness. A number of regular geometric solids are shown in Figure 160. These include:

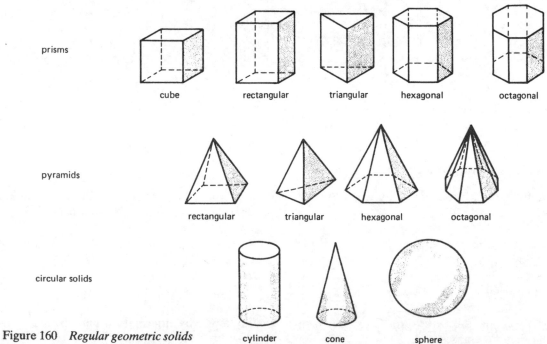

prisms   cube   rectangular   triangular   hexagonal   octagonal

pyramids   rectangular   triangular   hexagonal   octagonal

circular solids   cylinder   cone   sphere

Figure 160   *Regular geometric solids*

Table 28 **Plane figures**

Bounded by	Name of figure	Shape	Bounded by	Name of figure	Shape
1 line	circle			trapezium	
	ellipse			trapezoid	
2 lines	semicircle/segment			*polygons* (regular or irregular)	
3 lines	sector		5 lines	pentagon	
	triangle		6 lines	hexagon	
	quadrilaterals		7 lines	hectagon	
4 lines	square		8 lines	octagon	
	rectangle		9 lines	nonagon	
	rhombus		10 lines	decagon	
	parallelogram				

Cube   This is a solid figure formed by six faces, all of which are squares.

Prism   A solid figure formed by plane surfaces which are parallel to each other, named according to the shape of its base.

Pyramid   This is also named according to its base shape, and is a solid figure formed by its base and triangular sloping sides.

Circular solids   These include cylinders, cones and spheres.

Cylinder   A solid figure described by the revolution of a rectangle about one of its sides, which remains fixed and is called its axis. The base or ends of a cylinder are circular in shape.

Cone   A cone is a solid figure described by the revolution of a right-angled triangle about one of its sides, which remains fixed and is called its axis. The base of a cone is circular in shape.

Sphere   A sphere is a solid figure described by the revolution of a semi-circle about its diameter, which remains fixed and is called its axis.

Solids may be described as being either right or oblique. The central axis of right solids is vertical, while oblique solids have a central axis that is inclined. Examples of right and oblique solids are shown in Figure 161.

Sections of solids

When a solid is cut through the cut surface is a section. A solid that has had its top cut off is called a truncated solid. The remaining portion is called the frustum of a solid. The problem usually encountered at a practical level is to determine the true shape of the cut section. This involves drawing the plan and elevation of the solid. The true shape of the cut section is determined by projecting lines at right angles to the cutting plane and drawing in the auxiliary view. Examples of this procedure are shown in Figures 162–167.

Development of solids

The development of a solid is a drawing of the shape of all its faces laid out flat in one plane. This can be done by unfolding or unrolling as illustrated by Figure 168. Examples of the procedures involved when developing solids, with pictorial sketches, are shown in Figures 169–173.

Interpenetration

When two surfaces intersect there will be a line of intersection common to both of them. The shape of these lines will depend upon the shape of the contacting surfaces. The lines of intersection of two plane surfaces will be straight, whereas the lines of intersection will be curved when one or both of the intersecting surfaces are curved. The geometry concerned with intersections is closely related to developments and true shapes. At least two views of the intersecting solids, normally a plan and elevation, will need to be drawn in order to determine the required line of intersection, the development and the true shapes. Examples of the geometry involved when solids intersect, along with a pictorial sketch of the intersecting solids, are shown in Figures 174–177.

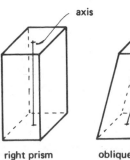
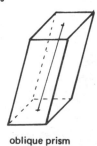
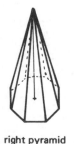

right prism   oblique prism   right pyramid   oblique pyramid   right cone   oblique cone

Figure 161   *Right and oblique solids*

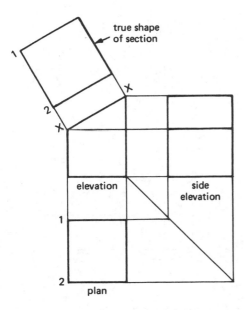

Figure 162   *True section of the frustum of a rectangular prism*

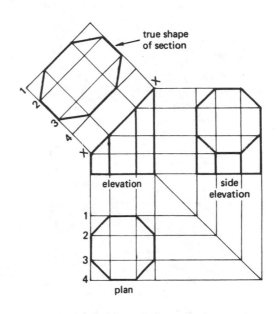

Figure 163   *True section of the frustum of an octagonal prism*

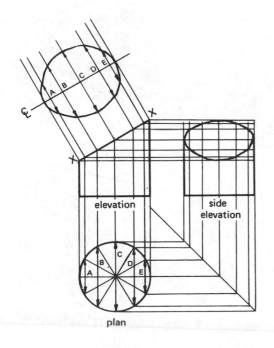

Figure 164   *True section of the frustum of a cylinder*

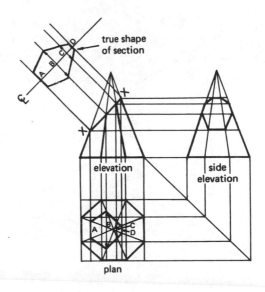

Figure 165   *True section of the frustum of an octagonal pyramid*

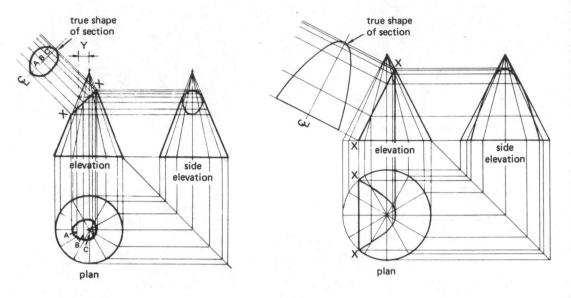

Figure 166   *True section of the frustum of a cone*

Figure 167   *True section of a cone*

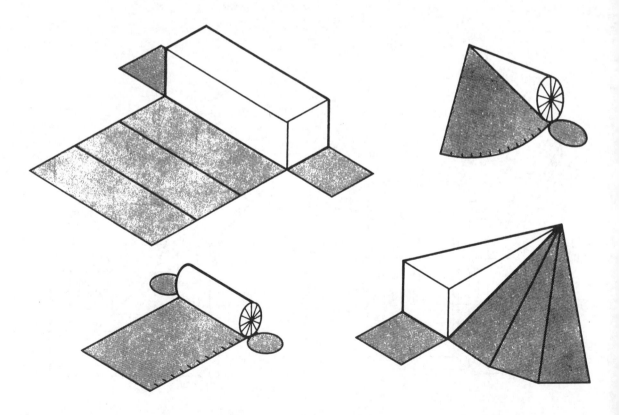

Figure 168   *Surface developments*

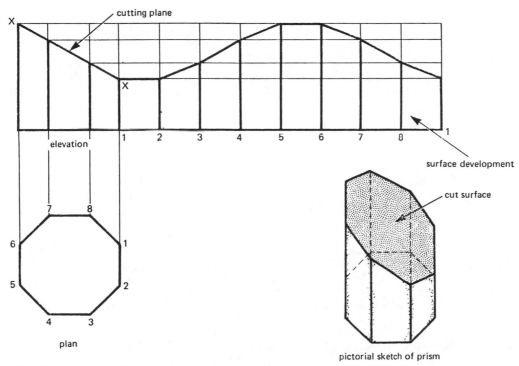

Figure 169   *Development of the frustum of an octagonal prism*

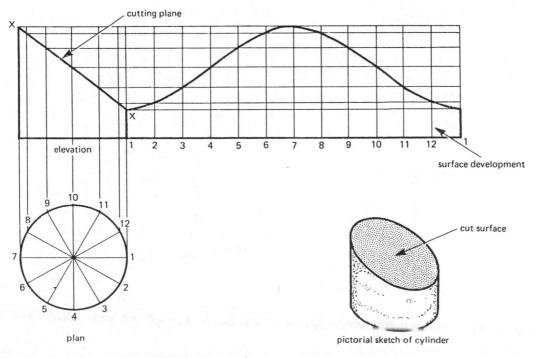

Figure 170   *Development of the frustum of a cylinder*

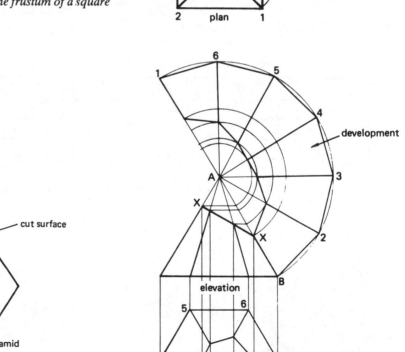

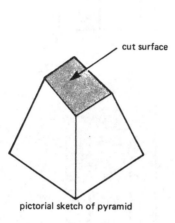

cut surface

pictorial sketch of pyramid

Figure 171   *Development of the frustum of a square pyramid*

cut surface

pictorial sketch of pyramid

Figure 172   *Development of the frustum of a hexagonal pyramid*

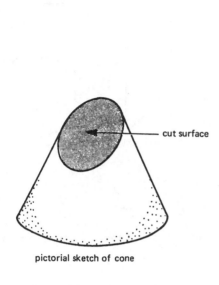

cut surface

pictorial sketch of cone

Figure 173 *Development of the frustum of a cone*

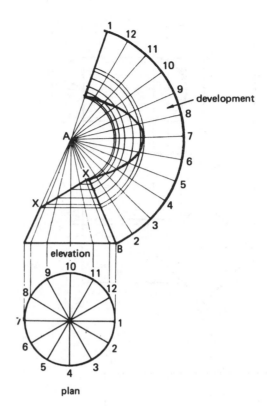

development

elevation

plan

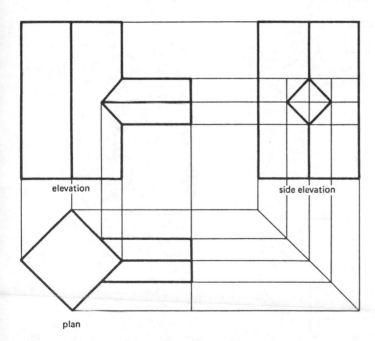

elevation

side elevation

plan

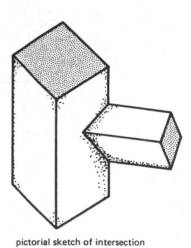

pictorial sketch of intersection

Figure 174 *Intersection of two prisms*

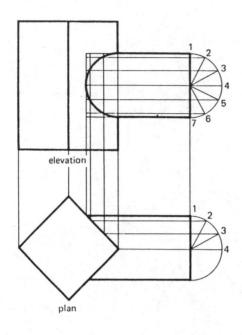

elevation

plan

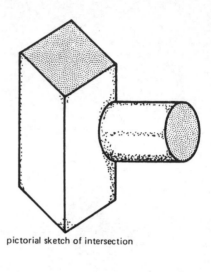

pictorial sketch of intersection

Figure 175   *Intersection of prism and cylinder*

Figure 176   *Intersection of two cylinders: perpendicular*

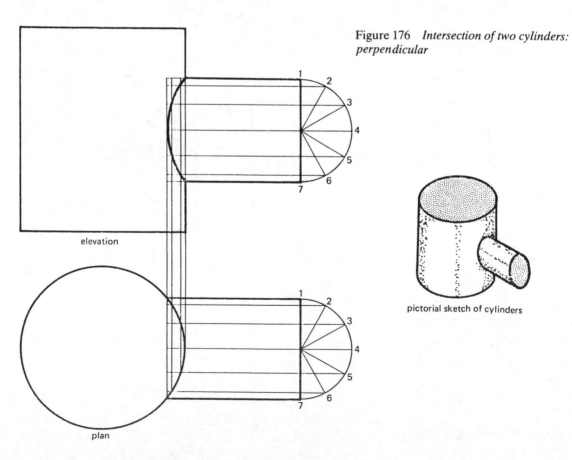

elevation

plan

pictorial sketch of cylinders

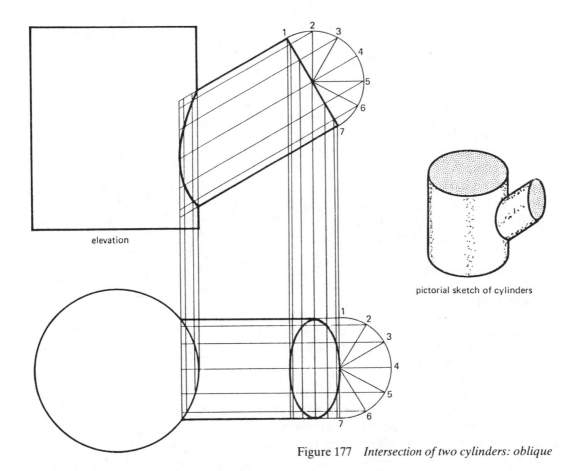

elevation

pictorial sketch of cylinders

Figure 177 *Intersection of two cylinders: oblique*

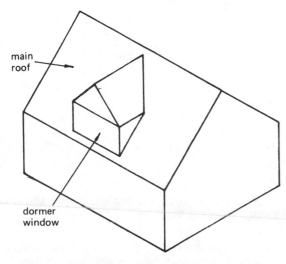

main roof

dormer window

Figure 178 *House with dormer window*

Practical examples

Dormer window in pitched roof

Figure 178 shows a sketch of a house with a dormer window in a pitched roof. The problem is to find the true shape of the opening in the main roof and the development of the dormer roof. The solution to this problem is shown in Figure 179. The method used is as follows:

Draw the plan and elevations.

Project up points A, B and C.

Mark points 1^1, 2^1 and 3^1 equal to distances 1, 2 and 3 taken from the elevation.

Draw lines to complete the true shape of the opening.

With centre E and radius ED, draw arc to give point F.

From F, project vertically down to G and from
G horizontally across on to plan.

Draw lines to give development of half of
dormer roof.

Segmental dormer in pitched roof

Figure 180 is a similar problem to the previous
example except in this case the dormer window
has a segmental-shaped roof. The solution is
shown in Figure 181. The method used is as
follows:

Draw the elevation and side elevation.

Divide the segmental roof into a number of
equal divisions 1, 2, 3, 4, 5 on the elevation
and project these points on to the main roof
line on the side elevation.

True shape of opening

Project lines down and across from the two
elevations and draw in the plan.

Project up the points of intersection on the main
roof line at right angles.

Draw in a centre line, which will carry 5^1.

Mark on either side of centre line points 1^1 to 4^1
equal to distances 1^1 to 4^1 on the elevation,
and draw lines from these points to form an
intersecting grid, with the right-angled projections from the main roof line.

Draw a smooth curve through the intersecting
grid to give the shape of the opening in the
main roof.

Development of dormer roof surface

Project points down from the plan and draw in
the centre line, which will carry point 5.

Mark on either side of the centre line points 1 to
4 equal to distances 1 to 4 on the elevation
and draw lines from these points to form an
intersecting grid with the projections from the
main roof line.

Draw a smooth curve through the intersecting
grid to give the development of the dormer
roof surface.

Intersection of two semicircular vaults

Figure 182 shows a pictorial sketch of two
intersecting semicircular vaults and the geometry required to determine the true shape of

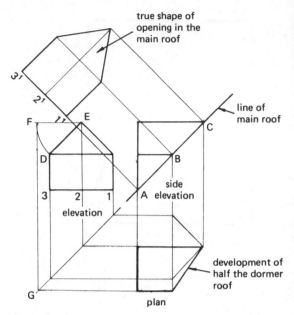

Figure 179   *Practical development (dormer window)*

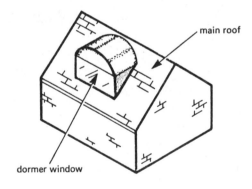

Figure 180   *House with dormer window with segmental roof*

intersection. This true shape is also known as the
groin.

Draw the plan and elevation.

Draw XY line parallel to the line of intersection.

Divide the arch in the elevation into a number of
equal divisions.

Project these points down on to the line of
intersection and then on past the XY line.

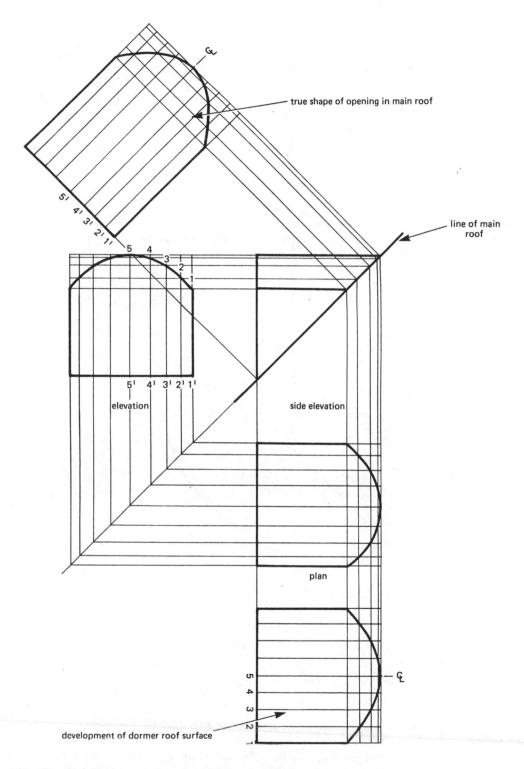

true shape of opening in main roof

line of main roof

elevation

side elevation

plan

development of dormer roof surface

Figure 181 *Practical development (segmental dormer window)*

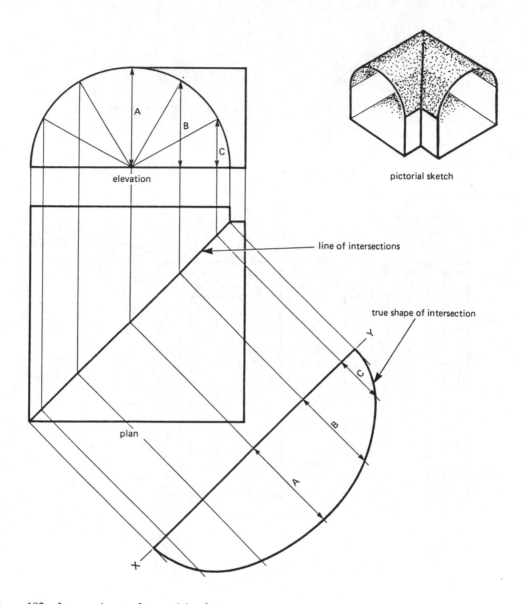

pictorial sketch

line of intersections

true shape of intersection

elevation

plan

Figure 182   *Intersecting vaults: semicircular*

Transfer distances A, B, C from the elevation and mark below the XY line.

Draw in a smooth curve to complete the true shape.

Intersection of two semi-elliptical vaults
Figure 183 shows a pictorial sketch of intersecting semi-elliptical vaults. The true shape of the groin or intersection is required to enable the

timber supporting structure for the brickwork or concrete to be formed. The geometry required is also shown in Figure 183. The method used is the same as that used in the previous example.

Domed roof with square plan
Figure 184 shows a semicircular domed roof which is square on plan. In order to construct the roof it is necessary to develop the true shape

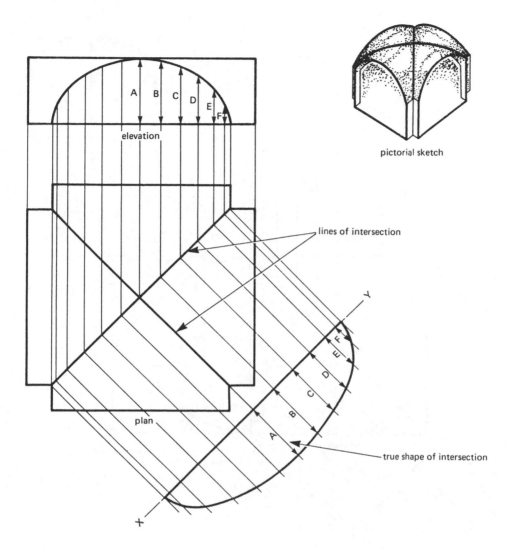

Figure 183 *Intersecting vaults: semi-elliptical*

of one surface of the roof, to determine the outine of the hip rib and backing bevel. The method used is as follows:

Development of surface

Draw plan and elevation of the roof.

Divide half the elevation into a number of equal divisions 1, 2, 3, 4, 5, 6, 7.

Project lines down from these points on to the plan to give a series of points on the hips.

Draw a horizontal line from each point on the hips.

Mark on the centre line points 1^1 to 7^1 equal to distances 1 to 7 on the elevation and draw lines through these points to form an intersecting grid with the horizontal lines.

Draw smooth curves through the intersecting grid to give the development of the roof surface.

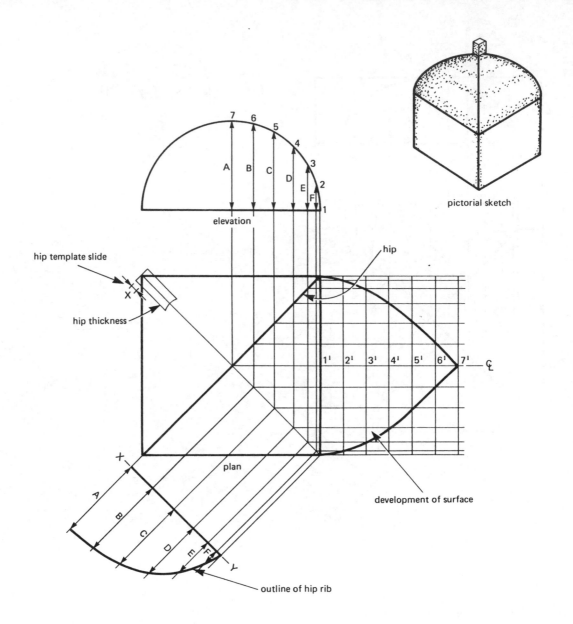

pictorial sketch

Figure 184   *Domed roof with square plan*

Outline of hip

Draw XY line parallel to one hip.

Project points from the hip at right angles through the XY line.

Transfer distances A, B, C, D, E, F from the elevation and mark below the XY line.

Draw in a smooth curve to give the outline of the hip rib (used to make hip template).

To form backing bevel

When the hip rib is cut to shape it will still require a backing bevel. This can be found by placing the hip template on the hip and sliding it sideways equal to distance X marked on the plan.

Mark around the template and repeat on the other side.

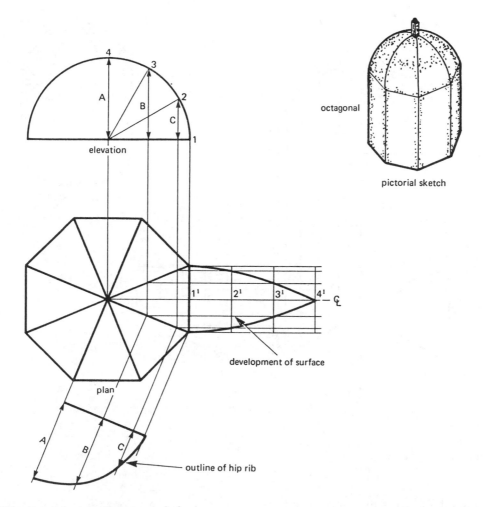

octagonal

pictorial sketch

elevation

development of surface

plan

outline of hip rib

Figure 185   *Domed roof with octagonal plan*

Mark the centre line on the top edge of the hip. Chamfer the edge to these lines to form the backing bevel.

Domed roof with octagonal plan
Figure 185 shows another example of a domed roof which in this case has an octagonal plan. The geometry involved is the same as that used in the previous example.

Hemispherical domed roof
Figure 186 shows a hemispherical domed roof. All that is required in this example is a development of one portion of the surface. The

outline of the hips will be the same as the elevation. It is not possible to develop accurately the surfaces of a hemisphere, but for practical purposes the method shown will give a close approximation. The method used is as follows:

Draw the plan and elevation.
Divide half of the elevation into a number of equal divisions 1, 2, 3, 4, 5, 6, 7.
Project lines down from these points on to the plan to give a series of points on the hips.
Draw a horizontal line from each point on the hips.
Mark on the centre line points 1^1 to 7^1 equal to distances 1 to 7 on the elevation and draw a

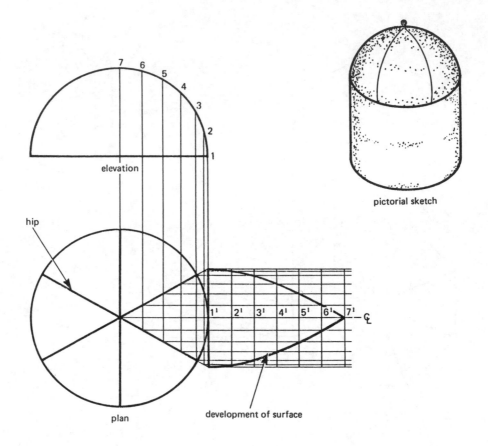

Figure 186   *Hemispherical domed roof*

line through these points to form an intersecting grid with the horizontal lines.

Draw smooth curves through the intersecting grid to give the approximate development of the roof surface.

Roofing geometry

Pitched roof geometry can be divided into three sections:

The development of roof surfaces
Finding the true length of rafters etc.
Finding the required angles for the cuts to the rafters and other components

Hipped-end roof with purlins

Figure 187 is a scale drawing of a part plan and section of a hipped-end roof with purlins. Indicated on the scale drawing are all the developments, angles and true lengths required to set out and construct the roof.

The geometry for each of these developments, angles and true lengths is considered separately in the following figures.

Rafter angles and lengths

Figure 188 shows the angles and true lengths for the common and hip rafters. The method used is as follows:

Draw, to a suitable scale, the plan and section of the roof.

Note: On regular plan roofs, the hip rafters will be at 45°. On irregular plan roofs the angle will have to be bisected.

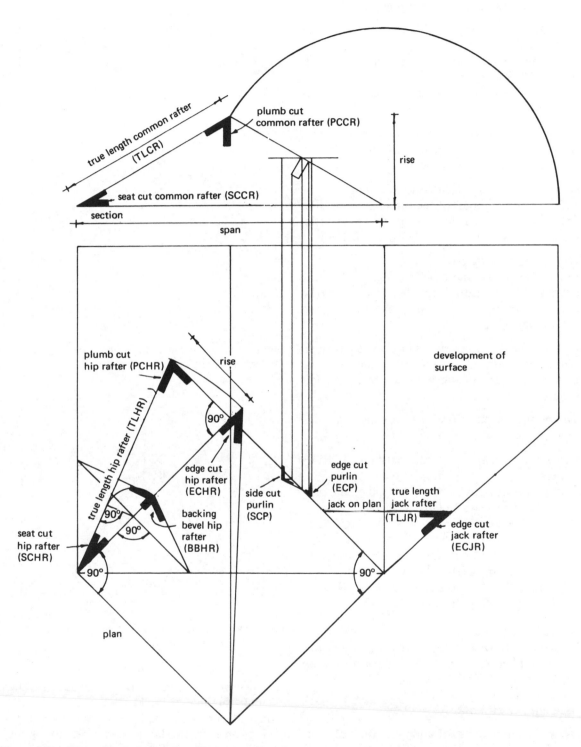

Figure 187   *Hipped-end roof with purlins*

Indicate on the section the following:

(a) The true length of the common rafter (TLCR)
(b) The plumb cut for the common rafter (PCCR)
(c) The seat cut for the common rafter (SCCR)

At right angles to one of the hips on the plan, draw line $A^1 B^1$ and mark on it the rise of the roof AB taken from the section.

Join B^1 to C and indicate the following:
(a) The true length of the hip rafter (TLHR)
(b) The plumb cut for the hip rafter (PCHR)
(c) The seat cut for the hip rafter (SCHR)

Hip rafter backing bevel

Figure 189 shows the dihedral angle or backing bevel for the hip rafter. The dihedral angle is the angle of intersection between the two sloping roof surfaces.

Note: The backing bevel is rarely used today in hipped roofing work for economic reasons. Instead the edge of the hip rafter is usually left square.

The method used to find the backing bevel is as follows:

Draw a plan of the roof and mark on TLHR as before.
Draw a line at right angles to the hip on the plan at D to touch wall plates at E and F.
Draw a line at right angles to TLHR at G to touch point D.
With centre D and radius DG, draw an arc to touch the hip on the plan at H.
Join point E to H and H to F. This gives the required backing bevel (BBHR).

Hip rafter edge cut

Figure 190 shows the edge cut to the hip rafter. This is applied to both sides to allow it to fit up to the ridge board between the crown and common rafters. The method used to find the edge cut is as follows:

Draw a plan of the roof and mark on TLHR as before.

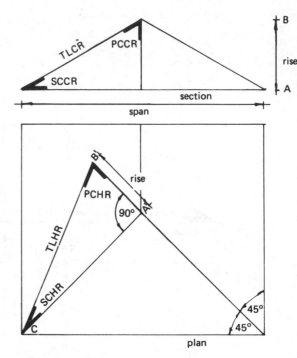

Figure 188   *Hipped-end roof with purlins: rafter angles and lengths*

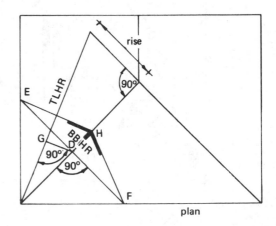

Figure 189   *Hip rafter backing bevel*

With centre I and radius IB, swing TLHR down to J (this makes IJ, TLHR).
Draw lines at right angles from the ends of the hips and extend the ridge line. All three lines will intersect at K.

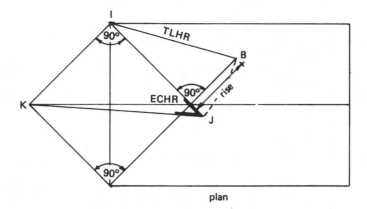

plan

Figure 190   *Hip rafter edge cut*

Join K to J. Angle IJK is the required edge cut
(ECHR).

Roof surface development and jack rafter cuts
Figure 191 shows the development of two of the
roof surfaces along with the true length of the
jack rafters (TLJR) and the edge cut for the jack
rafters (ECJR). The edge cut allows the jack
rafters to sit up against the hip.

The plumb and seat cuts for the jack rafters
are the same as those for the common rafters.
The method used to find the true lengths and
edge cut is as follows:

Draw the plan and section of roof. Mark on the
plan the jack rafters.
Develop roof surfaces by swinging TLCR down
to L and project down to M^1.
With centre N and radius NM^1, draw arc M^1O.
Join points M^1 and O to ends of hips as
shown.
Continue jack rafters on to development.
Mark the true length of jack rafter (TLJR) and
edge cut for jack rafter (ECJR).

Purlin cuts
Figure 192 shows the side and edge cut for the
purlin. The method used is as follows:

Draw a section of the common rafter with purlin
and plan of hip.
With centre B and radii BA and BC draw arcs
on to a horizontal line to give points D and E.

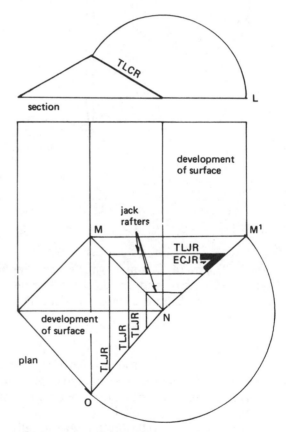

Figure 191   *Roof development*

Project D and E down on to plan.
Draw horizontal lines from A^1 and C^1 to give
points D^1 and E^1.
Angle DD^1B^1 is the side cut purlin (SCP) and
angle B^1E^1E is the edge cut purlin (ECP).

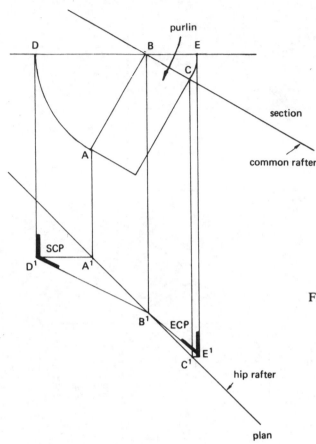

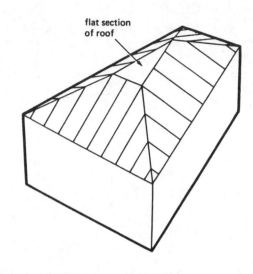

Figure 193   *Irregular plan roof*

Figure 192   *Purlin cuts*

Note: Where roofs contain valleys and cripples their true lengths and angles can be found by using similar methods as those used for hip and jack rafters.

Pitch line
The single line used in roof geometry represents the pitch line, which is a line marked up from the underside of the common rafter, one-third of its depth.

As the hip and valley rafters are usually of deeper section, the pitch line on these is marked down from the top edge at a distance equal to two-thirds the depth of the common rafter.

Irregular plan roofs
Figure 193 shows a hipped-end, equal-pitch roof on an irregular-shaped building.

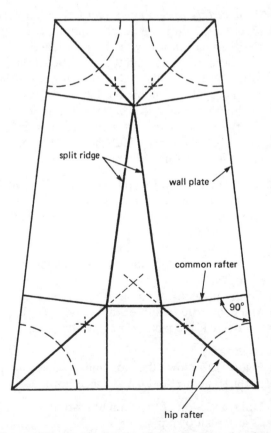

Figure 194   *Positioning members in an irregular plan roof*

The required true lengths and angles for this roof can be found using the methods covered in the previous examples, after first establishing the positions of the hips and split ridge. Figure 194 shows the required geometry. The method used is as follows:

Draw to a suitable scale the plan of the roof.

Bisect external angles and mark on line of hip rafters.

From the point where hips intersect at the narrow end, draw lines parallel to the wall plate to indicate split ridge.

Common and jack rafters can be indicated by drawing lines at right angles to the wall plates.

Ventilators

Figure 195 illustrates a gambrel roof with a louvre ventilator in the gablet.

Figure 196 shows the geometry required in order to make the ventilator. The method used is as follows:

Draw the elevation and vertical section of the ventilator.

Draw a rectangle to represent the development of inside surface of frame by projecting points on frame side over at right angles to the slope; the width of the rectangle equals the width of frame.

To obtain bevels for housing

Project points ABC and D across from the vertical section on to the development of inside surface of frame to give A' B' C' and D'.

Draw lines B' C' and A' D' to give width and bevel for housing.

The edge bevel for the housing is the same as the slope of the frame.

To obtain true shape and side bevel of blade

Project lines across from points E and F in the vertical section.

Draw centre line at same angle as the slope of the blades (45°). This gives points E' and F'.

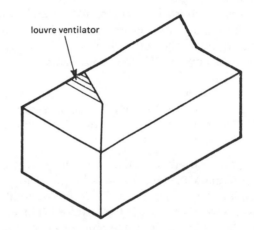

Figure 195   *Gambrel roof with ventilator*

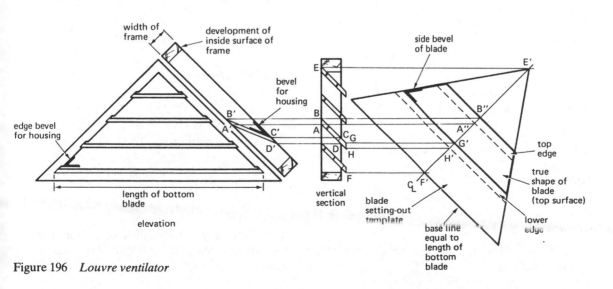

Figure 196   *Louvre ventilator*

Draw base line at right angles to centre line to pass through F′.

Make base line equal to length of bottom blade in elevation.

Draw lines from end of base line to E′. This gives outline for blade setting-out template.

Project lines from points A B G and H in the vertical section across to the centre line to give points A″ B″ G″ and H″.

Draw lines at right angles to the centre line from points A″ B″ G″ and H″ across width of template to give the true shape of blade and side bevel.

Centres for arches

In order to construct a centre for an arch, the carpenter must first set out the outline of the required arch. The setting out for various arch outlines is given in the following figures.

Segmental arch

Figure 197 shows the outline of a segmental arch. The method used to set out this arch is as follows:

Draw line AB equal to the span and bisect it.

From C mark the rise. Let this be point D.

Draw line AD and bisect it. The point where the two bisections cross is the required centre.

With the radius set from the centre to A, the arc can be drawn.

Equilateral Gothic arch

Figure 198 shows the outline of an equilateral Gothic arch. The method used to set out this arch is as follows:

Draw line AB equal to span.

With centres A and B and radius AB, draw arcs to intersect at C.

Note: Triangle ACB is an equilateral triangle.

Drop Gothic arch

Figure 199 shows the outline of a drop Gothic arch. The method used to set out this arch is as follows:

Draw lines AB and CD equal to the required span and rise.

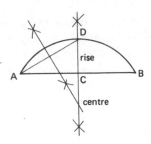

Figure 197   *Segmental arch*

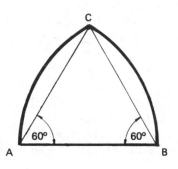

Figure 198   *Equilateral Gothic arch*

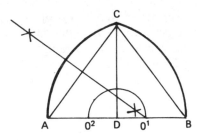

Figure 199   *Drop Gothic arch*

Bisect line AC to give point O^1.

With centre D and radius DO^1, draw arc to give point O^2.

With centres O^1 and O^2 and radius O^1A, draw arcs to intersect at C.

Lancet arch

Figure 200 shows the outline of a lancet arch. The method used to set out this arch is as follows:

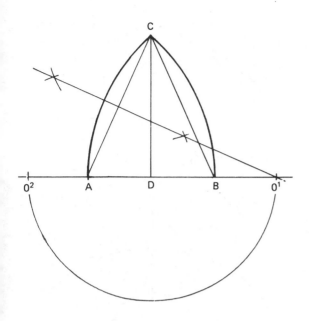

Figure 200 *Lancet arch*

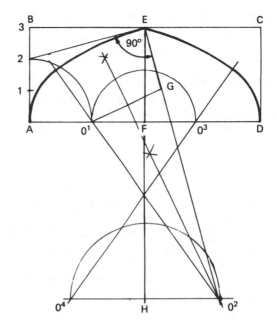

Figure 202 *Tudor arch*

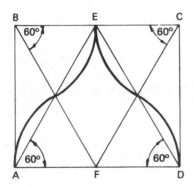

Figure 201 *Ogee arch*

Draw lines AB and CD equal to the required span and rise.
Bisect line AC to give point O^1.
With centre D and radius DO^1, draw arc to give point O^2.
With centres O^1 and O^2 and radius O^1A, draw arcs to intersect at C.

Ogee arch
Figure 201 shows the outline of an ogee arch.

The method used to set out this arch is as follows:

Draw equilateral triangle AED with base equal to the required span.
Complete rectangle ABCD.
Draw lines from B and C at 60° to give point F.
With centres F, B and C, draw arcs.

Tudor arch
Figure 202 shows the outline of a Tudor arch, which is also known as a four-centred arch. The method used to set out this arch is as follows:

Draw rectangle ABCD equal to the required span and rise.
Draw vertical line FE from the centre of AD.
Divide AB into three equal parts. Join point 2 to E.
Draw line EO^2 at right angles to line 2E.
Make EG equal to A2.
With centre A and radius A2, draw arch to give point O^1.
Draw line O^1G and bisect to give point O^2.
With centre F and radius FO^1, draw arc to give point O^3.

With centre H and radius HO^2, draw arc to give
   point O^4.
With centres O^1, O^2, O^3 and O^4, draw arcs.

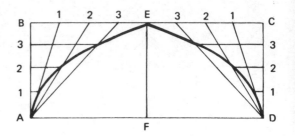

Figure 203   *Parabolic arch*

Parabolic arch
Figure 203 shows the outline of a pointed
parabolic arch. The method used to set out this
arch is as follows:

Draw rectangle ABCD equal to the required
   span and rise.
Draw vertical line FE from the centre of AD.
Divide lines AB, BE, CE and DC into the same
   number of equal parts.
Join points on BE to A and points on CE to D.
Draw horizontal lines from points on lines AB
   and DC.
Draw a smooth curve through points where
   same numbered lines intersect.

Three-centred elliptical arch
Figure 204 shows the outline of a three-centred
elliptical arch. This is also known as an
approximate or mock semi-elliptical arch. The
method used to set out this arch is as follows:

Draw the major and minor axes AB and CD.
Draw line AC.
With centre E and radius AE, draw arc AF.
With centre C and radius CF, draw arc FG.
Bisect line AG to give points H and I.
With centre E and radius EH, draw an arc to
   give H^1.
With centres H, H^1 and I, draw arcs to give the
   semi-ellipse.

Note: A true semi-elliptical arch outline,
although rarely used, can be marked out using
either the foci pins and string method or the
trammel method.

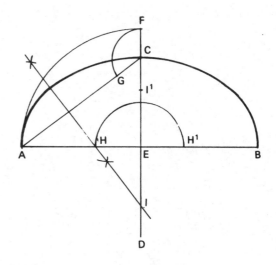

Figure 204   *Three-centred elliptical arch*

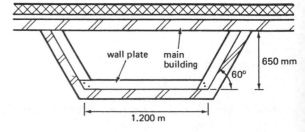

Figure 205

Self-assessment questions

1   A sloping concrete canopy is to be supported
    by 450 mm diameter concrete columns.
       Develop the true shape of the opening
    required in the soffit formwork of the canopy
    if it is inclined at 10° to the horizontal.

2   Draw the outline of a three-centred, semi-
    elliptical arch centre, having a span of
    2.800 m and a rise of 1.200 m.

3   Produce a scale drawing to show the true

lengths, plumb and seat cuts for the common and hip rafters of a rectangular plan, 30° pitched roof having a span of 6 m.

4 Figure 205 illustrates the plan at wall plate level of a cant bay window which is to have a 45° pitch hip roof. Draw to a scale of 1:20 the true shape of the three roof surfaces.

chapter 8

Site measurement

After reading this chapter the student should be able to:

1 Prepare a survey of an existing building.

2 List the sequence of operations used to set out a simple building.

3 Identify and describe the use of various types of setting-out equipment.

4 Recognize and state the significance of an Ordnance bench-mark.

Building survey

Whenever an existing building is to be extended, altered, or have major repairs undertaken, a measured survey should be carried out.

The extent of the measurements and details taken during the survey will depend on its purpose. It can be clearly seen that the requirements of a survey carried out for the complete refurbishment of an office block will be very different to those of a survey for replacement windows to a domestic house.

Procedure
Each survey is considered separately, sufficient measurements and details being taken in order to fulfil the survey's specific requirements. But a methodical approach is always required to avoid later confusion. The following survey procedures can be used to advantage in most circumstances.

Existing drawings
Make enquiries to the building's owner and the local authority *before* surveying, to determine whether there are any existing drawings concerning the property. If so these can simplify the task by forming the basis of the survey sketches.

Equipment
This will vary considerably depending on the survey requirements, but a list of basic equipment suitable for most tasks is as follows:

A4 or A3 sketch pad
Pens and pencils
30 m tape
2 m tape
2 m sectional measuring rod
1 m folding rule
Spirit level
2 m straight edge
Plumb-bob

In addition certain of the following items may be required for more detailed or specialist surveys:

Step ladder
Extension ladder
High-power torch
Moisture meter
Penknife
Camera
Binoculars
Moulding template
Hammer, bolster and floorboard saw

Reconnaissance
Before the actual survey the building should be

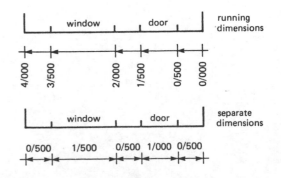

Figure 206 *Outline dimensions*

looked over, both internally and externally, to determine its general layout and any likely difficulties.

External survey

Sketch an outline plan and elevations of the building and then add the measurements. Wherever possible running dimensions are preferred to separate dimensions for plans (see Figure 206), since an error made in recording one separate dimension will throw all succeeding dimensions out of place and also make the total length incorrect.

Running dimensions are recorded at right angles to the line; an arrow head indicates each cumulative point. To avoid confusing the position of the decimal point, an oblique stroke is used to separate metres and millimetres.

Figure 207 *Typical external survey sketches*

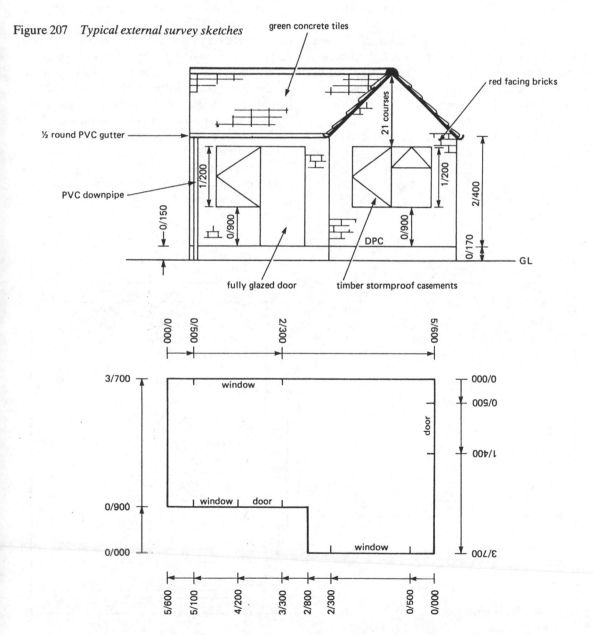

Separate dimensions are recorded on the line; their extent is indicated by arrow heads at either end. It is important that this distinction between the two methods is observed, as in certain situations it may be necessary to use both on the same sketch.

Typical external survey sketches are shown in Figure 207.

Running dimensions are taken in a clockwise direction around the building. Vertical dimensions on the elevations are taken from a level datum, often a damp-proof course. Where measurements cannot be taken because they are inaccessible (gable end or chimney etc.) they can be estimated by counting the brick courses and relating this to brickwork lower down that can be accurately measured.

All external details of materials and finishes etc. should be recorded on the elevation sketches. Photographs of the elevations are often taken as a back-up to the sketches, especially where fine or intricate details have to be shown.

Internal survey

Dimensioned sketches are made of each floor or room, starting at ground-floor level. All rooms should be named or numbered and corridors lettered. These sketches are traced from the external outline plan of the building. Measure through door or window openings to determine the thickness of the walls. Each floor plan should show a horizontal section through the building about one metre above floor level. Measurements should be taken and recorded on the sketches in a clockwise direction around each room. Diagonal measurements from corner to corner check the shape of the room and enable it to be redrawn later. Floor to ceiling heights are circled in the centre of each room. Floor construction and partition wall details are also shown on the floor plans. The floorboards run at right angles to the span of floor joists. The lines of nails indicate joist spacings (see Figure 208). Pattern staining on walls and ceilings indicates positions of grounds or battening and ceiling joists.

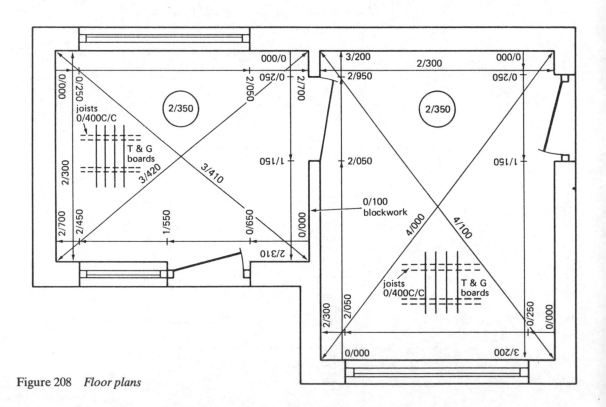

Figure 208   *Floor plans*

Walls can be identified by sounding them. When tapped with the fist, brick walls sound solid, thin blockwork walls tend to vibrate, and stud walls sound solid over the studs and hollow between them.

Where joinery items are to be repaired or replaced, full-size details of the sections and mouldings must be made to enable them to be matched later at the workshop. This task can be eased considerably by the use of a moulding template (see Figure 209). The pins of the template are pressed into the contours of the moulding. It is then placed on the sketch pad and drawn around. The exact location of where the moulding is taken should be noted, as these may vary from room to room.

Sketches of internal elevations or photographs may be required, especially where intricate details are concerned.

Sketches of the vertical sections taken at right

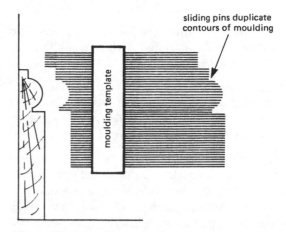

Figure 209   *Moulding templates*

angles to the building's external walls complete the main sketches. A typical section is shown in Figure 210. Sections should include door and window heights, as well as the internal height of

Figure 210   *Section through building*

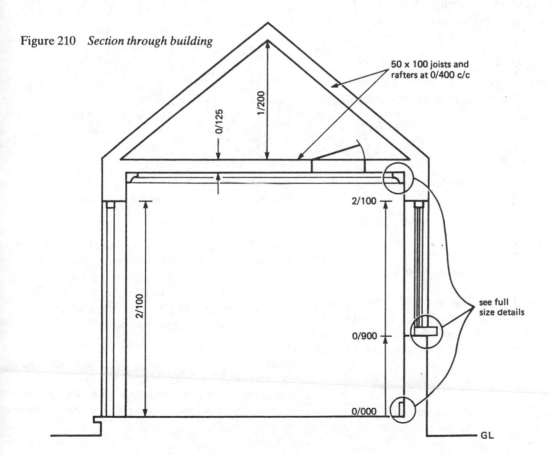

the roof. The thickness of upper floors and ceilings can be measured at the stairwell or loft trap door opening.

Note: Only details that can be seen and measured are sketched. No attempt should be made to guess details; therefore foundations, floor construction and lintels etc. are not shown.

Depending on the nature of the survey, service details such as outlets, sockets and switches for gas, water, electric, television, telephone etc. may be shown, although these are often recorded on separate 'service plans' to avoid overloading and confusing the main floor plans.

In addition brief notes should be taken, recording details of structural defects and signs of decay and deterioration. This may entail lifting several floorboards and the partial removal of panelling or casings etc.

On returning to the workshop or office the sketches can be 'drawn up' to produce a set of scale drawings, and the brief notes can be used to form the basis of the survey report. It is at this stage that the necessity of taking all the dimensions and details is realized. One vital missing dimension can be costly, as it will result in a further visit to the building at a later stage to take the dimension.

Site setting out

The setting out of a building can be divided into two distinct operations:

Establishing the position of the building and setting up profiles
Establishing a datum peg and transferring required levels to various positions

Establishing the position and setting up profiles
The basic requirements for establishing the position of a building are linear measurement (length), the setting out of angles and the setting out of curves.

Linear measurement
A 30 metre steel tape is most often used for setting out; linen or plastic tapes should be

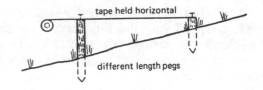

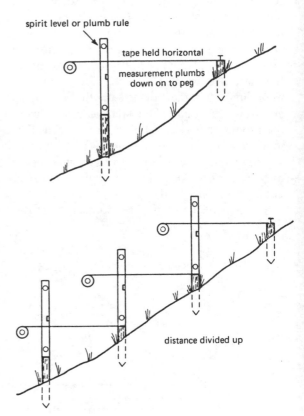

Figure 211   *Using a tape over sloping ground*

avoided as they are liable to stretch, resulting in serious errors. Inaccuracies can also occur when using steel tapes if they are not fully stretched out (tensioned). A constant tension handle is available for use with steel tapes, which reduces errors to less than 3 mm in 30 m.

Note: Linear measurements can also be made with surveyor's chains and other specialist equipment, such as electronic devices which utilize radio or light waves, or tacheometers: the use of these is not within the scope of your course.

Wherever linear measurements are made the tape must be kept horizontal if they are to be accurate. Where measurements are made over sloping ground the inaccuracies are potentially far greater. Figure 211 illustrates the correct methods to use. Where the slope is a slight one, pegs of different length can be used. On steeper slopes the tape must be held horizontal and the measurement plumbed down on to a peg. For longer measurements on steep slopes the distance should be divided and marked out in a number of stages.

Setting out angles
Right angles can be set out using any one of four main methods:

Using a builders' square
Using Pythagoras's 3:4:5 rule
Using an optical site square
Using an optical instrument with a graduated base ring (useful for all angles)

Builders' square (Figure 212)
A large builders' square is set up on packings so that one leg is against the building line. The side line should be positioned so that it runs parallel to the other leg of the square.

3:4:5 rule (Figure 213)
A triangle is marked out having sides of 3 units, 4 units and 5 units. A measurement of 3 units and 4 units can be marked on the front and side lines. The side line can then be positioned so that the distances between the two marked points is five units.

Optical site square (Figure 214)
The method of use is as follows:

Set up the instrument over corner peg A.
Sight through lower telescope towards peg B. This is the furthest front corner of the building.
Adjust the fine setting screw and tilt the telescope until the spot on view is seen

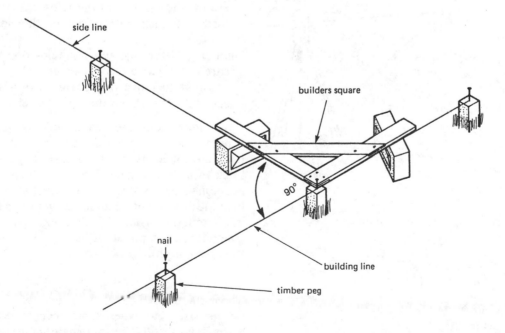

Figure 212 *Using a builders' square*

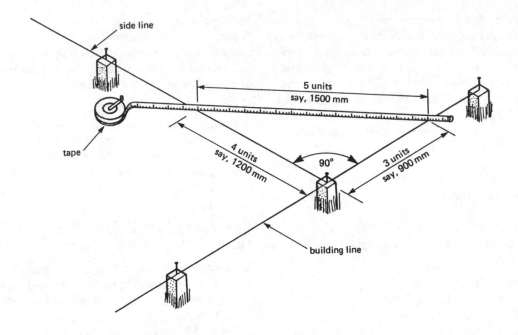

Figure 213 *Setting out a right angle with a tape measure*

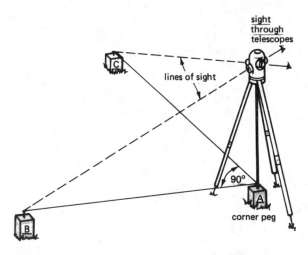

Figure 214 *Using an optical site square*

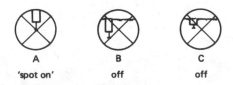

Figure 215 *View through sight*

through it (see Figure 215). The view through the telescope shown in Figure 215(b) and (c) are off the mark, and the telescope requires further adjustment to obtain the spot on view.

Sight peg C through the top telescope taking care not to move the instrument. Direct your assistant to move peg C sideways until the spot on view is seen through the telescope.

Projections from the main building for bay windows etc. are often set out using a timber template made up to the actual shape of the brickwork (see Figure 216). The template is positioned on packings up against the building line; the position of the foundation trench can be measured out from it. After excavation and concreting the template is used again to set out the position of the brickwork.

Setting out curves
The methods used to set out a curve will depend on its size and whether its centre point is accessible or not. The four main methods used are:

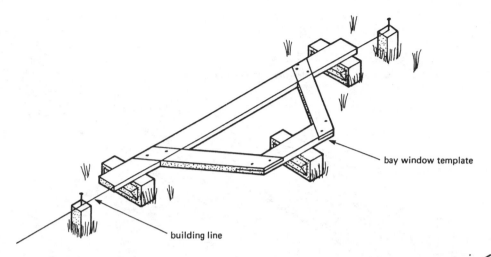

Figure 216 *Bay window template*

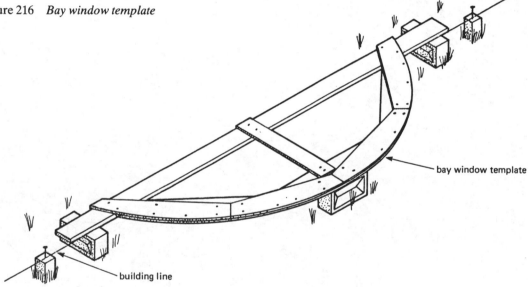

Figure 217 *Using a segmental bay window template*

Timber template
Radius rod
Triangular frame
Calculated ordinates

Small repetitive curves for bay windows etc. are also set out using a timber template; Figure 217 shows a segmental bay window template in use.

A radius rod can be used to accurately set out all curved work of up to about 4 m radius (see Figure 218). Where the radius length is exces-

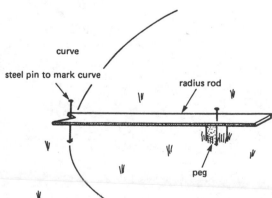

Figure 218 *Radius rod*

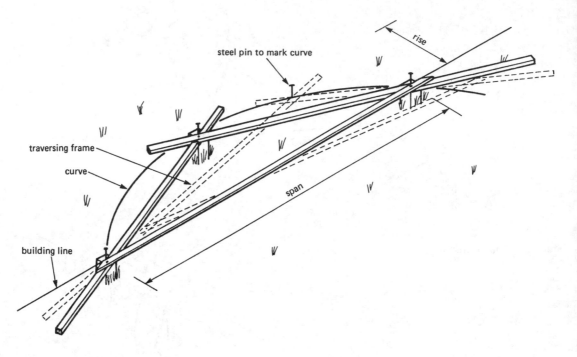

Figure 219   *Timber triangular frame*

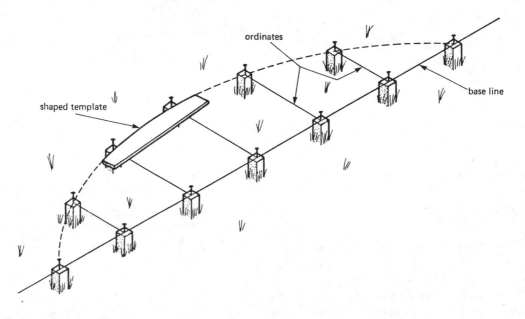

Figure 220   *Setting out a curve using calculated ordinates*

sive, or in situations where the centre point is inaccessible, a timber triangular frame can be used. Two pegs are positioned on the building line indicating the ends of the curve. The third peg is positioned at right angles to the building line indicating the maximum rise of the curve. For accuracy nails are driven into the tops of the pegs to indicate the exact dimensions. A lightweight timber frame is then made over the pegs as shown in Figure 219. When the centre nail is taken out the frame can be moved across while still keeping it in contact with the other two nails, using a steel pin at the apex to mark the required curve.

The previous methods are inappropriate for setting out curves of very large radius, as the size of the equipment makes it awkward to handle. One method that may be used is to calculate a number of ordinate lengths and peg these out from the base line. A shaped template is used between the pegs to mark the smooth line of the curve, as shown in Figure 220.

Pythagoras's Theorem is used to calculate the ordinate lengths.

Example
To calculate the lengths of the ordinate required to set out a curve having a chord length of 20 m and rise of 2 m, first find the radius using the intersecting chord rule (see Figure 221):

$$A \times B = C \times D$$

$$\frac{A \times B}{C} = D$$

$$\frac{10 \times 10}{2} = D$$

$$50 = D$$

Therefore:

diameter = 52 m $(D + C)$
radius   = 26 m

Divide the chord length into a number of equal parts, say at 2 m centres, giving ordinates 1–9 as shown in Figure 222.

Note: Only ordinates 1–4 need to be calculated

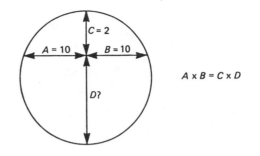

Figure 221   *Intersecting chord rule*

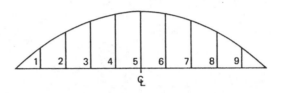

Figure 222   *Chord divided into equal parts*

since 1 = 9, 2 = 8, 3 = 7, 4 = 6 and ordinate 5 is the rise.

Use Pythagoras's Theorem to calculate each individual ordinate length in turn. Figure 223 shows the method used to calculate the length of ordinate 1. Line Z is the distance between the chord and the centre point (radius – rise) in the right-angled triangle ABC.

AC = radius
BC = distance of ordinate from centre line.

Ordinate 1
$$a^2 + b^2 = c^2$$
$$a^2 = c^2 - b^2$$
$$a^2 = 26^2 - 8^2$$
$$a^2 = 676 - 64$$
$$a^2 = 612$$
$$a = \sqrt{612}$$
$$a = 24.739$$

Therefore:
ordinate 1 = 24.739 – z
           = 24.739 – 24
           = 739 mm

The length of ordinates 2–4 is found using the same procedure.

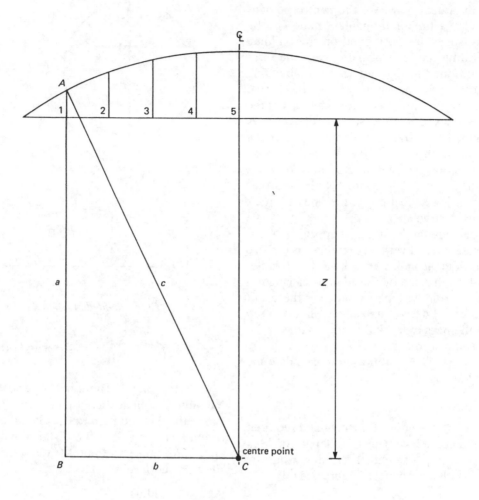

Figure 223   *Using Pythagoras's Theorem*

Ordinate 2
$$a^2 = c^2 - b^2$$
$$a^2 = 26^2 - 6^2$$
$$a^2 = 676 - 36$$
$$a^2 = 640$$
$$a = \sqrt{640}$$
$$a = 25.298$$

Therefore:
ordinate 2 $= 25.298 - 24$
$ = 1.298$ m

Ordinate 3
$$a^2 = c^2 - b^2$$
$$a^2 = 26^2 - 4^2$$
$$a^2 = 676 - 16$$
$$a^2 = 660$$
$$a = \sqrt{660}$$
$$a = 25.690$$

Therefore:
ordinate 3 $= 25.690 - 24$
$ = 1.690$ m

Ordinate 4
$$a^2 = c^2 - b^2$$
$$a^2 = 26^2 - 2^2$$
$$a^2 = 676 - 4$$
$$a^2 = 672$$
$$a = \sqrt{672}$$
$$a = 25.923$$

Therefore:
ordinate 4 $= 25.923 - 24$
$ = 1.923$ m

Establishing the position of a small building

To establish the position of a small building the procedures illustrated in Figure 224 can be used, as follows.

All setting out is done from the building line. This will be indicated on the block plan and its position is decided by the local authority. The line is established by driving in 50 mm × 50 mm softwood pegs A and B on the side boundaries at the correct distance from, and parallel to, the centre line of the road. A nail in the top of the peg indicates the exact position of the line. Strain a line between these two nails.

Drive two pegs C and D along the building line to indicate the front corners of the building. The position of the building in relation to the side boundaries will be indicated on the architect's drawings. Drive nails into the tops of the pegs to indicate the exact position of the corners on the building line.

Set out lines at right angles to pegs C and D and establish pegs E and F. Drive nails into the tops of pegs E and F to indicate the exact positions and tension lines between the four pegs.

Measure along lines CE and DF to establish pegs G and H in the far corners of the building. It is advisable at this stage to check the diagonals CH and DG. If these diagonals measure the same, the building must be square and the setting out can continue. When the diagonals are not the same, a check must be made through the previous stages to discover and rectify the inaccuracy before proceeding to the next stage.

Peg out the positions of offset I, J and K. Check the smaller diagonals which have been formed, to ensure accuracy.

Set up profile boards just clear of the trench runs at all of the corners and wall intersections of the building as shown in Figure 225. Transfer positions of setting-out lines to the profile boards (see Figure 226).

Four nails are driven into the top of each profile board to indicate the edges of the foundation trench and the edges of the brickwork. An alternative which is sometimes used instead of the nails is to mark the positions on top of the profile boards with four saw cuts.

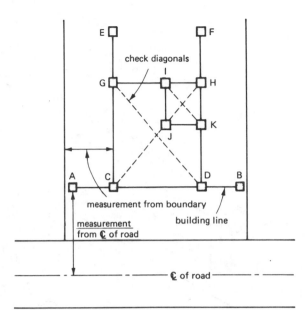

Figure 224 *Setting out a small building*

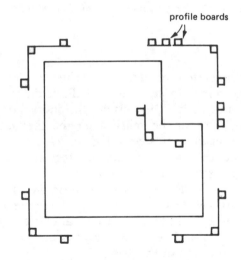

Figure 225 *Layout of profile boards*

Lines can be strained between the nails on the profiles to indicate the exact positions for the excavators and bricklayers. During excavation these lines will be removed, and therefore the position of the trench should be marked by sprinkling sand on the ground directly under the lines to indicate the sides of the trenches.

Once the foundations have been excavated

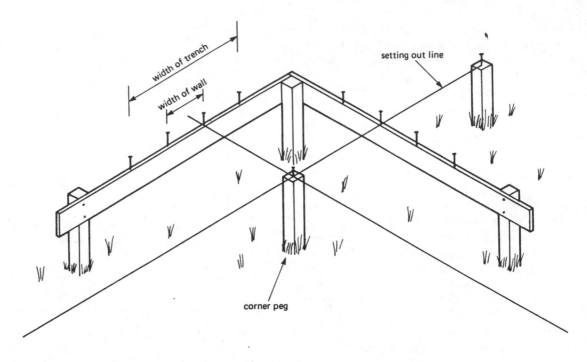

Figure 226   *Transferring setting-out lines to profile boards*

and concreted, one line is restrained around the nails on the profile boards to indicate the face of the brickwork. From this line the position of the brickwork can be marked on the foundation concrete as illustrated in Figure 227.

Steel or concrete frame buildings are set out using a structural grid. The centre lines of the columns, walls and beams etc. form the basis of this grid, which can also be used as a referencing system to identify each structural element (see Figure 228). The following procedure can be used to establish the grid.

Establish the four corner pegs of the building using the same method as before. Set up continuous profile boards along each side of the building (see Figure 229). These should be well clear of the work so as not to obstruct the excavators. Transfer corner points on to profiles. From these points mark out and drive nails along the profiles to indicate the centre lines of the columns and beams. Strain lines between the nails to indicate the centre line positions of the

column bases etc., which can be marked out by plumbing down from the line intersections (see Figure 230).

Establishing a datum peg and transferring levels
A datum peg is a timber or steel peg, driven into the ground to a suitable level and then set in concrete (see Figure 231).

In order to establish the value of the datum peg one must refer it back to an Ordnance bench-mark (OBM). OBMs are to be found cut into the walls of churches and public buildings. An OBM is illustrated in Figure 232. the level value of an OBM can be obtained from the relevant Ordnance Survey map, or from the local planning authority's office. The level given will be a fixed height above the Ordnance datum. The Ordnance datum is the mean sea level at Newlyn in Cornwall. The OBM may be some distance away from the site, and will have to be transferred back to a datum peg on the site.

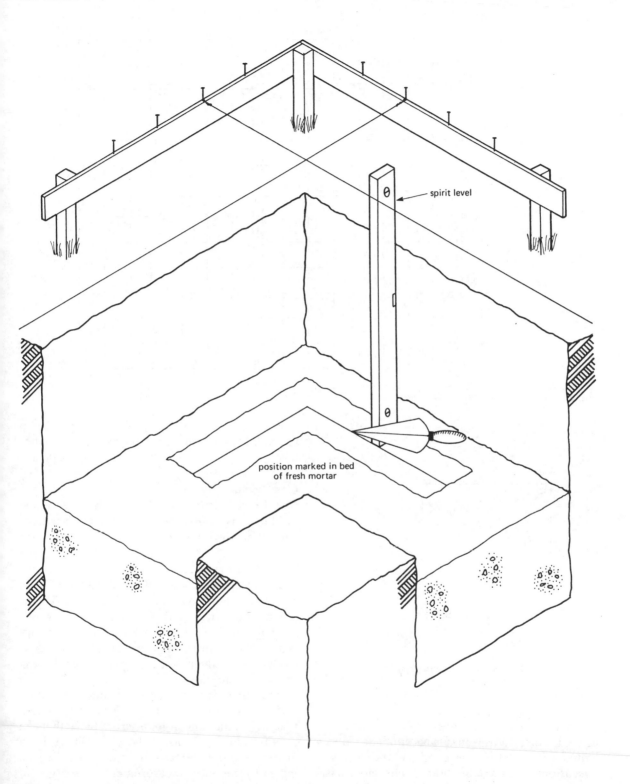

spirit level

position marked in bed
of fresh mortar

Figure 227 *Marking out from a profile board*

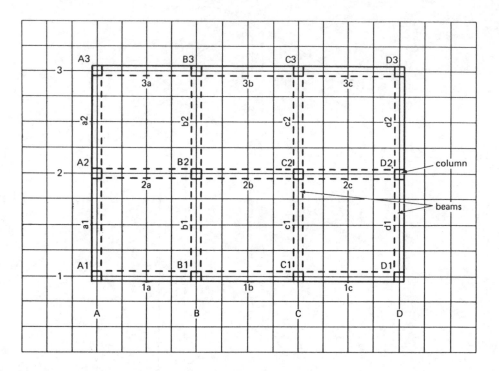

Figure 228   *Using a structural reference grid*

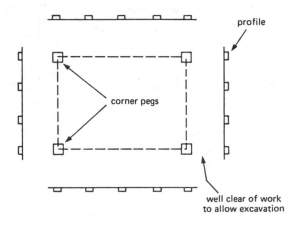

Figure 229   *Setting out a structural grid*

Levels on site are normally transferred to their required positions using either a Cowley automatic level or a quickset tilting level. Occasionally on small works certain more basic methods may be used, including a straight-edge and spirit level, line level, boning rods and water level.

Cowley automatic level

The Cowley automatic level is a very simple levelling instrument which is widely used for general site levelling operations. The instrument consists of three main parts – the head, the tripod and the staff.

The rectangular metal-cased head (Figure 233) contains a dual system of mirrors. This is mounted on the tripod, the centre pin of which must point upwards when the tripod is set up. When the instrument's metal-cased head is inserted on to the pin, a catch is released, setting the level ready for use.

The instrument is used in conjunction with a staff. This consists of a graduated aluminium pole with a moving target or cross-piece that can be adjusted up or down the pole. There is an arrow on the target or cross-piece which indicates the exact measurement on the graduated pole.

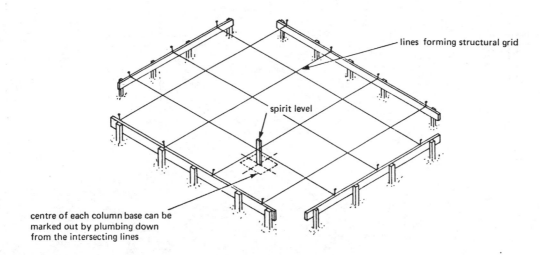

centre of each column base can be
marked out by plumbing down
from the intersecting lines

Figure 230 *Marking out from a structural grid*

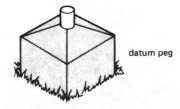

Figure 231 *Datum peg*

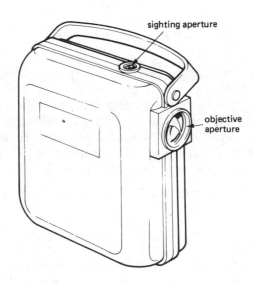

Figure 233 *Cowley automatic level head*

Method of use
The correct procedure for transferring a level
from one point to another is described below
and illustrated in Figure 234.

Set up the tripod and insert the level on the

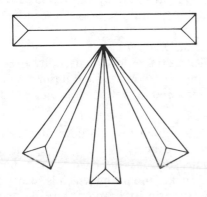

Figure 232 *Ordnance bench-mark*

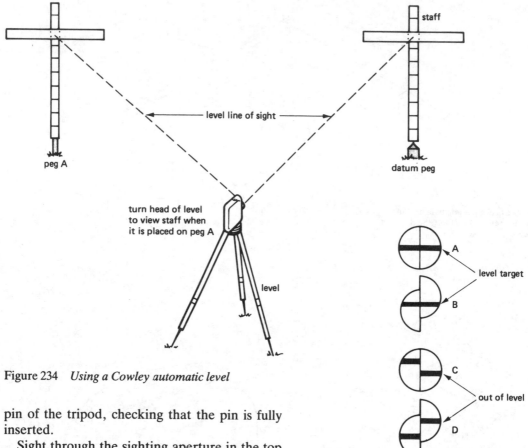

Figure 234   *Using a Cowley automatic level*

Figure 235   *View through Cowley automatic level*

pin of the tripod, checking that the pin is fully inserted.

Sight through the sighting aperture in the top of the level and adjust the tripod so that the two mirrors are seen to form an approximate circle.

Have an assistant hold the staff on the datum peg or temporary bench-mark (TBM).

Note: The assistant should ensure that the staff is held upright.

Sight through the sighting aperture at the staff and have the assistant slide the target up or down until the target is seen level, as in Figure 235 view A or B. If view C or D is seen, the target requires further adjustment up or down the staff.

Lock the slide in position on the staff. Get the assistant to drive the peg into the ground until the target is once again sighted level. Peg A is now horizontally level to the datum peg or TBM.

Note: Reduced or increased levels in relation

to the TBM can be found by moving the target up or down the staff by the required distance and resighting until the target is seen level.

Quickset tilting level
The quickset tilting level is basically a telescope with a spirit level on the side; it is mounted on a tripod and used in conjunction with a staff.

Level
A quickset tilting level is illustrated in Figure 236. The instrument is easily set up (hence the name quickset). It is attached to the tripod by a ball-and-socket mounting which is secured from underneath using the screw thread, once the circular bubble has been centralized.

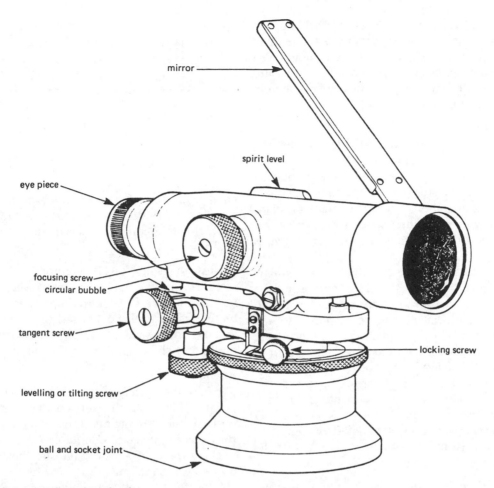

Figure 236   *Quickset tilting level*

Earlier types of level (dumpy level) were more time consuming to set up, as the mounting consisted of a horizontal plate and three levelling footscrews, each requiring adjustment.

Staff

The most common is the telescopic staff, available in either wood or aluminium. It consists of three box sections which slide within each other. When fully extended it has a total length of 4 to 5 m. The staff is graduated to give readings in metre, 100 mm and 10 mm divisions. Millimetres are read by estimation (see Figure 237). Care must be taken when reading the staff, as most levels give an inverted image, causing the staff to be seen upside-down as shown in

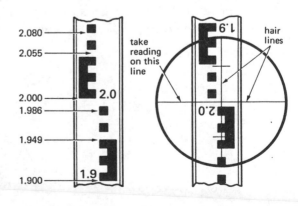

Figure 237   *Staff*

Figure 238   *Inverted image of staff*

Figure 238. Ensure that the staff is held upright when readings are taken, otherwise the reading will be high (see Figure 239). Care should also be taken when using an extended staff to ensure that it is fully extended and the catch located in its correct position.

Setting up

Open up the tripod; extend the legs so that the instrument will be approximately at the user's eye level. Firm the tripod into the ground by treading on the steps at the bottom of each leg. Ensure all nuts, bolts and screws are tight. Place the instrument on the tripod, locate the screw thread and tighten when the circular bubble is central.

Adjust the eyepiece to focus the cross-hairs (see Figure 236). This is done by placing the palm of one hand just in front of the telescope to direct a uniform amount of lighting to the instrument. Then, sighting through the eyepiece, rotate it until the cross-hairs appear as black and as sharp as possible.

Adjust the focusing screw to focus the telescope. This is done by sighting the staff through the telescope and then slowly rotating the focusing screw until the staff is seen clear and sharp. Rotate the tangent screw so that the staff is central.

Note: Care must be taken when adjusting the cross-hairs and focus as, if this is done incorrectly, errors in reading can occur owing to parallax. Parallax can be defined as the apparent separation between the cross-hairs and the staff image. This will be noticed by the user as a

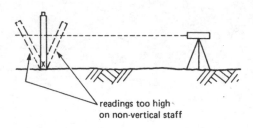

readings too high
on non-vertical staff

Figure 239   *Staff reading error*

change in the staff reading when he moves his eyes up and down. This is used as a check each time the telescope is focused on a new staff position.

Adjust the spirit level by rotating the tilting screw so that the bubble is central when viewed in the mirror. It is most important that the bubble is centralized each time a reading is taken. Failure to do so results in inaccuracies, as the line of sight is not truly horizontal.

Method of use

To find the differential in level between two points (Figure 240), set up the instrument midway between the points concerned using the previous sequence of operations.

Have the assistant hold the staff on the sight and take the reading.

Transfer the staff to the other point. Sight the new staff position, focus, adjust level, take the reading.

The difference between the two readings will be the difference in level between the two points.

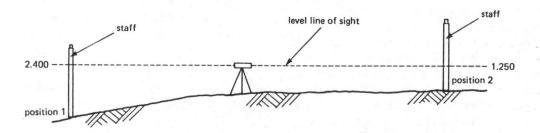

Figure 240   *Using a quickset tilting level*

high reading = lower level
low reading = higher level
  position 1 = 2.400
  position 2 = 1.250
  difference = 1.150

Therefore position 1 is 1.150 m lower than position 2.

The following terms are used when transferring levels:

Backsight The first reading taken once the instrument has been set up in position.
Foresight The last reading taken before moving the instrument.
Intermediate sight All the readings taken between the backsight and foresight.
Height of collimation The height of the line of site above the Ordnance datum.
Reduced level The height of any position above the Ordnance datum.

Note: Levelling in this course is limited to the transference of levels from one fixed position, i.e. without moving the instrument.

Site levelling: recording readings

Staff readings should be recorded in a levelling book as they are taken, using either the collimation method or the rise and fall method. There is little to choose between the two methods, but the collimation method has been used in the following examples.

Example
To establish a site datum peg (TBM)
  The procedure to follow is shown in Figure 241.
  Set up the instrument midway between the nearest OBM and the intended position of the TBM. This should be in an accessible position

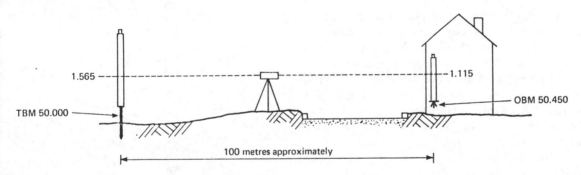

Figure 241 *Establishing a site datum peg*

Table 29 **Page from a collimation level book**

Back sight	Intermediate sight	Fore sight	Height of collimation	Reduced level	Notes
1.115			51.565	50.450	From OBM
		1.565		50.000	To TBM
	Check	FS 1.565	FRL 50.450		
		BS 1.115	LRL 50.000		
		0.450	0.450		

Differences equal OK ✓

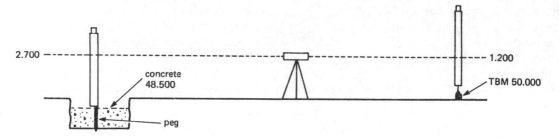

Figure 242   *Setting a foundation peg*

just inside the site boundary but out of the way of site works and traffic etc.

Note: When the distance between the two positions is greater than about 100 m a series of levels will have to be taken, or the reduced level of a convenient manhole cover may be available which could be used as a TBM.

Take a reading with staff placed on the OBM: 1.115. This is a backsight and is recorded in the backsight column. See Table 29 for a page of a levelling book. Since the reading is taken on the OBM its reduced level of 50.450 is recorded in the reduced-level column. The backsight and reduced level are added together to give the height of collimation, 51.565, which is recorded in the appropriate column.

To fix the valve of the TBM, resight the staff with it placed on the TBM. It is often convenient to set this at the same reduced level as the ground floor slab of the new building, in this case a reduced level of say 50.000.

This reduced level must be subtracted from the height of collimation to find the required staff reading:

height of collimation   =   51.565
  reduced-level TBM   =   50.000
                                         1.565

Therefore the datum peg must be driven until a reading of 1.565 is achieved. This will be the foresight and is recorded in the foresight column. The reduced level of the foresight, 50.000, has been recorded in the reduced-level column.

As a check for calculation or recording errors, the difference between the sum of the backsights and the sum of the foresights should equal the

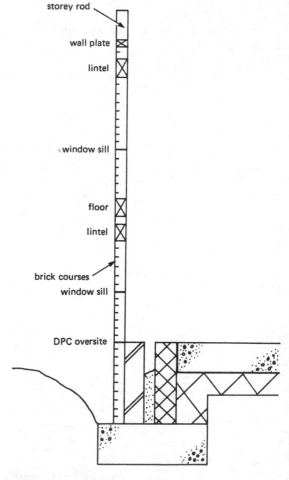

Figure 243   *Storey rod*

difference between the first and last reduced level.

Example
To set a peg in the bottom of a foundation trench as a guide for concreting.

Take the reduced level of the top of the foundation concrete to be 48.500 and the reduced level of the TBM to be 50.000.

The procedure to follow is shown in Figure 242.
Set up level.
Sight staff on TBM. Record backsight 1.200. Add backsight to reduced level of TBM: 1.200 + 50.000. Record height of collimation 51.200.
Position peg in foundation trench.
Sight staff on peg and drive until reading is 2.700. This is found by taking the reduced level of the foundation 48.500, away from the height of collimation 51.200. Record the foresight 2.700 and the reduced level 48.500. Then check.

From the previous examples it is clear that the staff reading required to set any reduced level can be found by subtracting the reduced level from the height of collimation.

Example
To set formwork.

Formwork to the sides of a ground beam are to be set at a reduced level of 98.450. What staff reading is required if the reduced level of the TBM is 100.000 and the staff reading on the TBM is 1.225?

height of collimation = TBM + staff reading on TBM
= 100.000 + 1.225
= 101.225

staff reading required = height of collimation – reduced level
= 101.225 – 98.450
= 2.775

Verticality
The verticality (plumb) of a building can be controlled using a spirit level or a suspended plumb-bob. More specialist techniques may be employed on larger structures (theodolite, optical autoplumb or laser beam).

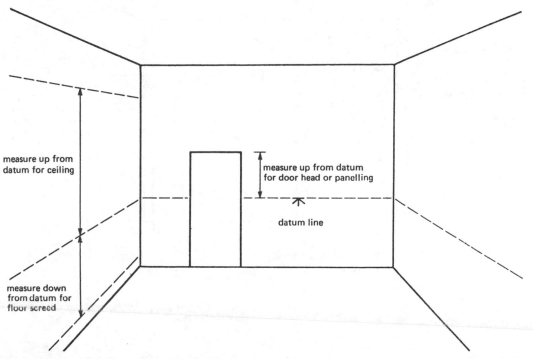

measure up from datum for ceiling

measure up from datum for door head or panelling

datum line

measure down from datum for floor screed

Figure 244   *Measuring from internal datum line*

Vertical positioning of windows, floors and wall plates etc. can be achieved with the use of a storey rod (Figure 243), which is marked out before work commences and fixed in one corner of the building.

Internal datum

Datum positions or lines are often marked around the walls inside a building, particularly in large areas. They should be indicated thus ⟋⟍ . The datum line is etablished at a convenient height, say 1 m above finished floor level (FFL). From this the position of other building components and finishes can be measured up or down; for example, the heights of floor screed, suspended ceilings, door heads and wall panelling etc., as shown in Figure 244.

To establish the datum line, transfer a level position to each corner of the room using either a water level as shown in Figure 245 or an optical instrument as shown in Figure 246.

Having established the corner positions, stretch a chalk line between each two marks in turn and spring it in the middle, leaving a horizontal chalk dust line on the wall.

Note: Before using a water level it must be prepared by filling it from one end with water, taking care not to trap air bubbles. Check by holding up the two glass tubes side by side: the levels of the water should settle to the same height.

Self-assessment questions

1 What is an OBM?

2 Why are diagonal room measurements taken when surveying an existing building?

3 What is the purpose of the eyepiece adjustment on a quickset level?

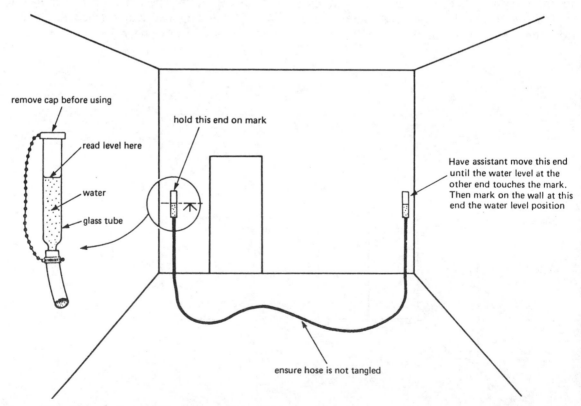

remove cap before using

read level here

water

glass tube

hold this end on mark

Have assistant move this end until the water level at the other end touches the mark. Then mark on the wall at this end the water level position

ensure hose is not tangled

Figure 245   *Using a water level to establish datum line*

4 What is the difference between running and separate dimensions?

5 How could a large-radius curve be set out if its centre point is inaccessible?

6 What staff reading is required to establish a reduced level of 47.550 if a reading of 1.250 is recorded with the staff set on a TBM of 50.000?

7 What is the purpose of a profile board?

8 What is the purpose of a storey rod?

9 What checks should be applied after a set of levels have been recorded?

10 (a) Briefly state what is parallax
    (b) Describe how it can be recognized and avoided

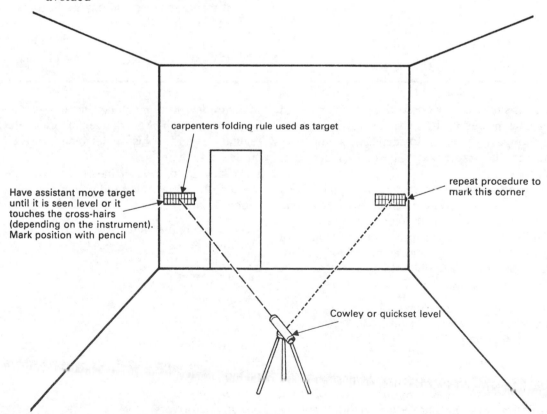

carpenters folding rule used as target

Have assistant move target until it is seen level or it touches the cross-hairs (depending on the instrument). Mark position with pencil

repeat procedure to mark this corner

Cowley or quickset level

Figure 246 *Using an optical instrument*

chapter 9

Machine utilization

After reading this chapter the student should be able to:

1 Distinguish between the various power sources and state the safe working procedures for each.

2 List general and individual safety precautions to be observed while using the following woodworking machines and portable power tools:
   (a) Circular saw, band saw and surface planer
   (b) Drill, screwdriver, orbital sander and belt sander
   (c) Circular saw, jig saw, chain saw, planer and router
   (d) Automatic drivers and ballistic tool

3 State the requirements of The Woodworking Machines Regulations 1974 applicable to each machine.

4 List the main requirements applicable to site work of The Abrasive Wheels Regulations 1970 and The Protective Eyes Regulations 1974.

The on-site use of woodworking machines and portable power tools is increasing. This stems from industry's need to increase productivity and at the same time become more cost effective.

The provision of equipment will vary widely from site to site, ranging from as little as one electric drill to a comprehensively equipped shop. Even though this provision is normally of a short-term or temporary nature, the appropriate legislation must still be fully complied with. This includes in particular:

The Woodworking Machines Regulations 1974
The Abrasive Wheels Regulations 1970
The Protection of Eyes Regulations 1974

It is the duty of every employer and employee, in places where woodworking machines are used, to ensure that they are aware of these regulations and that they are carried out in their entirety. It is therefore essential that every user of a woodworking machine, including students, has a thorough knowledge of the relevant regulations and in his or her own interest fully implements them.

At advanced level, the study and use of woodworking machines and powered hand tools is limited to:

Woodworking machines
Circular saw
Band saw
Surface planer

Power tools
Drill
Screwdriver
Sanders: orbital, belt
Saws: circular, jig, chain
Planer
Router
Automatic drivers
Ballistic tools

It is not possible to gain skills in the use of woodworking machines and powered hand tools by reading alone. Therefore this chapter sets out to identify the various machines and powered tools and their safe working procedures.

Power supply

Electricity

Electricity is virtually indispensible on a mechanized building site. Although an invaluable aid to site productivity, it is also a major safety hazard: unlike most other hazards it is invisible and instantaneous in effect. Its degree of hazard is directly related to the level of current and the duration of contact. Low levels of current may only cause an unpleasant tingling sensation, but the momentary lack of concentration may be sufficient to cause other injury (contact with moving parts, or fall etc.). Medium levels of current result in muscular tension and burning. Higher levels of current, in addition to the burning, affect the heart, often resulting in death.

Since clearly the lower the voltage the lower the risk, reduced-voltage schemes are the accepted procedure for safe site working. Reduced-voltage equipment operates on 110 volts supplied through step-down transformers with a centrally tapped earth, so that in the event of a fault the maximum shock that the operator should receive would be not more than 65 volts on the three-phase circuit and 55 volts on the single-phase circuit.

In addition, most power tools are now manufactured using the double-insulated principle whereby the motor and other live parts are isolated, making it impossible for the operator to receive a shock should a fault occur. Double-insulated tools which bear the BS 2769 (kitemark) and the double-squares symbol do not require an earth wire, although the risk of shock is still present if the cable is damaged.

Moisture is a good conductor of electricity. Therefore the risk of an electric shock in these circumstances is greatly increased, not only from the machine or power tool but also from the supply flex if it is frayed, damaged or jointed.

On-site supply

The electricity supply on site is usually provided by the local electricity board from the national grid. In circumstances where this form of mains supply is not available, portable petrol/diesel-powered electricity generators may be used.

Mains supply

The electricity board will provide supply to a lockable covered incoming unit which houses a meter, main fuses and master switch. This unit is connected to a main distribution unit from which distribution cables connect up to transformer units, outlet units and extension outlet units as shown in Figure 247. Thus a supply at the correct voltage (see Table 30) is provided to the entire site.

The use of supply outlets, plugs and couplings complying with BS 4343 make it impossible for a piece of equipment operating on one voltage to be plugged into an outlet of a different voltage. This is achieved by keys and keyways in different positions in the plugs and sockets and a

Table 30   **Site voltage requirements**

415 volts three phase	Heavy plant, e.g. tower crane, batching equipment etc.
240 volts single phase	Site accommodation, fixed high-level floodlighting
110 volts three phase	Lightweight plant e.g. circular saw, concrete mixer etc.
110 volts single phase	Portable power tools, movable plant, site lighting, portable hand lamps
50 or 25 volts single phase	Portable hand lamps for use in damp or confined spaces

Figure 247   *On-site electrical distribution*

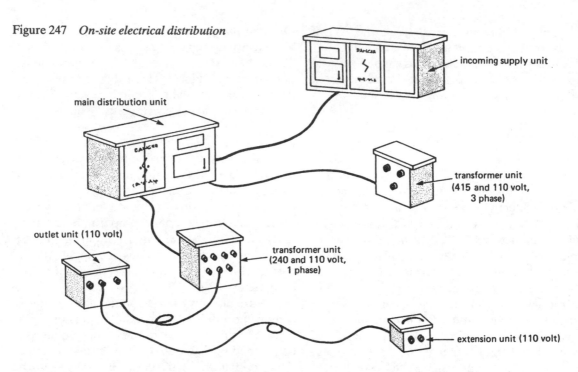

colour coding. Figure 248 illustrates one of these plugs and sockets. The colour coding is as follows:

Red   415 volts
Blue   240 volts
Yellow   110 volts
White   50 volts
Violet   25 volts

The complete electrical installation on site, including the wiring up of plugs to individual items of equipment, must be carried out and regularly inspected by a competent electrician.

When power tools are being used in an existing building from the 240 volts mains supply, a 110 volt portable step-down transformer should be used. In cases where an extension lead is required these should be used on the 110 volt side, kept as short as possible, and routed safely out of the way to prevent risk of tripping or damage. If the extension lead is stored on a drum, it must be fully unwound before use in order to prevent overheating.

Generators
Where electricity is provided by an on-site generator, care must be taken in its siting in order to minimize any nuisance from the emission of fumes and noise. The site distribution system from the generator will be the same as that previously mentioned for mains supply.

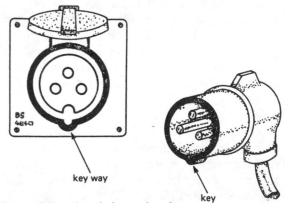

Figure 248   *Keyed plug and socket*

Figure 249 shows a portable petrol 110 volt single-phase generator; this has an output of four kilowatts.

In damp, confined or isolated conditions it is well worth considering the use of rechargeable battery-powered hand tools and lighting.

Figure 249   *110 V portable generator*

Compressed air

Air above the atmospheric pressure of 1 bar is used as the power source for a range of pneumatic tools on building sites. The majority of these tools operate at pressures of between 5 and 8 bar. This is normally produced by a mobile compressor unit, as illustrated in Figure 250. This may be powered by either a petrol/diesel or an electric motor.

Reciprocating-type compressors are normally used for building work. In these the air is sucked through a filter into a cylinder, compressed by a piston and passed on into an air receiver.

A single-stage compressor draws in the air and compresses it by a single stroke of the piston.

Two-stage or multistage compressors compress the air in successive stages until the final pressure is achieved.

Air receivers are incorporated into compressors to even out the pulsating delivery and provide a store of air that is available for discharge at a constant pressure. A system of hoses is used to transport the compressed air to the required working position. The size of the air hose must be compatible with the tool being used: any variation in the bore of the hose will result in a variation of the power supplied to the tool.

Ideally the compressor should be positioned as close as possible to the work. Long runs cause pressure drop through friction, and create hazards. Where long air hose runs are unavoidable, large-bore air hoses should be run to the

Figure 250   *Mobile compressor unit*

work area, where a shut-off valve can be fitted. This valve, in addition to reducing the bore of the air hoses to that compatible with the tool, also enables the tool to be isolated when not in use.

In order to work efficiently, and prevent overheating through friction and excessive wear, it is most important that compressed air tools are supplied with clean air and constant correct lubrication. Therefore every air hose should be equipped with an efficient air filter and lubricator to provide a supply of clean, constantly lubricated air.

Safety procedures

Compressed air equipment can be perfectly safe if correctly used, but can result in severe personal injury if misused. Compressed air entering the body causes painful swelling. If it is allowed to enter the bloodstream it can make its way to the brain, burst the blood vessels and cause death.

The following safety points must be observed whenever compressed air equipment is used:

1 The compressor must be in the control of a fully trained competent person at all times.
2 All equipment must be regularly inspected and maintained.
3 Training must be given to all persons who will use compressed air equipment.
4 Position the compressor in a well-ventilated area.
5 Ensure that all hose connections are properly cramped.
6 Route all air hoses to prevent snaking, the risk of persons tripping, or traffic crossing them, as any squeezing of the hose causes excess pressure on the couplings, which may fail.
7 Always isolate the tool from the air supply before investigating any fault.
8 Never disconnect any air hose unless it is protected by a valve.
9 Never use an air hose to clean away waste material or anything else that may result in flying particles.
10 Never use compressed air to clean down yourself or anyone else, as this creates a great risk of injury to the eyes, ears, nostrils and rectum.

Site woodworking machines

Owing to the relatively short duration of building work on site, the on-site woodworking machine shop is often of a very basic nature. At the very minimum it should consist of a level concrete base, covered with some form of carport type roof. Each machine should be provided with its own individual waterproof covering for after-work protection.

It is normal practice for the machine shop to be controlled by one person who will personally do all the machining required, although on some sites any carpenter may be asked to carry out the machining. In either case it is essential that the following basic common-sense rules are observed at all times.

Common-sense rules
Before use
1 Do not use any machine unless you have been fully instructed in its operation and you are capable of operating it.
2 Check that the machine is isolated from the power supply before setting it up.
3 Ensure that the machine and the working area around it is clean and free from obstruction, offcuts and shavings etc.
4 Check that the cutters are in good condition and suitable for the work in hand.
5 Ensure that all the guards, guides and fences are correctly set up and held securely in place.
6 Make sure that push sticks and or a push block are close to hand.

During use
7 Never feed timber into a machine until the cutters have reached maximum speed.
8 Never make any adjustments to a machine while the cutter is moving.

Note: Even after switching off, many machines take a considerable time to stop.

9 Never leave a machine until its cutters have stopped moving.
10 Never allow yourself to become distracted while operating a machine.
11 Never pass your hands over the cutters, even on top of the timber being machined.
12 Always isolate the machine, clean it down and cover after use.

General safety requirements
The safety requirements of the Woodworking Machines Regulations 1974, which are imposed wherever woodworking machines are in use, may be summarized as follows:

1 The cutters of every machine must be enclosed by a substantial guard to the maximum extent possible.
2 In general no adjustment should be made to the guards or any other part of the machine while the cutters are in motion.
3 Every machine must have an efficient starting and stopping device. This should be located so that it is easily used by the operator especially in an emergency.

4 The working area around a machine must be free from obstruction, offcuts and shavings etc.

5 The floor surface of the work area must be level, non-slip and maintained in good condition.

6 A reasonable temperature must be maintained in the workplace, and in any case must not fall below 13 °C, or 10 °C in a sawmill. Where this is not possible because the machine is situated in the open air, radiant heaters must be provided near or adjacent to the work area to enable operators to warm themselves periodically.

7 No person must use any woodworking machine unless they have been properly trained for the work being carried out or unless they are under close supervision as part of their training.

8 Machine operators must:

(a) Use correctly all guards and safety devices required by the Regulations.

(b) Report to the supervisor or employer any faults or contraventions of the Regulations.

9 Any person who sells or hires a woodworking machine must ensure that it complies with the Regulations.

Circular saws

Circular saw benches are the most common type of woodworking machine used on site. Models are available with petrol, diesel or electric motors.

Figure 251 shows the type of machine in general use. Although these are of a more basic design than those found in a joinery shop, they

Figure 251 *Site circular saw bench*

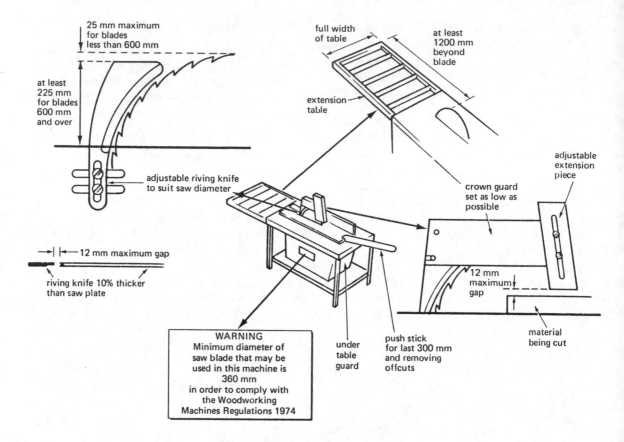

Figure 252   *Circular saw safety requirements*

must still comply with the same safety requirements. These requirements are illustrated in Figure 252 and briefly described as follows:

1 The part of the saw blade which is below the saw table must be enclosed to the maximum extent possible.

2 A strong, adjustable riving knife must be fitted directly behind the saw blade. Its purpose is to part the timber as it proceeds through the saw and thus prevent it jamming on the blade and being thrown back towards the operator.

3 The upper part of the saw blade must be fitted with a strong adjustable crown guard which has flanges that cover the full depth of the saw teeth. The adjustable extension piece should be positioned to within 12 mm of the surface of the material being cut.

4 The diameter of the saw blade must never be less than six-tenths (60 per cent) of the largest saw blade for which the machine is designed. In the case of a multispeed machine the diameter of the saw blade must never be less than 60 per cent of the largest saw blade which can be properly used at the highest speed. There must be a notice fixed to each machine clearly stating the minimum diameter of the saw blade that may be used.

5 Circular saws must not:

(a) Be used for cutting tenons, grooves, rebates or moulding unless effectively guarded. These normally take the form of Shaw tunnel type guards, which in addition to enclosing the blade also apply pressure to the workpiece, keeping it in place.

(b)   Be used for ripping unless the saw teeth project above the timber, i.e. deeping large-sectional material in two cuts is not permissible.

6   A suitable push stick must be provided and kept readily available at all times. It must be used for:

(a)   Feeding material where the cut is 300 mm or less
(b)   Feeding material over the last 300 mm of the cut
(c)   Removing cut pieces from between the saw blade and fence

7   Anyone working at the machine except the operator must stand at the delivery end. A full-width table extension must be fitted so that the distance between the nearest part of the saw blade and the end of the table is at least 1200 mm (except in the case of a portable saw bench having a saw of 450 mm or less in diameter).

Band saw (Figure 253)

These are rarely seen on site except where a large amount of fabrication or adjustment is required. They are particularly useful for conversion and rehabilitation work. Although a band saw can be used for straight cutting, its main use is for curved work. The smallest radius which may be cut is related to the width of the blade. Use a wide blade for straight or large-radius work and a narrow blade for small-radius work.

The regulations applicable to band saws are illustrated in Figure 254 and summarized as follows:

1   All moving parts must be totally enclosed, with the exception of the cutting section.
2   The part of the blade between the top wheel and the thrust wheel must be guarded at the front and one side, the front being as close as practicable to the blade and the side extending beyond the back of the blade.
3   In use the thrust wheel and therefore the guard must be kept adjusted as close as possible to the machine table.

Figure 253   *Band saw*

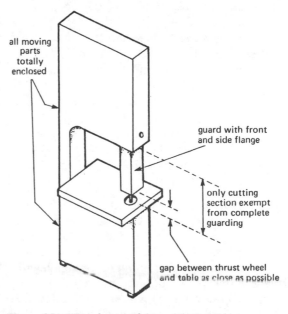

all moving parts totally enclosed

guard with front and side flange

only cutting section exempt from complete guarding

gap between thrust wheel and table as close as possible

Figure 254   *Band saw safety requirements*

Surface planer (Figure 255)

Again, this machine is rarely seen on site. The main exceptions are very large sites with an extended contract period, or conversion or rehabilitation jobs where the nature of the work makes it economic to set up a reasonably well-equipped on-site machine shop.

The Regulations applicable to a hand-fed surface planer can be summarized as follows and are illustrated in Figure 256:

1 The cutter block surface must be cylindrical.
2 The gap between the cutting circle and the outfeed table (delivery table) must not exceed 6 mm measured radially from the block's centre. The gap between the two tables must be kept to a minimum.
3 Every machine must be equipped with an easily adjustable bridge guard fitted centrally over the cutter block. This guard must be long enough to cover the cutter block and be at least as wide as the diameter of the cutter block.
4 In use the bridge guard must be adjusted so that:

   (a) When *surfacing* the gap between itself and the fence does not exceed 10 mm, and the gap between itself and the timber does not exceed 10 mm.
   (b) When *edging* the gap between itself and the table does not exceed 10 mm, and the gap between itself and the timber does not exceed 10 mm.
   (c) When *surfacing and edging* in operations one after the other, the gap between itself and the timber when being surfaced does not exceed 10 mm, and the gap between itself and the timber when being edged does not exceed 10 mm

5 An easily adjustable guard must be fitted to cover the exposed table gap behind the fence.
6 A push block should be used when machining timber less than about 450 mm in length.
7 Rebating or moulding etc. must not be carried out on a planing machine unless it is effectively guarded, normally by a Shaw

Figure 255   *Surface planer*

guard. The bridge guard is not considered effective for these operations.

Extraction equipment

The machines previously mentioned do not require extraction equipment, but if any of the machines on the following list are used an effective chip and dust extraction and collection system must be fitted.

(a) Thicknesser (panel planer)
(b) Vertical spindle moulder (if used for more than six hours per week)
(c) Multicutter moulding machine
(d) Automatic lathe
(e) Tenoning machine (if used for more than six hours per week)
(f) High-speed router

Maintenance

All machines must be maintained in good condition and where practicable be securely anchored.

Lighting

An efficient lighting system should be provided in any machine shop. Direct rays of natural or artificial light must be shaded to prevent glare and so avoid dazzling the machine operator.

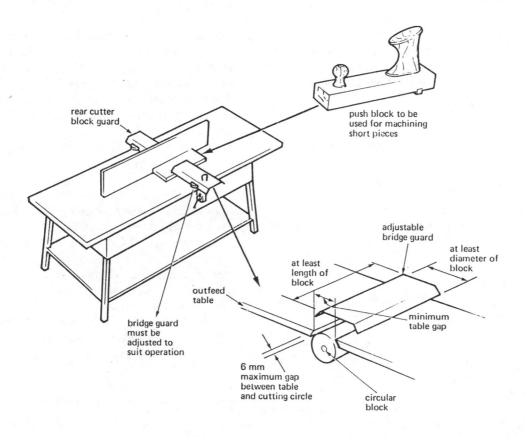

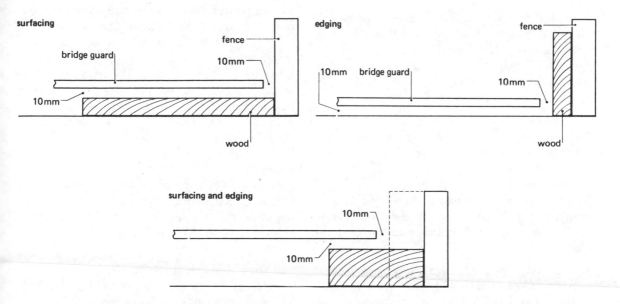

Figure 256　*Surface planer safety requirements*

Noise

Suitable ear protectors must be readily available and used where any person is likely to be exposed to noise levels of 90 dB(A) for eight hours or more per day.

Eye protection

The Protection of Eyes Regulations 1974, as amended in 1975, make provision for the protection of eyes of employees in several specific areas of construction work.

The following areas of work applicable to the carpenter and joiner require the use of eye protectors.

1 Striking masonry nails by hand tool or powered hand tool.
2 Any work with a hand-held cartridge-operated tool including loading and unloading.
3 Any high-speed metal cutting saw or abrasive cutting-off wheel.
4 Dry grinding of materials or articles where fragments may be thrown off.
5 Drilling into brick, tiles, blocks or concrete with a portable power tool.
6 Using compressed air to remove dust or other particles.

In addition it is advisable to use eye protectors when carrying out any operation that is likely to produce dust, chips, sparks etc.

Suitable eye protectors must be supplied to employees where their use is specified in the Regulations. All employees for their part must:

Take reasonable care of them
Report immediately any loss or damage
Use them to protect their eyes

Abrasive wheels

The mounting and use of abrasive wheels must comply with the Abrasive Wheels Regulations 1970. The following points summarize these Regulations:

1 'Abrasive wheels' means any cones, cylinders, discs or wheels having abrasive particles and intended to be power driven for cutting various materials.

2 All abrasive wheels must be clearly marked to indicate their maximum permissible (r.p.m.) speed as specified by its manufacturer. Abrasive wheels less than 55 mm diameter must have their maximum permissible speed clearly indicated on an adjacent notice.
3 Every machine which uses an abrasive wheel must be clearly marked with its spindle speed.
4 Only fully trained competent persons appointed in writing by their employers may mount (set up for use) an abrasive wheel.
5 Substantial guards must enclose abrasive wheels to the maximum possible extent. These should be capable of containing a wheel in the event of a fracture.
6 Where work or tool rests are used they must be of substantial construction and adjusted as close as practicable to the wheel.
7 All persons who use an abrasive wheel have an obligation to do so in a safe and proper manner. All guards, rests and personal protection (goggles) must be used.

Portable powered hand tools

The carpenter has at his disposal a wide range of powered hand tools, enabling many operations to be carried out with increased speed, efficiency and accuracy. In many circumstances there is little to choose between the various power sources available, although some particular advantages and disadvantages are associated with each type. Table 31 gives a comparison of these.

Safety

Although each type of power tool has its own individual safe working procedures, the following basic safety rules should be followed when using any powered tool:

1 Never use a power tool unless you have been properly trained in its use.
2 Never use a power tool unless you have your supervisor's permission.
3 Always select the correct tool for the work

Table 31 **Comparison of power sources**

Electric	Compressed air	Rechargeable battery
Advantages		
Power supply readily available	Tools are lighter	Suitable for use in damp conditions
Wide range of tools	Suitable for use in damp conditions	No leads or hoses
	Certain tools may be used under water	Ideal for use in isolated or confined conditions where there is no power supply
	No risk of motor burning out under load	
	Normally more powerful	
Disadvantages		
High risk of motor burning out under load	Limited range of tools	Limited range of tools
Trailing cables	Requires use of compressor	Limited motor power
Risk of shock	Compressor noise and fumes	Need to recharge batteries
Not suitable for use in damp conditions	Long trailing air hoses limit access	

in hand (if in doubt consult the manufacturer's instructions).

4. Ensure that the power tool and supply are compatible.

5 Ensure that the tool's cable and air hose is:

   (a) Free from knots and damage
   (b) Firmly secured at all connections
   (c) Unable to come into contact with the cutting edge or become fouled during the tool's operation.

6 Before making any adjustments always disconnect the tool from its power supply.

7 Always use the tool's safety guards correctly and never remove or tie them back.

8 Never put a tool down until all the rotating parts have stopped moving.

9 Always wear the correct protective equipment for the job. These may include:

   (a) Safety goggles
   (b) Dust mask
   (c) Ear protectors
   (d) Safety helmet

Note: Loose clothing and long hair should be tied up so that they cannot be caught up in the tool.

10 All power tools should be properly maintained and serviced at regular intervals by a suitably trained person. Never attempt to service or repair a power tool yourself. If it is not working correctly or its safety is suspect, return it to the storeman with a note stating why it has been returned. In any case it should be returned to the stores for inspection at least once every seven days.

11 Ensure that the material or workpiece is firmly cramped or fixed in position so that it will not move during the tool's operation.

12 In general compressed air tools must be started and stopped under load, whereas electric tools must not.

13 Never use an electric tool where combustible liquids or gases are present.

14 Never carry, drag or suspend a tool by its cable or hose.

15 Think before and during use. Tools cannot be careless but their operators can. Most accidents are caused by simple carelessness.

Drill

This is the most common type of portable power tool. The two main types available are:

Figure 257   *Drill*

Figure 258   *Back handle drill*

The palm grip type
The heavy-duty back handle type

Both are available in two- or multispeed versions, which makes them more versatile as it allows the user to adjust the speed to suit the size of hole and material being worked.

In general use a fast speed for drilling small-diameter holes and a slow speed for larger-diameter holes.

Figure 257 shows a drill with a palm grip handle. This design ensures that the pressure is exerted directly in line with the drill bit, thus assisting the cutting action.

Figure 258 shows a back handle heavy-duty drill, which is designed for two-handed operation. This type is often fitted with a percussion or hammer action for drilling masonry and concrete, with special percussion tungsten-carbide-tipped drills.

Twist drills and bits
Only high-quality twist drills and bits capable of withstanding the pressure and heat generated when drilling at speed should be used. They must be fully inserted into the jaws of the chuck and tightened using a chuck key in all three positions, so that the jaws grip the shank of the drill evenly.

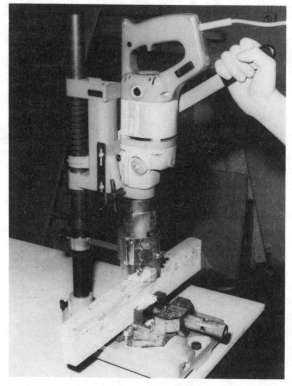

Figure 259   *Drill stand*

A useful hint is to tape the chuck key to the power tool flex near the plug, thus ensuring that the chuck is tightened and the key removed before the drill is plugged in and operated.

Drill stand

For repetitive work and light mortising a drill can be fitted into a drill stand as illustrated in Figure 259, thus combining accuracy and speed of production. In order to comply with safety requirements the stand is fitted with a retractable chuck and drill guard which must always be in position when drilling.

Operation

During use:

1　Hold the drill firmly.
2　Cramp the workpiece.
3　Do not force the drill; allow it to work at its own pace.
4　Withdraw the drill from the hole frequently to clear the dust and allow it to cool.
5　Drill a small pilot hole first to act as a guide when drilling large holes.
6　Reduce the pressure applied on the drill as it is about to break through, to avoid snatching or twisting.

Screwdriver

When large numbers of screws have to be driven, or nuts tightened, the use of a power screwdriver will greatly speed up the process. Figure 260 shows a power screwdriver. The body and motor is similar to that of an electric power drill, although a reduction gear is fitted to give the correct speed for screwdriving. Where a two-speed tool is used, the slow speed should be used for wood screws and the high speed for self-tapping screws. Most tools are manufactured with a reverse gear to enable screws to be removed as well as inserted.

The front housing of the tool holds the screwdriver bits and contains a clutch assembly. This operates in two stages:

1　The tool's motor will run but the screwdriver bit will not rotate until sufficient pressure is exerted to enable the clutch to operate and engage the main drive.
2　When the screws are tight and in the required position, the second stage of the clutch operates and stops the screwdriver bit rotating.

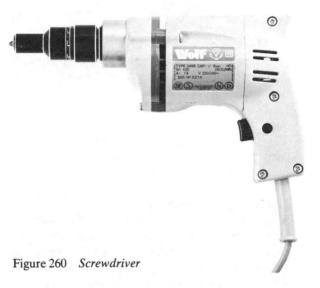

Figure 260　*Screwdriver*

The clutch can be adjusted by tightening or loosening the spring as required. If the adjustment is not suitable for the work in hand, the clutch spring can be changed for a weaker or stronger one. Four strengths are normally available. The weakest is used for driving smaller screws or screws which are to be left proud of the surface, and the strongest for large or deeply driven screws. The two intermediate strength springs are used for a variety of operations in between these two extremes.

Screwdriver bits and sockets

Various screwdriver bits and sockets are available to suit different types and sizes of screws. It is a simple operation to change the type of bit when required. The hexagonal shank of the bit is simply pushed into the front housing of the tool and retained in position by a spring-loaded steel ball which locates in a groove around the top of the shank. The bit is removed by simply pulling it out of the front housing.

Operation of screwdriver

During use:

1　Select a screwdriver bit that is compatible with the tool being used.
2　Drill a pilot hole, clearance hole and countersink where required before screwing

to avoid overloading the motor and splitting the material.

3   Maintain a steady, firm pressure on the screwdriver so that the bit cannot 'jump out' and damage the screw head or the workpiece.

Sanders

The two main types of sander used by the carpenter on site are the orbital sander and the belt sander.

Orbital sander (Figure 261)

This type is also known as the finishing sander, as it is mainly used for fine finishing work. The sander's base has a 3 mm orbit which operates at 12,000 r.p.m. Various grades of abrasive paper may be clipped to the sander's base. It is best to start off with a coarse grade to remove any high spots or roughness and follow on with finer grades until the required finish is obtained. However, where the surface of the timber has machine marks or there is a definite difference in the levels of adjacent material the surface should be levelled by planing before any sanding is commenced.

Belt sander (Figure 262)

This is used for jobs requiring rapid stock removal. When fitted with the correct grade of abrasive belt, it can be used for a wide range of operations such as smoothing and finishing joinery items, block flooring, and even the removal of old paint and varnish finishes.

The sanding or abrasive belt is fitted over two rollers. The front roller is spring loaded and can be moved backwards and forwards by the belt tensioning lever. This movement allows the belt to be changed easily and it also applies the correct tension to the belt. When changing the belt it is necessary to ensure that it will rotate in the correct direction. This is indicated on the inside of the belt by an arrow. If the belt is inadvertently put on the wrong way round the lap joint which runs diagonally across the belt will tend to peel. This could result in the belt breaking, with possible damage to the work surface. To keep the belt running central on the

Figure 261   *Orbital sander*

Figure 262   *Belt sander*

Figure 263   *Circular saw*

rollers there is a tracking control knob on the sander which adjusts the front roller by tilting it to either the left or the right as required. The tracking is adjusted by turning the sander bottom upwards with the belt running and rotating the tracking knob until the belt runs evenly in the centre without deviating to either side.

Operation of sanders
During use:

1 Always start the sander before bringing it into contact with the work surface, and remove it from the work surface before switching off. This is because slow-moving abrasive particles will deeply scratch the work surface.
2 Do not press down on a sander in use. The weight of the machine itself is sufficient pressure. Excessive pressure causes clogging of the abrasive material and overheating of the motor.
3 For best results lightly guide the sander over the surface with parallel overlapping strokes in line with the grain.
4 Always use the abrasive belts and sheets specifically recommended by the manufacturer for the particular model, as makeshift belts and sheets are inefficient and dangerous.
5 Always use the dust collecting bag where one is fitted. In any case always wear a dust mask, as inhaling the dust from many species of wood causes coughing, sneezing, running eyes and nose.

Saws
There are three types of portable saw in common use by the carpenter on site, each with its own specific range of functions: the circular saw, the jig saw and the chain saw.

Circular saw (Figure 263)
This is often known as a 'skill' saw and is used by the carpenter on site for a wide range of sawing operations. The saw is capable of cross-cutting, rip sawing, bevel cutting and compound bevel cutting.

Tungsten-carbide-tipped saw blades are preferable for site use. These give a longer working service before the need for resharpening. When cutting plywood, chipboard, fibreboard, plastic laminates and abrasive timbers they are especially useful.

Operation of a circular saw
1 Select and fit correct blade for work in hand (rip, cross-cut, combination or tungsten tipped etc.).
2 Adjust depth of cut so that the gullets of the teeth just clear the material to be cut.
3 Check that the blade guard is working properly. It should spring back and cover the blade when the saw is removed from the timber.
4 Set the saw to the required cutting angle. This is indicated by a pointer on the pivot slide.
5 Insert rip fence (if required) and set to the width required.

Note: When cutting sheet material or timber where the rip fence will not adjust to the required width, a straight batten can be temporarily fixed along the board to act as a guide for the sole plate of the saw to run against.

6 Check to ensure that all adjustment levers and thumbscrews are tight.
7 Ensure that the material to be cut is properly supported and securely fixed down.

Note: As the saw cuts from the bottom upwards, the face side of the material should be placed downwards. This ensures that any breaking out which may occur does not spoil the face of the material.

8 Rest the front of the saw on the material to be cut and pull the trigger to start the saw.
9 Allow the blade to reach its full speed before starting to cut. Feed the saw into the work smoothly and without using excess pressure.

Note: The blade guard will automatically retract as the saw is fed into the work.

10 If the saw binds in the work, ease it back until the blade runs free.
11 When the end of the cut is reached, remove the saw from the work, allowing the blade guard to spring back into place, and then release the trigger.

Note: Do not release the trigger before the end of the cut has been reached.

Jig saws (Figure 264)
These are also known as reciprocating saws. Although they may be used with a fence for straight cutting, they are particularly useful for circular, shaped and pierced work. In addition many models have adjustable sole plates, enabling bevel cutting to be carried out.

Figure 264   *Jig saw*

A range of different blades is available, suitable for cutting a wide variety of materials.

Operation of a jig saw
1 Select the correct blade for the work in hand.
2 Select the correct speed – slow speed for curved work and high speed for straight cutting.
3 Ensure that the material to be cut is properly supported and securely fixed down.
4 Rest the front of the saw on the material to be cut and pull the trigger to start the saw.
5 When the blade has reached its full speed, steadily feed the saw into the work, but do not force it.
6 When the end of the cut is reached release the trigger, keeping the sole plate of the saw against the workpiece, but making sure the blade is not in contact.

Figure 265   *Chain saw*

Pocket cutting
Both the circular saw and the jig saw may be used for pocket cutting. The circular saw is suitable for cutting access traps in completed floors. The jig saw is useful for cutting sink top holes in worktops etc. without the need for templates. See *Carpentry and Joinery for Building Craft Students*, Volume 2, pp.18–19 for pocket cutting techniques.

Chain saw (Figure 265)
This saw, although more usually associated with timber felling, can be useful on site for rough cutting to length of large-sectioned timbers, e.g. floor joists and shoring members.

There are a large number of models available, only the smaller of which tend to be electrically powered. The larger models are normally powered by an integral two-stroke petrol/oil motor.

The cutting is achieved by a special saw chain, with regularly spaced sharpened teeth, which runs through the motor and around the guide bar.

As well as the obvious safety hazard of the chain coming into contact with a part of the body, other hazards arise from vibration, exhaust fumes and noise, particularly in confined spaces.

Operation of a chain saw
1 Hold the chain saw firmly with both hands.

Figure 266 *Planer*

2 Maintain a well-balanced feet-apart stance.
3 Always use the bottom of the guide bar when cutting. Any attempt to use the tip will cause kickback. This is the rapid upward movement of the saw which often results in serious injury to the operator.
4 Never cut towards yourself or a helper.

Planer (Figure 266)

The portable planer is mainly used for edging work, although it is capable of being used for both chamfering and rebating. On site it is extremely useful for door hanging. Surfacing and cleaning up of timber can be carried out when required, but it tends to leave ridges on surfaces which are wider than the length of the cutters.

Operation of a planer

1 Check that the cutters are sharp and set correctly.
2 Adjust the fence to run along the edge of the work as a guide.
3 Rest the front of the plane on the workpiece, ensuring that the cutters are not in contact with the timber.
4 Pull the trigger and allow cutters to gain speed.
5 Move the plane forward, keeping pressure on the front knob.

Note: The depth of the cut can be altered by rotating this knob.

Figure 267 *Router*

6 Continue planing, keeping pressure both down and up against the fence.
7 When completing the cut, ease the pressure off the front knob and increase the pressure on the back.

Note: This prevents the plane tipping forward, causing the cutter to dig in when the end of the cut is reached.

8 Allow the cutters to stop before putting the plane down; otherwise the plane could take off on the revolving cutters.

Rebating and chamfering is carried out using a similar procedure. When surfacing, a number of overlapping strokes will be required.

Router (Figure 267)

This is a very versatile tool which is capable of performing a wide variety of operations including rebating, housing, grooving, moulding, slot mortising, dovetailing and, on many types, drilling and plunge cutting. However, it is mainly used on site for the trimming of plastic laminates and the recessing of hinges and locks.

Mechanically the router is a fairly basic piece of equipment. It consists of a motor driving a central shaft with a chuck at one end. The cutters are held in the chuck by a tapered collet which grips the shank of the cutter as the locking nut of the chuck is tightened.

Cutters

High-speed steel cutters are suitable for most softwoods, although tungsten-tipped cutters are recommended when working with abrasive timbers, laminates, plastics, plywood, chipboard and fibreboard.

Operation of a router

Recessing

This operation requires the fitting of a template guide to the base plate of the router and a template of the recess required.

When making the template an allowance must be made all round equal to the distance between the cutting edge of the bit and the outside edge of the template guide. Figure 268 shows a typical template for recessing a hinge.

1 Fix the template in the required position.
2 Place the router base on the template. Take a firm grip on the router, start the motor and allow it to attain maximum speed. Plunge the router to the preset depth and lock.
3 Applying a firm downward pressure, move the router around the edge of the template before working the centre. It is most important to feed the router in the opposite direction to the rotation of the cutter.
4 On completion, retract the cutter, switch off the motor and allow the cutter to stop rotating before putting the router down.

Note: Rounded corners will be left by the cutter; these can easily be squared up with a chisel.

Laminate trimming

Small routers for single-hand operation are manufactured specifically for laminate trim-

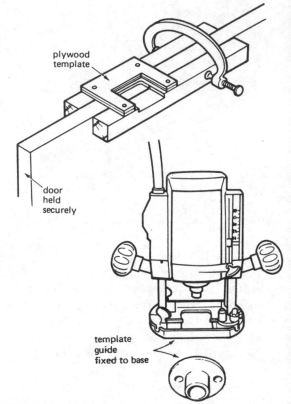

Figure 268   *Router template for recessing*

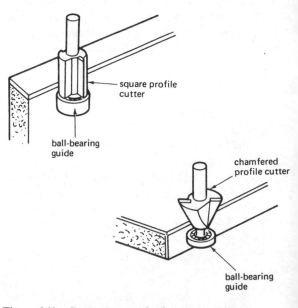

Figure 269   *Router cutters for laminate trimming*

ming, although it is possible to fit a ballbearing-guided laminate trimmer to a standard plunging router.

Figure 269 shows two router cutters suitable for laminate trimming. The square profile is used for trimming the edging strip and the chamfered one for trimming the top.

Automatic drivers

Various types of automatic drivers or tackers are available to suit a wide range of fixings.

The smaller tackers are usually operated by spring power and the larger ones by compressed air, although a limited range of electric tackers are available.

Operation of automatic drivers

This will vary depending on the type being used, but the following are a number of general points:

1 Do not operate the trigger until the base plate is in contact with the surface which is to be fixed.
2 Keep fingers clear of the base plate.
3 Maintain a firm pressure with the fixing surface during use. Failure to do so can result in kickback of the tool and ricochet of the nail or staple.
4 On tools with a variable power adjuster, carry out trial fixings at a low setting and gradually increase until the required penetration is achieved.

Figure 270 shows a spring stapler that is useful for fixing ceiling tiles, insulation and moisture/vapour barriers etc. To operate, the tacker is placed firmly in position and the operating lever pressed downwards.

Figure 271 illustrates a heavier type spring-operated stapler that is designed to drive a staple when swung against a surface in a hammer-like fashion.

Figure 272 illustrates a pneumatic nailer/stapler that is capable of firing nails and staples of up to 75 mm in length. This makes it suitable for a wide range of site fixings including carcassing and the surface nailing of flooring, cladding, sheathing and plasterboard etc.

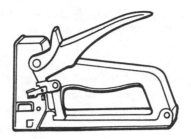

Figure 270   *Spring stapler*

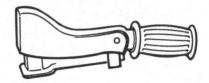

Figure 271   *Hammer-action stapler*

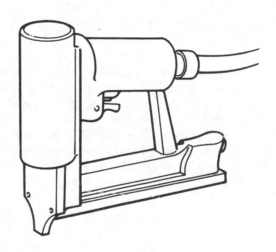

Figure 272   *Pneumatic nailer*

Secret nailing of tongued-and-grooved boarding can be carried out with the use of an angled base plate.

Cartridge-operated fixing tools (Figure 273)

The cartridge-operated fixing tool is an invaluable aid to making fast and reliable fixings to a variety of materials including concrete, brick and steel.

The two types of tool in use are the direct acting and the indirect acting.

Direct acting

In this type of tool the expanding gas from the detonated cartridge acts directly on the fastener, accelerating it from rest down the barrel to strike the base material at a velocity of up to 500 m/s (metres per second). At no time are the fasteners' propulsion or depth of penetration controlled. Should for any reason the base material be inconsistent, there is a danger that the fastener could penetrate through or ricochet and cause untold damage in the surrounding area.

Direct-acting tools are also known as high-velocity tools. They are operated by pulling a trigger which releases a spring to detonate the cartridge.

Indirect-acting tool

This type of tool has a piston in its barrel. When the cartridge is detonated, the released gas acts on the piston, accelerating it from rest to drive the fastener into the base material at a maximum velocity of up to 100 m/s. The piston is held captive in the tool and once the piston stops so will the fastener. This virtually eliminates the risk of through-penetration or ricochets, even if the base material is inconsistent. Indirect-acting tools are also known as low-velocity tools. They may be operated in one of two ways, depending on the make and type of tool being used. The cartridge may be detonated by an externally applied blow. This blow is normally from a club hammer. Alternatively, the cartridge is detonated by a spring which is released when the trigger is pulled.

Indirect-acting low-velocity tools are considered to be the safest type of cartridge-operated tool available.

Operation of cartridge-operated fixing tools

Safe working procedures are most important when using cartridge tools, and these can never be overemphasized. Before operating a tool, always run through the following dos and don'ts checklist.

Figure 273   *Cartridge tool*

Dos

Do ensure the tool is in good repair (cleaned and serviced daily).

Do ensure you have had the correct training.

Do ensure you understand the misfire procedure (given in the manufacturer's handbook).

Do wear recommended safety equipment (goggles, helmet and ear protectors).

Do ensure the base material is suitable (try the hand hammer test).

Do ensure the tool is used at right angles to the fixing surface.

Do ensure the fixing surface is free from cracks and damage.

Do insert fixing device before inserting cartridge.

Do ensure the correct pin, piston and cartridge combination is used.

Do ensure you understand the handling and storage of cartridges (stored in a metal box, in a secure store, to which only authorized persons have access).

Don'ts

Don't use a suspect tool (if in doubt return to the manufacturer for overhaul).

Don't use a tool you have not been trained for (manufacturers provide on-site training for operators).

Don't use force when loading a cartridge (it could detonate in your hand).

Don't load a cartridge before you need it.

Don't leave a loaded tool lying about.

Don't point the tool at any person.

Don't drive into brittle material.

Don't drive into very soft material.

Don't drive less than 63 mm from the edge of brick and concrete.

Don't drive less than 13 mm from the edge of steel.

Don't drive within 50 mm of a weld.

Don't drive into a damaged surface.

Don't drive where another fixing has failed.

Don't strip the tool without checking that it is unloaded.

Don't use the tool without recommended safety equipment.

Don't use other manufacturers' cartridges.

Don't use other manufacturers' fixing devices.

When cartridge fixing into a suspect material, the best procedure to follow is to carry out the hand hammer test. This is carried out by attempting to hand hammer a fastener into the material. A cartridge fixing is not suitable if any of the following occur:

The point of the fastener is blunted.

The fastener fails to penetrate at least 1.6 mm.

The surface of the material cracks, crazes or is damaged.

Where the strength of the material into which a fixing is being made is not known, a test fixing should be carried out in order to establish the required cartridge strength. Always make test fixings using the lowest strength cartridge first, increasing by one strength each time until the required fixing is achieved.

Further information on cartridge-operated fixing tools is given in *Carpentry and Joinery for Building Craft Students 2,* pages 22–8.

Health hazards associated with wood dust

The wood dust created when machining certain timbers has a known irritant effect. The most harmful effects are created by the fine airborne

Table 32 **Common irritant timbers**

	Severity			Harmful effect	
	Highly irritant	Irritant	Mildly irritant	Respiratory irritation: coughing, sneezing, inflamed and running eyes and nose, nosebleeds and in severe cases breathing difficulties	Skin irritation: dermatitis, reddening of skin, itching, swelling, dry flaking skin and in severe cases blisters and weeping sores
Idigbo			*		*
Obeche			*	*	
Western red cedar	*			*	*
Mahogany African	*				*
Keruing		*			*
Yew		*		*	*
Afrormosia		*			*
Agba			*		*
Iroko	*				*
Teak		*			*
Makore	*			*	
Rosewood		*			*

dust produced when sanding or sawing in confined, poorly ventilated areas, although the severity of the effect will depend on the sensitivity of the individual concerned.

The common timbers that are known to have irritant properties are listed in Table 32 along with its type and degree of effect.

Precautions

Since it is the dust that causes the problems, the most effective precaution is the use of dust extraction equipment. However, this is only part of the answer, as a certain amount of airborne dust cannot be avoided. Therefore, when working with a timber that has irritant properties, the following precautions should be taken:

1   Always use a dust mask or respirator.
2   Wear properly designed dustproof protective clothing.
3   Use barrier cream or disposable plastic gloves.
4   Thoroughly wash or shower as soon as possible after exposure to remove all traces of dust.

Self-assessment questions

1   List *four* operations where the use of eye protection is statutory.

2   Name *three* items of protective equipment and give examples where *each* might be used.

3   Electricity or compressed air may be used as the power source for powered hand tools. State *one* advantage and *one* disadvantage of using *each*.

4   List *five* safety points to be observed when using electrically powered hand tools.

5   Briefly state with the aid of a sketch the requirements of the Woodworking Machines Regulations 1974 applicable to a circular saw bench.

6   State *two* main differences between direct- and indirect-acting cartridge-operated fixing tools.

7   Sketch the position of the bridge guard when facing and edging a piece of 45 mm × 100 mm timber in consecutive operations.

8   List *three* main requirements relating to the floor around woodworking machines.

9   List *six* points of safety concerning the use of cartridge-operated fixing tools.

10 What do the Woodworking Machines Regulations state in regard to the temperature in work areas?

chapter 10

Construction work

After reading this chapter the student should be able to:

1 State the principles involved in the following items of construction work:

Floors
Roofs
Suspended ceilings
Timber framed buildings
Panelling
Partitions
Fixing joinery units
Doors and associated ironmongery
Stairs

2 Identify the components of these various items.

3 Produce sketches to show typical working details of these various items.

4 State any Building Regulations that are relevant to a given item of construction.

5 List the sequence of operations of a given job.

6 Select the most suitable detail or method of construction for a given situation.

Timber upper floor construction

It is normal for the joists in upper floors to span the shortest width. They must be of a deeper section than those used for ground floors because no intermediate supports in the form of sleeper walls are available.

The depth of the joist depends on its span – as the span increases, so must its depth. Therefore in order to use an economic depth of joist, the maximum span for simple floors is normally restricted to 4.8 m. For spans in excess of this, a more complex form of construction is required.

Upper floors may be classified into three groups, according to their method of construction: single floors; double floors; and triple or framed floors.

Single floors (Figure 274)
These are the most common type of upper floor for domestic house construction. They are used

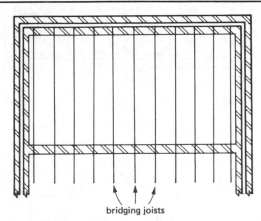

bridging joists

Figure 274   *Single floor*

for spans up to 4.8 m where common or bridging joists span from wall to wall.

Double floors (Figure 275)
These are used where the shortest span of the roof is over 4.8 m and up to about 6 m. The

room is divided up into a number of bays, each of which is not more than 4.8 m long, by binders which provide intermediate support for the bridging joists. These binders may be of steel (commonly known as a universal beam (UB)), timber (usually either solid glulam or a plywood box beam) or concrete. These are illustrated in Figure 276. Depending on the space available and the depth of floor they may be accommodated below, above, within or partly within the floor.

Triple or framed floors (Figure 277)
These are now almost obsolete, as for floors where the span is over 6 m reinforced concrete or other forms of floor construction are used.

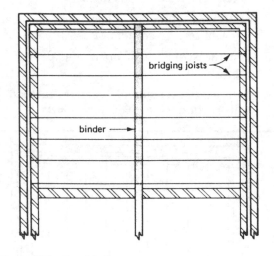

Figure 275   *Double floor*

However, when one is engaged in maintenance or renovation work, triple floors may be encountered. The room is divided up into bays by very heavy, large-sectioned steel universal beams or concrete beams. These beams provide support for the binders, which in turn provide support for the bridging joists.

Joist supports
The ends of the joists may be supported in a number of different ways. The three most common are described here.

Built in (Figure 278)
The ends of the joists are treated with a preservative and built into the inner leaf of the brickwork. An improvement of this method is to incorporate a steel bearing bar under the joists.

Note: Ends of joists are splayed off to prevent them from penetrating into the cavity and possibly catching mortar droppings. Also as a fire precaution, this method cannot be used for supporting joists in a party or separating wall.

Hangers (Figure 279)
The ends of the joist are supported by galvanized joist hangers which are built into the brickwork. An advantage of this method is that the joists can be fixed after the wall is completely built, unlike the previous method where the bricklayers have to wait for the carpenters to position the joists before they can continue with the brickwork.

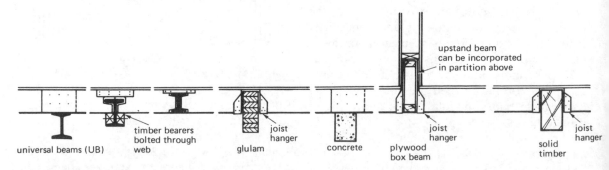

Figure 276   *Binders*

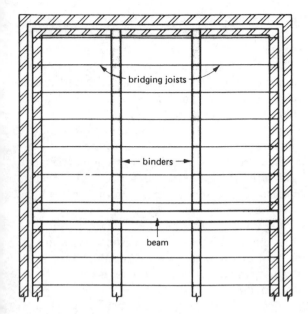

Figure 277   *Triple floor*

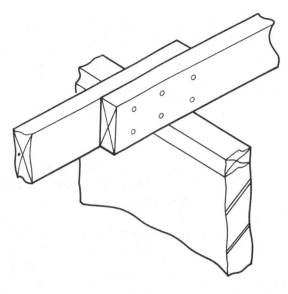

Figure 280   *Supporting joist on internal partition*

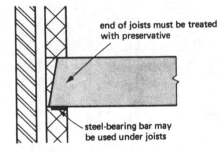

Figure 278   *Joist built in*

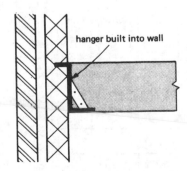

Figure 279   *Joist on hanger*

Wall plate (Figure 280)

The ends of the joists may be supported by a wall plate bedded on top of a load-bearing internal partition. Often the joists from either side meet on an internal partition. It is usual to nail them together side by side with overlaps of about 300 mm. This method is not suitable for use in an external wall.

Trimming

Whenever an opening occurs in a floor, the joists require framing around the opening so as to be self-supporting. This is known as trimming and it is achieved using trimmed, trimmer and trimming joists. These terms are defined below.

Trimmed joist

A bridging joist that has been cut short (trimmed) to form an opening in the floor is known as a 'trimmed joist'.

Trimmer joist

A joist placed at right angles to the bridging joist, in order to support the cut ends of the trimmed joists.

Trimming joist

A joist with a span the same as the bridging joist, but supporting the end of a trimmer joist.

Note: As both the trimmer and the trimming joist take a greater load, they are usually 25 mm thicker than the bridging joists.

Layout of floor joists

The positioning of floor joists is fairly simple. The outside bridging joists are placed in position first, leaving a 50 mm gap between them and the wall. The other joists are then spaced out evenly in the remaining space.

However, when openings for fireplaces and stairwells etc. are required in the floor, the layout of the floor joists is governed by these openings. This is because the bridging must be cut short in order to form the opening. This necessitates the use of a trimmer and trimming joists. The trimming and outside bridging joists are the first to be positioned, once again leaving

a 50 mm gap between the joist and the wall. The other joists are then spaced out in the remaining space.

Although fireplace openings in upper floors are virtually obsolete, they are covered in this chapter because they may be met in maintenance or rehabilitation work.

Figure 281 shows the layout of joists for a single floor with a fireplace opening.

The dovetail strips shown in Figures 281 and 282 are bedded into the top of the concrete hearth to provide a fixing for the ends of the floorboards.

Figure 283 shows another section through the fire hearth. The 6 mm asbestos, which is supported on the brickwork and the batten fixed to the trimmer, acts as permanent formwork for the concrete.

The Building Regulations Part J Heat Producing Appliances, states that the construction around heat producing appliances should minimize the risk of the building catching fire. In order

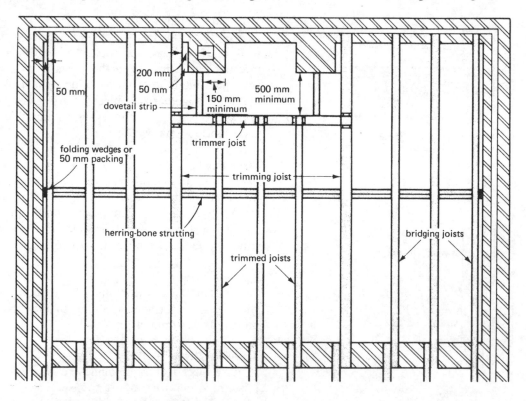

Figure 281   *Layout of floor around fireplace*

to comply with this requirement the use of combustible material in the vicinity of a fireplace, chimney or flue is restricted. The following requirements comply with AD: J

No timber is to be built into the flue, or be within 200 mm of the flue lining, or be nearer than 40 mm to the outer surface of a chimney or fireplace recess (a 50 mm air space between any joist and wall is standard practice). The exceptions to this requirement are: flooring; skirting; architrave; mantel shelf and other trim. Any metal fixings associated with these must be at least 50 mm from the flue.

There must be a 125 mm minimum thickness solid non-combustible hearth which extends at least 500 mm in front of the fireplace recess and a 150 mm one either side.

Combustible material used underneath the hearth is to be separated from the hearth by an airspace of at least 50 mm or be at least 250 mm from the hearth's top surface. Combustible material supporting the edge of the hearth is permitted.

Figure 284 shows the layout of joists around a stairwell. It can be seen that this is a similar arrangement to the trimming around the fireplace.

Often to provide sufficient headroom for quarter-turn stairs, an L-shaped stairwell opening is required. Figure 285 shows how the landing is formed using cantilever joists which must be carried through the wall and across the adjacent room. Solid strutting should be fixed diagonally across the landing for strength. Where the joists meet at the external angle a dovetail joint can be used.

Trimming joints

Traditionally, tusk mortise and tenon joints were used between the trimmer and the trimming joists, while housing joints were used between the trimmed joists and the trimmer. The joints along with their proportions are shown in Figure 286.

Joist hangers are a quicker, modern alternative to the traditional joints. As these hangers

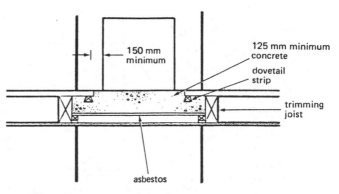

Figure 282 *Section through fire hearth showing dovetail strips*

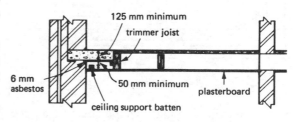

Figure 283 *Section through fire hearth*

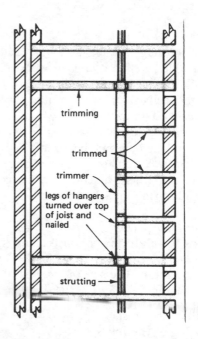

Figure 284 *Trimming to stairwell*

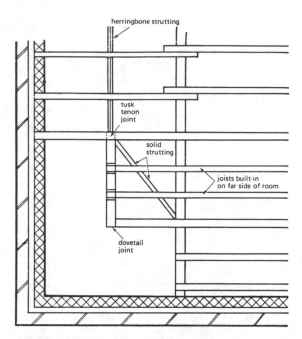

Figure 285   *L-shaped stairwell*

are made from thin material they do not require notching in, but they must be securely nailed to both joists with 32 mm galvanized plasterboard nails or square twisted shank nails.

Levelling joists
After positioning, the joists should be checked for line and level. This is done by working round the building using a straight edge and spirit level to find the highest point. The other joists can then be packed up to this level, where required, thus ensuring a level surface on to which the flooring and ceiling can be fixed. Temporary battens can be nailed across the top of the joists to ensure that their spacing remains constant before and during their building in.

Joist sizes and spacing
The joists for all forms of construction must be large enough to carry safely the loads which are imposed on them. The size of the joists depends on three factors:

The span of the joists
The spacing of the joists
The load per m^2 on the floor

A suitable sectional size for floor joists can be determined using one of three methods:

1   The Building Regulations, AD A Tables B, gives the required size of joists for various spans, spacing and loads.
2   By calculation using the formula and procedures covered previously in chapter 5.
3   The approximate depth of 50 mm thick joists spaced at 400 mm centres can be found by using the following rule of thumb method. This is suitable for normal domestic use, although the sections will be on the generous side:

(span of joist in millimetres/20) + 20
= depth of joist

Notches and holes
The position of notches for pipes and holes for cables in joists should have been determined at the design stage and indicated on the drawings. Since it is necessary to make an allowance for them when calculating sectional sizes.

BS 5268: Part 2: 1984 Structural Use of Timber, states that it is not necessary to make an allowance for notches and holes when calculating sectional sizes for floor joists of up to 250 mm in depth, providing that:

Notches of up to 0.125 of the joist's depth are located between 0.07 and 0.25 of the span from either support.

Holes of up to 0.25 of the joist's depth are drilled on the neutral stress line and are located between 0.25 and 0.4 of the span from either support. In addition adjacent holes should be separated by at least three times their diameter (centre to centre).

Figure 287 illustrates the Permissible Positions for notches and holes.

Example: Position and sizes for notches and holes for a 200 mm deep joist spanning 4 m are:

Notches: between 280 mm and 1 m in from each end of joists and up to 25 mm deep.

Holes: between 1 m and 1.6 m in from each end of joists and up to 50 mm diameter.

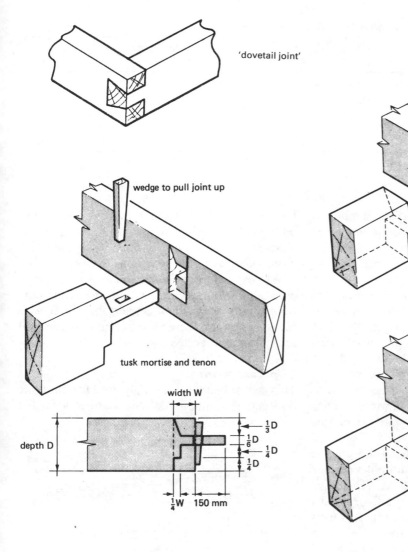

Figure 286 *Traditional trimming joists*

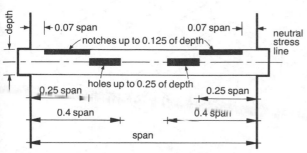

Figure 287 *Positions for notches and holes*

Span of flooring

Table 33 gives the spacing for joists in relation to the type of boarding used.

Floorboarding

Softwood flooring usually consists of 25 mm × 150 mm tongued-and-grooved boarding. This can be fixed either by floor brads nailed through the surface of the boards and punched in, or by lost-head nails secret-fixed through the tongue. Square butted or splayed heading joints are introduced as required to utilize offcuts of board

Table 33   **Joist spacing according to boards used**

Material	Finished thickness (mm)	Maximum spacing of joists (mm)
Softwood T & G boarding	16	450
Softwood T & G boarding	19	600
Flooring-grade chipboard	18	400–450
Flooring-grade chipboard	22	600

and avoid wastage. Heading joints should be staggered evenly throughout the floor and never be placed adjacent to each other.

Laying floorboards

This can begin once the plumbing and electrical underfloor carcassing work has been completed and the building made weather-tight. The first board is fixed 10 mm away from the outside wall or in front of the fire hearth. The remainder of the boards are laid four to six at a time, cramped up with floorboard cramps and surface nailed to the joists. Boards up to 100 mm in width require one nail to each joist, while boards over this require two nails.

Two alternatives to the use of floorboard cramps are folding or wedging, although neither of these is so quick or efficient. They are illustrated in Figure 288. Folding a floor entails fixing two boards spaced apart 10 mm less than the width of five boards. The five boards can then be placed with their tongues and grooves engaged. A short board is laid across the centre and 'jumped on' to press the boards in position. This process is then repeated across the rest of the floor. Alternatively, the boards may be cramped, four to six at a time using dogs and wedges.

Secret-fixed boards must be laid and tightened individually and cramping is therefore not practical. They may be tightened by levering them forward with a firmer chisel driven into the top of the joist, or with the aid of a floorboard nailer. This tightens the boards and drives the nail when the plunger is struck with a hard mallet. Both of these methods are illustrated in

Figure 289. Secret fixing is normally only used on high-class work or hardwood flooring, as the increased laying time makes it considerably more expensive.

Where services such as water and gas pipes or electric cables are run within the floor, the floorboards over them should be fixed with recessed cups and screws to permit easy removal for subsequent access.

Chipboard flooring

This is now being increasingly used for domestic flooring. Flooring-grade chipboard is available

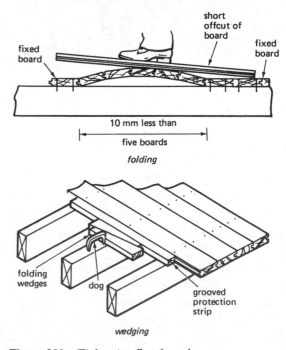

Figure 288   *Tightening floorboards*

with square edges in 1220 mm × 2440 mm sheets, and with tongue-and-groove edges in 600 mm × 2440 mm sheets. Square-edged sheets are normally laid with their long edges over a joist. Noggins must be fixed between the joists to support the short ends. Tongue-and-groove sheets are usually laid with their long edges at right angles to the joists and their short edges joining over the joist. Both types require noggins between the joists where the sheet abuts a wall.

Fixing

Sheets are laid staggered and fixed at 200 mm to 300 mm centres with 50 mm lost-head nails. A gap of 10 mm must be left along each wall to allow for expansion.

For protection it is recommended that the floor is covered with building paper after laying and that this is left in position until the building is occupied.

Strip flooring

Hardwood strip flooring is used where the floor itself is to be a decorative feature. It is made

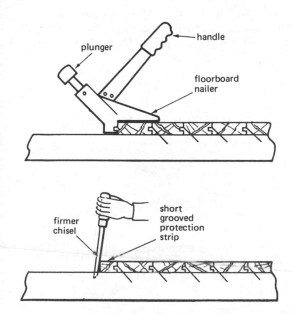

Figure 289   *Tightening secret-fixed floorboards*

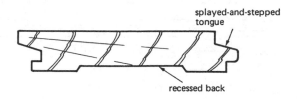

Figure 290   *Hardwood strip floorboards*

from narrow strips of tongued-and-grooved hardwood. These are usually random lengths up to 1.8 m long and 50 mm to 100 mm in width. The heading joints are also usually tongued and grooved.

Figure 290 shows a section through a piece of hardwood strip floorboard. It has a splayed-and-stepped tongue to ease nailing and also to reduce any likelihood of the tongue splitting. The purpose of the recessed back is to ensure positive contact between the board and joist.

It is essential that the newly laid hardwood strip flooring is protected from possible damage by completely covering it with building paper or a polythene sheet, which should remain in position until the building is ready for occupation.

Timber finish to solid floors

There are two main methods which can be used to provide a timber finish to solid floors. The first is to use timber bearers or battens, either bedded in or clipped to the solid floor. These bearers, which are spaced at about 400 mm centres, act as floor joists and thus provide a means of fixing the floorboards. This is illustrated in Figure 291.

The alternative method is to bed the flooring directly to the solid floor using a bituminous mastic compound. This is mostly used for laying wood block or parquet floor finishes. An expansion gap around the perimeter of the floor is required. This should be filled wih either polystyrene or cork so that the blocks are allowed an amount of moisture movement, but are prevented from 'creeping' and closing the gap.

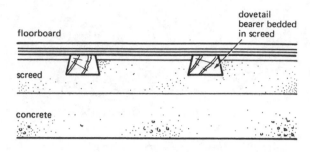

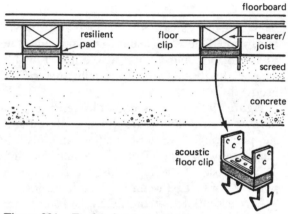

Figure 291 *Timber finish to solid floors*

Fire protection of universal beams

Where universal beams are used in floor construction they must be protected as a fire precaution. This protection is required in order to prevent early structural collapse resulting from the fact that the strength of steel rapidly decreases at temperatures above 300 °C. Various methods of protection include:

A sprayed coat of non-combustible insulating material

A solid casing of concrete

Encasing in expanded metal lathing and plastered

Encasing with plasterboard or other non-combustible material

Figure 292 shows a typical method of encasing a steel beam using plasterboard and a skim coat of finishing plaster. The plasterboard has been fixed to timber cradling members nailed to each joist.

Roofs

Timber roofs are classified according to their shape. The most common types are illustrated in Figure 293.

Flat roof

A flat roof is one where the slope or pitch of the roof surface does not exceed 10°.

Pitched roof

A pitched roof is one where the slope or pitch of the roof surface exceeds 10°. These may be further divided into a number of types:

Lean-to

This is a single or monopitched roof (only one sloping surface).

Gable-end roof

This is a double-pitched roof (having two sloping surfaces) terminating at one or both ends with a triangular section of brickwork.

Hipped-end roof

A double-pitched roof where the roof slope is returned around the shorter sides of the building to form a sloping triangular end.

Mansard roof

A double-pitched roof where each slope of the roof has two pitches. The lower part has a steep pitch, while the upper part rarely exceeds 30°. May be finished with either gable or hipped ends.

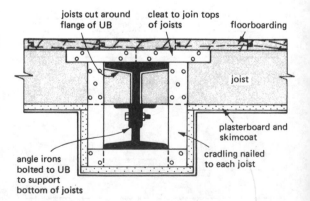

Figure 292 *Cradling to a universal beam*

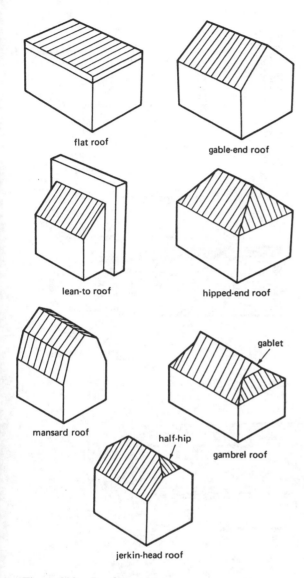

flat roof

gable-end roof

lean-to roof

hipped-end roof

mansard roof

gablet

gambrel roof

half-hip

jerkin-head roof

Figure 293   *Roof types*

Gambrel roof
A double-pitched roof having a small gable or gablet at the ridge and the lower part a half-hip.
Jerkin-head roof
A double-pitched roof which is hipped from the ridge part way to the eaves, and the remainder gabled.

Flat roof construction
Although the surface of the roof is flat, it is not horizontal. It should have a slope or fall on its top surface of about 25 mm for every metre run of the joist (1 in 40). This ensures that rainwater will be quickly cleared and will not accumulate on the roof. There are three ways of forming the slope, as follows.

Level joists (Figure 294)
The joists are laid level and the slope is formed by nailing long tapering pieces of timber (firring pieces) to their top edges. This is the most common method as it forms a level ceiling.

Note: The thinnest end of the firring pieces should be at least 25 mm thick.

Sloping joists (Figure 295)
The joists themselves are laid to the required slope and therefore no firrings are required. The disadvantage is that this forms a sloping ceiling.

Diminishing firrings (Figure 296)
The joists are laid level at right angles to the slope. This method is rarely seen, but it is a useful method when timber boards are used for the roof decking as these should be fixed parallel to the roof slope. This is because the boards are prone to become slightly 'cupped', and if they

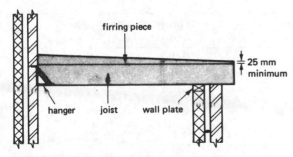

firring piece

25 mm minimum

hanger   joist   wall plate

Figure 294   *Level joist*

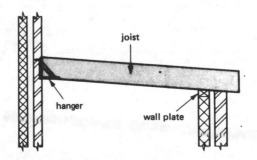

joist

hanger

wall plate

Figure 295   *Sloping joist*

were fixed at right angles to the fall the cupping would restrict the flow of rainwater off the roof and tend to form puddles.

Note: This problem can be overcome to some extent where timber boards are used for the first two forms of flat roof construction, by fixing the boarding diagonally across the roof.

Joist size and spacing

The size of flat roof joists can be found in the same way as floor joists, that is, through the Building Regulations, AD A Tables B, or calculation.

The spacing of the joists depends on the type of material used for the decking. The chart shown in Table 34 can be used as a guide.

Layout of joists

The positioning and levelling of flat roof joists is similar to the positioning and levelling of floor joists, except that flat roofs only occasionally have to be trimmed around openings, e.g. roof lights, chimney stacks etc.

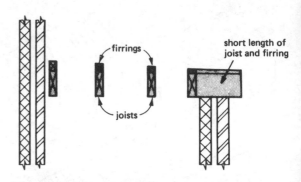

Figure 296   *Diminishing firrings*

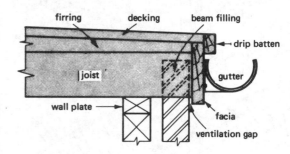

Figure 297   *Flush eaves*

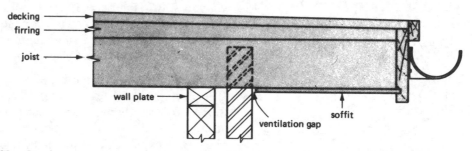

Figure 298   *Overhanging eaves*

Table 34   **Flat roof joist spacing**

Decking material	Finished thickness (mm)	Maximum spacing of joists (mm)
Softwood T & G boarding	19	600
Chipboard	18	450
Chipboard	22	600
Plywood	12	400
Plywood	18	600
Woodwool	50	600

Note: Flat roofs, like floors, also require some form of strutting at their mid-span or at 1.8 m centres.

Eaves details

The section of the roof where the ends of the joist overhang the wall and terminate with the fascia board are known as the eaves. The ends of the joists which run at right angles to the wall can be finished at the eaves in one of two ways:

Flush eaves (Figure 297)
Overhanging eaves (Figure 298)

Both of these methods involve the use of a deep fascia board. An alternative to this is to reduce the depth of the joists at the eaves. Figure 299 shows that this may be done with a splay or square cut to the ends of the joists.

Note: The brickwork is normally continued partially up between the joists to stiffen the joists at their ends. This is called beam filling. The cavity should also be closed, for example with a damp-proof course cavity closer.

Rainwater is discharged from the roof surface into the gutter at the lowest eaves. An angle fillet should be used around the other edges of the roof as shown in Figure 300. This prevents the rainwater from dripping or being blown over the edges of the roof.

Note: An angle fillet should also be fixed along the edges of the roof which abut the brickwork, to enable the roof covering (bitumen roofing felt etc.) to be turned up into the brickwork joint.

In order to finish the eaves which are parallel to the main joists, short joists must be fixed to these at right angles. Figure 301 and 302 show two alternative details that may be used:

Returned eaves   Where short joists are fixed to the main joists using joist hangers.
Ladder frame eaves   Where a ladder frame is made up and fixed to the last joist.

Anchoring joists

In order to prevent strong winds lifting the roof, the joists must be anchored to the walls at a

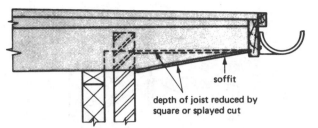

Figure 299   *Reducing joist depth at eaves*

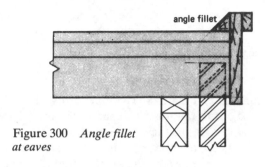

Figure 300   *Angle fillet at eaves*

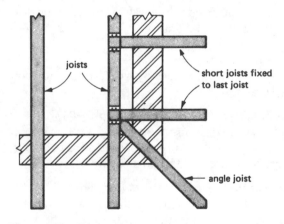

Figure 301   *Returned eaves*

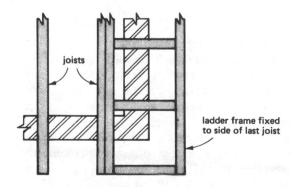

Figure 302   *Ladder frame eaves*

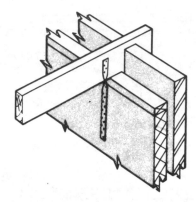

Figure 303   *Anchoring flat roof joist*

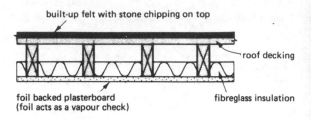

Figure 304   *Insulation in roof space*

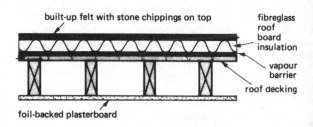

Figure 305   *Insulation above roof space*

maximum of 2 m centres. This anchoring must be carried out to the joists that run both parallel and at right angles to the wall. Figure 303 shows a flat roof joist anchored to the wall using an anchoring strap. The strap is nailed to the side of the joist and fixed to the wall by either nailing or plugging and screwing.

Thermal insulation

There are two methods by which a flat roof can be insulated.

Insulation in the roof space (Figure 304)

This has thermal insulation and a vapour check at ceiling level. The roof space itself is cold and must be vented to the outside air.

Insulation above the roof space (Figure 305)

This has its thermal insulation and vapour barrier placed over the roof decking. The roof space is kept warmer than the outside air temperature.

Sheet-metal-covered flat roofs

When sheet metal such as lead, copper or zinc is used as a flat roof covering material, wood-cored rolls in the direction of the fall and stepped drips across the fall must be incorporated in the roof construction. This is to enable sheets to be joined and also limit the size of the sheets to combat the effects of expansion in warm weather. Figure 306 shows a part plan and section through a lead flat roof with rolls, drips and a box gutter.

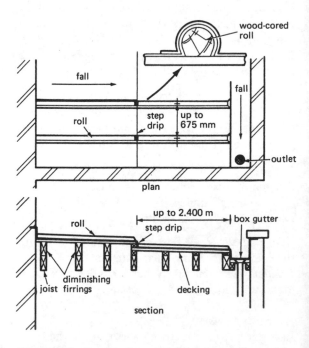

Figure 306   *Section through lead-covered flat roof*

Pitched roof construction

Timber pitched roofs may be divided into two broad but distinct categories:

Traditional framed roofs Entirely constructed *in situ* from loose timber sections and utilizing simple jointing methods.

Prefabricated trussed rafters and roof trusses Normally manufactured in factory conditions.

Traditional roofs

These may be constructed as either single or double roofs according to their span (see Figure 307). The rafters in single roofs span from wall plate to the ridge without any intermediate support.

Roofs of greater span have rafters of such a length that they require an intermediate support to prevent sagging. This support is normally provided by the use of a purlin in mid-span.

Figure 308 shows a section through a single close-couple roof suitable for limited spans. A central binder may be hung from the ridge to bind together and prevent any sagging in the ceiling joists.

Single roofs are not economically viable for large spans because of the large-section timbers required. Where the span of the roof exceeds about 5.5 m, a double roof should be used.

Figure 309 shows a section through a double roof which is suitable for spans up to 7.2 m. It consists of the following components:

Common rafters These are cut to the ridge and bird's mouthed over the wall plate as usual.
Purlin This is best notched into the struts.

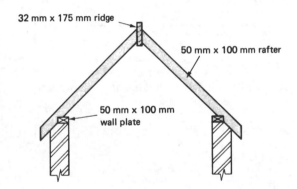

Figure 307 *Sections through single and double roofs*

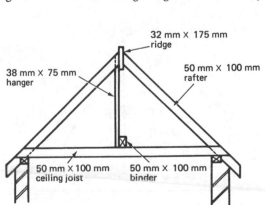

Figure 308 *Close-couple roof*

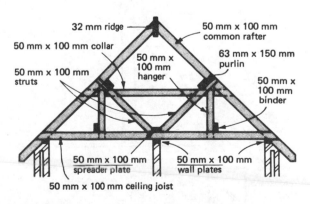

Figure 309 *Double roof for spans up to 7.2 m*

Struts These transfer the loads imposed by the purlins on to a load-bearing partition wall.

Spreader plate This provides a suitable bearing for the struts.

Collar This acts as a collar tie and also provides some support for the purlins.

Ceiling joists As well as being joists on which the ceiling is fixed, these also act as ties for each pair of rafters at wall plate level.

Binders and hangers These stiffen and support the ceiling joists in their mid-span, to prevent them from sagging and distorting the ceiling.

Note: The struts, collars and hangers are spaced evenly along the roof at every third or fourth pair of rafters.

Mansard roofs are constructed so that accommodation can be provided in the roof space. Traditionally the roof was constructed from framed mansard roof trusses which were a combination of a king post truss and a queen post truss, as illustrated in Figure 310. The modern method of forming a mansard roof is illustrated in Figure 311. This detail is suitable for roofs up to 6 m in span.

Pitched roof end and intersections

The ends of pitched roofs may be terminated with either a gable wall or a sloping hip-end roof or a combination of both, e.g. gambrel roof and jerkin roof. Figure 312 shows the finish to a gable end, and Figure 313 gives the typical finish to a hip end.

Where two pitched roofs intersect a valley is formed between the two sloping surfaces. This valley may be constructed in one of two ways. Either a valley rafter is used and the feet of the

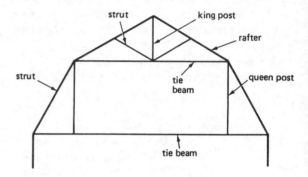

Figure 310   *Outline of traditional mansard roof*

Figure 311   *Mansard roof*

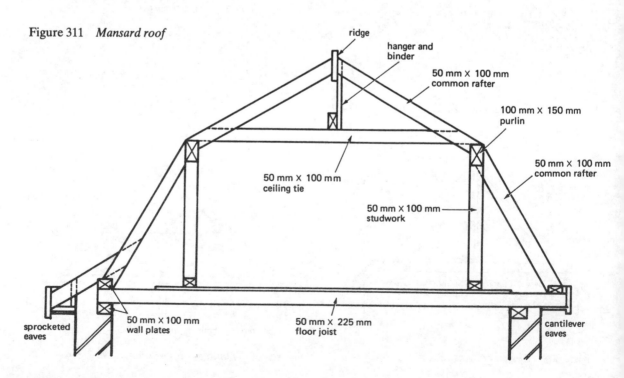

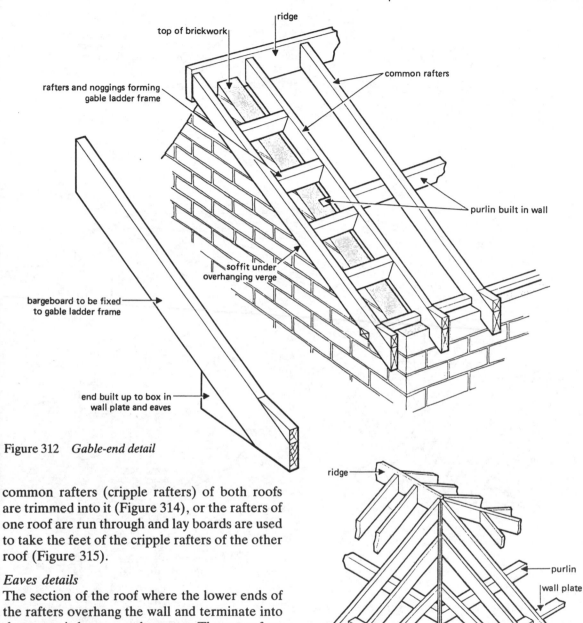

Figure 312   *Gable-end detail*

common rafters (cripple rafters) of both roofs
are trimmed into it (Figure 314), or the rafters of
one roof are run through and lay boards are used
to take the feet of the cripple rafters of the other
roof (Figure 315).

Eaves details
The section of the roof where the lower ends of
the rafters overhang the wall and terminate into
the gutter is known as the eaves. There are four
methods of finishing eaves in common use.
These are illustrated in Figure 316.

Flush eaves
In this method the ends of the rafters are cut off
10 mm – 15 mm past the face of the brickwork
and the fascia board is nailed directly to them to
provide a fixing point for the gutter. The small
gap between the back of the fascia board and the
brickwork allows for roof space ventilation.

Figure 313   *Hip-end detail*

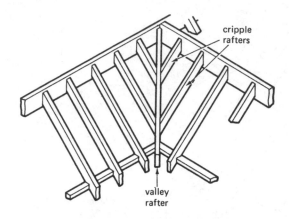

Figure 314   *Valley using valley rafter*

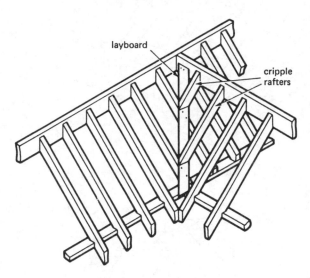

Figure 315   *Valley using lay board*

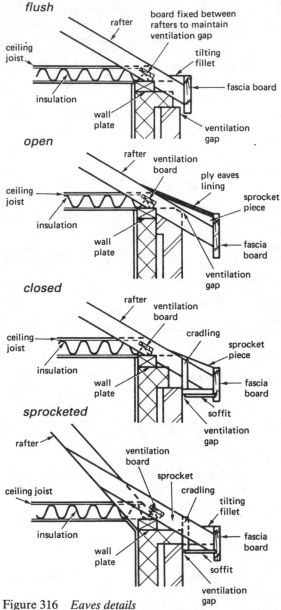

Figure 316   *Eaves details*

Open eaves

These project well past the face of the wall to provide additional weather protection. The ends of the rafters should be prepared as they are exposed to view from the ground. In cheaper-quality work the fascia boards are often omitted and the gutter brackets fixed directly to the side of the rafter.

Closed eaves

These overhang the face of the wall the same as open eaves except that the ends of the rafters are closed in with a soffit. Cradling brackets are nailed to the sides of the rafters to support the soffit at the wall edge.

Sprocketed eaves

On steeply pitched roofs the flow of rainwater off the roof surface has a tendency to overshoot the gutter. Sprockets can be nailed to the sides of each rafter to slow down the rainwater before it reaches the eaves and thus reduce the likelihood of it overshooting. In addition they also enhance the appearance of the roof, giving it a 'bell-cast' finish.

Note: Provision for roof space ventilation must be made in all eaves details; that is, all roofs must be cross-ventilated by permanent vents which have an area equivalent to a continuous gap along both sides of the roof of 10 mm, or 25 mm when the roof has a pitch which is less than 15 degrees.

Parapet gutter

Where a pitched roof terminates at a parapet wall, framework for a lead- or zinc-lined parapet gutter must be formed. Figure 317 illustrates typical details of a parapet gutter.

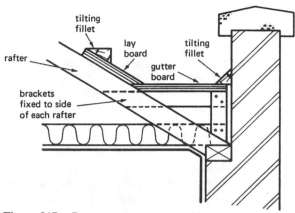

Figure 317 *Parapet gutter*

Trimming

Where openings occur in roofs, in either the rafters or ceiling joists or both, these have to be trimmed. Framing anchors or housing joints are used to join the trimmers, trimmings and trimmed components together.

Figure 318 is a section through a ceiling hatch showing the trimmed opening and hatch lining.

Figure 319 is a part plan and section through a roof showing the trimming around a chimney stack and the back gutter detail.

Note: To comply with the Building Regulations, no combustible material, including timber, is to be placed within 200 mm of the inside of the flue lining; or, where the thickness of the chimney surrounding the flue is less than 200 mm, no combustible material must be placed within 40 mm of the chimney.

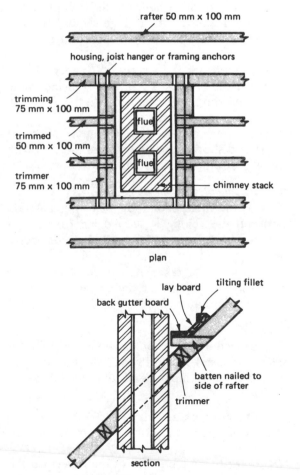

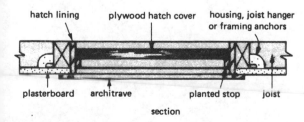

Figure 318 *Trimming to loft hatch*

Figure 319 *Trimming to chimney stack*

Whenever possible, openings for loft hatches and chimneys in roofs made up of trussed rafters, should be accommodated within the trussed rafter spacing. If a larger opening is required for the chimney stack, a trussed rafter is placed on either side of the stack and the space between is infilled using normal rafters and ceiling joists.

Water tank platforms

These are ideally situated centrally over a load-bearing wall. The platform should consist of boarding supported by joists laid on top of the ceiling joists and at right angles to them. Figure 320 shows a typical water tank platform.

Anchoring roofs

Rafters can be skew nailed to the wall plates or, in areas noted for their high winds, framing anchors or truss clips where appropriate can be used.

Wall plates must be secured to the wall with straps at 2 m centres. The rafters adjacent to the gable end should also be tied into the wall with straps at 2 m centres.

The rafters and ceiling joists adjacent to the gable end should also be tied into the wall with metal restraint straps at 2 m centres.

Thermal insulation in pitched roofs

This is normally done by placing insulation between the ceiling joists and incorporating a vapour check, such as foil-backed plasterboard, at ceiling level.

Care must be taken not to block the eaves with the insulating material as the roof space must be ventilated (see Figure 316).

Roof erection

The procedure for roof erection is similar for most untrussed types of roof. The procedure of erection for a hipped-end roof would be as follows:

1   The wall plate, having been bedded and levelled by the bricklayer, must be tied down.
2   Mark out the position of the rafters on the wall plate.
3   Make up two temporary A-frames. These

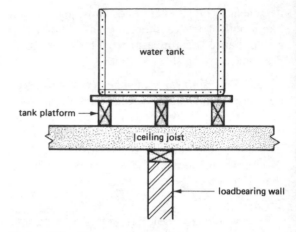

Figure 320   *Water tank platform*

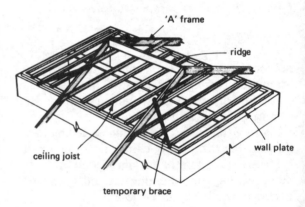

Figure 321   *Roof erection*

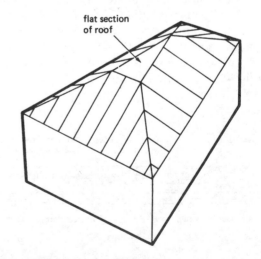

Figure 322   *Irregular plan roof*

each consist of two common rafters with a temporary tie joining them at the top, leaving a space for the ridge and a temporary tie nailed to them in the position of the ceiling joists.

4 Fix ceiling joists in position.
5 Stand up the A-frames at either end of the roof in the position of the last common rafter and skew nail to the wall plate.
6 Fix temporary braces to hold the A-frames upright.
7 Mark out the spacing of the rafters on the ridge and fix in position (see Figure 321).
8 Fix the crown and hip rafters.
9 Fix the purlins, struts and binders.
10 Fix the remaining common rafters and jack rafters.
11 Fix the collars and the hangers.
12 Finish the roof at the eaves with fascia and soffit as required.

Irregular plan roofs

In general most buildings are regular on plan and have equally pitched roofs, i.e. they have square corners and both sides of the roof sloping. Sometimes, to create an architectural feature or to make use of a limited tapering site, buildings are constructed with an irregular plan. This therefore requires the use of irregular roof shapes and unequal pitches.

Figure 322 illustrates an equal-pitched hip-end

roof on a building whose long sides are not parallel.

Note: All of the rafters are kept square on plan to their respective wall plate, to avoid splayed plumb and seat cuts to the common rafters.

This necessitates a split ridge and a flat section to the top of the roof. The alternatives to this, which are impractical, would result in a sloping ridge and cut courses of roof tiles, or sloping eaves.

Figure 323 shows a method of forming the split ridge where the flat section is a maximum of about 300 mm. Figure 324 shows the detail for wider flat sections.

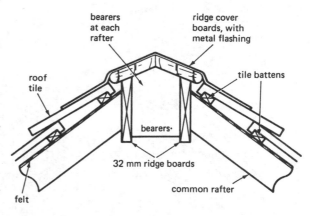

Figure 323   *Split-ridge details*

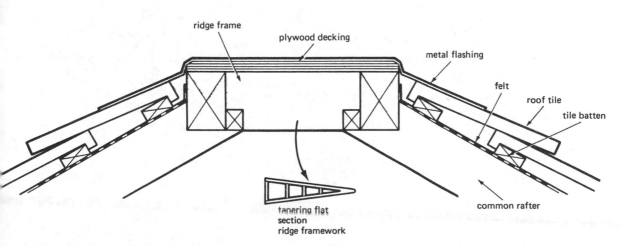

Figure 324   *Split-ridge detail for wider flat section*

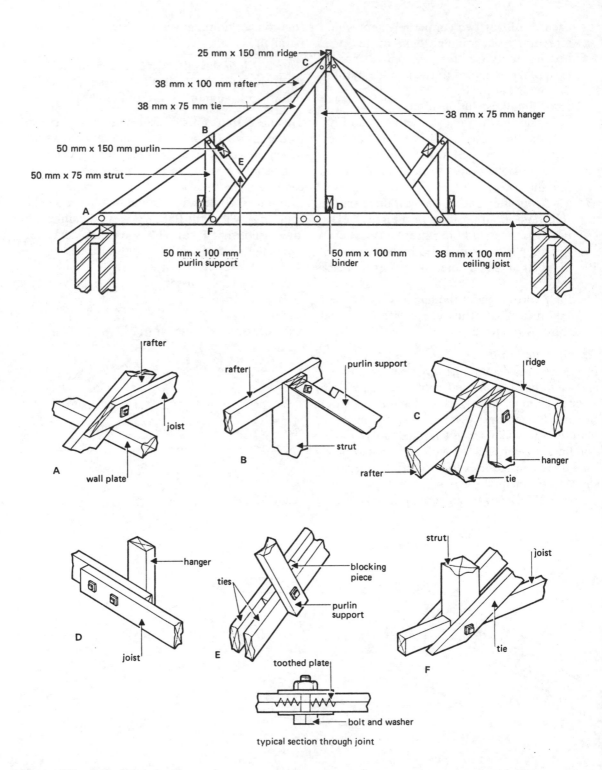

Figure 325   *Bolted truss details*

Prefabricated trussed rafters and roof trusses
Prefabricated roof components developed because of the need to:

Reduce the amount of timber in a roof
Simplify the often complicated on-site cutting of
  a roof
Enable large spans without the need for
  intermediate supporting walls

The earlier designs were bolted roof trusses,
which developed from the traditional king and
queen post trusses. Then came nail plate trussed
rafters. The essential difference between the two
is that in a trussed rafter roof every rafter is
trussed and carries only its own proportion of
the total load, whereas bolted roof trusses
support a purlin and carry the roof loads from a
number of adjacent common rafters.

Bolted roof trusses
The component parts of bolted trusses have
overlapped joints which are connected up using
bolts and toothed plates. They are normally
prefabricated in a shop and arrive on site in two
easily managed halves, which must be bolted
together once the truss has been positioned.

Figure 325 shows a typical bolted truss with
enlarged joint details. The trusses are spaced
along the roof at about 1.8 m centres, to support
the roof components. The purlins and ceiling
binders are then fixed to these. The spaces
between the trusses are infilled with normal
common rafters and ceiling joists. Figure 326 is a
line diagram of this arrangement. Half-trusses
are used in place of the crown rafter for
hipped-end roofs, normal hip and jack rafters
being inserted as required.

Timber roof trusses for industrial buildings
are rarely encountered in new work as these are
almost exclusively made of steel, although the
type of trusses detailed in Figure 327 may be met
in maintenance and rehabilitation work.

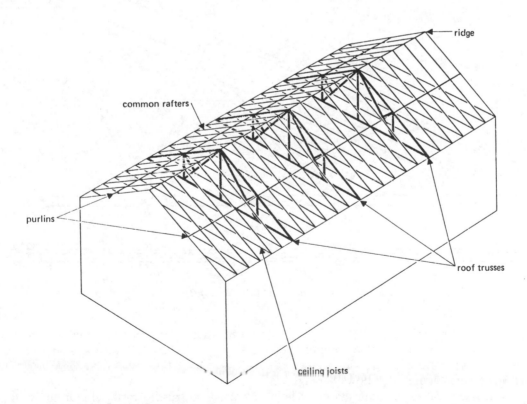

Figure 326   *Roof arrangement using bolted trusses*

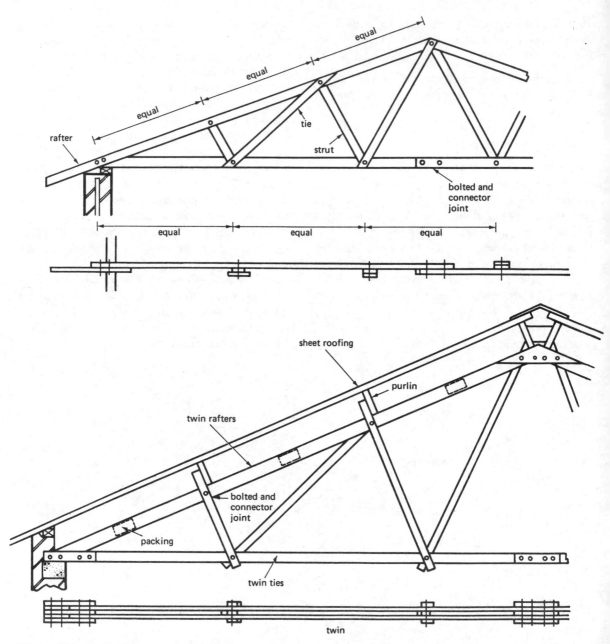

Figure 327   *Half-elevation and plan of two alternative industrial roof trusses*

Nail plate trussed rafters
These are prefabricated by a number of specialist manufacturers in a wide range of shapes and sizes. Figure 328 shows a range of standard trussed rafter configurations. They consist of prepared timber laid out in one plane, with their butt joints fastened with nail plates.

Figure 329 shows a typical design for a trussed rafter.

Note: The trussed rafter sits on the wall plate and is not bird's mouthed over it.

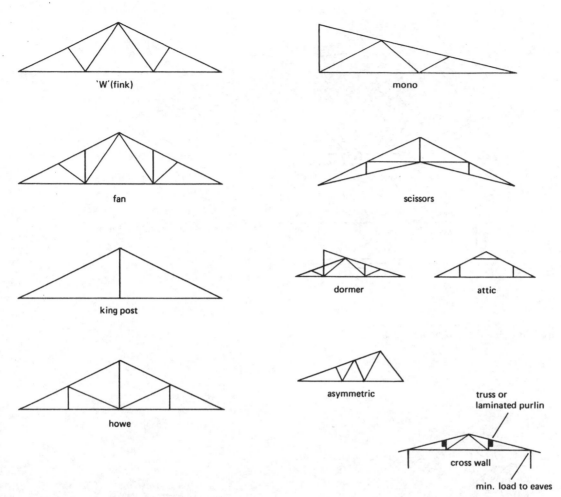

Figure 328 *Standard trussed rafter configurations*

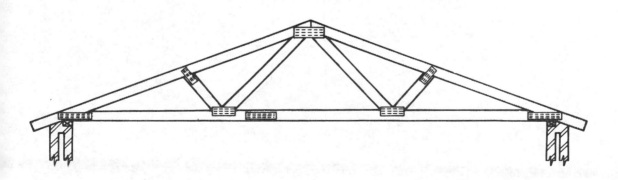

Figure 329 *Nail plate trussed rafter*

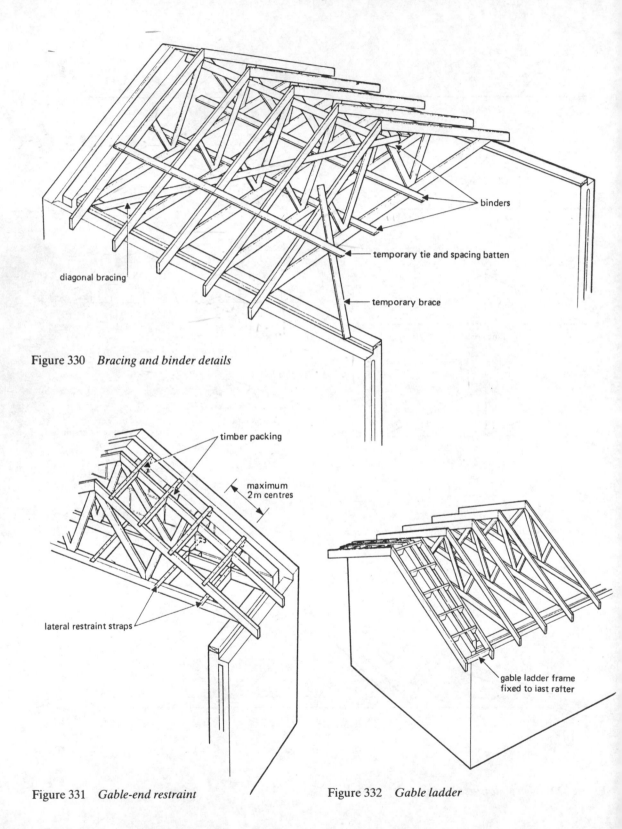

Figure 330   *Bracing and binder details*

binders

temporary tie and spacing batten

temporary brace

diagonal bracing

timber packing

maximum 2 m centres

lateral restraint straps

gable ladder frame fixed to last rafter

Figure 331   *Gable-end restraint*

Figure 332   *Gable ladder*

In use the trusses are spaced along the roof at between 400 mm and 600 mm centres and fixed to the wall plate, preferably using truss clips.

In order to provide lateral stability the roof requires binders at both ceiling and apex level and diagonal rafter bracing fixed to the underside of the rafters (see Figure 330). These must be fixed in accordance with the individual manufacturer's requirements.

Figure 331 shows how the gable wall must be tied back to the roof for support. This is done using lateral restraint straps at 2 m maximum centres both up the rafter slope and along the ceiling tie.

Roof end and intersections using trussed rafters
Prefabricated gable ladders as shown in Figure 332 can be fixed to the last truss when an overhanging verge is required. Bargeboards and soffits are in turn nailed directly to the ladder.

Where hip ends and valleys occur in trussed rafter roofs, these may be formed either by using loose timber and cutting normal hip and valley rafters etc. in the traditional manner, or by using specially manufactured components.

Figure 333 illustrates how a hip end may be formed using a compound hip girder truss to support hip mono trusses. Loose hip rafters, infill jack rafters and ceiling joists must still be cut and fixed in the normal way.

Figure 334 shows how a valley may be formed where two roofs intersect at a tee junction, using diminishing jack rafter frames nailed on to lay boards. The ends of the rafters on the main roof are carried across the opening by suspending them from the compound girder truss using suitable joist hangers.

Trimming
Wherever possible, openings in roofs for chimney stacks and loft hatches should be accommodated within the trussed rafter spacing. If larger openings are required the method shown in Figure 335 can be used. This entails positioning a trussed rafter on either side of the opening and infilling the space between with normal rafters, purlins and ceiling joists. For safety reasons, on no account should trussed rafters be trimmed or otherwise modified without the structural designers' approval.

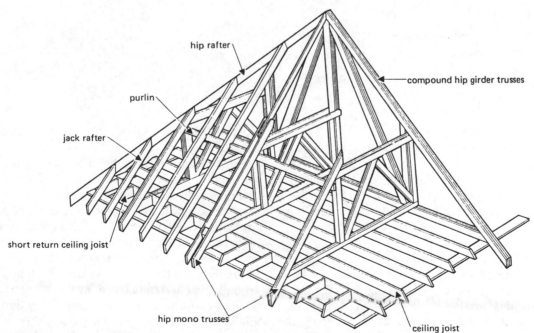

Figure 333 *Hip-end detail*

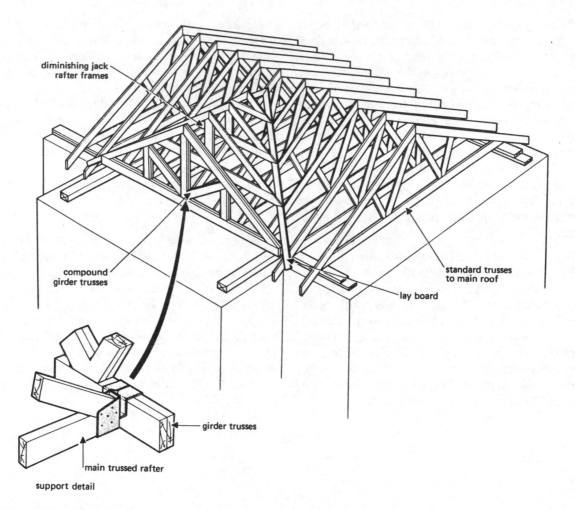

diminishing jack
rafter frames

compound
girder trusses

standard trusses
to main roof

lay board

girder trusses

main trussed rafter

support detail

Figure 334   *Valley detail*

Water tank platforms

These should be placed centrally in the roof with the load spread over at least three trussed rafters. The lower bearers of the platform should be positioned so that the load is transferred as near as possible to the mid-third points of the span (see Figure 336).

Erection of trussed rafters

The main problem encountered with the erection of trussed rafters is handling. In order not to strain the joints of the trussed rafters they should be lifted from the eaves, keeping the rafter in a vertical plane with its apex upper-

most. Inadequate labour or care will lead to truss damage.

Trussed rafters may be lifted into position with the aid of a crane, either singly from the node joints using a spreader bar and slings, or in banded sets. In both cases these should be controlled from the ground using a guide rope to prevent swinging. In addition, where large cranes are available, the entire roof may be assembled, braced, felted and battened at ground level and then lifted into position as one whole weatherproof unit, requiring only tiling at a later stage. This method is particularly suited to the rapid erection of timber frame buildings.

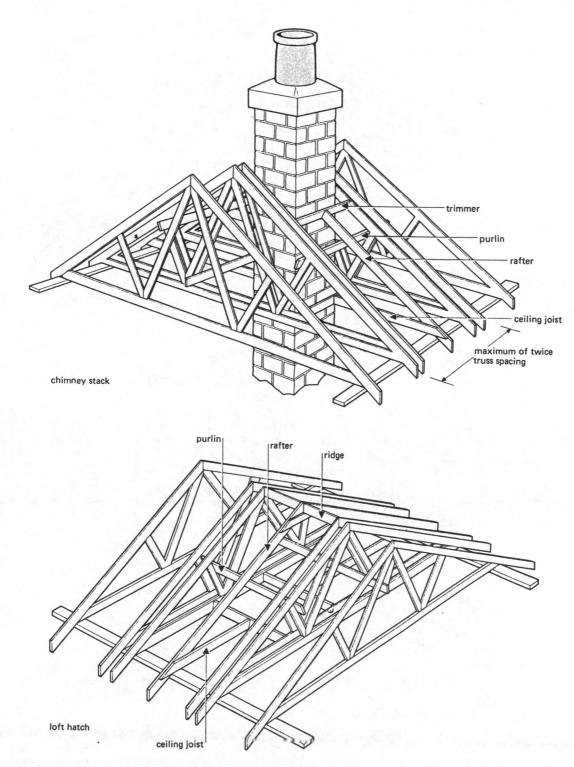

Figure 335   *Trimming to openings*

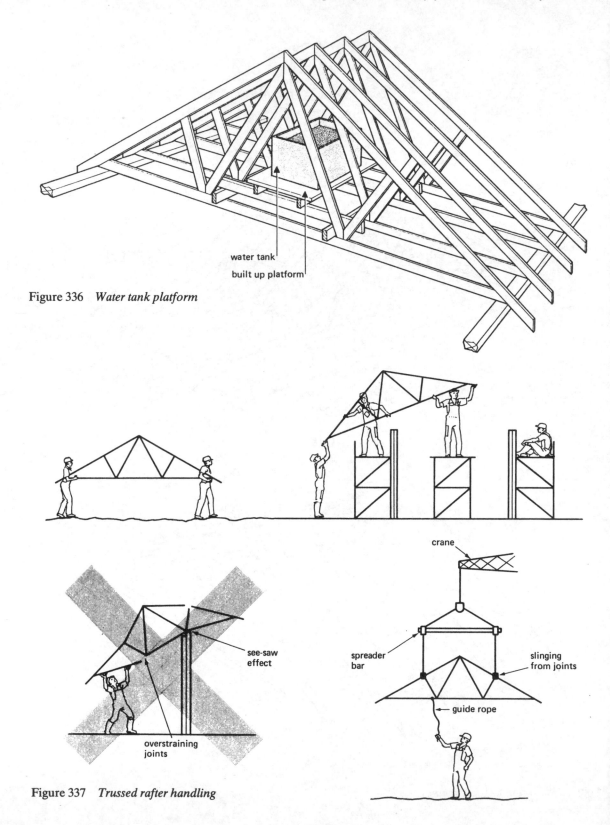

Figure 336   *Water tank platform*

water tank

built up platform

see-saw
effect

overstraining
joints

Figure 337   *Trussed rafter handling*

crane

spreader
bar

slinging
from joints

guide rope

Figure 337 illustrates the handling of trussed rafters.

The erection procedure

The erection procedure for a gable-end roof using trussed rafters is as follows:

1 Mark the position of the trusses along the wall plates (see Figure 338).
2 Once up on the roof, the first trussed rafter can be placed in position at the end of the under-rafter diagonal bracing. It can then be fixed at the eaves, plumbed and temporarily braced.
3 Fix the remaining trussed rafters in position one at a time up to the gable end, temporarily tying each rafter to the preceding one with a batten.
4 Fix diagonal bracing and binders.
5 Repeat the previous procedure at the other end of the roof.
6 Position and fix the trusses between the two braced ends one at a time, and fix binders.
7 Fix ladder frames and restraint straps.
8 Finish the roof at the eaves and verge with fascia, bargeboard and soffit as required.

Dormer windows

These are vertical windows that project from a sloping roof surface to provide daylight and ventilation to a room in the roof space. The triangular sides of the dormer (cheeks) above the main roof are framed out with studding and covered with tiles, sheet metal or timber cladding.

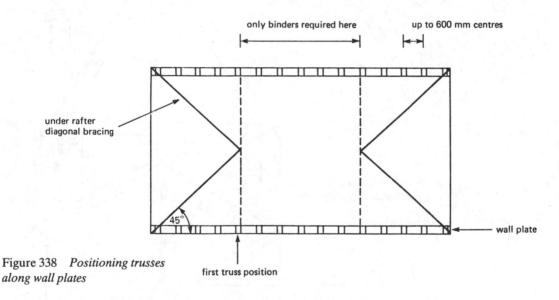

Figure 338 *Positioning trusses along wall plates*

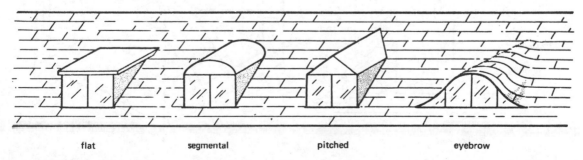

flat   segmental   pitched   eyebrow

Figure 339 *Dormer roofs*

The actual roof over the dormer window which extends from the main roof can be constructed in various ways, as illustrated in Figure 339, although flat or pitched roofs are most commonly used.

Figure 340 is an isometric view of the basic framework construction for a flat roof dormer. Twin rafters are used on either side of the opening to carry the increased load.

Figure 341 illustrates a section through a dormer window showing typical construction details.

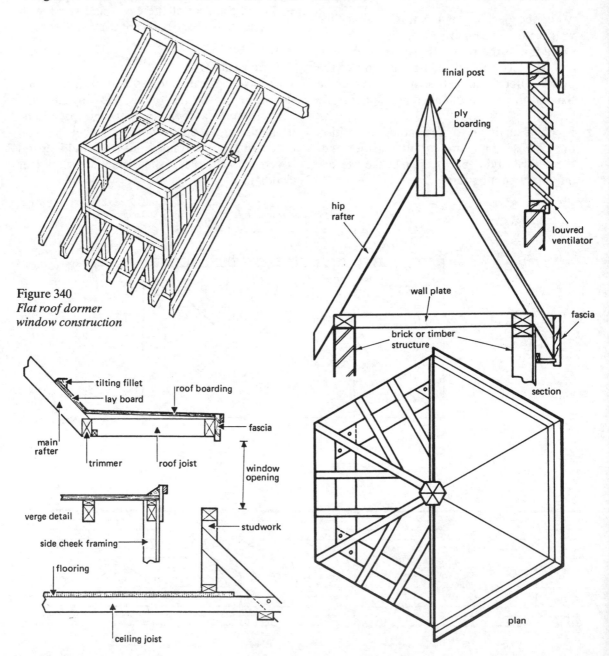

Figure 340
Flat roof dormer
window construction

Figure 341   *Dormer details*

Figure 342   *Hexagonal turret roof details*

Ornamental roofs

This classification includes turrets, spires and domes. These are all forms of fairly small decorative roofs, normally weatherproofed in sheet lead, copper or zinc and used to cover small structures such as bell towers and church steeples etc. The construction of each roof is basically the same irrespective of its plan shape, which may be square, polygonal or circular.

Figure 342 shows the plan and section of a hexagonal turret roof which may be mounted on a brick or timber structure. It consists of a wall plate, halved together to form the plan shape. Hip rafters are bird's mouthed over the wall plate at their lower end and are tenoned into a finial post at the top. The hips should be backed to enable the roof to be boarded. Jack rafters are used between the hips.

Also illustrated in Figure 342 is a section through a louvred ventilator, which is often incorporated in the supporting structure at the top of a tower to provide ventilation.

The main differences in the construction of turrets, spires and domes may be stated briefly. Spires tend to be taller and more steeply pitched than turrets. These therefore require special consideration in the method of tying down to the main structure, because of the considerable wind pressures they are subjected to. Domes have exactly the same construction details as turrets except that the top edges of the hips and jacks will have been precut to the required curve before erection.

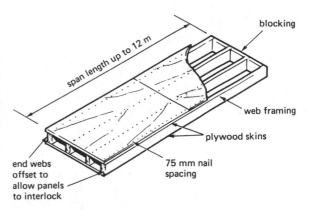

Figure 343 *Stressed skin panel*

Stressed skin panels

A stressed skin plywood panel consists of timber framing members called webs, onto which a skin of plywood is fixed. The panels can be single skin for most situations or double skin for use in high-load conditions; a double-skin panel is illustrated in Figure 343. The panels are used as prefabricated floor or roof panels, especially where long uninterrupted spans are required.

Stressed skin panels differ from normal joists and boarding in that the plywood, in addition to supporting the load between the framing, also contributes to the strength and stiffness of the framing itself. This is because the plywood is glued and nailed to the framing. Thus the panels function as an efficient structural unit transmitting the stresses between the plywood and framing.

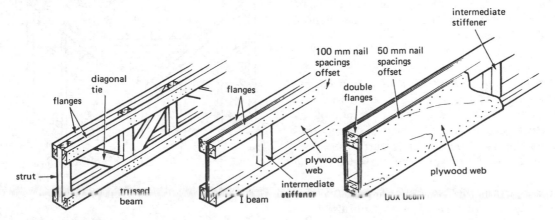

Figure 344 *Built-up beams*

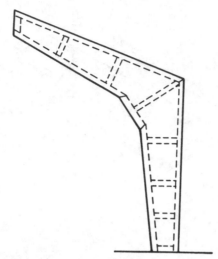

Figure 345   *Plywood portal frame*

Built-up beams

Built-up nailed and glued beams have a distinct advantage over solid timber sections or glulam. Figure 344 illustrates typical details of three different methods of forming built-up beams. Each consists of top and bottom flanges, spaced by either ties and struts or plywood webs and stiffeners. It is possible to use built-up beams for far greater spans than solid timber, and they have a much better weight to strength and stiffness ratio than either solid timber or glulam sections.

They may be used as purlins or support beams in roof construction and as binders or main support beams in double or framed floors. It is possible to manufacture portal frames using either the I or box beam method of construction, as illustrated in Figure 345.

Shell roof construction

A timber shell roof consists of a thin curved lightweight membrane acting as a stressed skin that obtains its strength as a result of its curvature. Laminated edge beams are incorporated around the perimeter to carry the membrane's forces and strengthen the edge of the shell.

Apart from the aesthetic appeal of this exciting geometric form of roof, shells also have the advantage of being able to form large clear

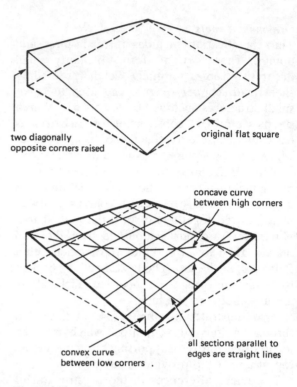

Figure 346   *Hyperbolic paraboloid formation*

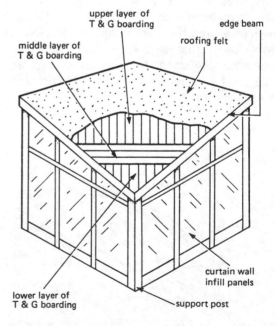

Figure 347   *Hyperbolic paraboloid shell roof*

spans without the need for intermediate support. In addition their lightweight construction enables the enclosing walls to be of a mainly non-load-bearing nature, which in turn allows smaller more simple foundations.

Timber shell roofs have been used in various forms to cover many different types of building, including schools, churches, factories, libraries, sports complexes and leisure centres.

The form of shell roof most often used is the hyperbolic paraboloid. It is created by raising the two diagonally opposite corners of a square to a higher level than the other two corners (see Figure 346). The roof derives its name from the curves produced between its diagonally opposite corners. Between the low corners a convex curve is produced and between the high corners a concave curve, whereas all cross sections parallel to the edges of the shell will be straight lines.

Note: In general, shells with a greater curvature, i.e. those with a greater rise between high and low corners, are stiffer than shells of the same plan size but with a lesser curvature, i.e. a smaller rise between high and low corners.

The hyperbolic paraboloid timber shell roof shown in Figure 347 is formed by three layers of tongued-and-grooved boards glued with a synthetic resin adhesive and nailed together with square twisted-shank or annular nails. Scaffolding is erected before construction to allow access to the underside of the roof, and more importantly to provide support for the lower layer of boarding. The middle layer is nailed to the lower layer, while the nails in the upper should penetrate right through the middle layer and into the lower layer. It can be seen that these boards are laid diagonally across the roof with the grain direction at right angles to its adjacent layers.

Any end jointing of the boards in the upper layers may be simple butts, although for strength it is normally recommended that the bottom layer is finger jointed. It is also advisable to use a better quality timber on the bottom layer as this will be varnished to provide the finished ceiling.

Note: Two layers of boarding may be used for the membrane of limited span shell roofs.

The edge beams, normally glulam, can be either made in one piece and positioned below the boarding or made in two pieces and positioned half above and half below the boarding as shown in Figure 348.

In order to stop the shell flattening out, the low corners are tied together with the aid of a mild steel tie bar that has been threaded at each end. Figure 349 illustrates this tie bar and also the method of fixing the edge beams in position.

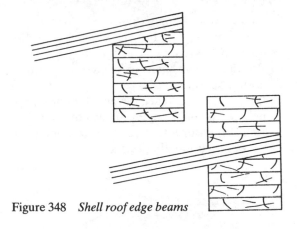

Figure 348   *Shell roof edge beams*

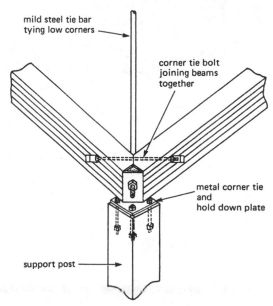

Figure 349   *Shell roof tie bar*

Alternatively some form of buttress can be used to withstand the outward diagonal thrust of the shell at its low corners.

Wherever possible the edge beams should be given support by posts, walls or curtain walling mullions. In any case the low corners must be well supported as these take the main load of the roof. Also the high corners must be tied down to prevent lifting by wind forces.

Sequence of operations

The sequence of operations for the erection of a hyperbolic paraboloid shell roof is as follows:

1 Erect corner support posts.
2 Assemble scaffolding to support the first layer of boards.
3 Position lower half of beams and bolt to corner support posts.
4 Glue and nail each layer of boarding in position at right angles to each other, taking care to ensure that a close contact exists between all meeting surfaces.

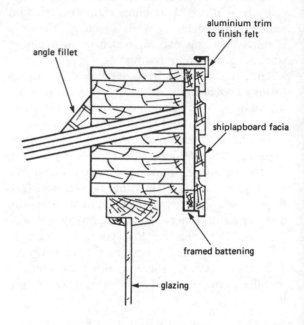

Figure 350 *Shell roof edge detail*

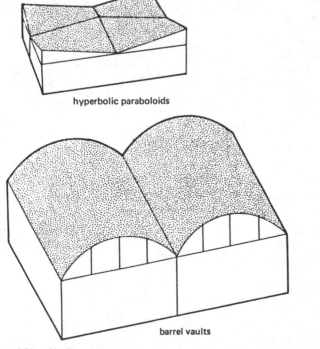

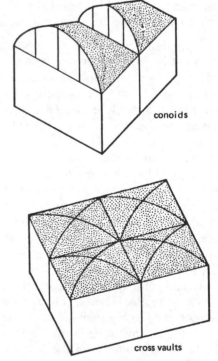

Figure 351 *Shell roof forms*

5 Position upper half of beams. These are glued and fixed using either long square twisted-shank nails or coach screws.
6 Fix angle fillets to facilitate the dressing of the roofing felt over the edge beam. See Figure 350 for a typical edge detail.
7 Fix fascia.
8 Dismantle scaffolding.
9 Felt over the roof to make it watertight.

Alternative forms of shell

Multiple hyperbolic paraboloid shell roofs can be formed by joining a number of shells side by side (see Figure 351). Many other forms of shell roof are possible, some of which are also shown in Figure 351. Although vastly different in shape, these shells have a similar formation in that they all consist of a curved layered membrane.

Suspended ceilings

These are also known as false ceilings. They are mainly used in concrete or steel frame buildings, such as offices, shops, factories and schools, to provide a decorative finished ceiling.

The main reasons for the installation of suspended ceilings are as follows:

To improve the thermal insulation and so reduce heat loss
For sound insulation purposes
For structural fire protection
To conceal structural beams
To route and conceal services, heating ventilation ducts and sprinkler systems etc.
To create integrated lighting

In addition suspended ceilings may be used in houses, particularly older ones with high ceilings. This is usually to reduce the height of the

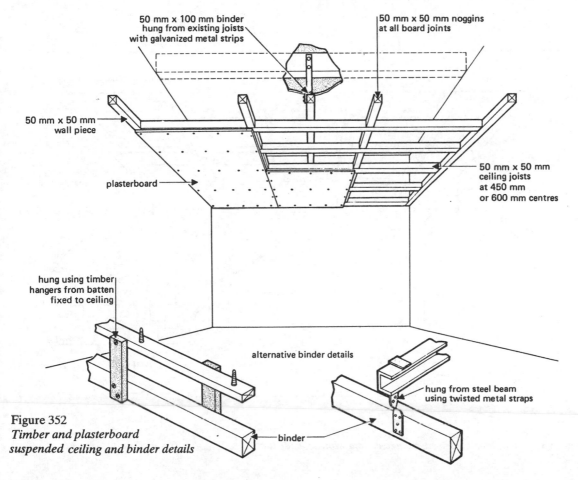

Figure 352
*Timber and plasterboard
suspended ceiling and binder details*

ceiling, thus creating a better-proportioned room, or to conceal an existing ceiling which may be in a bad state of repair.

Ceilings may be suspended from the underside of roof or floor structures using either a timber framework or a proprietary system.

Timber-framed suspended ceilings

A timber and plasterboard suspended ceiling is shown in Figure 352. This consists of ceiling joists spanning the shortest dimension of the area and skew nailed between the wall pieces which have been previously fixed at the required height. Binders are hung at intervals from the main structure to provide intermediate support to the ceiling joists and prevent them sagging. The method used to hang the binders will depend on the type of main structure and the distances between it and the suspended ceiling.

Alternative binder details are also given in Figure 352.

The actual ceiling finish will normally be either tongued-and-grooved matchboarding, acoustic tiles or plasterboard. Where plasterboard is used, the boards should be staggered and noggins fixed between the ceiling joists to support the joints.

A counter-battened suspended ceiling is shown in Figure 353. This method, which is also known as brandering, is used when the existing ceiling base surface is not level enough or is otherwise unsuitable for the application of the required ceiling finish. The counter-battens are fixed to the ceiling base surface, lined in and packed down as required to provide a level surface.

The ceiling finish itself can again be either tongued-and-grooved matchboarding, acoustic tiles or plasterboard. Figure 353 illustrates an

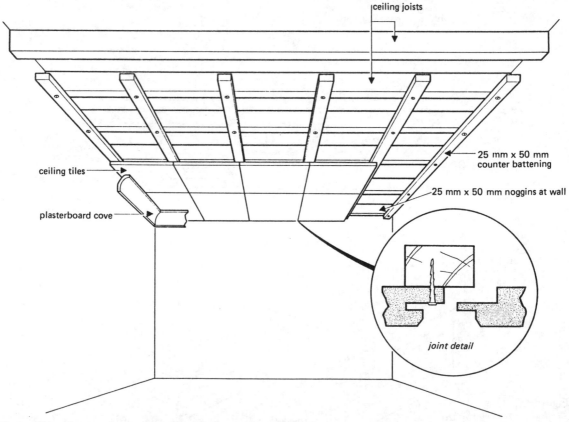

Figure 353   *Counter-batten suspended ceiling with acoustic tiles*

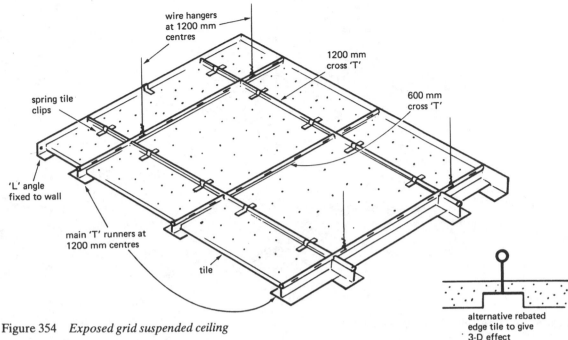

Figure 354   *Exposed grid suspended ceiling*

acoustic tile finish. These tiles have a stepped tongued-and-grooved joint to enable a secret nailed fixing, although they may also be stuck in position with an impact adhesive. The joint between the wall and ceiling in this example has been masked with a plasterboard cove.

Proprietary systems

There are two main metal suspended grid ceiling systems in use: the exposed grid system and the concealed Z-bar system.

Exposed grid system (Figure 354)

The exposed grid system is used to support either 600 mm × 1200 mm or 600 mm square plasterboard, or acoustic or other decorative infill tiles. The grid consists of galvanized steel main T-section runners spaced at 1200 mm centres and hung on wires from the structural soffit or on straps fixed to timber joists. 1200 mm cross-tees interlock into the main runners at 600 mm centres. Where 600 mm square tiles are to be used, 600 mm cross-tees are interlocked into the centre of the 1200 mm cross-tees. An L-sectioned angle is fixed around the perimeter of the room to support and finish the edge.

The exposed parts of the grid are stove enamelled or capped in aluminium. A wide variety of finishes is available, including white, black, silver and timber effect.

The tiles are simply dropped in place between the T-sections and secured using spring clips. A number of tiles are normally left unclipped in order to provide a convenient access to the space above. The ceiling may be given a three-dimensional effect by using rebated edge tiles.

Concealed Z-bar system (Figure 355)

This is a concealed grid system for supporting various types of grooved-edge tiles. The system consists of galvanized main channels which support the Z-sections. The Z-sections are clipped to the main channels at either 300 mm or 600 mm centres (depending on the tile size). The bottom flanges of the Z-section provide support for the two opposite sides of the tiles, the other sides of the tiles being joined by a metal splice or noggin tee.

L-section angles are used to support the tiles and finish the ceiling where it abuts the walls.

Before fixing, the layout of the components must be planned so that the tiles are centralized

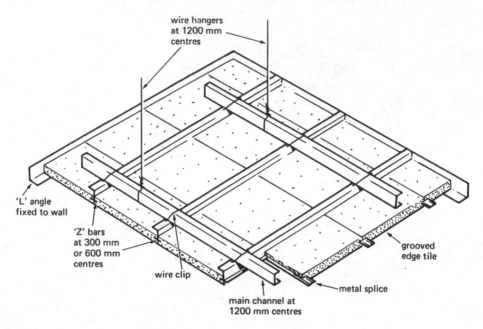

wire hangers
at 1200 mm
centres

'L' angle
fixed to wall

'Z' bars
at 300 mm
or 600 mm
centres

wire clip

grooved
edge tile

metal splice

main channel at
1200 mm centres

Figure 355   *Concealed Z-bar suspended ceiling*

and any cut tiles around the perimeter are the same width on opposite sides of the room.

Levelling

The levelling of both timber framed and proprietary suspended ceilings is extremely important, as any distortion or misalignment will be evident in its finished appearance.

To achieve a level ceiling in each case the first operation is to establish the position and fix the wall pieces. All of the other components must then be lined into these. The position of the wall pieces may be marked out by measuring up a set distance from a datum line. This will have been previously established using either a water level or an optical levelling instrument as mentioned in Chapter 8. However, specialist erectors working on large office or industrial contracts are increasingly using electronic and laser levelling instruments to establish datums.

Timber-frame construction

In the United Kingdom permanent timber frame buildings are normally prefabricated under factory conditions and then transported to the site for erection on prepared foundations. In Canada and the USA, on the other hand, the 'stick-built' method of timber frame is utilized. This is where the timber is delivered to the site as separate loose timbers and framed up adjacent to where it will subsequently be erected. The stick-built method is rarely used in the United Kingdom because of our variable climatic conditions, but it is suitable for one-off projects and small extensions.

In timber frame buildings all of the structural parts above the damp-proof course, that is the walls, floor and roof, are constructed from timber and plywood. The external cladding merely provides a weatherproof finish and may include bricks, stone, tiles, cement rendering and various types of timber boarding.

Timber frame construction methods have a number of advantages over other forms of construction. These include:

1   A reduction in the site erection time.
2   Improved standards of thermal insulation.
3   Wide variety of external finishes available.
4   Dry construction methods allow quicker occupation as no drying out time is required.

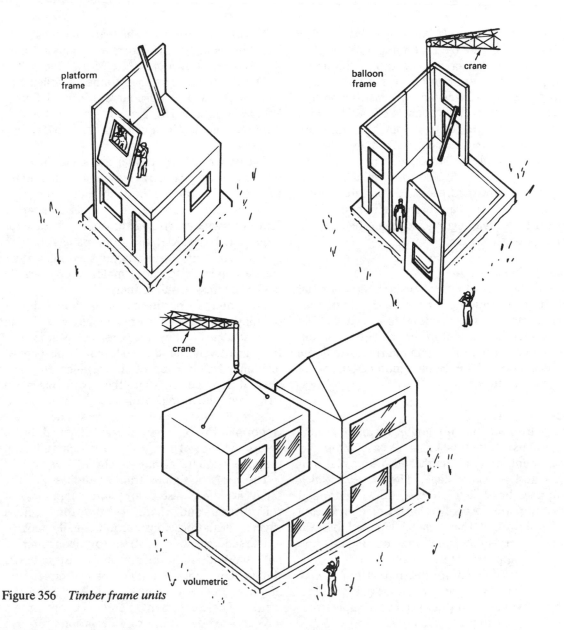

Figure 356   *Timber frame units*

5 No subsequent remedial work as a result of shrinkage is necessary.
6 Adverse weather conditions do not greatly affect the construction progress.
7 Prefabricated components are manufactured under ideal factory conditions.

Main types

The two principal designs of timber frame units are illustrated in Figure 356. These are platform frame (small panel, large panel, volumetric) and balloon frame (large panel).

Platform frame

This is by far the most used method of timber frame construction. The walls are built in single-storey-height sections. Once the first wall sections have been erected on the ground floor, the first-floor joist and floor covering are fixed on top of them. This creates a platform on which the second-storey walls can be erected. Further floors are formed by continuing this process. Finally the roof is erected on top of the upper wall panels. A variation of the platform frame method, which utilizes factory construction to a much larger extent, is volumetric housing units. In this, complete box or room size units are delivered to the site and stacked together to form the completed structure. These are normally fully decorated and in certain circumstances even furnished, thus reducing the on-site construction time to an absolute minimum. They have the disadvantage of requiring the use of a large, powerful crane.

Balloon frame

This method uses timber frames that are the full height of the building. The studs are continuous from damp-proof course level to the eaves. The wall panels are therefore erected to their full height in one operation, with intermediate floors being supported on ribbons notched into the continuous studs.

Methods of construction

The platform frame method is normally preferred because of its smaller, more easily managed components and the fact that a working platform is erected at each stage. The panels, which comprise head and sole plates, studs and sheathing, are normally related to the maximum size and weight that can be handled by two people. This gives panel sizes of single-storey height by approximately 3.600 m.

Unsheathed panels for internal partitions may be considerably larger. In situations where a crane is available on site to erect the superstructure, the maximum panel size restriction is removed. This enables the use of balloon frames and larger platform frames. This method is often known as the large-panel erection system. It allows full house width and depth panels to be used; in addition, these panels are often more highly factory finished, including windows, glazing, insulation, internal lining and, where appropriate, external cladding. This has the advantage of reducing the on-site time and enables more rapid completion.

Typical examples of the external wall construction using both platform and balloon frame methods are shown in Figure 357(a) and (b).

The majority of timber frame buildings are constructed with solid concrete ground floors. Where a suspended timber ground floor is required, the detail shown in Figure 357(c) may be used.

The upper floors of timber frame buildings are normally simply constructed on site using loose joists and boarded over with either tongued-and-grooved boarding or sheet material. However, where a contractor is using a crane for large panel erection, the floor panels may be prefabricated in large sections, using either standard joists and sheet material or specially designed stressed skin panels.

The internal partitions of a timber frame building are normally erected along with the main structure. They are constructed in exactly the same way as the external wall panels, including lintels over door openings etc. The only difference is that they will have no structural sheathing prefixed. This tends to make them unstable when handled. Therefore it is normal to fix a temporary diagonal brace across the face of the studs to stiffen and keep the panels square during erection.

The roofs of timber frame buildings are the same as those used for other methods of construction and therefore the roof details covered in the previous section equally apply.

The sequence of operations for the erection of both methods of timber frame construction is similar. Once the foundations are complete the major components may be delivered from the factory. These can then be erected in one or two days to provide a fully weatherproof structure. Finishing work can be carried out inside at the same time as the external cladding is laid on.

Figure 358 illustrates the major components and erection sequences for both methods of construction.

Care must be taken during erection as, until the shell is fully completed, including floor decking, roof coverings and glazing, the timber frame may be structurally unstable. This creates an obvious risk during the erection; to a great

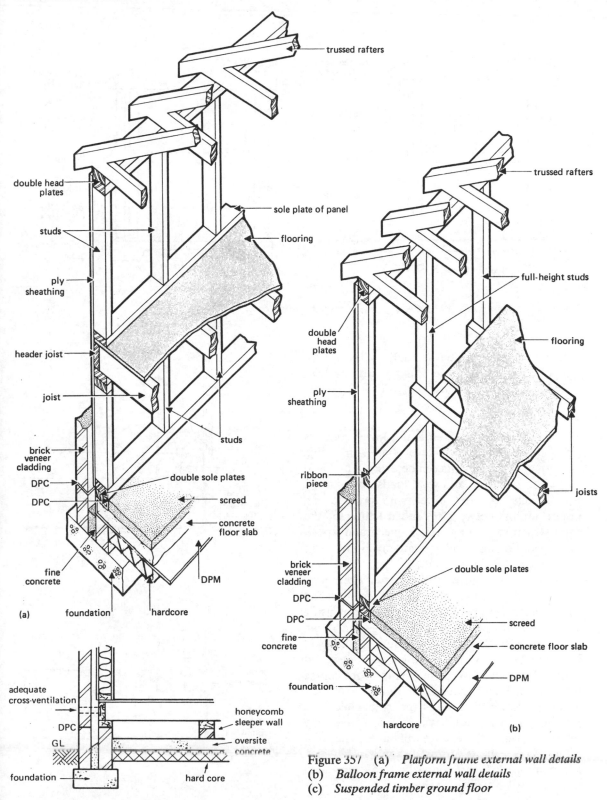

trussed rafters

double head plates

studs

ply sheathing

header joist

joist

brick veneer cladding

DPC

DPC

fine concrete

foundation

hardcore

(a)

sole plate of panel

flooring

studs

double sole plates

screed

concrete floor slab

DPM

trussed rafters

full-height studs

double head plates

ply sheathing

ribbon piece

flooring

joists

brick veneer cladding

DPC

DPC

fine concrete

foundation

double sole plates

screed

concrete floor slab

DPM

hardcore

(b)

adequate cross-ventilation

DPC

GL

foundation

honeycomb sleeper wall

oversite concrete

hard core

Figure 357   (a)   *Platform frame external wall details*
(b)   *Balloon frame external wall details*
(c)   *Suspended timber ground floor*

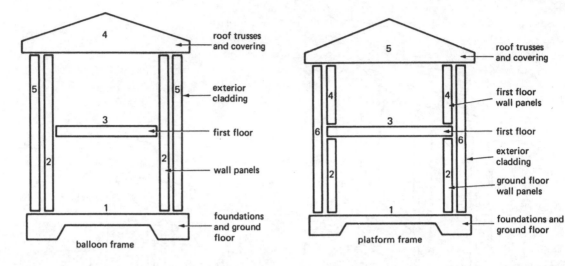

Figure 358   *Components and erection sequences for timber frame buildings*

extent this risk may be avoided by the use of temporary diagonal braces and struts, particularly in windy conditions.

Fixings

The first item to be fixed is the lower sole. Its purpose is to form a level base on which subsequent components can be erected and also to transmit vertical and wind loads down to the foundations. As the lower sole provides an important link between the substructure and the superstructure, care taken in accurately positioning and fixing it will prevent any inaccuracies being repeated throughout the structure.

Illustrated in Figure 359(a) are two alternative methods of fixing the sole plate, either by nailing with a cartridge-operated fixing tool or by using some form of rag bolt or expanding bolt. It can be clearly seen that the use of either method will hole the DPC. With nails this problem is not considered significant as the damp-proof course tends to self-seal around the tight perforation made by the nail, and as the sole plates are pressure impregnated with preservative any minute amount of moisture will have no harmful effect. Where bolts are used, any gap between the damp-proof course and bolt can be sealed with mastic or a fibre washer.

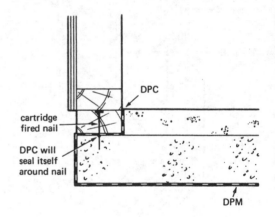

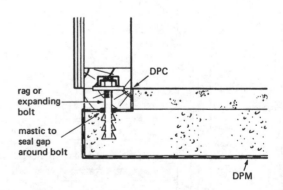

Figure 359   (a)   *Sole plate fixings*

The fixing down of the sole plate, the nailing of the panels to it and the nailing of adjacent panels to each other are a critical part of the structural design. Each timber frame designer will therefore produce a comprehensive nailing schedule which must be fully complied with both during manufacture and on site. A typical nailing schedule is illustrated in Figure 359(b).

External wall panels

These normally consist of prepared 50 mm × 100 mm MGS or MSS stress-graded softwood studwork. The studs, which are spaced at 400 mm or 600 mm centres to suit the sheet sizes, are simply butt jointed and nailed to the head and sole plates. No noggins or diagonal braces are required as the plywood sheathing which is nailed to the studs provides the required

rigidity. An additional head plate is used to bind the panels together, line them and provide additional strength, so joist and trussed rafter spacing are not dependent on the stud positions. Where wall panels intersect additional studs should be used to provide a fixing for the internal lining (see Figure 360). It should be noted that the head plate joints are staggered at wall panel intersections to tie them together.

Lintels must be provided over openings where these occur in external walls. This is normally two pieces of 50 mm × 150 mm timber fixed together and stood on edge. This is supported on either side of the opening by double studs, one stud being cut shorter (cripple stud) to provide a bearing for the lintel (see Figure 361).

Where wall panels contain a door opening it is advisable to leave the sole plate in position

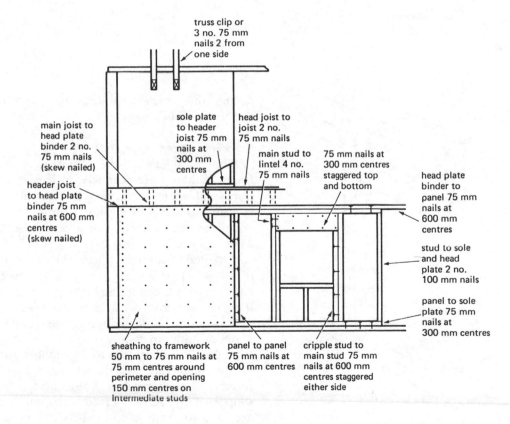

(b)   *Typical nailing schedule*

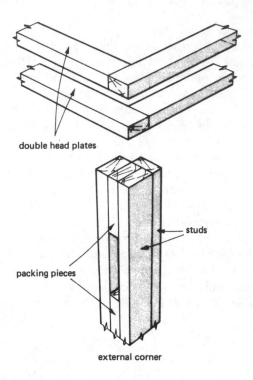

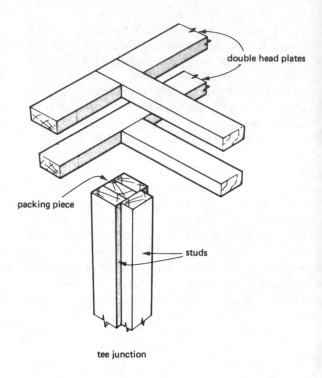

Figure 360   *Corner details*

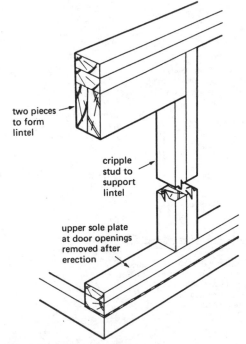

Figure 361   *Opening details*

during the erection process to avoid panel distortion and damage.

Site construction (stick built)
Although in general the majority of timber frame buildings are produced in factory conditions and some even by computer-controlled cutting and assembly machines, timber frame is equally suited to the on-site stick-built method. This is especially true of the one-off design constructed by a small builder. All of the details to follow will still apply to the on-site method, and if care is taken in the making of the panels the same accuracy in sizes as achieved by the factory method is possible, e.g. plus 0 mm minus 3 mm in both directions.

Figure 362 illustrates a jig suitable for the on-site manufacture of timber frame panels. It consists of a plywood deck on timber bearers, supported by trestles. Fixed stops and wedges are used to locate the members and cramp up the panel.

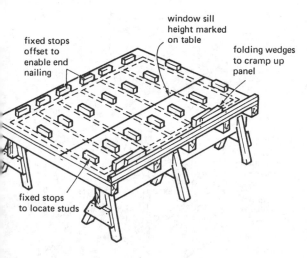

Figure 362 *Jig for on-site panel-making*

Preservative treatment

All external wall timbers, sole plates, battens, plywood, cavity barriers and timber cladding should be preservative treated to protect them against decay and insect attack, preferably using a vacuum or pressure treatment. All timbers cut after treatment, whether in the factory or on-site, must be given two flood brush applications of the preservative on the cut surfaces.

Insulation

In accordance with the Building Regulations, all buildings and extensions must be thermally insulated to a high standard. This is easily achieved in timber frame buildings by installing rock fibre or fibreglass insulation in the spaces between the studs of the external walls and between the ceiling joists in the roof space.

Although at present there is no insulation requirement for ground floors it can be advantageous to improve energy efficiency by insulating them. Suspended ground floors may be insulated between the joists with rock fibre or fibreglass supported on galvanized wire or plastic mesh fixed to the underside of the joist. Solid ground floors can be insulated by placing a suitable material, e.g. 50 mm thick polystyrene sheet, between the floor slab and screed.

Barriers

Two essential barriers must be incorporated in the construction. These are a vapour barrier and a moisture barrier.

Vapour barrier

It is most important that a vapour barrier is used on the warm side of the insulation. Its purpose is to minimize the passage of water vapour from the moist interior of the building passing into the structure and condensing (interstitial condensation). If this were allowed to take place the wall materials would become saturated, thus making the insulation ineffective and creating the ideal conditions for the development of timber decay.

The vapour barrier, which is normally of 250 – 500 gauge polythene sheet should be situated between the insulation and plasterboard. It should be fixed to the head and sole plates, around openings and overlaps with staples at approximately 250 mm. All joints should be overlapped by at least 100 mm and occur over a stud.

Note: Although foil-backed plasterboard provides a vapour check, its use for this purpose on its own is not permitted by the National House Building Council.

Care should be taken in fixing the polythene to ensure that it covers the entire wall surface, including the sole plate, head plate, studs, lintels and reveals. Any holes around services or tears in the barrier must be repaired with a suitable adhesive tape to seal any gaps before the plasterboard is fixed.

So as not to seal moisture within the wall structure, it is most important that the moisture content of the framework is checked prior to the fixing of the vapour barrier. This should always be less than 20 per cent.

It is impossible for a vapour barrier to be 100 per cent effective because of the joints in it and fixings through it. Therefore a breather-type moisture barrier is installed on the outside of the timber frame under the cladding so that any water vapour that has penetrated through the vapour is allowed to escape or 'breathe' to the outside air.

Moisture barrier

A moisture barrier must be waterproof but at the same time must allow water vapour to pass through it. Fixed on top of the sheathing, it 'weathers' the timber frame shell immediately after erection. In addition it also provides a second line of protection against the penetration of wind-driven moisture that might penetrate the cladding. Moisture barriers also seal any gaps in the panel joints and thus act as a draughtproofer.

Moisture barriers are usually special light-weight building paper or felt, designed to be both waterproof and vapour permeable (able to breathe). They are fixed to the sheathing starting at the bottom of the wall in horizontal widths around the building.

They should be fixed to the head and sole plates, studs, around openings and overlaps with staples at approximately 250 mm centres. Horizontal laps should be at least 100 mm, with the upper layer overlapping the lower one. Vertical laps should be at least 150 mm and staggered in adjacent layers (see Figure 363).

Staples may be driven through narrow plastic strips. This avoids the barrier pulling over the staples, particularly when exposed to windy conditions. In addition the strips also serve to indicate the stud positions for subsequent wall tie fixing.

Fire stops and cavity barriers

The Building Regulations require fire stops and cavity barriers to be fitted in the timber frame construction to control the spread of flame or smoke through cavities.

A fire stop is a non-combustible material used to divide the separating wall cavities of semi-detached or terraced buildings from the external wall or roof cavity (see Figure 364). In addition fire stops are also required where services pass through the timber structure.

Timbers of at least 38 mm section are often used as cavity barriers. They must be fixed to seal the cavity between the timber frame and cladding, horizontally at each floor and roof level, around all door and window openings and vertically at intervals of not more than 8 metres.

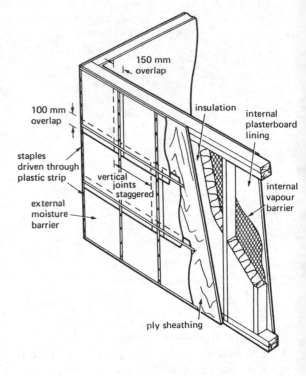

Figure 363   *Wall panel insulation and barriers*

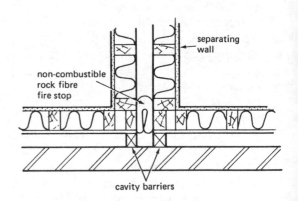

Figure 364   *Fire stop*

In addition vertical cavity barriers are required to separate the external wall cavities of semidetached or terraced buildings (see Figure 365 for details).

Figure 366 illustrates how cavity barriers should be protected from the external wall by a damp-proof course.

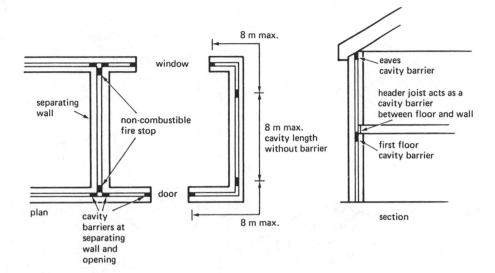

Figure 365   *Cavity barriers*

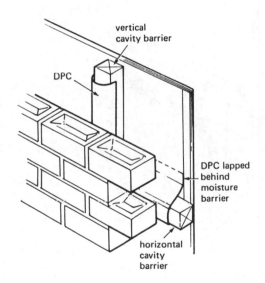

Figure 366   *Protecting cavity barriers*

Cladding

Various types and arrangements of material can be used for cladding the exterior of timber frame buildings. The cladding provides a visually acceptable and sufficiently durable weatherproof finish. The main types of cladding in common use are illustrated in Figure 367.

The most popular cladding is brick veneer, which gives the building a traditional appearance, although this is often used in conjunction with large areas of timber cladding, tile hanging or cement rendering.

Brick cladding

This must be effectively connected to the timber frame for stability. Since there will be differing amounts of movement between the timber frame and the brick cladding, flexible wall ties must be used. In addition, gaps should be left between the brickwork and the timber to allow for movement at the eaves and around window and door frames that are fixed to the timber frame. These gaps around the window and door frames should be sealed with a compressible mastic to prevent rain penetration.

The cavity between the brick cladding and the timber frame should be ventilated at the eaves and below the damp-proof course level, by raking out the vertical brick joints (perpends) at 1.500 m intervals. The lower open joints also serve as weep-holes to drain the cavity.

Other lightweight cladding

Timber, tile hanging and cement rendering are preferably fixed to vertical battens nailed to the

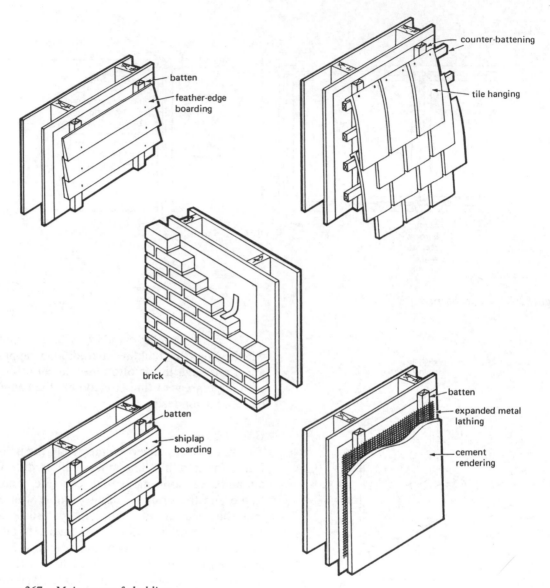

Figure 367   *Main types of cladding*

studs or horizontal and vertical counter-battening. This allows for free movement of air so that the cladding is ventilated on both sides. When timber boards are used, care must be taken when nailing to ensure that the boarding is nailed near one edge only and that the nails do not penetrate two boards. This is to ensure that each board is able to move more freely, without danger of splitting, when subsequent moisture movement takes place. Horizontal timber boarding is nailed near the bottom edge of the board. The top edge is held by the overlapping edge of the board above.

The length of nails used to fix the cladding must be 2½ times the cladding thickness and should be treated to resist corrosion or be made of a non-corrosive metal.

Naturally durable timber cladding such as Western red cedar may be used without preservative treatment or any subsequent finish.

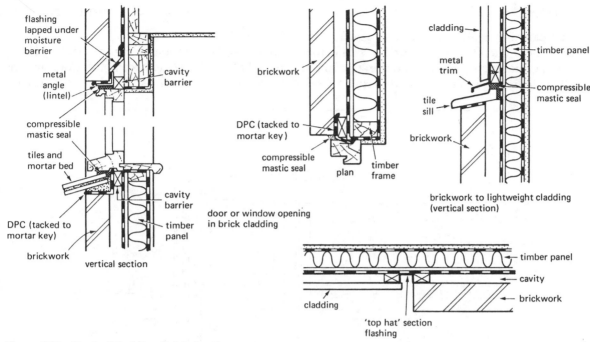

Figure 368 *Typical cladding finish details*

Other timbers that are not naturally durable must be preservative treated. They may also have a further finish applied for decorative reasons or to prevent natural fading.

Paints and varnishes are the commonest finish. However, they are not particularly suitable as cracks in the film soon appear along the large number of joints in the cladding. This allows moisture to penetrate, causing the paint or varnish to peel.

Exterior wood stains are available in a wide range of colours. These are more suitable than paints or varnishes as they give the cladding a water-repellent surface without forming a film, and therefore cannot crack and peel off. Stains may be applied by brush, or by pressure impregnation at the same time as the preservative treatment.

Cladding details

Careful detailing to allow for differing movement and prevent rain penetration is required where claddings finish around door and window openings or where different claddings join.

Figure 368 illustrates a number of typical cladding details.

Curtain walling

Timber framed panels can be used as non-load-bearing infill wall units (curtain walling) for skeleton frame structures of either steel or reinforced concrete and for brick or concrete cross-wall construction.

These panels may be constructed as large window frames using a combination of glazed openings and insulated infill sections. Alternatively they may be constructed as timber framed and clad panels using standard timber-frame construction methods and principles.

The panels must be securely fixed to the structural frame or cross-walls, normally using metal brackets or straps.

Careful detailing is required in order to allow for the differential movement between the curtain walling and the main structure while at the same time maintaining a weatherproof joint. This is done by filling the joint with a resilient strip and sealing with a compressible mastic.

Panelling

Wall panelling is the general term given to the covering of the internal wall surface with timber or other materials to create a decorative finish. All panelling may be classified in one of two ways, either by its method of construction or by its height.

Dado-height panelling (Figure 369) This is panelling that extends from the floor up the walls to the window-sill level or chair-back

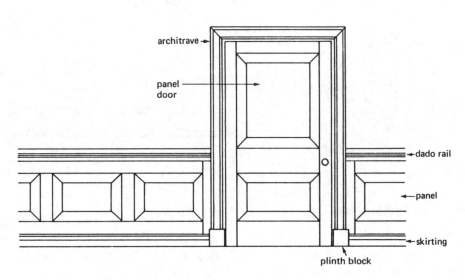

Figure 369   *Dado-height panelling*

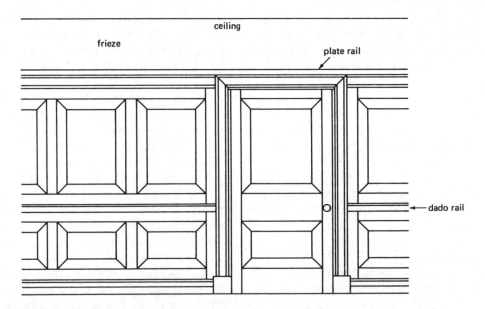

Figure 370   *Three-quarter-height panelling*

height, i.e. about 1 m, and is known as dado panelling.

Three-quarter-height panelling (Figure 370) This type of panelling is also known as frieze-height panelling. It extends from the floor up the walls to the top of the door i.e. about 2 m. Traditionally a plate shelf was incorporated on top of this type of panelling to display plates and other frieze ornaments.

Full-height panelling (Figure 371) This, as its name suggests, covers the whole of the wall from floor to ceiling.

Methods of construction

Traditionally all panelling was made up from solid timbers. It consisted of framing, mortised and tenoned together to receive decorative, flat or raised panels and other solid mouldings. The modern practice is to utilize sheet materials as far as possible, either in a traditional framed surround or on their own without framing to give a flush appearance. This flush appearance can be given a traditional look by tacking planted mouldings to its surface to form mock panels. In addition to framed or sheet panelling, strip panelling made from narrow strips of boarding (T&G and V-jointed) are also used.

Whichever method of construction is used, most of the work will have been carried out off site in a joiner's shop. The panels should be delivered to site at the latest stage possible in easy to handle sections of up to 3.600 m in length.

As this is a site practice book, this section deals with the fixing of panelling rather than its manufacture.

Grounds

Probably the most important requirement of panelling is a straight and level surface on which to fix it. Any distortion will be exaggerated in the finished panelling and will mar its appearance. This straight and level surface can be provided by battening out the walls with grounds. These are normally preservative-treated softwood. They may have been framed up using halvings or mortise-and-tenon joints or alternatively supplied in lengths for use as separate grounds or counter-battening (see Figure 372).

The method used to fix the grounds will vary depending on the material they are being fixed to, e.g. brick, block, concrete or steel, but will be either by plugging and screwing, nailing into

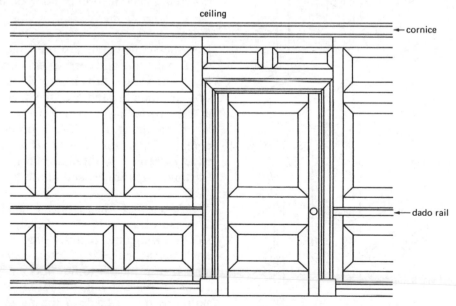

Figure 371 *Full-height panelling*

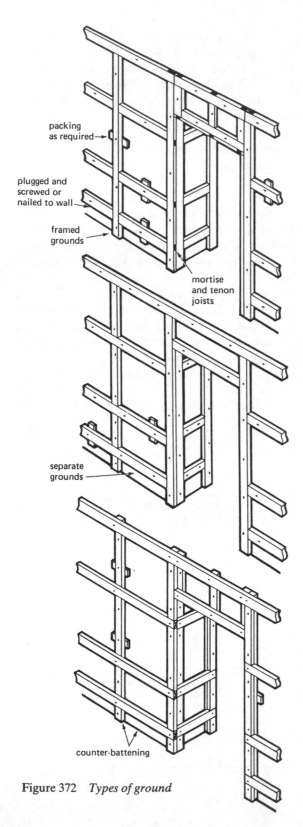

packing
as required

plugged and
screwed or
nailed to wall

framed
grounds

mortise
and tenon
joists

separate
grounds

counter-battening

Figure 372   *Types of ground*

twisted timber plugs, nailing direct to the wall with cut or hardened steel nails, or by using a cartridge fixing tool.

Uneven wall surfaces will require packings behind the grounds to achieve a flat surface. A level and straight edge can be used to test the wall in order to find any high spots. The grounds can then be fixed, packed out and lined in to this level. As framed grounds are made up with the panelling in the joiner's shop, they will have been planned to suit each other, but when separate grounds or counter-battens are used it is essential that these are correctly positioned in order to provide the desired fixings for the panelling. These positions will be shown on the full-size setting-out rods of the panelling supplied by the joiner's shop.

Fixing panelling

The fixing of panelling to the grounds should be concealed as far as possible. There are various methods of achieving this. Figure 373 illustrates the following concealed or 'secret' fixings.

Interlocking grounds

Splayed or rebated grounds are fixed to the back of the panelling and the wall. As the panelling is lowered it is hooked in position on the grounds.

Slot screwing

Keyhole-shaped slots are prepared in the back of the panelling and corresponding countersunk-head screws are driven into the grounds. The slots are then located over the projecting screws and the panelling tapped down so that the head is driven along the slot to provide a secure completely secret fixing. This method was widely used in traditional panelling for fixing skirtings, architraves and plinth blocks.

Slotted and interlocking metal plates

The use of keyhole slotted plates is similar to slot screwing, the plates being recessed in the back of the panelling. Interlocking plates are similar in principle to interlocking grounds, the cranked plate being fitted in corresponding positions in the back of the panelling and the face of the grounds. An alternative method is to

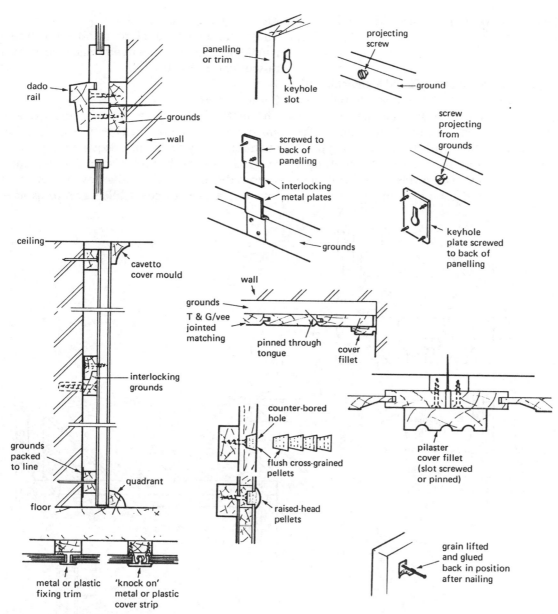

Figure 373   *Concealed fixings*

fit the plates so that the panels can slide in sideways.

Pellets

Screw holes are counter-bored, and cross-grained pellets made from the same material as the panelling are glued and inserted in the hole. Care must be taken in matching the grain and cleaning the pellet back flush with the surface. Dome-headed pellets are also available to provide a featured fixing.

Cover fillets

Panelling can be surface screwed to the grounds and then covered with a fillet pinned in place. This may be moulded to form a feature or may in fact be the skirting, cornice, frieze rail, dado rail or pilaster.

Nailing

Strip panelling such as T&G and V matchboarding may be secret fixed by pinning through the tongue. In other sections the nails may be partly concealed by pinning through a quirk in the moulding and filling with a matching stopping, or secret fixed through the surface by lifting a thin sliver of grain with a chisel, nailing behind this and gluing the grain back in position.

Metal or plastic trim

These are mainly used to fix sheet material panelling, and in most circumstances provide a raised feature joint.

Corner details

The method of forming internal and external angles will depend on the type of panelling, but in any case they should be adequately supported by grounds fixed behind. Figure 374 illustrates various details. Tongue-and-groove joints, loose tongues, rebates or cover fillets and trims have

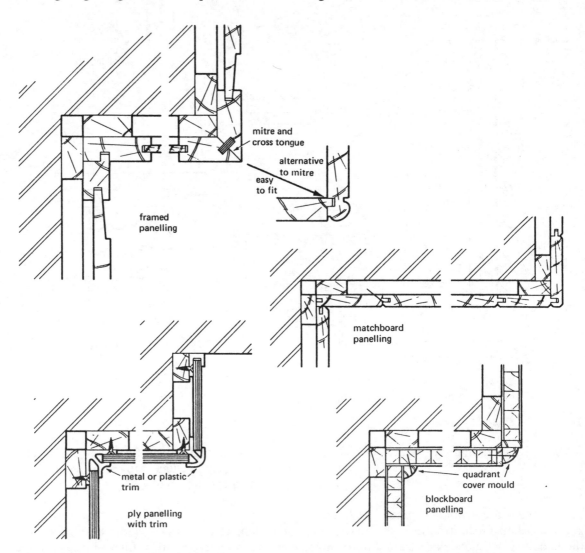

Figure 374   *Corner details*

been used to locate the panelling members and at the same time conceal the effects of moisture movement.

Panel moulds

Where bolection mouldings are used, these should be slot screwed through the panel from behind. The length of the slot must be at right angles to the grain in order to allow panel movement without any possibility of splitting (see Figure 375). Also shown in Figure 375 is a method used to fix planted panel moulds. They should be pinned to the framing only and not the panel. This again allows a certain amount of panel movement without splitting.

General requirements of panelling

1 Before any panelling commences it is essential that the wall construction has dried sufficiently.
2 All timber should be of the moisture content required for the respective situation (equilibrium moisture content M/C).
3 The backs of the panelling sections should be sealed prior to fixing, thus preventing moisture absorption.
4 Timber for grounds should be preservative treated.
5 A ventilated air space is desirable between the panelling and the wall.
6 Provision must be made for a slight amount of moisture movement in both the panelling sections and the trim.
7 The positioning of the grounds must be planned to suit the panelling.
8 The fixing of the panelling to the grounds should be so designed that it is concealed as far as possible.

Partitions

Partition walls are normally lightweight and non-load-bearing, their use being to divide large areas into smaller areas. The two main types of partition wall as far as the carpenter is concerned are stud partitions and proprietary partition systems.

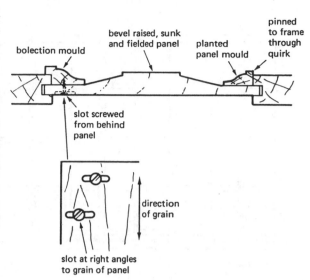

Figure 375 *Bolection moulds and planted panel moulds*

Stud partitions

These consist of vertical timbers called studs (hence the name, stud partitions) which are fixed to two horizontal timbers, one at the ceiling level, called a head plate, and the other at floor level, called a sole plate. Short horizontal timbers called noggins are fixed between the studs to stiffen them and provide additional fixing points for the covering material.

The actual covering material can be plasterboard, plywood, insulation board, hardboard, matchboarding etc.

It is most important that the material to be used is known before the stud is erected as the studs must be spaced accordingly. Most sheet materials require a stud on either edge and two intermediate studs. This makes the stud spacing approximately 400 mm. The positions for the noggins also vary with the covering material, but in general noggins are fixed at skirting height, knee height (600 mm), waist height (1.2 m) and shoulder height (1.8 m), these being the most vulnerable points. Additional noggins are fixed where horizontal joints occur between sheet material.

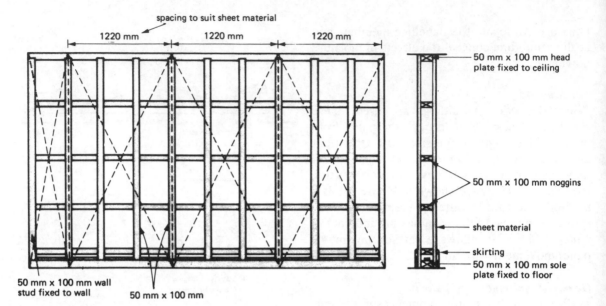

Figure 376   *Stud partitions*

Figure 376 shows a typical stud partition. The position of the sheet material covering is indicated in the elevation by the diagonal broken lines.

Figure 377 shows the joints used between the studs and the head and sole plates. These joints must be fixed with nails. The noggins are butt jointed and skew nailed. On cheaper work the studs are also butt jointed and skew nailed. An alternative to both methods would be to use framing anchors.

Figure 378 shows the arrangement of studs where two partitions join at right angles.

Note: Using this method, one partition must be erected and sheeted on one side before the other partition is erected. Alternatively, additional studs can be inserted to take the plasterboard.

Where openings are required in the studwork for doors, hatches, borrowed lights, etc. the studs and noggins must be positioned accordingly (see Figure 379).

Proprietary partitions
Various proprietary partition systems are available from a number of manufacturers, but

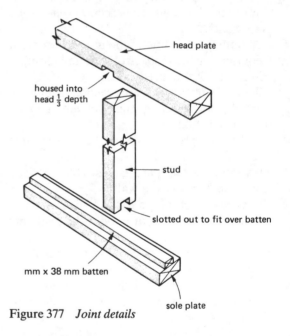

Figure 377   *Joint details*

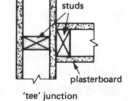

Figure 378   *Corner details*

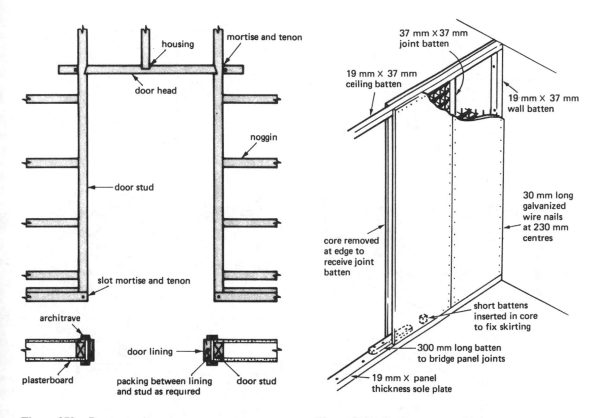

Figure 379   *Door opening*

Figure 380   *Paramount partitions*

probably the most popular for domestic work is the Paramount dry partition system. This is constructed using prefabricated panels which consist of two sheets of plasterboard separated by a cellular core.

These are available in panel widths of 600 mm, 900 mm, and 1200 mm, thicknesses of 50 mm, 57 mm and 63 mm, and heights from 1.8 m up to 3.6 m, with either ivory faces for direct decoration or grey faces for plastering. The panels rest on timber sole plates fixed to the floor and fit over timber battens which are fixed to the wall and ceiling. Battens are also fixed between adjacent panels (see Figure 380). The batten sizes refer to 57 mm and 63 mm partitions. 50 mm partitions require 19 mm × 30 mm and 30 mm × 37 mm battens. In all cases these should be a press fit in the panel, and therefore may require some easing.

A range of typical fixing details is illustrated in

Figure 381. It is essential in order to give adequate strength that battens are inserted into the cellular core and secured with galvanized wire nails at all panel joints, wall intersections and openings. Electric cables and other similar services up to about 30 mm in diameter can be accommodated in the cellular core. Timber plugs of a suitable section can be inserted into the cellular core in various positions during erection, to provide later fixing points for cisterns, radiators, washbasins etc. The sound and thermal insulation properties of these partitions increase with the panel thickness. They also provide good fire protection. The sound thermal and fire properties of the partition may be further improved by bonding an additional layer of plasterboard to one or both sides with a suitable adhesive. For the greatest benefit the joints between the panels and sheets should be staggered.

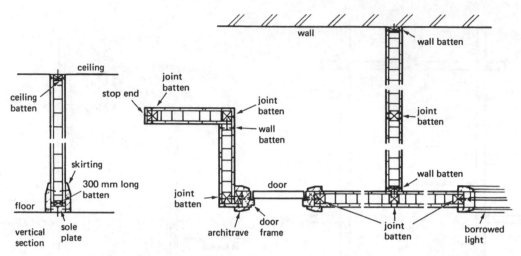

Figure 381   *Paramount partition details*

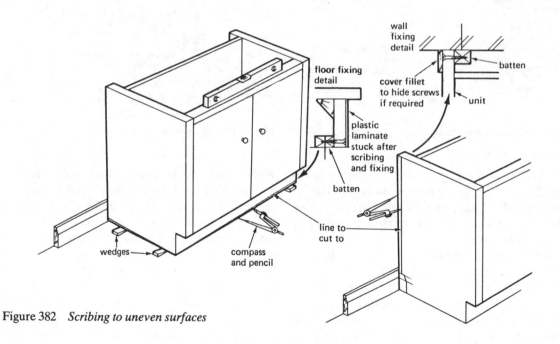

Figure 382   *Scribing to uneven surfaces*

Joinery units

This category includes screens, partitions, cupboards etc. These will have been made in a joiner's shop, and most are fully assembled prior to their arrival on site. However, budget-priced units (kitchen cupboards, wardrobes etc.) are often sent in knock-down form for simple on-site assembly, normally involving either screws and dowels or proprietary joint devices.

Figure 382 shows a method of scribing and fixing cupboard units to uneven floor and wall surfaces. The units should be wedged up off the ground until they are plumb and level. A compass can be set to the widest gap and used to mark a line parallel with the floor. This is then

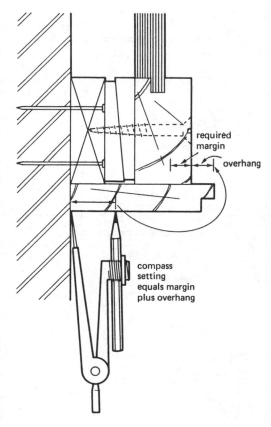

required margin

overhang

compass setting equals margin plus overhang

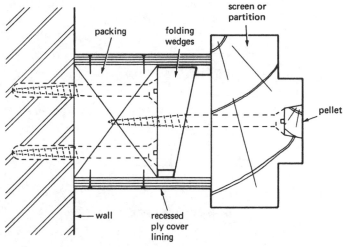

packing

folding wedges

screen or partition

pellet

wall

recessed ply cover lining

cut and the operation repeated to scribe to the wall. The unit can then be screwed to battens fixed to the wall and floor.

Partitions, screens and units are normally made slightly smaller than the opening in which they are to fit. This enables them to be packed or wedged out and suitable cover strips or linings applied to conceal the joint (see Figure 383).

Figure 384 shows how a framed dwarf screen

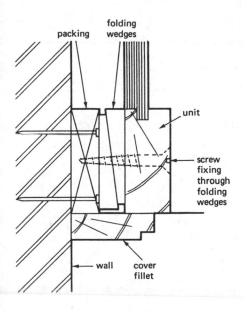

packing

folding wedges

unit

screw fixing through folding wedges

wall

cover fillet

Figure 383 *Fixing joinery*

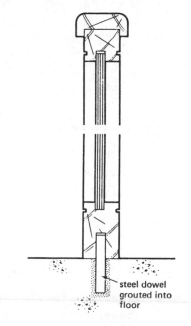

steel dowel grouted into floor

Figure 384 *Fixing a dwarf screen*

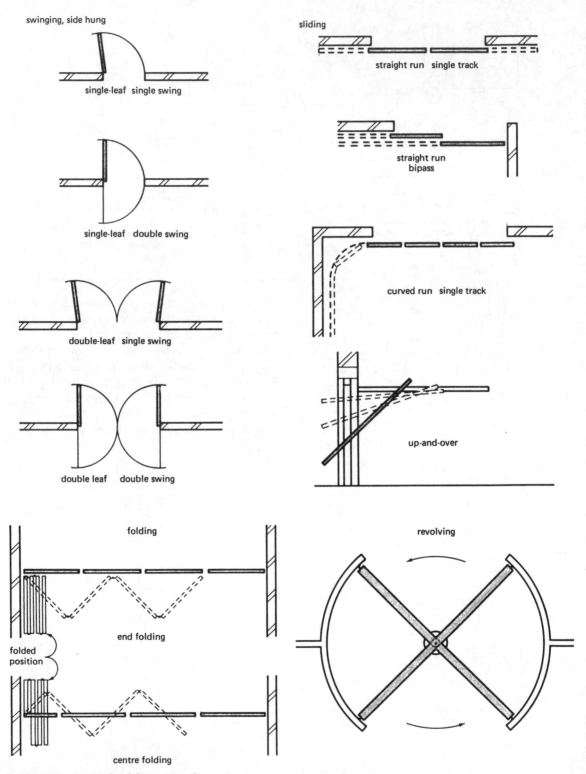

Figure 385   *Methods of door operation*

may be fixed to the floor by inserting steel dowels into the bottom rail and grouting these into holes in the floor. Often the free end of this type of screen terminates with a post. This may be fixed to the floor in a similar way to a newel post, either by inserting a steel dowel partly into the bottom of the post and grouting it into the concrete, or in the case of a timber floor continuing the post through the floor and bolting it to a joist.

Doors and associated ironmongery

A door can be defined as a movable barrier used to cover an opening in a structure. Its main function is to allow access into a building and passage between the interior spaces. But a door must be carefully designed and detailed so that it is capable of doing this while at the same time maintaining its other various performance requirements, e.g. weather protection, fire resistance, sound and thermal insulation, security, privacy, ease of operation and durability.

A door's method of operation will be determined by its location, construction and desired performance requirements. Figure 385 illustrates various methods of door operation. These include swinging, sliding, folding and revolving.

The selection of ironmongery is closely linked to the door's desired performance requirements and its method of operation.

Door ironmongery can be considered under the following three headings:

Fittings which allow movement (hinges, pivots, and sliding gear)
Fittings which give security (locks, latches and bolts)
Miscellaneous items (letter plates, finger plates and door stops)

Swinging doors

This method is the most suitable for pedestrian use and also the most effective for weather protection, fire resistance, sound and thermal insulation.

The most common means of swinging a door is to side hinge it, although top and pivots are

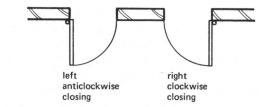

Figure 386 *Typical handing diagram*

more effective where constant use is expected, e.g. shops, office reception areas etc. The hands of doors are required to enable the correct items of ironmongery to be selected. To determine the hand of a door it must be viewed from the hinge knuckle side; if they are on the left the door is left handed, whereas if they are on the right the door is right handed. They may also be defined as either anticlockwise or clockwise closing (see Figure 386).

Movement fittings

Hinges
Figure 387 illustrates a range of hinges, which are readily available in a variety of materials. Brass hinges should be used for hardwood doors. Steel hinges should not be used in external locations, and aluminium or plastic hinges should not be used for fire-check or fire-resistant doors.

Butt hinge is suitable for most applications. As a general rule the leaf with the greatest number of knuckles is fixed to the door frame.
Washered butt hinges are used for heavier doors to reduce knuckle wear and prevent squeaking.
Parliament hinges have extended knuckles to enable doors to fold back against a wall, clearing deep architraves etc.
Rising butts are designed to lift the door as it opens to clear any obstruction e.g. mats and rugs. They also give the door some degree of self-closing. In order to prevent the top edge of the door fouling the frame as the door closes, this edge must be eased.
Double- and single-action spring hinges are designed to make a door self-closing. Their large

knuckles contain helical springs which can be adjusted to give the required closing action by using a 'tommy bar' and moving the small pin at the top of the knuckles into a different hole. Where double-action hinges are used, they should not be cut into the door frame but screwed to a planted section the same width as the door and fixed to the frame.

Hawgood hinges are another type of spring hinge and are suitable for industrial and heavy-duty double-swing doors. The spring housed in the cylinder is mortised and recessed into the door frame, and the moving shoe fits around both sides of the door. A twin-spring Hawgood hinge is available for use as the top hinge of very heavy doors.

Positioning of hinges

Lightweight internal doors require one pair of 75 mm hinges, whereas glazed, half-hour fire-check and other heavyweight doors need one pair of 100 mm hinges. All external doors and one-hour fire-check doors require 1½ pairs of 100 mm hinges.

Figure 388 illustrates the standard hinge positions for flush doors, although on glazed and panelled doors the tops of the hinges are often fixed in line with the rails to produce a more balanced effect.

Pivoted floor spring

Pivoted floor springs are the best method of swinging and controlling both single- and

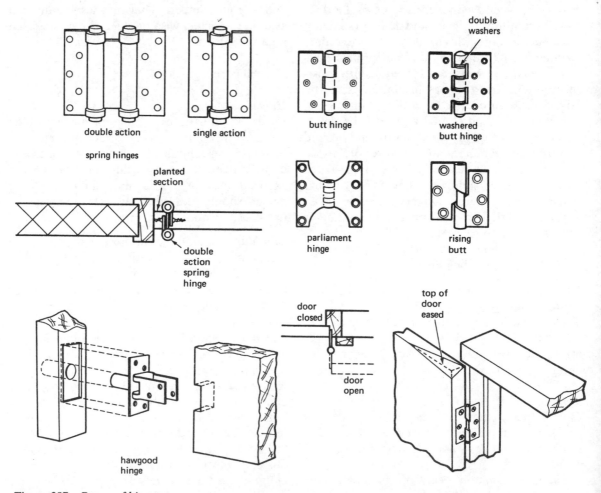

Figure 387   *Range of hinges*

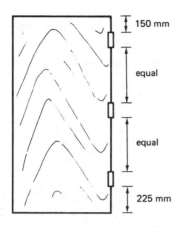

Figure 388   *Hinge positions for flush doors*

double-action doors, although their use is restricted mainly to shops and offices etc. because of their expense.

Figure 389 illustrates single and double floor springs. Both consist of:

A spring contained within a metal box which is bedded into the floor screed.
A shoe which is fixed to the bottom of the door and locates over the pivot spindle.
A two-part top pivot, of which one part is fixed to the head of the frame and the other to the door.

It is essential for the later smooth operation of the door that the loose box and floor spring is set into the floor at the correct position to the frame

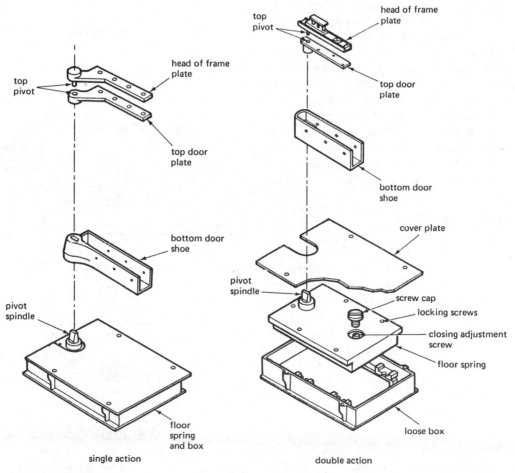

Figure 389   *Pivoted floor springs*

(see Figure 390). This is determined by the finished thickness of the door plus an allowance between the door in its opening position and frame of between 3 mm and 6 mm.

The closing action of a door fitted with a floor spring is illustrated in Figure 391. A stand-open position, normally at 90°, can be included to hold the door in the open position, although the stand-open device is not suitable for fire doors.

The delayed closing action over the first few degrees can delay the closing of the door for up to one minute before it reverts to its normal closing speed and is therefore suitable where goods and trolleys etc. have to pass through. The closing action may be varied by turning the closing adjustment screw in the floor spring. The single-action doors may be removed from the frame by unscrewing the head of the frame plate, tilting the door slightly outwards to clear the frame and lifting it off the bottom pivot spindle. Double-action doors are removed by first retracting the top pivot pin. This is achieved by turning the adjustment screw in the head of the frame plate. The door can then be tilted slightly outwards and lifted off the bottom pivot.

Brush or rubber seals may be required around the edges of double-action doors to prevent the passage of smoke and draughts. These may also include intumescent strips for fire doors (see Figure 392).

Door closers (Figure 393)

These are mainly used in offices, shops and industrial premises to give their normally larger and heavier doors a controlled self-closing action, and also to enable the door to be held in the open position when required. The speed of closing may be altered by turning the adjustment screw, which is normally under the main cover. Certain types of closer are fitted with a temperature-sensitive device that automatically closes the door from the held-open position in the event of a fire.

Others are available with:

A delayed closing action as with floor springs
A snap action over the last few degrees of travel
   to ensure that the door closes fully into the
   latch

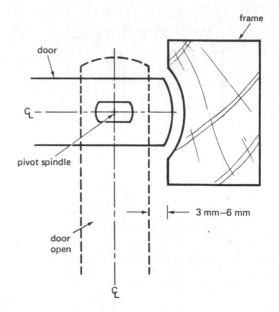

Figure 390   *Floor spring loose box*

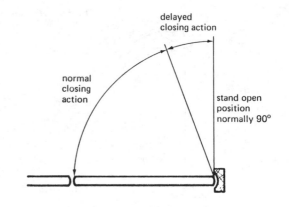

Figure 391   *Action of door with floor spring*

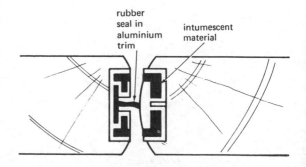

Figure 392   *Seals and strips on double-action doors*

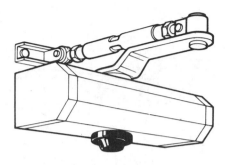

Figure 393　*Overhead door closer*

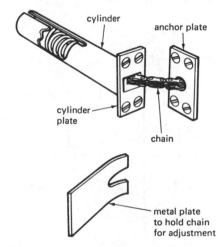

Figure 394　*Concealed door closer*

A back check action. This controls the last few degrees of opening travel, thus preventing the door from slamming into a return wall adjacent to the opening

Figure 394 shows another type of spring door closer which is concealed when the door is closed. The cylinder which contains the spring is mortised into the edge of the door and the plate recessed flush. The anchor plate is recessed in and screwed to the frame. Adjustment to the closing action is achieved by inserting the metal plate near the cylinder plate to hold the chain, unscrewing the anchor plate and turning it either clockwise to speed the action or anticlockwise to slow the closing action.

The hydraulic door check and holder shown in Figure 395 can be used in conjunction with door closers or spring hinges to control the last few degrees of closing travel. This prevents slamming and holds the door firmly closed against strong winds.

In order to ensure that self-closing double doors with rebated stiles close in the correct sequence, a door selector must be fitted (see Figure 396).

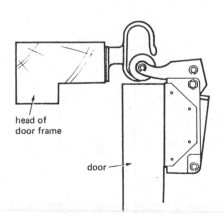

Figure 395　*Hydraulic door check and holder*

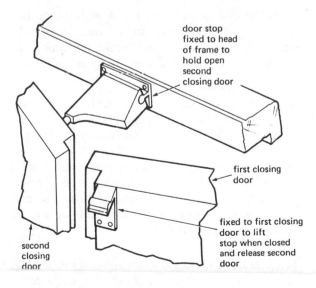

Figure 396　*Double-door selector*

Security fittings

Cylinder rim latches are mainly used for entrance doors to domestic property but, as they are only a latch, provide little security on their own. When fitted, the door can be opened from the outside with the use of a key and from the inside by turning the handle. Some types have a double-locking facility which improves their security (Figure 397).

Mortise deadlock provides a straightforward key-operated locking action, and is often used to provide additional security on entrance doors where cylinder rim latches are fitted. They are also used on doors where simple security is required, e.g. storerooms (Figure 398).

Mortise latch is used mainly for internal doors that do not require locking. The latch which holds the door in the closed position can be operated from either side of the door by turning the handle (Figure 399).

Mortise lock/latch is available in two types (Figure 400):

Horizontal type: little used nowadays because of its length, which means that it can only be fitted to substantial doors.

Vertical type: the more modern type, and can be fitted to most types of doors. It is often known as a narrow-stile lock/latch.

Both types can be used for a wide range of general purpose doors in a wide range of locations. They are in essence, a combination of the mortise deadlock and the mortise latch.

Rebated mortise lock/latch should be used when fixing a lock/latch in double doors that have rebated stiles. The front end of this lock is cranked to fit the rebate on the stiles (Figure 401).

Knobset consists of a small mortise latch and a pair of knob handles that can be locked both internally and externally. Knobsets can also be obtained without the lock in the knob for use as a latch only (Figure 402).

Miscellaneous fittings

Knob furniture is for use with the horizontal mortise lock/latch. It should not be used with the

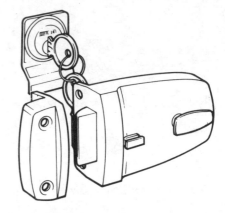

Figure 397   *Cylinder rim latch*

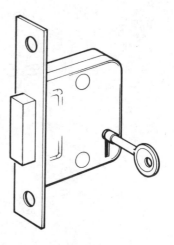

Figure 398   *Mortise deadlock*

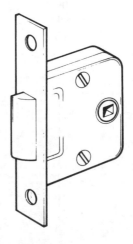

Figure 399   *Mortise latch*

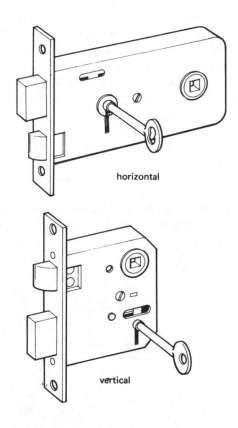

horizontal

vertical

Figure 400 *Mortise lock/latches*

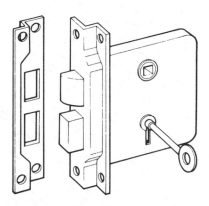

Figure 401 *Rebated mortise lock/latch*

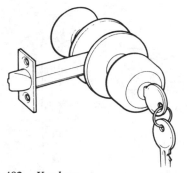

Figure 402 *Knobset*

vertical as hand injuries will result (Figure 403).
Keyhole escutcheon plates are used to provide a neat finish to the keyhole of both deadlocks and horizontal mortise lock/latches (Figure 404).
Lever furniture is available in a wide range of patterns, for use with mortise latches and mortise lock/latches (Figure 405).
Barrel bolts are used on external doors and gates to lock them from the inside. Two bolts are normally used, one at the top of the door and the other at the bottom (Figure 406).
Flush bolt is flush fitting and therefore requires recessing into the timber. It is used for better-quality work on the inside of external doors to provide additional security and also on double doors and French windows to bolt one door in the closed position. Two bolts are normally used, one at the top of the door and the other at the bottom (Figure 407).

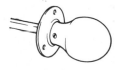

Figure 403 *Knob furniture*

Figure 404 *Escutcheon plate*

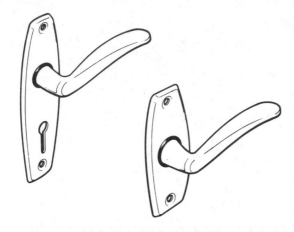

Figure 405   *Lever furniture*

Security chains   can be fixed on front entrance doors, the slide to the door and the chain to the frame. When the chain is inserted into the slide, the door will only open a limited amount until the identity of the caller is checked (Figure 408). *Door holders*   are foot operated and hold doors and gates in the open position. They are particularly useful for holding side-hung garage doors open while driving into or out of the garage (Figure 409).

Panic bolts   are used on the inside of emergency exit doors to bolt them closed. Pressure applied to the push bar will disengage the bolts. They can be fitted with an audible alarm to deter unauthorised use (Figure 410).

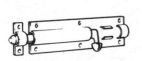

Figure 406   *Barrel bolt*

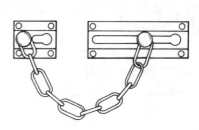

Figure 407   *Flush bolt*   Figure 408   *Security chain*   Figure 409 *Door holder*

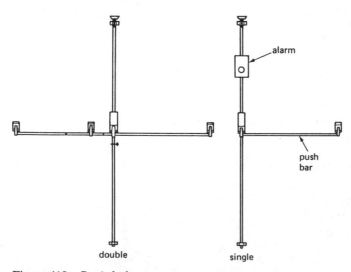

double   single

Figure 410   *Panic bolts*

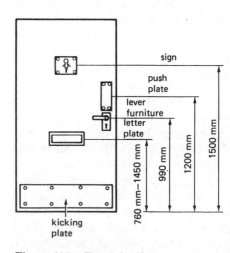

Figure 411   *Fixing heights*

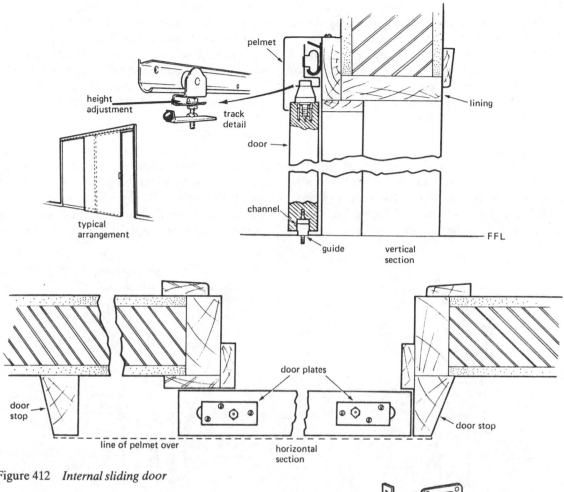

Figure 412   *Internal sliding door*

Figure 411 illustrates the recommended fixing height for various items.

Sliding doors

Sliding doors may be used either to economize on space where it is not possible to swing a door or where large openings are required that would be difficult to close with swinging doors.

Various types of sliding gear are available, for straight sliding, by-passing and around the corner arrangements. In general top sliding gear is used for lightweight doors and bottom sliding gear is used for heavier doors.

Figure 412 shows typical details and sections of an internal sliding door which is top hung. The bottom of the door is controlled by a small

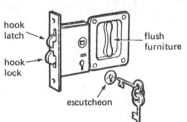

Figure 413   *Sliding door mortise lock/latch*

nylon guide that runs in a channel, set in the bottom of the door.

Sliding doors require special locks and latches with hook-shaped bolts which prevent the door being slid open. The furniture is usually flush fitting so that the doors are able to slide without fouling (see Figure 413).

Folding doors

Folding doors are in fact folding sliding doors. They can be used either as movable internal partitions to divide up large areas or as commercial folding doors for warehouse and showroom entrances etc. They may be either end folding or centre folding. Top-hung or bottom-roller gear is available for both types.

End folding

End-folding units should consist of an even number of leaves, up to six, hinged on either jamb of the frame. For extra wide openings, additional 'floating' units of four or six leaves not hinged to either jamb may be added. An extra leaf can be added if a swinging access door is required. A leaf width of between 600 mm and 900 mm is recommended. These must have solid top and bottom rails so that a firm fixing for the edge-fitting hangers and guides can be achieved.

Figure 414 shows the arrangement and section of an external end-folding top-hung unit.

Centre folding

Centre-folding units are of a similar construction to edge-folding units except that there will always be a half-leaf hinged to the frame to permit the centre folding arrangement.

From 1½ to 7½ leaves may be hinged together on either jamb of the frame. An extra

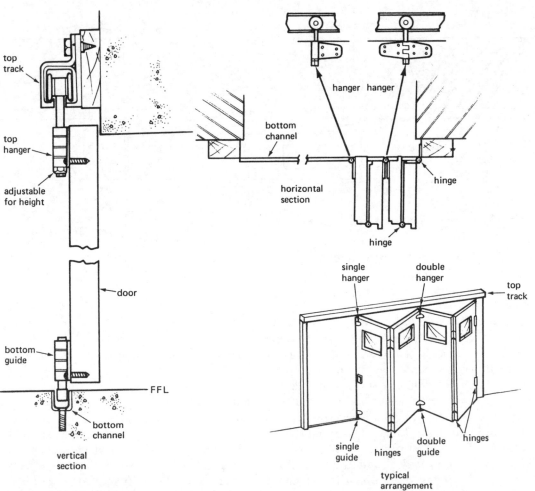

Figure 414   *End-folding doors*

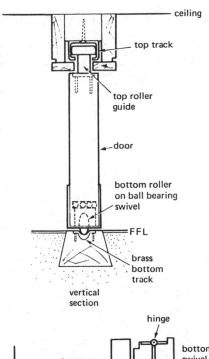

vertical
section

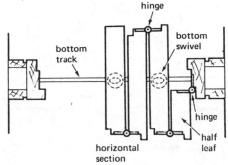

horizontal
section

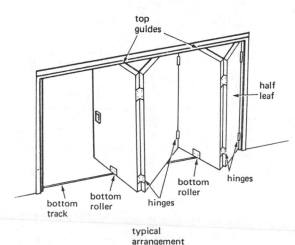

typical
arrangement

Figure 415   *Centre-folding doors*

leaf can be added if a swinging access door is required.

Figure 415 shows details and sections of an internal centre-folding bottom-running partition.

Revolving doors

Revolving doors may be used as main entrances to hotels, offices and shops etc. They allow a fairly constant flow of traffic while reducing draughts and heat loss, although they are often used adjacent to swinging doors in order to accommodate extra traffic and goods etc.

The design, construction and installation of revolving doors is normally carried out by a specialist firm.

Stairs

A stairway can be defined as a series of steps (combination of tread and riser) giving floor-to-floor access. Each continuous set of steps is called a flight. Landings are introduced between floor levels either to break up a long flight, thus giving a rest point, or to change the direction of the stair where there is a restricted going.

Types of stair

Stairs can be classified according to their plan shape. The main ones are:

Straight-flight stair
Quarter-turn stair
Half-turn stair
Geometrical stair

In addition, each type can be further classified by its method of construction e.g. close string, open string, open riser, carriage beam, spine beam etc.

Straight-flight stair

These run in one direction for the entire length. Figure 416 shows three different variations.

The flight which is closed between two walls, also known as a cottage stair, is the simplest and most economical to make. Its handrail is usually a simple section fixed either directly on to the wall or on brackets.

The flight fixed against one wall is said to be open one side. This open or outer string is normally terminated and supported at either end by a newel post. A balustrade must be fixed to this side to provide protection. The infilling of this can be either open or closed and is usually capped by a handrail. Where the width of the flight exceeds one metre in width a wall handrail will also be required.

Where the flight is free standing, neither side being against a wall, it is said to be open both sides. The open sides are treated in the same way as for the flight open one side.

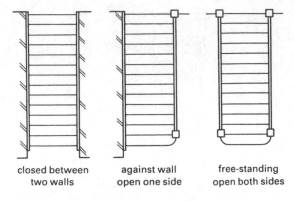

closed between   against wall   free-standing
two walls   open one side   open both sides

Figure 416   *Straight-flight stairs*

Quarter-turn stair

As its name suggests, this type of stair changes direction 90° to the left or right by means of either a quarter-space landing or tapered steps (see Figure 417).

Tapered steps, although economizing on space because of the introduction of the extra steps in place of the landing, are potentially dangerous owing to the narrowness of the treads on the inside of the turn. They should therefore be avoided where at all possible, especially in situations where they are likely to be used by young children or elderly persons, or at least be located at the bottom rather than at the top of the flight.

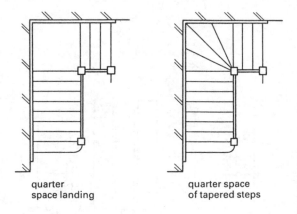

quarter   quarter space
space landing   of tapered steps

Figure 417   *Quarter-turn stairs*

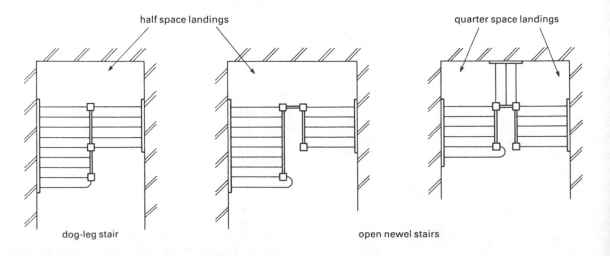

half space landings   quarter space landings

dog-leg stair   open newel stairs

Figure 418   *Half-turn stairs*

Half-turn stair

This stair reverses its direction through 180°, normally by a half-space landing. Figure 418 illustrates the two main types.

One is the dog-leg stair, where the outer strings of the upper and lower flights are joined into a common newel immediately above each other. This stair takes its name from the appearance of its sectional elevation.

The other type is the open-newel stair. This is also known as an open-well stair. Two newels are used at landing level. This separates the string of the upper and lower flights and thus creating a central space or well. A short flight is often introduced between the two newels at landing level, thereby creating two quarter-space landings and at the same time economizing on space.

In addition, tapered steps could also be used instead of landings to negotiate turns in both dog-leg and open-newel stairs.

Geometrical stair

The previous more robust types of stair utilize newels to change direction and also to terminate and support the outer strings. This gives them an image of strength and rigidity. A geometrical stair, as shown in Figure 419, presents a graceful, more aesthetic appearance. It has an outer string and a handrail that are continuous from one flight to another throughout the entire stairway. As both the string and handrail rise to suit the stairs throughout the curve they are said to be 'wreathed'.

Although the use of newels is not essential they are sometimes used at the top and bottom of a stair to support the scrolled handrail above. This type of stair is the most expensive and is thus rarely encountered in new work, except in 'one-off' very high-quality construction.

In addition to the stair illustrated, an infinite variety of design for geometrical stairs may be devised, including helical (often misnamed spiral) and elliptical stairs.

Building Regulations

The design and construction of stairs is very closely controlled by the Building Regulations:

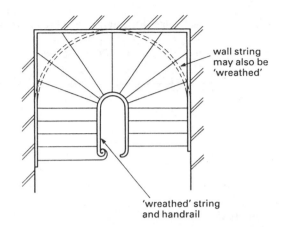

Figure 419   *Geometrical stair*

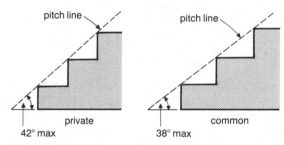

Figure 420   *Pitch*

1985: Part K. These lay down different requirements for stairs depending on the use of the building, these are summarized as follows and illustrated in Figures 420 to 427.

Note: These requirements do not apply to stairways outside a building; ladders; or a stairway with a rise of less than 600 mm, except where the drop at the side is more than 600 mm.

Pitch   The pitch or steepness is limited to a maximum of 42 degrees for a private stair (a stairway used only by one dwelling) and a maximum of 38 degrees for a common stair (a stairway used by two or more dwellings (see Figure 420).

Rise and going   For straight flights the steps should all have the same rise and the same going. Limits to these dimensions are applied to different stairs. In all cases twice the rise plus the going 2 R + G should fall between 550–700 (see Figure 421 and Table 35A).

Table 35A **Specific requirements for stairs: rise and going**

Description of stair	Max. rise (mm)	Min. going (mm)	Range (mm) (to meet pitch limitation)
Private stair	220	220	155–220 rise used with 245 to 260 going or 165–200 rise used with 220 to 305 going
Common stair	190	240	155–190 rise used with 240–320 going
Stairway in institutional building (except stairs only used by staff)	180	280	
Stairway in assembly area (except areas under 100 m²)	180	280	
Any other stairway	190	250	

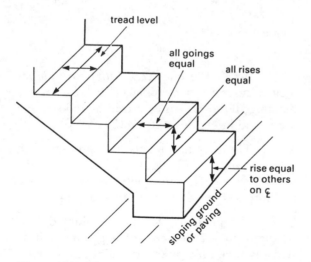

Figure 421   *Risers*

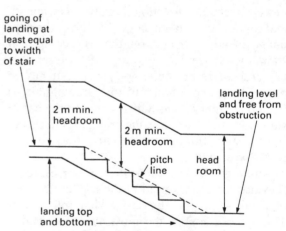

Figure 422   *Headroom and landing*

The rise is measured from the top surface of one tread to the top surface of the next tread. Goings are measured from face of riser to face of riser, and where there are not any risers from nosing to nosing.

Headroom   A minimum headroom of 2 m is required over the pitch line of all flights and over landings (see Figure 422).

Steps   All steps should have level treads, where steps have open risers the treads should overlap each other by at least 15 mm. The gaps in open riser steps must not permit the passage of a

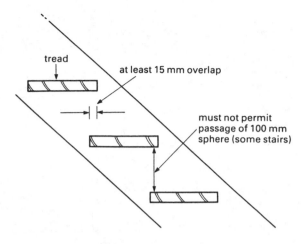

Figure 423   *Open-riser stairs*

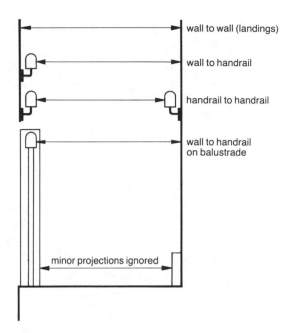

Figure 424   *Measuring minimum width*

100 mm diameter sphere when the stairway is in a dwelling (private and common); any other residential building; or an institutional building (where it is likely to be used by children under five years of age) (see Figure 423).

Width   Minimum widths for stairways depend on the type of stair, as shown in Table 35B.

These minimum dimensions are unobstructed widths (see Figure 424), although minor projections such as skirting strings and newels are ignored. Wide flights over 1.800 m should be sub-divided in width to form separate flights.

Length   No more than 36 risers are permitted in consecutive flights unless there is a change of direction of at least 30 degrees. Flights forming part of the stairway in a shop or an assembly area are limited to a maximum of 16 risers.

Landings   Landings are required at both ends of any flight. They should be free of obstruction and be at least equal in width and depth, to the width of its adjoining stairway. All landings should be level except where they are firm made-up or paved ground, when a slope up to 1 in 12 is permitted (see Figures 421 and 422).

Door swings should not obstruct a landing except at the bottom of a flight if it still leaves at least 400 mm clear across the full width of the bottom riser.

Tapered treads   These must conform to the previously mentioned rise and going restrictions,

Table 35B Specific requirements for stairs: minimum width

Description of stair	Minimum width (mm)
Private stair giving access to one room only (except kitchens and living room)	600
Other private stair	800
Common stair	900
Stairway in institutional building (except stairs only used by staff)	1000
Stairway in assembly area (except areas under 100 m²)	1000
Other stairway serving an area that can be used by more than 50 people	1000
Any other stairway	800

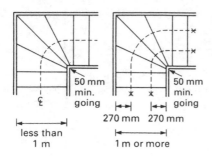

Figure 425   *Tapered tread details*

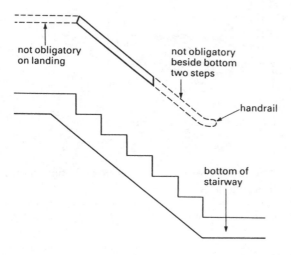

Figure 426   *Handrails*

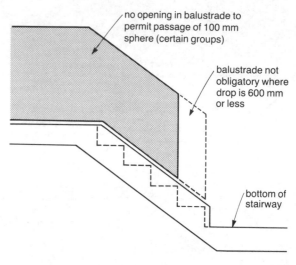

Figure 427   *Guarding of stairways*

measured as follows: flights less than 1 m wide in the middle; flights 1 m or wider, 270 mm in from each edge (see Figure 425). The minimum width of tread at the narrow end is 50 mm. All consecutive tapered treads should have the same taper.

Handrails   All flights less than 1 m wide require a handrail on one side, wider flights should have a handrail on both sides. These should be fixed between 840 mm and 1 m measured vertically above the pitch line. Handrails are not required; beside the bottom two steps of the stairway (see Figure 426).

Guarding   A balustrade or other suitable guard is required at the open sides of all flights and landings. Except where the drop is 600 mm or less. For all private and common stairways, those in institutional buildings likely to be used by children under five years of age, and any other residential building, openings in balustrades must not permit the passage of 100 mm diameter sphere; in addition its design should prevent children readily climbing up it. See Figure 427 and Table 35C.

Note: The purpose of prohibiting the passage of a 100 mm diameter sphere, through open risers and openings in balustrades, is to prevent children from getting their heads stuck in them.

The height of the balustrade depends on the type of stair.

***Table 35C* Specific requirements for stairs: minimum balustrade heights**

Description of stair	Minimum balustrade height (mm)	
	Flight	Landing
Private stairway	840	900
Common stairway	900	1000
Other stairway	900	1100

Alternative approach　An alternative approach to the stairway design requirements given in the Building Regulations AD: K is to use BS 5395 stairs, ladders and walkways. The BS is more comprehensive in that it states optimum sizes in addition to the minimum ones.

In certain aspects the BS is more restrictive than the AD and in others it is more lenient. Stairways must be designed in their entirety to conform with either the BS or AD. It is not permissible to pick the best requirements from both and mix them.

Means of escape　Stairways that are in offices, shops, dwellings of three or more storeys, or form part of the only means of escape for disabled persons, may need to conform to additional requirements. See mandatory rules for means of escape in case of fire published by HMSO.

Installation

The installation of any staircase on site follows the same basic procedure, although there will be differences depending on the type of stair and the nature of the site.

Stairs are normally delivered to site assembled as far as possible. However, for ease of handling each flight will be separate, its newels, handrail, balustrade and any tapered treads being supplied loose ready for on-site completion.

For maximum strength and rigidity the stairs should be fixed as shown in Figures 428, 429 and 430. The top newel is notched over the landing or floor trimmer and either bolted or coach

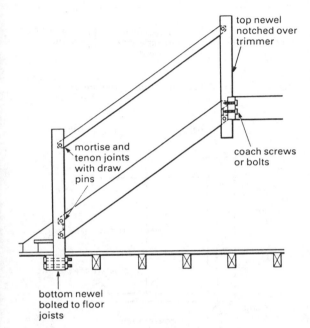

Figure 428　*Fixing outer string and handrail*

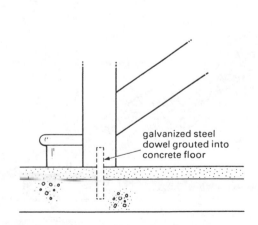

Figure 429　*Newel fixing*

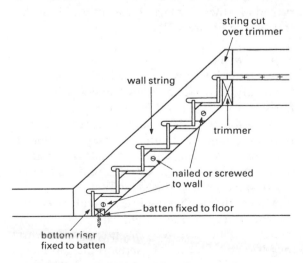

Figure 430　*Fixing wall string*

screwed to it. The lower newel should be carried through the landing or floor and bolted to the joists (see Figure 428). The lower newel on a solid ground floor can be fixed by inserting a steel dowel partly into the newel and grouting this into the concrete (Figure 429).

Figure 428 also shows that the outer string and handrail are mortised into the newels at either end. With the flight in position these joints are glued and then closed up and fixed using hardwood draw pins.

The wall string is cut over the trimmer at the top and cut nailed or screwed to the wall from the underside as illustrated in Figure 430. Also shown is how the bottom of a flight may be secured by screwing it to a batten fixed to the floor.

Illustrated in Figure 431 is a section across a flight fixed up against one wall showing typical finishing details.

Figure 432 shows how the trimmer around the stairwell opening is finished with an apron lining and nosing.

Where the width of the stair exceeds about 1 metre, a carriage may be fixed under the flight to support the centre of the treads and risers. To securely fix the carriage it is bird's mouthed at both ends, at the top over the trimmer and at the bottom over a plate fixed to the floor. Brackets are nailed to alternate sides of the carriage to provide further support across the width of the treads (see Figure 433).

Tapered treads

Any tapered treads are fixed after the main flights are in position. They should fit in place fairly easily as they will have been prefitted dry in the joiner's shop and disassembled for transportation. In practice a certain amount of adjustment is often required to take account of on-site conditions, e.g. slightly out of square or out of plumb brickwork etc.

After fitting the tapered treads and risers into the housings in the string, they should be wedged up and screwed. Because of their extra length some form of support is normally required under the tapered treads. This can be provided as shown in Figure 434 by bearers

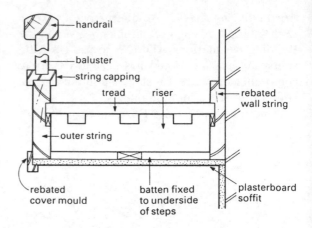

Figure 431   *Section across flight open one side*

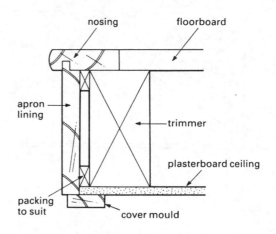

Figure 432   *Landing detail*

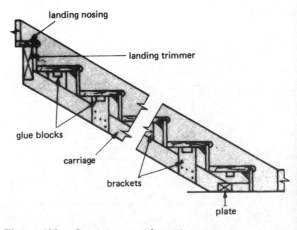

Figure 433   *Carriage on wider stairs*

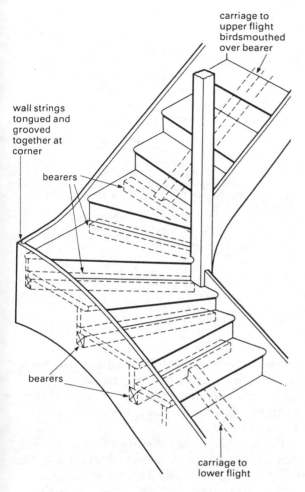

carriage to upper flight birdsmouthed over bearer

wall strings tongued and grooved together at corner

bearers

bearers

carriage to lower flight

Figure 434 *Tapered treads*

under the riser of each step. These are fixed between the two strings or between the string and the newel. Also shown is how the carriages of the main flights are bird's mouthed over these bearers.

Landings

The construction of landings and the materials used are normally similar to the upper floor.

Figure 435 shows details of a half-space landing. The trimmer joist spans between two walls and supports the end of the trimmed joists spanning the landing.

The free end of the trimmer for a quarter-space landing is normally supported by extending the newel post down to the floor, as shown in Figure 436. Alternatively either a landing frame or some form of cantilever landing could be used.

Figure 437 shows a typical landing support framework. This would be subsequently boxed in or made into a cupboard, creating extra storage space.

The cantilever landing shown in Figure 438 consists of a diagonal joist built in to the wall at both ends. This provides a bearing midway along the cantilever joist which is built in to the

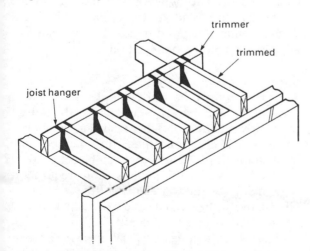

trimmer

trimmed

joist hanger

Figure 435 *Half-space landing details*

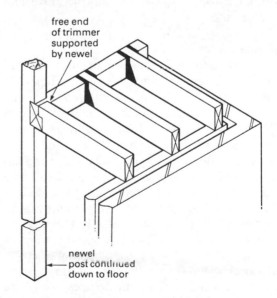

free end of trimmer supported by newel

newel post continued down to floor

Figure 436 *Quarter-space landing details*

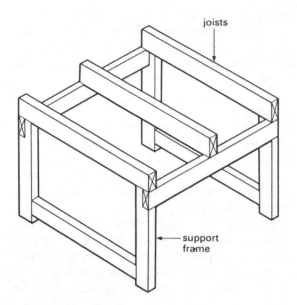

Figure 437   *Landing support framework*

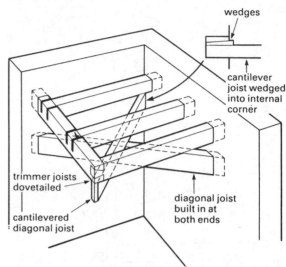

Figure 438   *Cantilever landing*

internal angle of the wall. The landing trimmer joists are dovetailed together and supported on their free end by the cantilevered joist. This method of support has the advantage of giving a clear space under the stair. It is essential that the timber used is well seasoned, as even slight shrinkage will cause the landing to move and creak in use.

Geometrical stair

These are supplied in a number of easily handled sections, the tapered treads being assembled on site as before. The main difference in the installation is the fixing of the 'wreathed' portion of the string. This will have been previously formed and permanently fixed at one end to the string. The other end of the wreathed string has to be fixed to its adjoining string on site. These are jointed one rise past the turn with a cross-grained tongue. A counter-cramp can be used to pull the two ends tightly together, as shown in Figure 439. This also has the effect of stiffening the stair and preventing movement at the joint. The cramp consists of three short pieces mortised to take the wedges. They are screwed to the strings initially only at one end,

the two outside pieces to the wreathed string and the middle piece with its mortise slightly off-centre to the straight string. After driving the wedges to pull up the joint, the other ends can be screwed.

The outer or wreathed string of a geometrical stair is usually of a cut-and-bracketed type illustrated in Figure 440. This shows the general construction, much of which will have been completed prior to delivery with the exception of the balusters and return nosing. Where a section contains tapered treads they will normally be completely assembled on site.

Open-riser stair

The fixing of open-riser or open-plan stairs with close strings and newels is the same as the stairs previously mentioned. Where carriage or spine beam stairs are concerned the method of installation differs. Both types can be completely prefabricated in the joiner's shop, requiring only fixing at the top and bottom on site. Alternatively they can be delivered in knock-down form for on-site assembly.

Figure 441 illustrates a typical open-riser stair supported on carriages. The upper ends of the

Figure 439   *Counter-cramp for fixing geometrical stair*

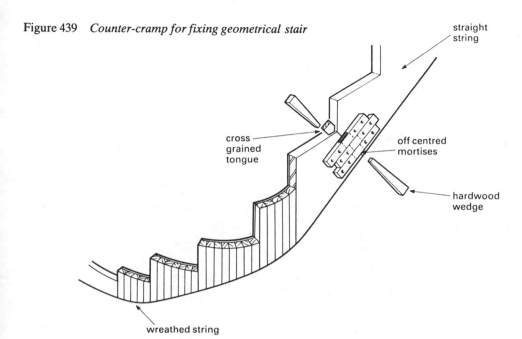

straight
string

cross
grained
tongue

off centred
mortises

hardwood
wedge

wreathed string

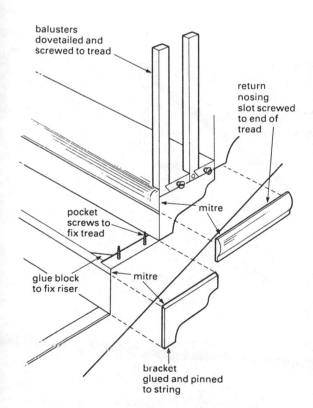

balusters
dovetailed and
screwed to tread

return
nosing
slot screwed
to end of
tread

mitre

pocket
screws to
fix tread

mitre

glue block
to fix riser

bracket
glued and pinned
to string

Figure 440   *Cut-and-bracketed geometrical stair*

carriages are bird's mouthed around the trimmer, while the lower ends of the carriages are fixed to the floor with metal angle brackets. The treads are supported by and screwed and pelleting to timber brackets, which are themselves glued and dowelled to the carriages. Newel posts are fixed at either end of the flight on to which the ranch-style plank balustrading is screwed and pelleted.

Illustrated in Figure 442 is a spine beam stair which is also known as a monocarriage stair. The spine beam is a large glulam section that is often tapered or curved on its underside to reduce its somewhat bulky appearance. Both ends of the spine beam are fixed to metal brackets that have been cast in the concrete; because of the great stresses and likelihood of movement at the junction between the tread and beam, it is essential that these are securely fixed. The shaped bearers would be bolted, screwed or fixed with metal brackets to the beam. The treads can then be screwed and pelleted on to the bearers. Metal rod balusters are often used for this type of stair. They are secured at one end to the tread. A mild steel core rail is used to secure the tops of the balusters. This is fixed

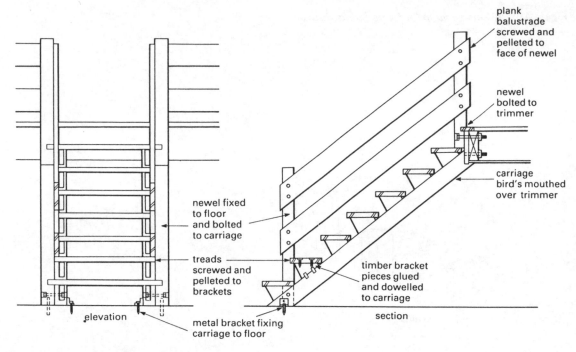

Figure 441   *Open-riser stair*

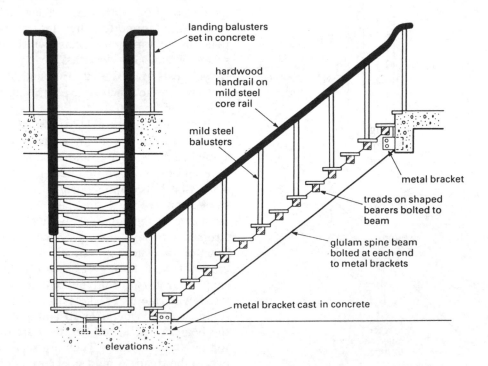

Figure 442   *Spine beam stair*

using set screws into the baluster after drilling
and tapping. The hardwood handrail is grooved
on the under side to conceal the core rail,
through which it is screwed. An enlarged detail
of this is shown in Figure 443.

On certain flights where the gap between the
treads is restricted, a partial riser tongued to
either the top or the underside of the tread can
be used. Figure 444 illustrates these two
alternative methods.

Treads of open-riser stairs are often found to
be noisy and slippery in use. They can be made
safer by fitting non-slip nosings to the front
edges of the treads. Alternatively, to cut down
on the noise and at the same time make them
less slippery, carpet may be either wrapped
around the treads between the carriages and
tacked or fitted into recesses that have been cut
into the top of each tread (see Figure 445).

Balustrade

Balustrading to stairs and landings can be
formed in many ways other than the standard
balusters, metal balusters and ranch-style plank
balustrading covered in previous examples.
Other methods of forming balustrades range
from framed panelling with a variety of infill,
including laminated or toughened glass, to
decorative wrought iron work in various designs.

Handrails

Handrails to straight flights with newels as
illustrated in previous examples are tenoned into
the face of the newel posts. In better-quality
work they will also be housed into the face of the
newel by about 6 mm so that any shrinkage will
not result in an open, unsightly joint.

Wall handrails either may be fixed by
plugging, screwing and pelleting direct to the
wall, or may stand clear of the wall on metal
brackets fixed at about 1 metre centres. Figure
446 illustrates a traditional section and a modern
built-up section fixed direct to the wall, as well
as one on brackets.

Where a handrail changes direction around a
corner or from rake to level, the section fixed
directly to the wall may simply be mitred.
Handrails on brackets are not normally mitred

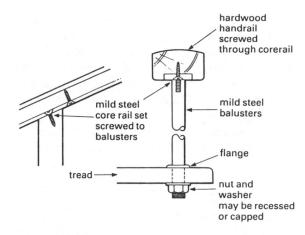

Figure 443   *Balustrade detail*

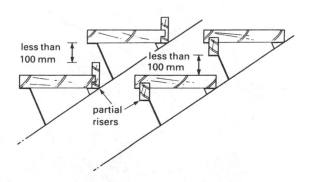

Figure 444   *Partial risers*

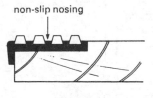

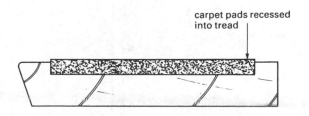

Figure 445   *Carpeting open-riser stairs*

but change direction with the aid of short tangential curved sections, jointed to the main straight lengths with handrail bolts and dowels. The nuts are set from the underside of the rail and the mortises are plugged with grain-matched inserts. Figure 447 illustrates a number of these curved sections.

A quadrant is used to turn a level handrail around a 90° bend. Ramps are either concave or convex and are used to join raked to level handrails. Wreaths are double-curvature sections. They are used where a raking handrail turns a corner, e.g. in stairs with tapered steps, or where a raking handrail turns a corner and changes to a level handrail, e.g. at the junction of stair and landing. Alternatively a ramp and mitre may be used. A half-newel can be used to give support to the handrail and balustrade where it meets the wall or a landing (see Figure 448).

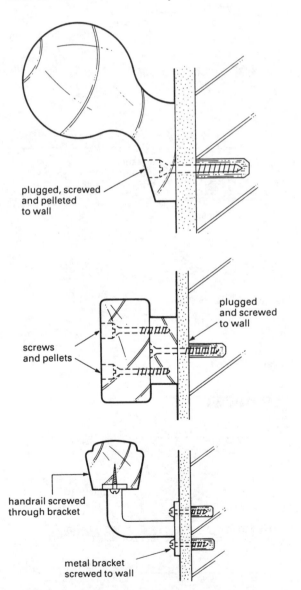

Figure 446   *Handrail sections*

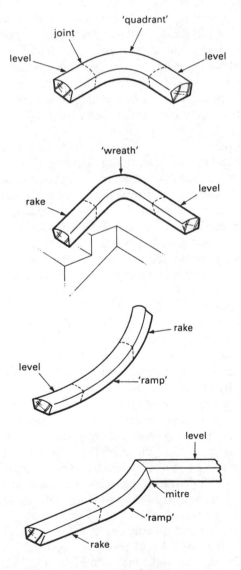

Figure 447   *Curved handrail sections*

The end of a handrail in a geometrical stair is supported by the balusters and may either terminate in a scroll or be mitred into the top of a decorative turned newel post, as shown in Figure 449. The setting out and making of geometrical handrails is the work of a highly specialized joiner.

Where the balustrading is of metal, as is often the case in present-day non-domestic construction, the handrail is fitted to a metal core rail. It

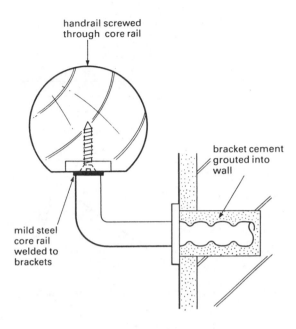

Figure 450 *Metal core rail and brackets*

is common practice for the handrail to be wreathed, grooved and jointed and then given to the metalworker to produce a suitable core rail. Details of fixing metal balustrades and core rails have been illustrated in previous examples. Wall handrails may also be fixed to core rails for additional strength.

Figure 450 shows a detail of a hardwood handrail that has been fitted to a metal core rail, welded on brackets and set in the wall.

Timber facings

Concrete stairs can be given a more pleasing appearance by the addition of hardwood treads, as shown in Figure 451. These are screwed and pelleted to dovetail blocks that have been cast into the concrete.

The landings may be given the same finish by secret fixing hardwood tongued-and-grooved flooring to dovetail bearers that have again been cast into the concrete.

In situations where the riser is also to be faced the detail shown in Figure 452 could also be used.

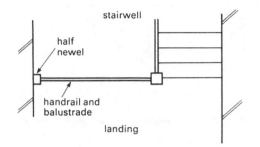

Figure 448 *Half newel detail*

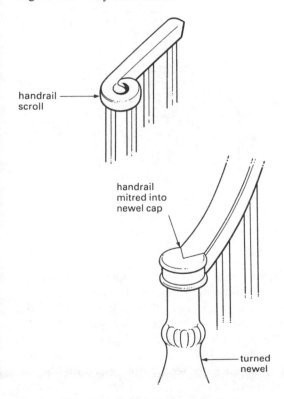

Figure 449 *Geometrical handrail*

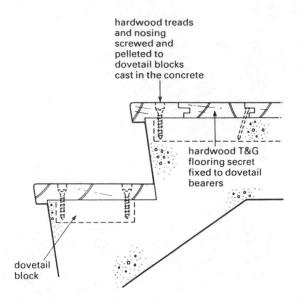

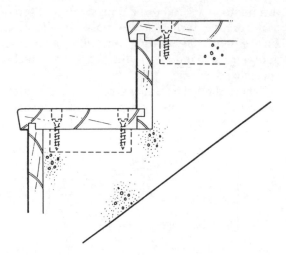

Figure 451   *Hardwood treads for concrete stairs*   Figure 452   *Hardwood risers for concrete stairs*

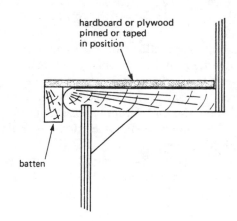

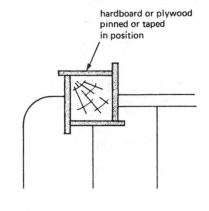

Figure 453   *Temporary protection of treads*   Figure 454   *Temporary protection of newels*

In certain circumstances a hardwood cut string is also used to finish the edge of a stair. This can be screwed and pelleted to fixing blocks.

Protection of completed work
After a new staircase has been installed, a short period spent taking measures to prevent damage during subsequent building work saves much more than it costs.

False treads made from strips of hardboard or plywood as shown in Figure 453 are pinned on to the top of each step. The batten fixed to the strips ensures the nosing is well protected.

On flights to be clear finished the false treads should be held in position with a strong adhesive tape, as pin-holes would not be acceptable.

Strips of hardboard or plywood are also used to protect newel posts. These can be either pinned or taped in position depending on the finish (see Figure 454).

Adequate protection of handrails and balustrades can be achieved by wrapping them in corrugated cardboard held in position with adhesive tape.

Self-assessment questions

1 Describe with the aid of sketches the correct methods of handling trussed rafters (a) by hand (b) by crane.

2 Sketch the plan arrangement of a centre-folding, bottom-running partition having four leaves.

3 State *two* alternative methods of obtaining the fall to a flat roof.

4 State the requirements of the Building Regulations applicable to the following:

(a) Tapered steps in a private residence
(b) Openings in the balustrade to a flight used by children under five years of age

5 Use sketches and brief notes to show the following construction details:

(a) The lateral restraint of a gable-end wall
(b) A method of fixing bolection mouldings to framed panelling

6 State the correct positions for the following barriers used in timber frame construction.

(a) Vapour barrier
(b) Moisture barrier
(c) Cavity barrier
(d) Fire stop

7 (a) Produce a labelled sketch to show a double stressed-skin plywood panel.
(b) Sketch *two* alternative methods of forming built-up timber beams.

8 (a) State the purpose of sealing the backs of panelling sections prior to fixing.
(b) Sketch *two* methods of secret fixing framed panelling to softwood grounds.

9 Use labelled sketches and brief notes to distinguish between balloon and platform frame methods of construction.

chapter 11

Temporary construction work

After reading this chapter the student should be able to:

1 State the principles involved in the following items of temporary construction:
   (a) Centres for arches
   (b) Shoring
   (c) Formwork for concrete

2 Identify the components of these various items.

3 Select the most suitable material for use in stated circumstances.

4 Produce sketches to show typical working details of these various items.

5 Select the most suitable detail or method of construction for a given situation.

Arch centres

To enable a bricklayer to build an arch he requires a temporary framework which is normally made of timber and is known as centring. There are two main types of supporting framework.

Turning piece

This is the simplest form of centre and is cut from a solid piece of timber. It is only suitable for flat or segmental arches which are of low rise, approximately 150 mm from the springing line (see Figure 455).

Built-up centres

These are used where the rise exceeds 150 mm. Centres for low rises up to approximately 200 mm can have solid ribs, as illustrated in Figure 456. For rises in excess of this, made-up or laminated rib frames are used. Figure 457 shows a built-up centre with rib frames made up from a double layer of separate ribs held together at the bottom with a tie. This is suitable for rises of approximately 500 mm. Where the width of the brickwork exceeds half a brick, cross-braces should be used to stiffen the centre. The two sets of ribs are spanned around the centre by lagging and at the bottom by bearers.

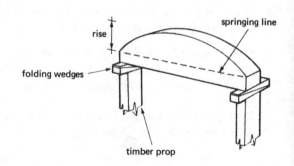

Figure 455   *Turning piece*

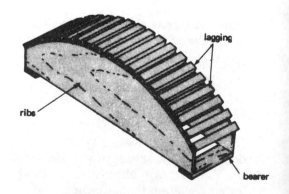

Figure 456   *Centre for low rise*

The laggings and bearers should be 20 mm shorter than the depth of the arch, thus ensuring that the centre will not obstruct the bricklayer in levelling and plumbing the brickwork. Timber battens or plywood may be used for the lagging, depending on the type of work in hand. In general plywood or closed timber lagging is used for brickwork and open timber laggings for stonework.

Figure 458 shows a centre for an equilateral or Gothic arch. Each rib frame is made from two separate ribs, held together at top and bottom with a tie, with a strut in the centre for additional support. Cross-braces are fixed to the struts to stiffen the centre.

Figure 459 shows a centre made up using two solid ribs cut from a sheet of 18 mm plywood.

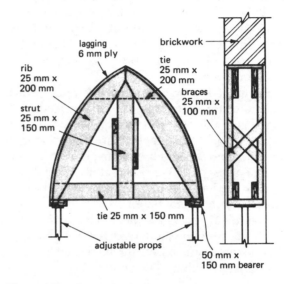

Figure 457 *Centre with rib frames*

Figure 458 *Centre for Gothic arch*

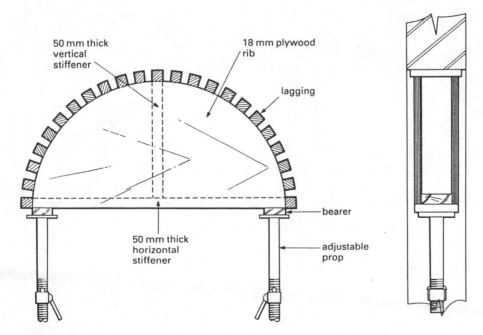

Figure 459 *Centre with two solid plywood ribs*

They are joined around the curve by lagging and at the bottom by bearers. The vertical and the horizontal timber stiffeners have been included to provide rigidity. These take the place of the cross-braces used in traditional centres.

The previous turning pieces and centres were suitable for arches with spans of up to approximately 1 m. Centres for larger spans can be made using the same form of construction, the only difference being that the size of the timber used should be increased to support the additional load.

Figure 460 shows a modern arch centre which is suitable for spans of up to 3 m. The method of making up this centre is very similar to a trussed rafter. The components are butt jointed together and secured by nailing plywood gussets or nail plates on either side. Before assembly the timber used should be prepared and individual ribs precut to a template.

Figure 461 shows a semi-elliptical arch centre made up using the modern gusset plate method. This method can be used for making up any arch centre irrespective of its outline shape.

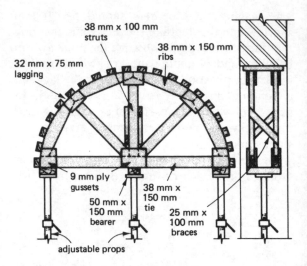

Figure 460   *Modern arch centre*

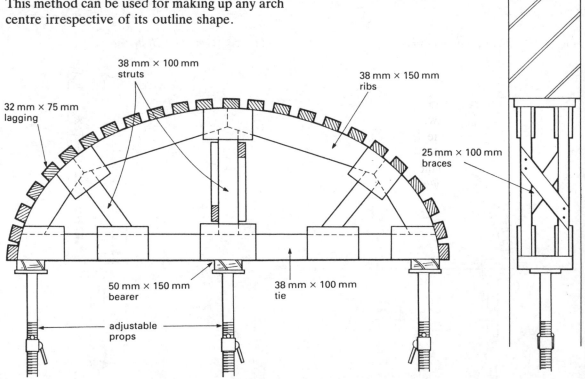

Figure 461   *Semi-elliptical modern arch centre*

Note: Arches with spans in excess of approximately 3 m are rarely encountered in normal building work. They are normally restricted to civil engineering work, such as bridge or tunnel construction.

Setting out and assembly

Segmental centres and turning pieces are set out using either the triangular frame method or a radius rod. Where the radius rod is used, the required radius will have to be calculated or the centre point found by bisection. Other arched centres are normally set out using a radius rod or trammel. The geometry required for setting out these and various other arch centre outlines is covered in Chapter 7.

Note: When making the outline of an arch an allowance must be made for the thickness of the laggings.

The rib frames for built-up centres should be assembled over a full-size outline of the centre which has been marked either on a sheet of ply or the workshop floor. This ensures the ribs are made up to the required shape. Figure 462 shows one rib frame for a small semicircular centre. The inner ribs, outer ribs, struts and tie are clench nailed together. The outline of the arch has been marked and the rib frame is ready to be cut on the band saw. Once the rib frames have been assembled the lagging bearers and braces can be nailed in position.

On site, where a band saw may not be available, a portable power jig saw can be used. The ribs for larger centres are normally precut to a template before the rib frames are assembled.

Support of centres

Turning pieces and centres can be supported, levelled and adjusted by means of either adjustable steel props or timber posts and folding wedges. The props or posts transfer the load imposed on the centre to the ground or other support: the adjustment given by the props or wedges enables the centre to be levelled and in addition facilitates the easing and striking (slight lowering and removal) of the centre without damage to the finished brick-

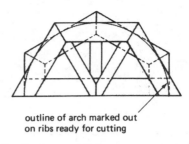

outline of arch marked out
on ribs ready for cutting

Figure 462 *Setting out rib frame*

work. Large-span centres require additional intermediate props in order to support their imposed load. Once the arch has been built and the mortar joints have set sufficiently, the centre can be removed; but before this, props or wedges should be gradually eased until the arch takes up the load of the structure.

Shoring

When a building is to be extensively altered or is considered to be structurally unsound, possibly owing to ground subsidence, it may be necessary to give temporary support to the walls of the building. This temporary support is called shoring. The three main types used are (Figure 463) vertical shores, raking shores and horizontal shores.

Vertical shores give vertical support; horizontal shores provide horizontal support; whereas raking shores fall somewhere between the two, providing a certain amount of both vertical and horizontal support. Often a combination of the two or more types are required.

Note: As an alternative to timber, tubular scaffolding or proprietary steel systems are often used. This discussion is restricted to timber.

Vertical shores

The purpose of vertical shores is to support the superimposed or dead loads of a section of a building during alteration or repair work. A typical situation where vertical shores are used would be where an opening is to be made in a loadbearing wall. The wall above the opening

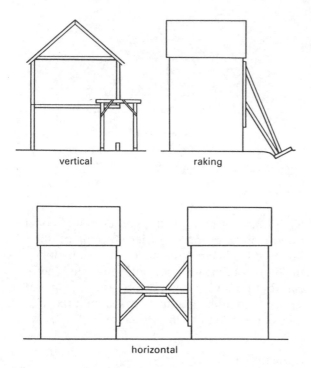

vertical   raking

horizontal

Figure 463 *Types of shoring*

must be supported while a lintel is inserted and the wall made good around the lintel.

Figure 464 shows a typical detail for vertical shores.

Sequence of operations

1   Strut all window openings. This is done by placing lengths of 50 mm × 75 mm timber in the window reveals and driving struts tightly between them.

2   Prop floors using 75 mm × 225 mm head and sole plates and adjustable steel props.

Note: On hollow ground floors, some boards should be removed so that the prop can extend down to the oversite concrete.

3   Cut holes in the wall for the needles. These should be spaced at 1.2 m centres under solid brickwork and not placed under windows etc.

4   Place the sole plates on firm ground both inside and outside the building, as these are going to spread the load.

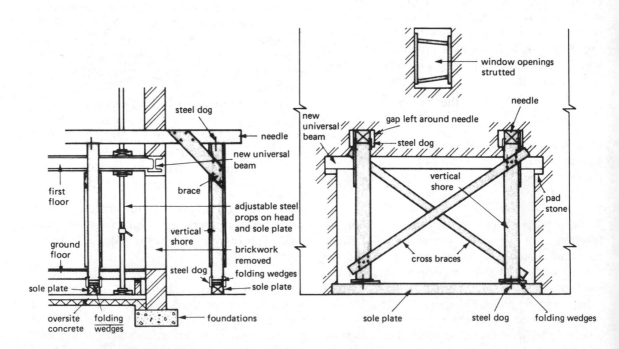

Figure 464 *Detail for vertical shores*

Note: It is a good idea to place the lintel in position on the floor before the shoring is erected, as access may be restricted afterwards.

5   Insert the needles through the wall and support them on dead shores. Drive hardwood folding wedges between the vertical shores and the sole plates, to bring the needles tight up under the brickwork. Packings may be needed between the needles and the brickwork.

Note: Where cement mortar is used for the packings it must be allowed to harden before any load is placed upon it.

6   Securely fix all joints between the sole plates, the vertical shores and the needles with steel dogs.
7   Cross-brace the vertical shores to prevent any possibility of them overturning.
8   Check all of the shoring for tightness, i.e. props, wedges, struts, bracing etc., and adjust if required.
9   Remove wall and build piers and padstones to support the lintel.
10 Insert the lintel. This is usually either a universal beam or a concrete lintel.
11 Make good the brickwork around the lintel and allow at least seven days for this to thoroughly set.
12 Ease and remove the shoring and make good the holes in the wall through which the needles passed.

Note: The easing entails partially slackening the wedges. After about one hour these should be checked. If they are still loose then all of the shoring can be removed using the reverse order to that in which it was erected. But if the wedges have tightened, some form of settlement has occurred. The new brickwork around the lintel should be checked for any signs of cracking. If this is satisfactory then only some initial settlement has taken place and the easing procedure can be repeated.

The size of timbers used for vertical shores will depend on the building to be supported, but an approximate method of determining a suitable section of timber for a two-storey building is to divide the shore's height by twenty. For example, vertical shores which are 3 m high require a section of $3000 \div 20 = 150$ mm. Therefore the section required is 150 mm $\times$ 150 mm.

Where the building exceeds two storeys, 50 mm should be added to the section for each additional storey. For example, vertical shores which are 3 m high for a three-storey building require a section of 150 mm + 50 mm. Therefore the section required is 200 mm $\times$ 200 mm.

In order to save on costs, second-hand timber can be used providing it is sound and free from defects. Where large-section timber is not available, this can be built up or laminated from smaller sections; for example, three lengths of 50 mm $\times$ 150 mm bolted together will give a 150 mm $\times$ 150 mm section.

Raking shores

These are shores that are inclined to the face of a building. Their purpose is to provide support to a building that is in danger of collapsing, or they may be used in conjunction with vertical shores for support during alteration or repair work.

In order to provide maximum support to the floors and to prevent 'pushing in' defective brickwork, the tops of the rakers must be positioned in relation to the floors (see Figure 465). When the joists are at right angles to the wall the centre line of the raker should, when extended, intersect with the centre of the joist's bearing. For joists that are parallel to the wall, the centre line of the floor, wall and raker should intersect. Figure 466 shows the front and side elevation of a single raking shore. These should be positioned at each end of the building and over intermediate cross-walls at between 2.5 m and 5 m apart, depending on the building's condition.

Note The term 'single raking shore' does not refer to the number of shores used but to the number of rakers in each shore, single, double, triple etc.

Figure 467 shows the jointing arrangement at the top of the raker. The raker is cut to fit the wallpiece and notched around the needle. This locates it and prevents lateral movement. A straight-grained hardwood must be used for the needle, which is mortised through the wallpiece and allowed to project into the brickwork by about 100 mm. The function of the wallpiece is to spread the thrust of the raker evenly over a large area of the wall. In order to do this

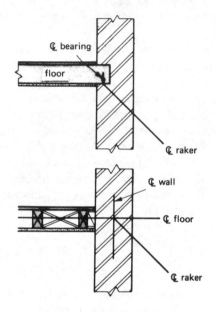

Figure 465   *Position of raking shores*

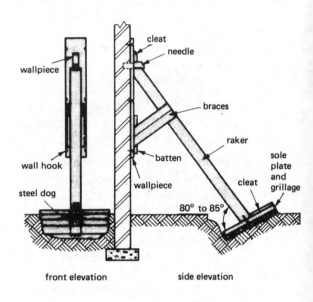

Figure 466   *Raking shore elevations*

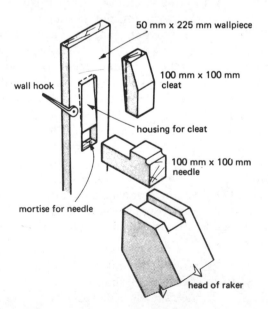

Figure 467   *Jointing arrangement at top of raker*

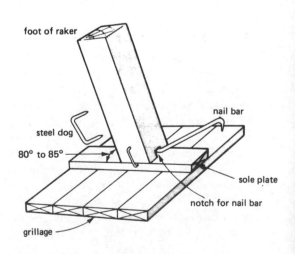

Figure 468   *Raker detail at ground level*

effectively it must be securely fixed back to the wall using wall hooks. The cleat which is housed into the wallpiece stiffens the needle.

Figure 468 shows the detail at ground level. This consists of the raker bearing on the sole plate at an angle of about 80–85°.

Note: This angle must always be less than 90° to enable the raker to be tightened when it is levered forward.

Where the ground is weak, a grid or grillage of sleepers can be placed under the sole plate to spread the load over a larger area.

Figure 469 shows a double raking shore to a two-storey building. The head of each raker must be positioned in relation to the floor as before. In any shore system the internal angles between the outer raker and the horizontal should be between 60° and 75°.

Figure 470 shows a multiple raking shore to a four-storey building. Where a sufficient length of timber is not available for the outer raker it may be made up using two pieces. The longest available length is used for the top rider shore. The remaining length is made up with a back shore that lays against the adjacent raker. Adjustment is made by tightening the folding wedges between the rider and back shore.

Sequence of operations
1 Strut windows as before
2 Cut out half-bricks in the wall to accommodate the needles.
3 Fix the needle and the cleat into the wallpiece.
4 Place the prepared wallpiece up against the wall and fix.
5 Prepare the sole plate and grillage.
6 Place the raker in position and tighten using a nail bar to lever it forward on the sole plate.

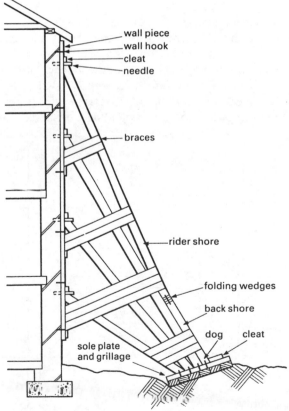

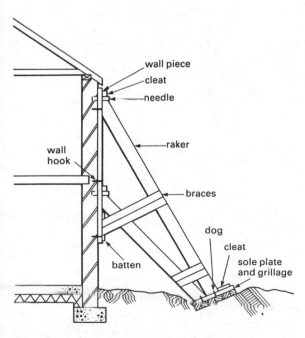

Figure 469 *Double raking shore to two-storey building*

Figure 470 *Multiple raking shore*

Note: Overtightening can be dangerous. The shore is there for support only. No attempt should be made to push back bulging brickwork.

7 Fix the foot of the raker with a cleat and dogs.
8 Brace the raker back to the wallpiece.

Note: Diagonal cross-braces and ties should be used between adjacent shores.

9 Check the shoring for tightness periodically and adjust as required.

Timber sizes again depend on the buildings being supported, but as a guide 150 mm × 150 mm rakers are suitable for single-shore systems, 175 mm × 175 mm for double and 225 mm × 225 mm for triple. As before, these sections can be laminated by bolting a number of smaller sections together.

Horizontal shores

These are also known as flying shores and are used to provide horizontal support between the walls of buildings that run parallel to each other. They are mainly used for support when an intermediate building of a terrace has to be demolished prior to rebuilding, or across a

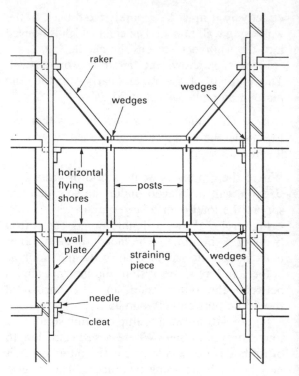

Figure 472   *Double horizontal shore*

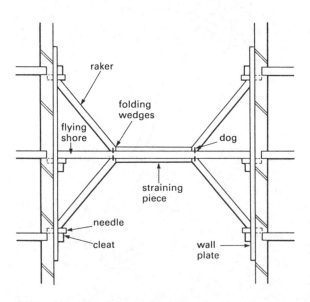

Figure 471   *Single horizontal shore*

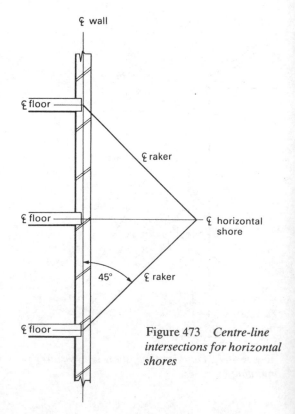

Figure 473   *Centre-line intersections for horizontal shores*

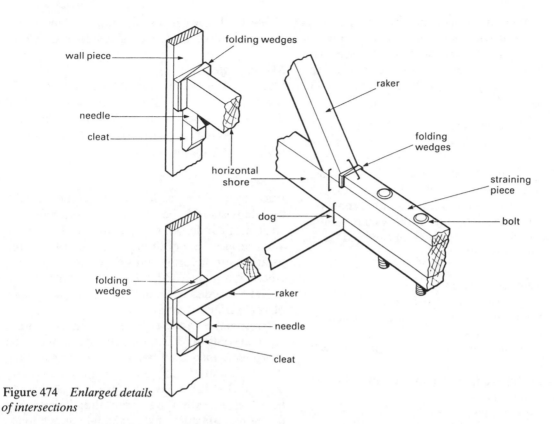

Figure 474 *Enlarged details of intersections*

narrow street or alley way, to support a weak wall off a sound one. In these situations the use of raking shores may be impracticable because of the limited space available or because of the obstruction they would cause at ground level.

Buildings of two storeys in height require only a single horizontal shore suitably strutted as shown in Figure 471. For taller buildings multiple horizontal shores may be required. Figure 472 shows the arrangement of a double horizontal shore.

The arrangement and position of the shores, wallpieces, needles and cleats are similar to those used for raking shores.

Figure 473 shows the centre-line intersections of floor, wall and shoring timbers. The positions of needles and cleats are inverted to support the horizontal shore and take the downward thrust from the lower rakers. Hardwood folding wedges are used to tighten the shore. Enlarged details are shown in Figure 474.

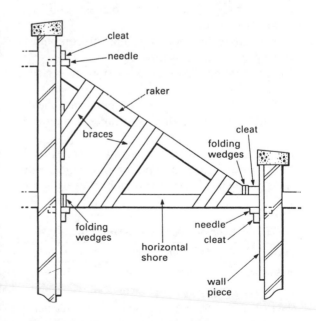

Figure 475 *Horizontal shore for different floor levels*

Note: Often more than one horizontal shore is required to provide sufficient support, in which case a system of shores can be used with individual sets of shores positioned near the ends of the opposite walls and at 2.5–5 m intervals.

Figure 475 illustrates the use of a horizontal shore where one building is higher than the other. The floor levels of the two opposing buildings do not always coincide. In these cases the floor levels of the weaker building should be used to determine the positions of the shores. A thicker wallpiece is used on the sound building to transfer the thrust to the floors and reduce the risk of 'pushing in' the wall.

Sequence of operations
1 Strut window opening (if any).
2 Cut out half-bricks in the wall to accommodate the needles.
3 Fix the needles and cleats into the wallpieces.
4 Place the prepared wallpieces up against the walls and fix.
5 Lay horizontal shores and posts in position and wedge up.
6 Place rakers and straining pieces in position and wedge up.
7 Nail all wedges and dog joints on completion to prevent lateral movement.
8 Fix diagonal cross-braces between adjacent sets of shores.
9 Check the shoring for tightness periodically and adjust by re-driving wedges if required.

Timber sizes in this case depend on the span of the horizontal shore and not on the height of the building. Typical sizes for members are given in

Table 36. These can also be laminated by bolting a number of smaller sections together as before.

Shoring safety
Shoring is normally carried out by specialist firms. However, in all cases the work must be designed and closely supervised during erection by an experienced person with extensive knowledge of shoring operations.

Inspections
Prior to erection a detailed inspection of the building should be made to determine its structural condition. Contact the local authority and service undertakings to determine the locations of underground sewers, water gas and electricity mains and telephone cables. These must be avoided when positioning the sole plates of vertical and raking shores.

Irrespective of the type of shoring to be used, all materials and component parts must be thoroughly inspected before erection. Anything that is found to be defective must be clearly marked that it is unsafe for use. Timber should be discarded. Metal parts can often be returned to the manufacturer for straightening or repair.

After erection every shoring system must be inspected at seven-day intervals and after adverse weather conditions for signs of distortion and movement. Points to check:

Distortion of members caused by overloading.
Tightness of members. Slackness can be caused by timber drying out, or by soil movement due to repetitive freezing and thawing or soaking and drying of the ground.
Displacement of timbers including wedges, possibly due to traffic vibration, moving plant or settlement of building.

Table 36 **Sizes for horizontal shore members**

Span	Horizontal shore	Raker posts	Straining piece	Wall piece
up to 4 m	100 mm × 150 mm	100 mm × 100 mm	50 mm × 100 mm	50 mm × 225 mm
4 m to 6 m	150 mm × 150 mm	100 mm × 100 mm	50 mm × 100 mm	50 mm × 225 mm
6 m to 9 m	150 mm × 225 mm	100 mm × 150 mm	50 mm × 100 mm	75 mm × 275 mm
9 m to 12 m	225 mm × 225 mm	150 mm × 150 mm	50 mm × 150 mm	75 mm × 275 mm

If further movement, cracking or bulging of the building is noticed, the designer of the shoring should be contacted immediately for advice, as such movement could possibly end in total collapse.

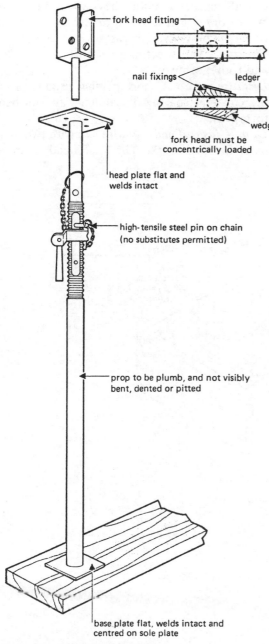

Figure 476   *Adjustable prop*

Removal of shoring

Horizontal or raking shores supporting a structurally unsound building cannot be removed until the defect has been remedied (walls rebuilt or foundations underpinned etc.) or the building has been completely demolished.

The procedure for striking is normally the reverse of that used for erection. This should be done in easy stages over several days so that the structure gradually takes up its full load. Look out for signs of building movement such as cracks in the brickwork or the opening up of mortar joints. If such movement is found, consult a structural specialist immediately.

Note: Raking or horizontal shores should be the first to be erected and the last to be removed when used in conjunction with vertical shores.

Formwork

Formwork can be defined as a temporary structure which is designed to shape and support the wet concrete until it cures sufficiently to become self-supporting, and thus includes not only the actual materials in contact with the concrete but all of the associated supporting structure.

Glossary of terms and basic principles

Adjustable prop (Figure 476)   A proprietary steel prop with provision for adjustment so that its length may be varied.

Beam box   The formwork for a beam, which includes the sides and the soffit.

Beam clamp (Figure 477)   A proprietary clamp

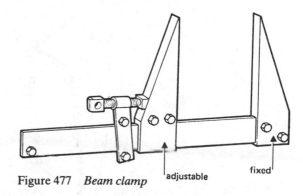

Figure 477   *Beam clamp*

or timber yoke which maintains a constant beam width during casting.

Blow hole A small hole or cavity in the concrete face caused by an air pocket, normally not more than 15 mm in diameter.

Box-out (Figure 478) The formwork for a pocket or opening in the concrete item, e.g. bolt hole, service duct opening, door opening etc.

Column box The formwork for a column.

Column cramp (Figure 479) A proprietary steel cramp or timber yoke which holds the column box tightly together during casting.

Cover The measurement between the concrete surface and the reinforcement. This protects the reinforcement from corrosion and increases the resistance to fire.

Cube test A number of standard-size cubes are cast on site from specified mixes. After curing one is placed in a press and subjected to an increasing load to determine its crushing or compressive strength. After curing for twenty-four hours in the metal moulds, the cubes are stored in water until they are sent to the laboratory for testing, normally at seven and twenty-eight days after casting.

Decking The sheeting or soffit of slab (floor and roof) formwork.

Distance piece A short member used to ensure the constant spacing of parallel wall and beam formwork.

Double-headed nail A wire nail with two heads used for formwork. The first head is driven

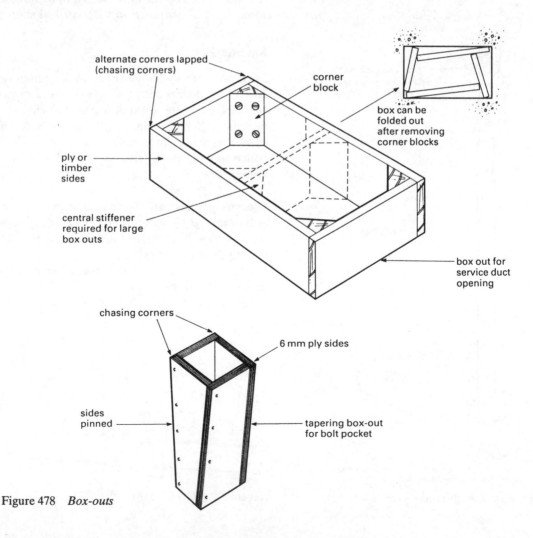

Figure 478   *Box-outs*

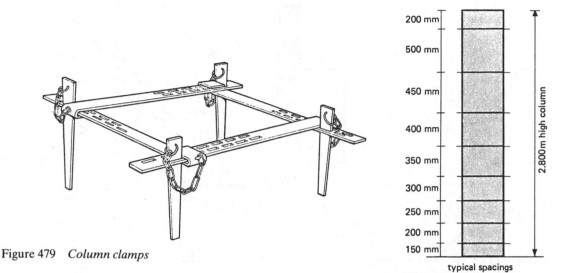

Figure 479   *Column clamps*

typical spacings

home for strength, the second is left projecting, enabling easy withdrawal.

Draw (Figure 480)   The lead or taper of a fillet to allow its ease of removal from the cast concrete. Large features may require a false lead or draw.

Edge form   The vertical formwork to the edge of a slab, path or road etc.

Expanded metal   An open-mesh sheet metal which is useful for forming box-outs and permanent stop ends. It is fairly easy to cut using shears. Reinforcing bars can be pushed through without difficulty. It has the advantage, when used as a stop end, that it provides a key for the subsequent pour.

Expanded polystyrene   A rigid plastic, obtainable in blocks or sheets. Its main use is for forming box-outs and other small pockets for holding-down bolts, metal handrails, and balusters. After use the polystyrene can be removed by breaking it up, burning it out, or softening it out with petrol.

Fair face   A high-quality plain concrete finish achieved straight from the form, without any subsequent making good or touching up.

Falsework   The temporary support structure which supports the forms. Normally only used to describe the support structure for bridges and other major civil engineering works.

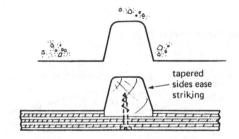

tapered sides ease striking

square feature false draw

this screw removed before striking

Figure 480   *Draw*

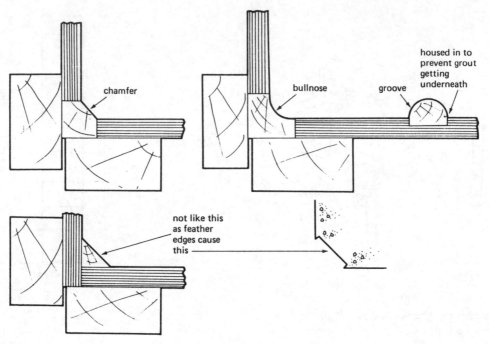

Figure 481   *Fillet*

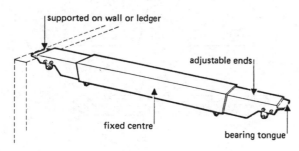

Figure 482   *Floor centre*

Fillet (Figure 481)   A small section of material fixed to the form face in order to produce a chamfer, bullnose or groove etc.

Floor centre (Figure 482)   A proprietary metal beam, normally of a lattice or box design, which is adjustable in length and used in place of ledgers in soffit formwork.

Form filler   A filler used to repair surface damage to sheathing materials and fill small gaps, nail and screw holes for fair-faced work. Repairs are normally overfilled and sanded down flush once the filler has hardened.

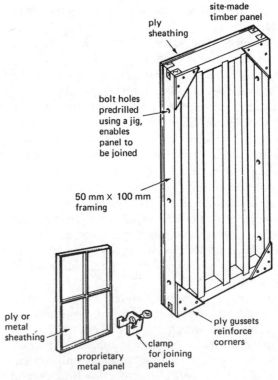

Figure 483   *Form panels*

Form lining The actual material used to line the inside of a form in order to produce the desired finish.

Form panel (Figure 483) A standard panel either of a proprietary metal, or of a framed design, or specifically made up using a timber frame and ply sheathing, normally based on standard sheet size. Prefabricated form panels can be used for a wide range of work including wall, slab construction and as base boards for precast work.

Form tape A waterproof adhesive tape used to seal joints in the form face, thus preventing grout leakage.

Form ties (Figure 484) A bolt or tie rod, often called a wall tie, used to hold the retaining sides

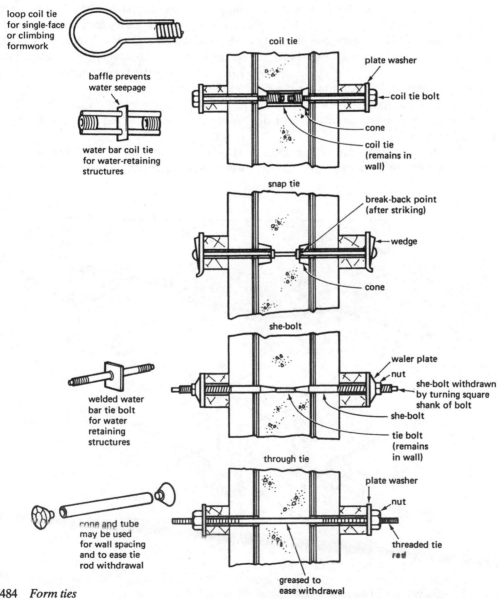

Figure 484 *Form ties*

of formwork in the correct location. The main types in current use are coil tie, snap tie, she-bolt and through tie.

Gang mould A precast mould to cast more than one unit in the same casting.

Grout loss The leakage at form joints of a mixture of cement, sand and water.

Hydrostatic pressure The pressure exerted on the formwork by the liquid concrete.

Insert A dovetail timber block or other proprietary item which is cast in the concrete to provide a subsequent fixing.

In situ cast concrete This is where the product is cast in the actual location or position where it is required.

Joist Normally 75 mm × 100 mm timbers used to support the decking material for concrete floor slabs. Proprietary aluminium joists are also available (see Figure 485).

Key A small indent or exposure of concrete surface to provide key for next casting.

Kicker A small upstand of concrete, the same plan size as the finished wall or column but only up to 150 mm in height. Its purpose is to locate the bottom of the form and prevent grout loss.

Lacing (Figure 486) Horizontal members used to space and tie together vertical supports. Their use converts adjustable steel props into a support system, thus greatly increasing their safe working load.

Ledger Normally 75 mm × 150 mm timbers, supported by adjustable steel props which in turn support the joists for concrete floor slabs. Also known as a runner. Proprietary aluminium ledgers are also available (see Figure 485).

Lift The height of concrete that is poured in one operation.

Live load The temporary load imposed on the formwork by workmen and concreting equipment.

Mould The formwork for a precast item.

Permanent form Formwork or the form face,

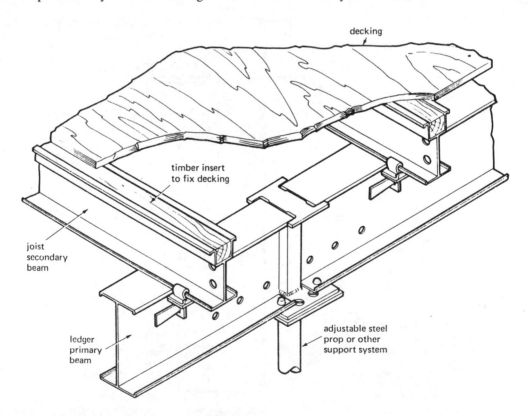

Figure 485   *Proprietary aluminium joists and ledger*

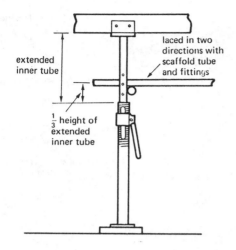

Figure 486   *Lacing*

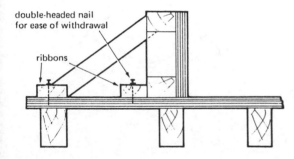

Figure 487   *Ribbon*

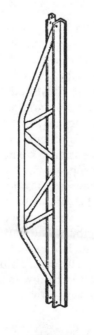

Figure 488   *Strong back*

which is left permanently in position after casting.

Precast concrete   This is where the product is cast out of location, on site or in a factory.

Release agent   A substance applied to the formwork to prevent adhesion between the form face and the concrete surface.

Ribbon (Figure 487)   A horizontal member fixed to a soffit, its purpose being to prevent beam sides and slab edges spreading. May be used to strut off.

Sheathing   The face of vertical forms.

Sill   A horizontal member, also known as a sole plate, used under vertical supports to evenly spread the load.

Slump test   An on-site test to measure the workability of concrete and compare its consistency between successive mixes of concrete. A metal slump cone is filled with concrete. After compaction the cone is removed and the slump measured. The workability of the mix increases with the slump.

Soffit   The underside of a floor slab or beam. Soffit formwork is known as decking.

Soldier   A vertical member to stiffen forms. Normally used in pairs in conjunction with form ties.

Stop end   A sheathing member used to form a construction or day joint at the end of a day's concreting.

Strike   To strike or striking is the removal of formwork after it has cured sufficiently to become self-supporting.

Strong back (Figure 488)   A proprietary soldier normally of a substantial metal construction and used where high pressures are anticipated.

Table form (Figure 489)   A proprietary decking and support system for soffits in the form of a table which can be struck, crane handled and repositioned in one piece.

Trough form   A hollow form used to produce trough-shaped recesses in the concrete soffit. Often made of glass-reinforced plastic.

Vibrator   A mechanical tool which imparts vibrations into the concrete to assist in its compaction. Types include an immersion vibrator, known as a poker, or an external vibrator attached to the outside of the formwork.

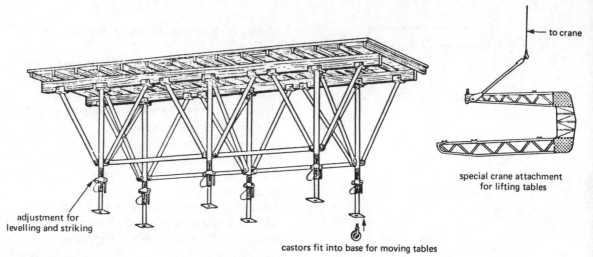

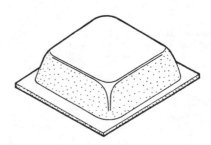
special crane attachment
for lifting tables

adjustment for
levelling and striking

castors fit into base for moving tables

Figure 489   *Table form*

Waffle form (Figure 490) A domed hollow form, square on plan, used to make recesses in the concrete soffit. Normally made of glass-reinforced plastic.

Waling A horizontal member to stiffen forms, and used in conjunction with soldiers or strong backs and wall ties.

Yoke The arrangement of members to encircle and secure a form, thus preventing movement. For column formwork these have now been superseded by proprietary metal column cramps.

Figure 490   *Waffle form*

Materials for formwork

When choosing the materials for formwork the following points should be born in mind:

Strength of materials
Economic use of materials
Ease of handling, making and erecting
Facilities for adjustment, levelling, easing and
    striking
The quality of the finish required

Timber

Softwood is the most commonly used material. The main reasons for this are:

Availability
Economy
Structural properties
Ease in working and handling

V grade European redwood, European whitewood and Western hemlock are the species most widely used. For heavily loaded members the extra cost of using stress-graded timber can often be justified.

It is common practice to use PAR timber, not only because of its uniform cross-section in any one parcel but also because it is better to handle and easier to clean off after any concrete spillage or seepage.

The use of solid timber in formwork, for both quality of finish and economic reasons, is almost exclusively restricted to the support and framing members and rarely the actual soffit or sheathing. The exception is where decorative board-marked feature finishes are required, in which case the formwork is lined with either prepared or sawn softwood boards.

The natural grain pattern, which is transferred to the finished concrete, may be enhanced by a prior soaking in water or a sand-blasting treatment.

The reuse potential of timber-boarded formwork is between one and ten uses, depending on the quality of finish required and the care taken in striking and handling.

Plywood

The two main types of plywood in common use are douglas fir and birch. The grain pattern of douglas fir plywood will be transferred to the concrete and can be used as a decorative feature, whereas birch plywood leaves a much smoother finish to the concrete.

Plywood for concrete formwork must be exterior quality. A/C or GIS grades are normally specified where a good smooth finish to the concrete is required. B/C, BB/C or select sheathing is used where minor surface irregularities in the concrete finish are permissible. C/C or sheathing may be specified for underground or covered work where the concrete finish is not important.

Surfaced plywoods are used almost exclusively for high-quality repetitive work. This gives a greater number of reuses and a smoother concrete finish, and also reduces the effects of moisture and abrasion. These factory-applied surface treatments include:

Barrier paints and varnishes
Cellulose film surface, impregnated with a phenolic resin
Overlay of glass fibre, impregnated with polyester or phenolic resin (GRP overlay)

On site any cut edges or holes must be sealed with a barrier paint or other waterproofing agent to prevent moisture absorption into the exposed layers, which would result in swelling and subsequent delamination.

Care in the handling of all types of plywood is essential, but more especially with surface plywoods as damaged surfaces are not so easily repaired.

The reuse potential of plywood varies widely depending on its handling and surface treat-

Table 37   Reuse values for plywood formwork

Type	Reuses (up to)
Untreated	10
Treated with barrier paint or varnish	20
Resin film surface	50
GRP overlay	100

Note: A compatible release agent must always be used with both untreated and treated plywoods

ment. Typical reuse values for plywood, assuming reasonable care in handling, are given in Table 37.

Profiled or textured surface plywoods are also obtainable. These impart a featured surface to the concrete. The reuse potential of these textured panels is limited as they become progressively more difficult to clean and maintain after each use.

As plywood is a laminated construction it has more layers parallel to the face grain than across it. This makes it stronger parallel to the face grain. Therefore for maximum strength the face grain should be placed at right angles to the panel supports. Where this is impracticable extra supports can be used.

Chipboard

Only exterior-grade chipboard or special-quality boards should be used as a structural sheathing material. Standard grades are unsuitable as they are not sufficiently resistant to moisture absorption; this leads to a large amount of moisture movement and a substantial loss in strength.

Special film-faced chipboards for formwork are also available. These have a fairly high reuse potential if properly treated and handled. In general, the number of reuses that can be expected from chipboard is less than that from the equivalent grade of plywood.

Fibreboard

This is used as a form lining material, and is normally nailed or glued to a supporting backing of timber or plywood. The two main qualities used for formwork are standard hardboard and oil-tempered hardboard.

The oil-tempered boards have a smoother surface and are less absorbent. They produce a better concrete finish. The oil-tempered boards are also stronger and stiffer but tend to be brittle; therefore the standard boards are more suitable for curved formwork as they can be bent to a smaller radius.

Hardboard's reuse potential is fairly limited. Standard boards are considered suitable for one use only, whereas oil-tempered boards if properly treated may give up to 10 uses. However, the quality of the concrete finish will rapidly deteriorate with each reuse.

Medium-density and softboards are sometimes used as absorbent form liners, thus reducing the risk of blow holes in the concrete finish and at the same time creating a fine surface texture. These boards are only suitable for one use.

Other form linings
A variety of other materials is available for lining forms. These include building paper, corrugated cardboard, plastic laminate, moulded rubber, expanded polystyrene etc. They are applied to the face of the form in order to obtain a specific concrete surface finish, e.g. smooth, textured or patterned.

Woodwool
Woodwool slabs are used as permanent formwork sheathing or decking for walls and flat floor slabs in addition to permanent waffle and trough forms. The open texture of the slabs provides an ideal key for the concrete and also any subsequent finish applied to the wall or ceiling. The use of woodwool slabs has the added advantage that they have good thermal acoustic and fire-resisting characteristics.

Metal
Steel and aluminium are normally used for formwork in circumstances where there is a high degree of repetitive work. The two main types of metal formwork available are:

Proprietary forms
Special purpose-made forms.

Proprietary forms
These consist of a wide range of equipment, including the following:

Steel framed panels with plywood or metal sheathing which may be used for walls, columns and slabs.
Aluminium beams for use as ledgers, joists and walings.
Adjustable props, table forms and other support systems.
Column cramps, beam cramps, wall ties and a variety of other ironmongery designed to secure formwork.

These proprietary systems are available for sale or hire from a number of specialist formwork suppliers.

The main advantages in using metal forms are their high strength, accuracy, smooth concrete finish, ease of erection and economy for repetitive use. Sometimes they have the disadvantages of being not readily adaptable, not readily acceptable of inserts, box-outs and fixing blocks, and generally heavier than other forms, thus requiring crane handling.

Special purpose-made forms
These are normally manufactured for one specific job. They tend to be used more in civil engineering rather than construction work. Typical applications include tunnelling, retaining walls, sea walls and slip forming etc. In addition the use of special purpose-made forms may be considered where a large number of identical components is required, e.g. precast moulds, column forms or complicated shapes such as mushroom-headed columns etc.

The reuse potential of metal forms is very high, and provided they are handled with care and thoroughly cleaned, oiled and maintained after each use, between 100 and 600 reuses can be expected. Where the forms have become damaged, distorted or otherwise defective, for both accuracy and safety reasons they should not be used. As the repair of these forms is a highly specialized operation they should either be discarded or returned to the manufacturer for repair or replacement.

Plastics

Sheet or foamed plastic can be an economical formwork material where repetitive use, high-quality finish and complicated shapes are required.

Glassfibre-reinforced plastics (GRP) are widely used for:

Waffle and trough moulds for floor construction
Profiled form liners, mainly for wall construction, to provide a patterned finish
Special purpose-made forms for complex shapes e.g. circular columns with mushroom heads etc.

The reuse potential of plastic is, in common with other formwork materials, dependent on its treatment and handling. In general one can expect up to 100 or more uses.

Plastics are particularly susceptible to impact damage and surface scratching; therefore extra care must be taken to avoid hitting the surface. Some plastic forms are specially designed to be removed by compressed air. After striking, the form face should be immediately cleaned to remove all traces of cement dust, using a special cleaning agent, clean soapy water or an oil-soaked cloth. Any hardened cement paste can be removed with a wooden scraper. The use of metal scrapers is not recommended as these damage the surface.

In addition to their high reuse value and their ability to form complex shapes and produce a high-quality finish, they also have the advantage of being low in weight.

Release agents

The correct use of release agents has a significant effect on the quality of the concrete finish and the reuse potential of the formwork. Their main functions are to:

Prevent adhesion between the form face and concrete surface
Aid the production of a high-quality blemish-free concrete finish
Enable the maximum reuse of formwork.

There are various types of release agent available. The choice is dependent on the form face material and quality of finish required. It is therefore essential that care is taken in choosing a release agent and that it is compatible with not only the form face but also any other formwork preparation such as barrier paints, fillers, surface retarders and waxes etc.

The main categories of release agent and surface coatings in general use, together with their main characteristics and suitable form faces, are given in Table 38.

Precautions in use

Whatever the category of release agent being used, the best results are obtained with a very thin film. Excessive application causes a poor concrete finish, presents a greater risk of it getting on to the reinforcement and also creates a safety hazard because of the risk of people slipping on horizontal surfaces.

Release agents contain substances which can be harmful to your health. They must therefore always be handled and used with care:

1 Always follow the manufacturer's instructions with regard to use and storage.
2 Avoid contact with skin, eyes or clothing.
3 Avoid breathing in the fumes, particularly when spraying.
4 Keep away from foodstuffs to avoid contamination.
5 Always wear protective clothing:
  (i) Barrier cream or disposable protective gloves
  (ii) A respirator when spraying.
6 Do not smoke or use near a source of ignition.
7 Ensure adequate ventilation when used internally.
8 Thoroughly wash your hands before eating and after work with soap and water or an appropriate hand cleanser.
9 In the case of accidental inhalation, swallowing or contact with the eyes, medical advice should be sought immediately.

Loads on formwork

The loads on formwork may be classified into:

Dead loads These consist of the self-weight of

Table 38   Release agents

Type	Characteristic	Brush	Squeegee	Spray	Sawn timber	Planed timber	Plywood (Unsealed)	Plywood (Sealed)	Metal	Plastic
		Method of application			Suitable form face					
Neat oil	Encourages the formation of blow holes and therefore not recommended									
Neat oils with surfactant	Contains a surface wetting agent to minimize the formation of blow holes	*		*	*	*	*	*	*	*
Mould cream emulsion	General-purpose release agent particularly suitable for absorbent surfaces	*	*		*	*	*			
Water-soluble emulsion	Causes discoloration and retardation of surface cement and is therefore not recommended for visual concrete									
Chemical release agent	Causes a chemical reaction at the form face, thus minutely retarding the concrete surface. Recommended for all high-quality work and particularly pretreated surfaces			*		*	*	*	*	*

the formwork and the deadweight of the concrete and reinforcing steel.

Imposed loads These can be considered as temporary loads and include the impact load of concrete being placed and the live loads of workmen and concreting equipment, in addition to the later storage of materials and forces from the permanent structure.

Environmental loading This includes wind loading and snow loading as well as accidental loading.

Hydrostatic pressure
Freshly poured unset concrete acts as a fluid which exerts an equal pressure in all directions. The amount of pressure is dependent on the height of the pour (lift) and is therefore only significant in vertical or steeply sloping formwork. As the concrete sets the pressure gradually disappears. The maximum hydrostatic pressure at any point within a form is equal to the amount of concrete above it. Therefore there will be minimum pressure at the top of the

Type	Characteristic	Method of application			Suitable form face					
		Brush	*Squeegee*	*Spray*	*Sawn timber*	*Planed timber*	*Plywood (Unsealed)*	*Plywood (Sealed)*	*Metal*	*Plastic*
Sealers and coatings, including barrier paints, waxes and other impermeable coatings	Mainly used as pretreatments. Not recommended for use without release agent. They prevent the absorption of release agents into the form face. Wax treatments are particularly useful for filling and sealing small imperfections in the form face	Often factory applied or as directed by the manufacturer			*	*	*	*	*	*
Other specialized release agents including wax emulsion	Formulated for specialized applications such as heated formwork systems and concrete forms	As directed by the manufacturer								
Surface retarders	Although these are not release agents they have the same effect as they retard the setting of the surface concrete. Surface retarders are in fact used to produce an exposed aggregate finish. The surface cement is brushed or washed away after striking the formwork	*	*	*	*	*	*	*	*	*

form which will steadily increase to the maximum at the bottom. Figure 491 shows the method of graphically illustrating the hydrostatic pressure exerted on the form face at any point in vertical formwork. The pressure at any point in a filled form may be calculated using the following formula:

maximum hydrostatic pressure at any point, P_{max} (kN/m^2)

Example
Calculate the maximum hydrostatic pressure at the base of a 3 m high column assuming the density of concrete is 2400 kg/m³.

$$P_{max} = \frac{\text{Density of concrete (kg/m}^3\text{)} \times \text{distance from top of form (m)}}{100 \text{ (converts to kN)}}$$

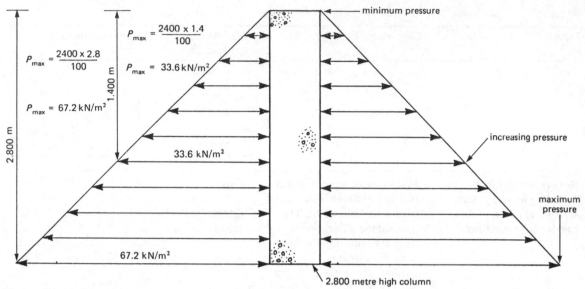

Figure 491 *Hydrostatic pressure*

Maximum hydrostatic pressure at any point, P_{max} $= \dfrac{\text{density of concrete} \times \text{distance from top of form}}{100}$

$$P_{max} = \frac{2400 \times 3}{100}$$

$$P_{max} = 72 \text{ kN/m}^2$$

Other factors which concern the development of pressure within formwork along with their effect are given in Table 39.

Basic formwork construction

Formwork plays a very important part in the finished appearance of a concrete structure. Therefore workmanship of a very high standard is required to produce high-quality concrete.

When making formwork, its construction depends on the following basic requirements:

Containment   It must be capable of shaping and supporting the wet concrete until it cures.
Strength   It must be capable of safely withstanding the dead, imposed and environmental loadings without distortion or danger.
Resistance to leakage   All joints in the form face must be close fitting or taped to prevent grout leakage.

Accuracy   The accuracy of the formwork must be consistent with the item being cast. Formwork for foundations is not normally required to be as accurate as formwork for the superstructure.

Ease of handling   All formwork should be designed and constructed to include facilities for adjustment, levelling, easing and striking without damage to the formwork or concrete.

Finish/reuse potential   The form face must be capable of consistently imparting the desired concrete finish and at the same time achieving the required number of reuses.

Access for concrete   The formwork arrangement must provide access for the placing of the concrete.

Table 39 **Factors affecting the development of pressure**

Factor	Effect on pressure
Density of concrete	Pressure increases in proportion to density
Workability	Pressure increases in proportion to increases in the slump of the mix
Rate of placing	Slow rates of placing enable lower levels of concrete to commence setting before the pour is complete, thus reducing pressure
Method of discharge	Discharge from a height causes a surge or impact loading
Concrete temperature	High temperatures quicken the setting and thus reduce pressure, whereas low temperatures have the opposite effect
Vibration	This makes the concrete flow and increases the pressure up to P_{max}
Height of pour	In theory P_{max} increases with the height of pour, although in practice during the time taken to fill the form the lower levels will have started setting, and therefore P_{max} over the full height is unlikely to be realized
Dimension of section	Pressure in walls and columns below 500 mm thick is reduced because of the arching or support effect of the aggregate between the formwork sides.
Reinforcement detail	Heavy steel reinforcement tends to provide support for the concrete and therefore reduces pressure

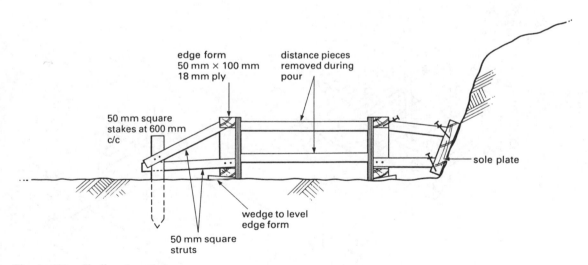

Figure 492   *Shallow foundation*

Foundations

In firm soil it is often possible to excavate foundations and cast the concrete against the excavated sides. In circumstances where this is not possible, formwork will be required.

Figure 492 shows typical details of a shallow foundation for a concrete strip, raft or ring beam. It consists of made-up form panels wedged, levelled and strutted in position. Strutting may be from stakes in the level ground or from a sole plate against the bank in deeper excavations. The distance pieces should be removed during pouring as the concrete reaches them.

Figure 493 shows typical details of a deep foundation for a column pad base or pile cap.

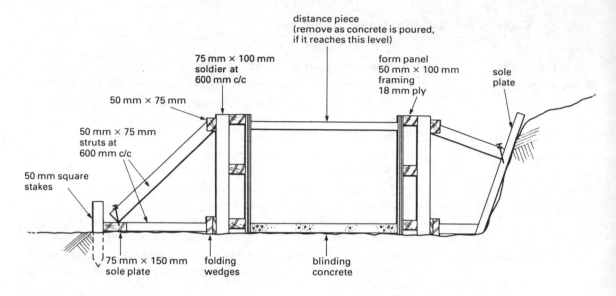

distance piece
(remove as concrete is poured,
if it reaches this level)

75 mm × 100 mm
soldier at
600 mm c/c

form panel
50 mm × 100 mm
framing
18 mm ply

sole
plate

50 mm × 75 mm

50 mm × 75 mm
struts at
600 mm c/c

50 mm square
stakes

75 mm × 150 mm
sole plate

folding
wedges

blinding
concrete

Figure 493   *Deep foundation*

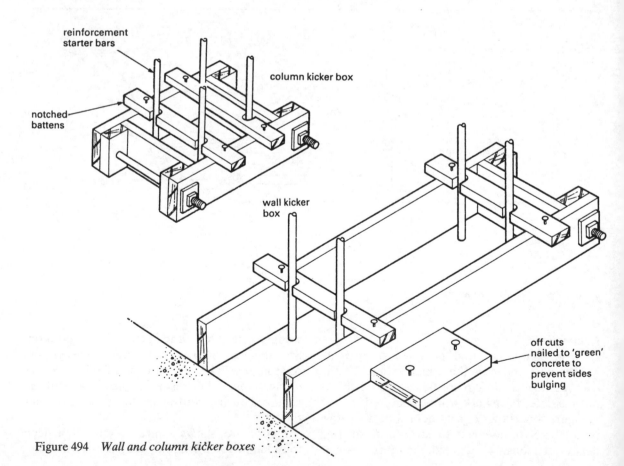

reinforcement
starter bars

column kicker box

notched
battens

wall kicker
box

off cuts
nailed to 'green'
concrete to
prevent sides
bulging

Figure 494   *Wall and column kicker boxes*

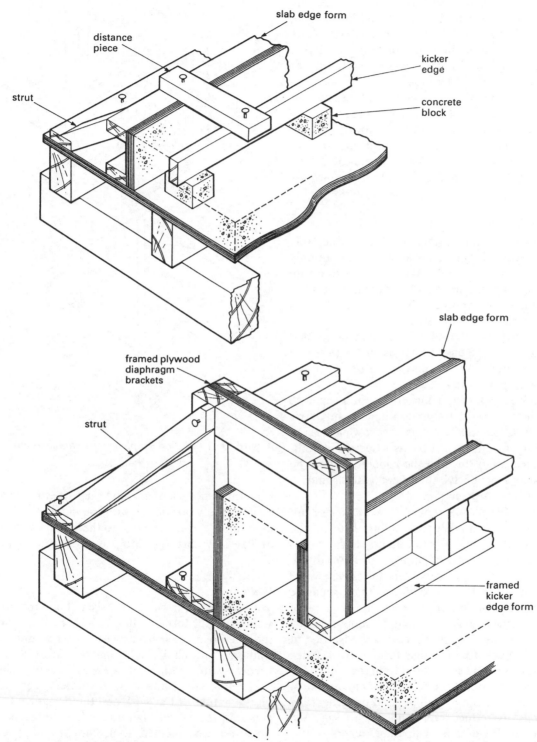

Figure 495 *Floating kickers*

Framed form panels are used for the sides and ends; these must be firmly strutted in position, again either from stakes or from the bank. Care taken in laying the blinding concrete means that it can form a kicker, thus positioning the forms and reducing grout leakage.

In situations where a number of bases or caps with different depth but same plan size are required, the forms can be made to the greatest depth. When these are used for the smaller depths the concrete level can be indicated by a batten tacked to the sides or nails driven into the sides.

Kickers

A kicker is a small upstand of concrete, the same plan size as the finished wall or column but only up to 150 mm in height. Its purpose is to locate the bottom of the form and prevent grout loss. It is an important component in concrete work as far as accuracy is concerned.

Kickers for walls and columns may be formed together with the base or slab as part of the same pour, or alternatively it may be formed later as a separate operation.

The ideal size for a kicker cast in a separate operation is about 150 mm in height; any more than this and accuracy is lost owing to the difficulty in ensuring that its sides are plumb. Much less than this and the concrete cannot be compacted properly, thus later causing movement at the intersection.

Figure 494 shows typical kickers. These are normally held in position by tying them off the reinforcement starter bars with notched battens.

Kickers that are cast along with the slab are known as floating kickers or upstands. These are often more difficult to form than separate kickers. Depending on their height, this type of kicker either may be simply supported by previously cast concrete blocks and also tied at intervals back to the edge form with distance pieces, or may be suspended from the edge form with the aid of plywood diaphragm brackets. Concrete blocks may still be used underneath at intervals to reduce any tendency to sag. See Figure 495 for details of floating kickers.

For reasons mainly of speed, kickers are

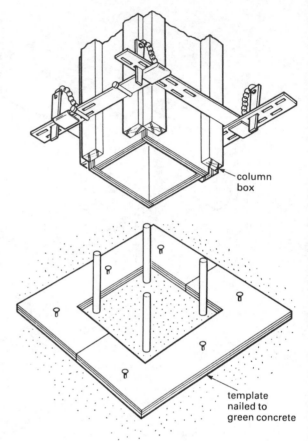

Figure 496   *Plywood template to position column*

sometimes not used, in which case the form may be accurately positioned with the aid of plywood templates, either nailed on to the green concrete or fixed by cartridge tool, as shown in Figure 496.

Walls

Wall formwork normally consists of a number of standard wall forms bolted together. These are then tied over their backs with either walings or soldiers. The choice of using the form panels vertical with horizontal walings, or of using horizontal panels and vertical soldiers, depends on the nature of the work and the designer. It is general practice for high lifts, where substantial pressures are expected, to use horizontal panels and vertical soldiers.

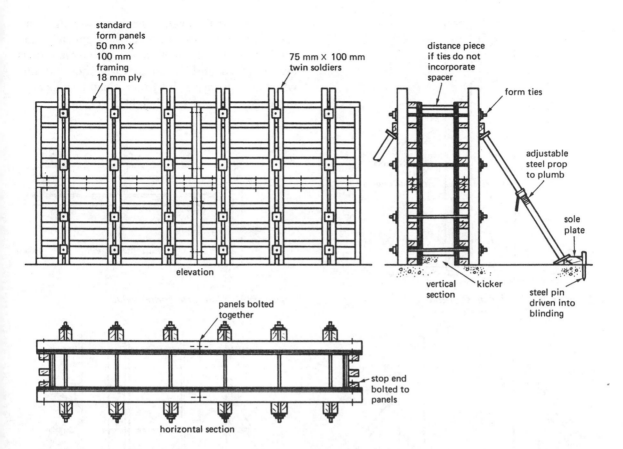

standard form panels 50 mm × 100 mm framing 18 mm ply

75 mm × 100 mm twin soldiers

distance piece if ties do not incorporate spacer

form ties

adjustable steel prop to plumb

sole plate

elevation

vertical section — kicker

steel pin driven into blinding

panels bolted together

stop end bolted to panels

horizontal section

Figure 497   *Wall forms*

Figure 497 shows typical details of a wall form using standard panels and form ties. These are erected against the previously cast kicker. The tie bolt positions are dependent on the wall height, thickness, method and rate of pour, as these factors greatly affect the development of concrete pressure within the forms.

Adjustable steel props are used at about one metre centres on both sides of the wall to plumb and hold the forms in position. A too steep prop angle should be avoided as this tends to lift the forms off the kicker. An allowance for shrinkage must be made on long walls. They are often therefore cast in a hit-and-miss pattern, so that shrinkage movement can take place before alternate bays are cast.

Where provision is required in the stop end

for the reinforcement starter bars to protrude into the next bay, the detail illustrated in Figure 498 can be used. This accommodates the starter bars and eases removal after striking the main panels, as the two halves of the ply stop end simply slide out from either side.

Figure 499 illustrates a corner detail. The outer panels are bolted together, and because of the increased pressure at the intersection an additional adjustable steel prop should be used at this point.

Walls are sometimes cast in a number of vertical lifts. This is either to reduce the concrete pressures of a high lift, or to obtain the maximum reuse from a minimum number of form panels. The formwork for this method is known as climbing wall forms.

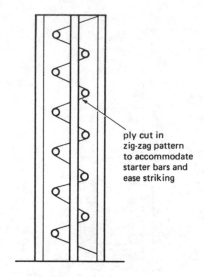

ply cut in
zig-zag pattern
to accommodate
starter bars and
ease striking

Figure 498   *Wall form stop end*

Figure 500 illustrates the basic arrangement for climbing forms. After casting and allowing the first lift to cure sufficiently, the form panels are removed and raised to form the next lift, which is then cast. This process can be repeated until the required wall height is reached.

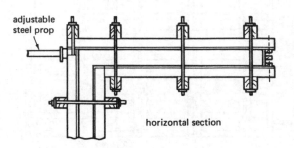

adjustable
steel prop

horizontal section

Figure 499   *Wall form corner detail*

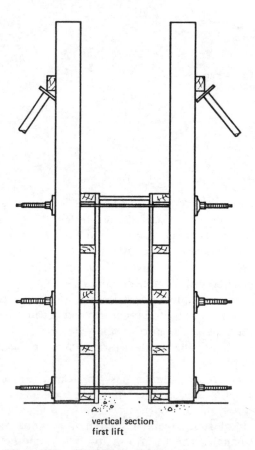

vertical section
first lift

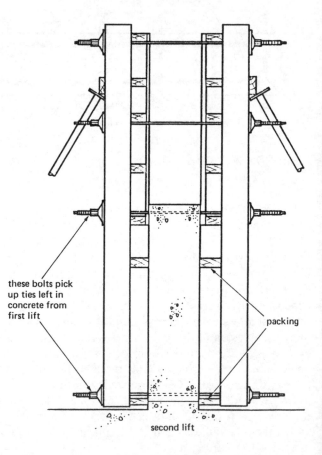

these bolts pick
up ties left in
concrete from
first lift

packing

second lift

Figure 500   *Climbing wall forms*

On fair-faced work the joint line created between lifts may be unsightly. This can be masked by adding a filler to the panel which forms a definite feature joint (see Figure 501). This detail is particularly useful on vertical joints in sawn board marked feature forms.

In situations where a wall has to be cast against a bank or other structure, the single-sided wall form arrangement shown in Figure 502 is used. This has standard form panels and proprietary strong backs. Because of the lack of ties it is essential that each strong back is anchored firmly to the kicker. In the example, this has been achieved by bolting the strong backs to loop coil ties which were previously cast in the kicker. Where an additional lift is required, loop coil ties could be cast at the top of the wall for subsequent anchorage.

Columns

A plan view of a typical square column box is shown in Figure 503. This is made up in four separate sections; two of these are the same width as the column, whereas the other two are made twice the thickness of the ply over size. Each side is made up so that the backing timbers overhang the edge of the plywood by its thickness, so that the box will be self-aligning when it is cramped up.

Large columns will require an additional backing timber placed centrally on each side, or noggins fixed between the backing timbers under each cramp. This is to prevent the ply bending.

Figure 504 illustrates the same column box assembled in position. The four sections are held together with steel column cramps and the whole column box is plumbed up and held in position by an adjustable steel prop on each side. The column must be plumbed in both directions. This can be done with the aid of a plumb bob or straight edge and level.

Figure 505 shows both of these methods. The props must be adjusted until the column is plumb. This operation must be repeated on the adjacent edge so that the column is plumb in both directions. When tightening any prop its opposite one must be slackened otherwise the

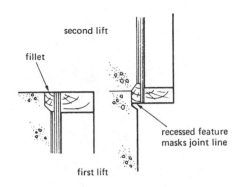

Figure 501 *Masking joint line*

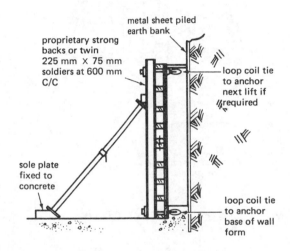

Figure 502 *Single-sided wall form*

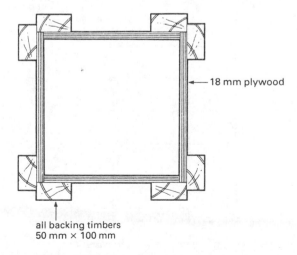

Figure 503 *Plan of square column box*

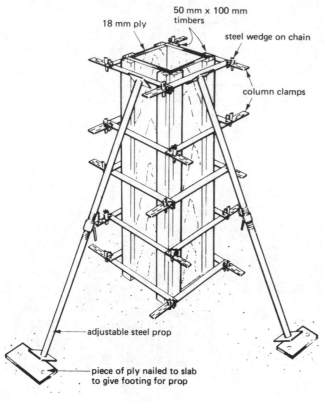

Figure 504   *Assembled square column box*

whole column box will be lifted from the kicker. Immediately after pouring the column must be rechecked for plumb and carefully adjusted if required, as it may have been knocked during the pouring process.

Note: The plumbing of wall forms is a similar operation.

Circular columns can be formed using a number of proprietary forms. Cardboard tube formers are available fairly economically, but these are only suitable for one-off usage.

Proprietary glass-reinforced plastic formers, although more expensive, can be cost effective when a large number of columns are required.

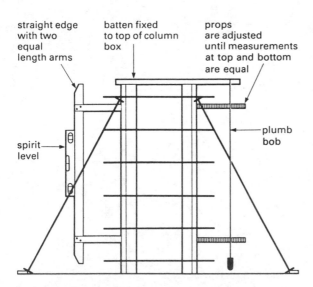

Figure 505   *Alternative method of plumbing the column*

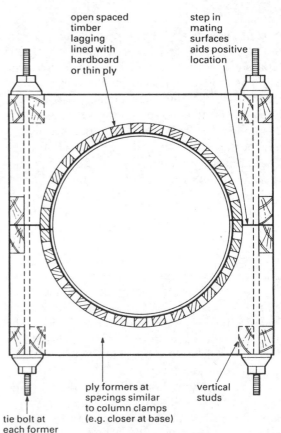

Figure 506   *Circular column form*

These are available with either a straight profile or conical-shaped head (known as a mushroom head).

Illustrated in Figure 506 is a method of forming a circular column in timber. It is made up of plywood formers, timber lagging and vertical studs in two separate halves which are later bolted together. Adjustable steel props are used for holding and plumbing in the same way as square columns.

Floors and beams

The decking for floor or roof slabs usually consists of plywood joists and ledgers supported on adjustable steel props, or one of the various proprietary formwork systems available, or a partial combination of both.

Figure 507 shows the arrangement of timbers and adjustable steel props for a typical floor slab. Scaffold tubes and fittings have been used for the lacing and diagonal sway bracing.

The spacing of formwork members will vary depending on the anticipated loads and pressures. As a general guide the following can be used:

Props   1.200 m centres
Ledgers   1.500 m centres
Joists   400 mm centres.

Figure 508 shows how a slab may be finished at

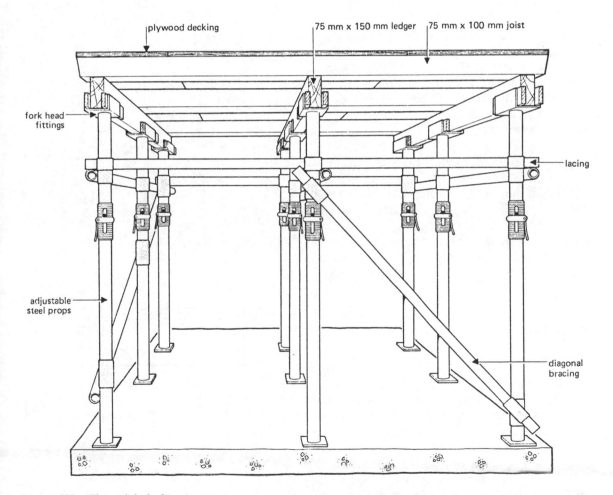

Figure 507   *Floor slab decking*

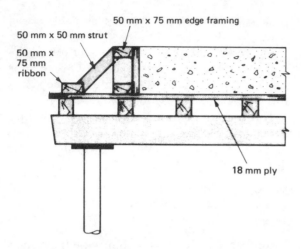

Figure 508   *Slab finishing at open edge*

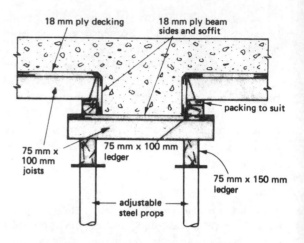

Figure 509   *Drop beam in slab*

an open edge. The edge, which sits on top of the decking, is framed up from 50 mm × 75 mm timbers and strutted in position off the 50 mm × 75 mm ribbon with 50 mm × 50 mm struts. The ends of the struts are shown bird's mouthed over the edge framing and ribbon, but in practice these are often cut square.

Figure 509 and 510 show details of the formwork required where beams are incorporated in the slab. Figure 509 shows a drop beam which is in the centre of a slab. The beam soffit is made up of 18 mm plywood, 75 mm × 100 mm joists and 75 mm × 100 mm ledgers and supported by adjustable steel props. The ends of the main joists are supported by the beam soffit. These are packed off a 75 mm × 100 mm ledger to the required height.

Note: The ends of the joists are splayed so that one end can be dropped when striking without binding.

Figure 510 shows the detail of an edge beam. The joists which support the beam soffit have been cantilevered out so that the beam side may be strutted. The cantilevered joists are often necessary at upper floor levels where no bearing is available for the base of the adjustable steel props.

In situations where the plywood sheets fit between brickwork or beams it is usual to

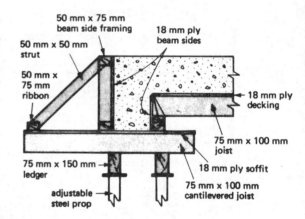

Figure 510   *Edge beam*

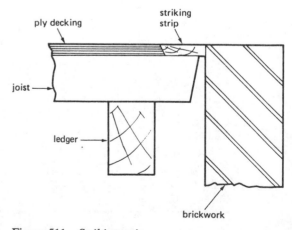

Figure 511   *Striking strip*

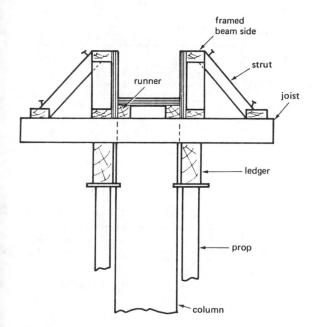

Figure 512   *Beam box*

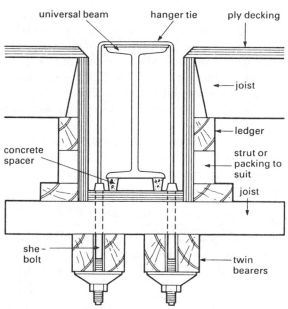

Figure 513   *Suspended formwork in steel framed buildings*

include a narrow striking piece along one edge to aid striking by preventing the sheet becoming 'trapped' (see Figure 511).

Although in general it is common practice to cast beams and slabs in one operation, beams are sometimes required to span between two supports on their own. Figure 512 illustrates the formwork for a beam spanning between two columns. The runners under the beam soffit are not essential, but their use enables wider spacing of the joist and permits easy variation of the beam depth.

Steel framed buildings have to be encased to protect against fire and corrosion. Where they are to be encased in concrete it is possible to suspend the formwork from the universal beams using hangers (see Figure 513).

Proprietary adjustable floor centres are useful for decking as they reduce not only the amount of timber but also the number of adjustable props required, thus easing the levelling operations and creating a less 'cluttered' under-slab area.

Figure 514 shows a typical example of the formwork for a floor slab using centres and standard form panels.

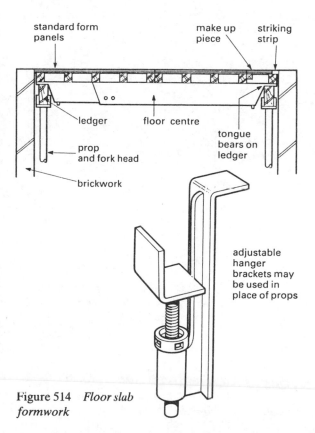

Figure 514   *Floor slab formwork*

Table forms are popular for the repetitive casting of floor slabs in medium- to high-rise structures. This is because they greatly reduce the time taken to erect, strike and re-erect, owing to the fact that these operations can be carried out without any dismantling.

Figure 515 illustrates a floor slab, and edge beam detail using table forms as the support system. Where edge beams are concerned, one essential requirement is that the table must be capable of being lowered sufficiently to get under the edge beam.

Stairs

In situ formwork for stairs is possibly one of the most expensive operations; therefore wherever possible designers tend to use precast stairs.

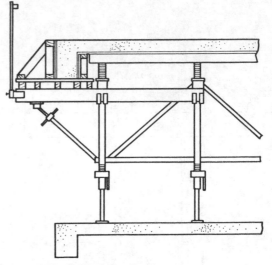

Figure 515   *Table form detail*

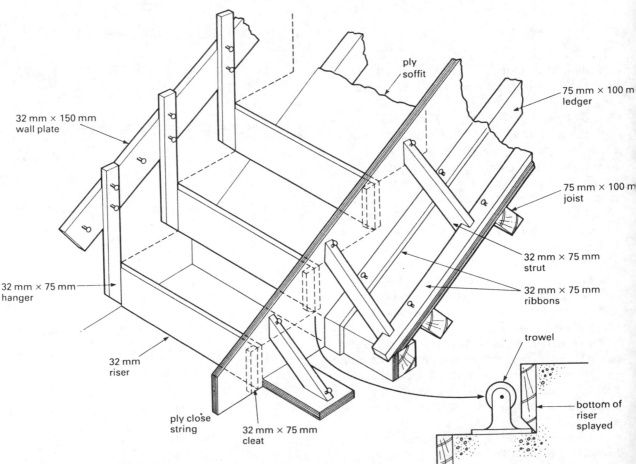

Figure 516   *Close string stairs*

When setting out formwork for stairs great care is necessary, as the finished result must obviously comply with all the requirements of the Building Regulations.

As the soffit of the stairs is basically a sloping slab, the supporting formwork will be similar to floor slabs. The step profile is formed by using strings and riser boards, which should have a splayed bottom edge to enable the entire tread surface to be trowelled off.

Figures 516 and 517 show isometric views of part of two alternative formwork arrangements which can be used for stairs that abut a wall on one side.

Pressed-steel risers as shown in Figure 518 could be used in place of timber risers. The radius along their edges acts as a stiffener as well as producing a neat pencil round on the finished step.

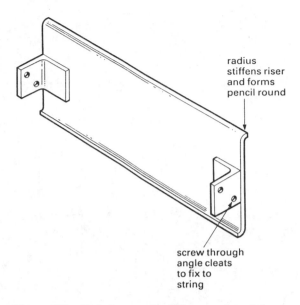

radius stiffens riser and forms pencil round

screw through angle cleats to fix to string

Figure 518   *Stair formwork using pressed steel risers*

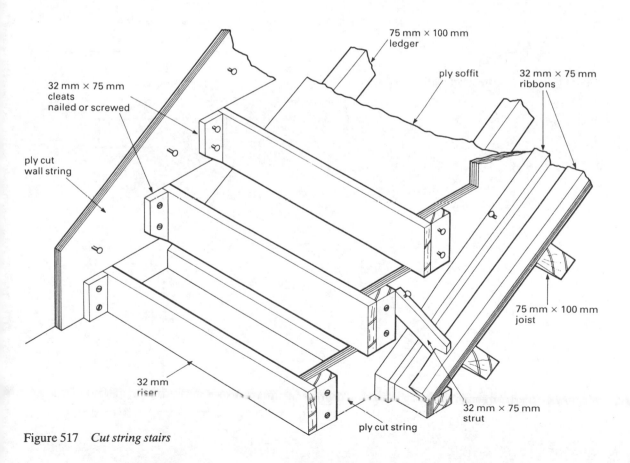

75 mm × 100 mm ledger

ply soffit

32 mm × 75 mm ribbons

32 mm × 75 mm cleats nailed or screwed

ply cut wall string

75 mm × 100 mm joist

32 mm riser

ply cut string

32 mm × 75 mm strut

Figure 517   *Cut string stairs*

Figure 519   *Section through stairs up to landing*

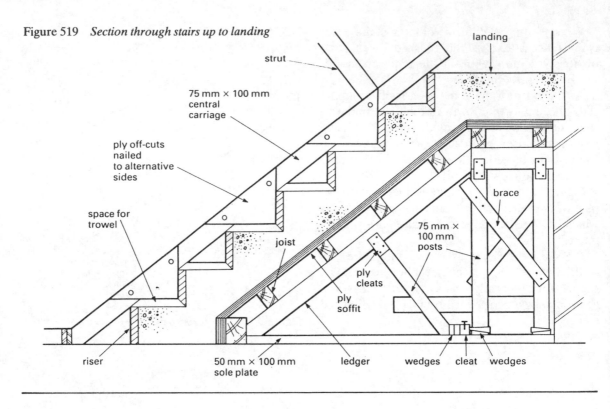

Labels in figure:
- landing
- strut
- 75 mm × 100 mm central carriage
- ply off-cuts nailed to alternative sides
- space for trowel
- joist
- brace
- 75 mm × 100 mm posts
- ply cleats
- ply soffit
- riser
- 50 mm × 100 mm sole plate
- ledger
- wedges
- cleat
- wedges

Figure 520   *Section through stairs from landing*

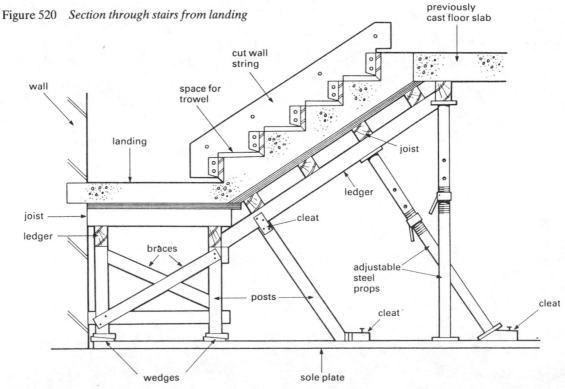

Labels in figure:
- previously cast floor slab
- cut wall string
- space for trowel
- wall
- landing
- joist
- ledger
- braces
- joist
- ledger
- cleat
- adjustable steel props
- posts
- cleat
- cleat
- wedges
- sole plate

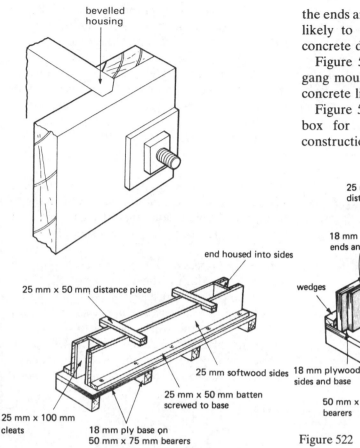

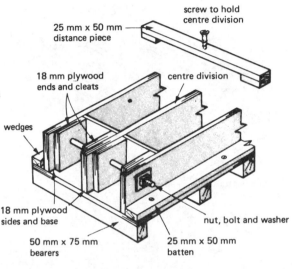

the ends and sides ensures a tight joint and is less likely to cause damage to the corner of the concrete during striking.

Figure 522 is an isometric view of part of a gang mould which can be used for casting two concrete lintels at a time.

Figure 523 shows a section through a mould box for a precast concrete sill. The basic construction is the same as a lintel mould box

Figure 521   *Precast knock-down lintel box*

Figure 522   *Gang mould for lintels*

Figures 519 and 520 give details of the formwork for short flights up to and from landings. These details would be suitable for quarter-turn and dog-leg flights. In wide flights a carriage is fixed down the centre of the stairs to resist any bulging in the risers as a result of the concrete pressures.

Precast moulds

Moulds for precast work in factories are mainly of steel or glassfibre-reinforced plastic constructions, although in this section only timber and plywood moulds for on-site construction are considered.

Figure 521 is an isometric view of a precast knock-down mould box suitable for casting lintels. The use of a bevelled housing between

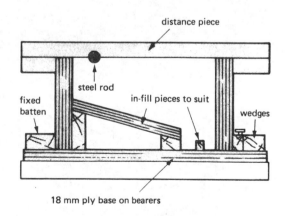

Figure 523   *Sill mould box*

with infill pieces inserted to form the required shape.

A drip groove can be formed by pressing

either a length of steel reinforcing rod or a piece of sash cord into the freshly poured concrete.

Figure 524 is an isometric view of part of the sill mould box showing the method of construction. Bolts are used to hold the sides of the mould together, and for easy removal the hole for these bolts can be slotted. Cleats are screwed to the sides to locate the plywood ends. The

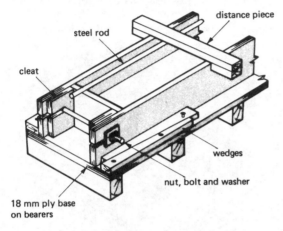

Figure 524   *Construction of sill mould box*

sides are prevented from spreading by the batten which is fixed to the base along one side and by long folding wedges fixed to the other.

Figure 525 illustrates a mould for precasting tapering concrete fence posts. This is similar to the lintel gang mould. Holes are usually required in the posts for bolts or straining wire. These are formed by placing well-greased or waxed steel rods through the mould in the required position and removing them shortly after the initial set.

In general most shaped precast items, e.g. sills, lintels, copings and posts, can be made by using the basic mould box design with infill pieces inserted to form the required profile.

Formwork inspection

At all times during the erection of the form-work, and both just prior to and during concreting, the formwork supervisor must keep a close eye on the work. This is to ensure that the formwork is to the engineer's specification, capable of producing the required quality (dimensions, tolerances and concrete finish)

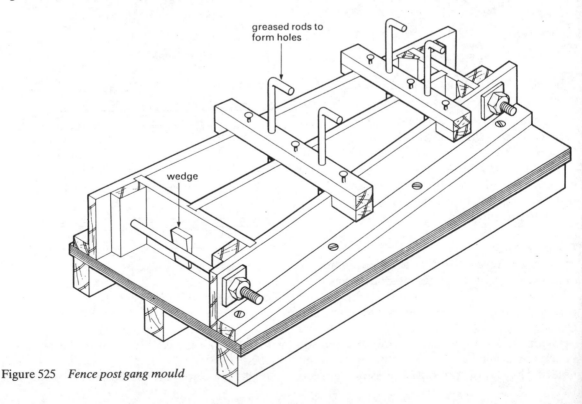

Figure 525   *Fence post gang mould*

and, most important of all, safe. The following checklist is useful for this purpose. Owing to the wide range of formwork constructions, the list includes items which may not be relevant to a particular job; therefore it must be amended to suit the work in hand. In addition to the formwork supervisor, similar checks should also be carried out by the general foreman, site engineer, clerk of the works and, where appointed, the falsework co-ordinator, one of whom will have the duty of giving permission to load or fill the formwork. During the actual pouring of the concrete it is essential that a fully experienced formworker is on 'stand-by' adjacent to the work to deal with minor adjustments during casting, replumbing, levelling or lining after casting and any other contingencies.

Checklist

Before concreting

1 Are all materials suitable and free from distortions, defects, rust and rot etc.?
2 Is the formwork in accordance with the design; in the right position; of the correct dimensions; plumb, level and in line?
3 Are all ties, supports, struts, cramps and braces, correctly positioned, tight and suitably tied or fixed to prevent later movement?
4 Has provision been made for ease of striking without causing damage to the concrete?
5 Have all the stop ends, features, fillets, inserts and box-outs etc. been correctly located and fixed?
6 Has a release agent been applied to the form face?
7 Have all holes, fixings and joints in the form face been suitably filled or taped?

During concreting

1 Look out, listen for and bring to the attention of the engineer any of the following:

Formwork straining noises (ties snapping, timber creaking etc.)
Any movement or distortion in the formwork
Any joints opening or grout leakage.

Each of these may be an indication of a possible formwork blowout or collapse.
2 Where appropriate, have distance pieces been removed and fixing blocks etc. inserted?

Note: There are other items which must be checked but are not usually the responsibility of the formworker. These include: safe access, steel reinforcement, key to previously poured surface, availability of concrete and equipment, method and rate of fill, curing etc.

Striking

The time between the pouring of the concrete and the striking of the formwork varies widely. This depends on the following:

The type of formwork, e.g. wall, column, slab or beam
The concrete used and the type of surface finish required
The weather conditions and exposure of the site

No formwork must be removed until the concrete has cured sufficiently for it to be self-supporting and capable of carrying any loads imposed upon it.

Vertical surfaces such as walls, columns and beam sides etc. can, in very good weather, be struck as little as nine hours after pouring.

Horizontal surfaces normally require a much longer time, and this can be up to twenty-eight days in poor winter weather. It is usual after striking horizontal formwork to reprop the concrete in strategic positions for up to a further fourteen days.

The final decision to strike must always rest with the site engineer, who has knowledge and experience of what is involved.

The safe time to strike the formwork can be determined by tests on cubes made from the same mix as the concrete and cured under similar conditions. In circumstances where compressive cube test results are not available, Table 40 from CP 110: *The Structural Use of Concrete*, can be used as a guide where ordinary Portland cement (OPC) has been used.

Table 40   **Minimum striking times**

Location of formwork	Temperature	
	16° C	7° C
Vertical surfaces:		
Walls, columns, beam sides	9 hours	12 hours
Horizontal surfaces:		
Slab, soffits (repropped)	4 days	7 days
Removal of repositioned props	11 days	14 days
Beams, soffits (repropped)	8 days	14 days
Removal of repositioned props	15 days	21 days

Safety

Striking is an important operation, the procedure for which must be carefully considered to avoid any safety risk to personnel, stress or damage to the completed building, and damage to the formwork itself.

In general, the procedure to adopt is the reverse of that used for erection. Observe the following precautions:

1   Always wear protective clothing (safety boots, helmet, gloves etc.).
2   Never stand or allow anyone else to stand close to the striking area.
3   Use hardwood wedges to ease the forms away from the concrete surface (the use of nail bars results in both form and concrete damage).
4   Always release loaded member gradually (ease). For example, props for floor slabs must be released in small stages (half a turn of the handle) starting from the centre and working out, then repeating the operation.
5   Always control the striking by removing a section at a time.
6   Never allow the formwork to fall (crash striking).
7   Always clean, denail, repair and store under cover, ready for reuse, all formwork material. In addition all props, cramps and bolts etc. should be cleaned, lubricated and coated with a rust inhibitor.

Self-assessment questions

1   List *four* points of safety concerning the use of adjustable steel props.

2   Sketch a plywood box-out to form a bolt pocket 300 mm deep × 125 mm square tapering to 75 mm square.

3   Briefly explain what is meant by easing in relation to arch centres.

4   Sketch details to show the construction of a segmental arch having a span of 3 m and a rise of 1 m.

5   State *two* methods of shoring and describe the typical circumstances in which *each* might be used.

6   Sketch the intersection between a raking shore and its sole plate, indicating the method of tightening.

7   Describe with the aid of a sketch *two* proprietary form ties.

8   Sketch a cross-section through a suitable timber and plywood formwork arrangement for the *in situ* casting of the column shown in Figure 526.

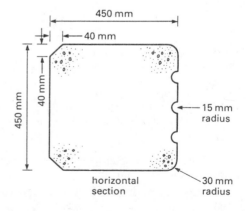

Figure 526

9 (a) Calculate the maximum hydrostatic pressure exerted at the bottom of a 2.4 m high wall form.
   (b) List *four* factors that affect the development of pressure within formwork.

10 (a) State a suitable release agent and method of application for use on:
        (a) Sawn board marked forms
        (b) Unsealed plywood
        (c) Glassfibre-reinforced plastic.
    (b) List *five* points of safety to be observed when using release agents.

A guide to advanced examinations and study

The main purpose of an advanced craft course of study is to develop practical ability in and theoretical knowledge of your chosen craft. Examinations are set to measure your achievement of the course objectives. In setting an examination question, examiners give you the opportunity to demonstrate your knowledge and understanding of a particular topic. Their aim is to obtain a true assessment of your abilities, not to confuse, mislead or fail you.

How examinations are set and marked

Setting
Subject experts from education or industry set draft question papers, based on an examination specification. These draft papers are submitted to a meeting of the subject moderating committee, who are also subject experts. At this meeting the draft paper is discussed as a whole and each question considered individually in detail. As a result of discussion between the examiner and moderators, questions may be replaced or amended. This process should ensure that the final version of the examination conforms to the specification and is clear, straightforward and valid.

Types of question
There are three main types of question that appear in an advanced craft examination:

1   Short-answer questions
2   Structured questions
3   Long-answer questions

Short-answer questions
This type of question consists of one or more problems to which you are required to give a limited written answer. The length of this answer may vary, depending on the topic, from one or two words to a short paragraph. In certain circumstances a sketch or simple calculation may be all that is required.

Example
State the meaning of the following abbreviations:
(a)   HMSO
(b)   BSI
(c)   BRE
(d)   BWF
(e)   TRADA
(f)   HASAWA
(g)   JCT
(h)   BEC
(i)   SMM
(j)   HSE

Typical answer
(a)   Her Majesty's Stationery Office
(b)   British Standards Institution
(c)   Building Research Establishment
(d)   British Woodworking Federation

(e)   Timber Research and Development Association

(f)   Health and Safety at Work etc. Act

(g)   Joint Contractors Tribunal

(h)   Building Employers' Confederation

(i)   Standard Method of Measurement

(j)   Health and Safety Executive

Structured questions

These normally start with a statement which gives a certain amount of information, followed by a series of subquestions in logical order. The length of your answer for each subquestion may again vary depending on the topic from one or two words to a short paragraph, a labelled sketch, scale drawing, detailed calculation or a combination of these, but at each stage the question will make it clear what is required.

Example

After felling, timber is converted into usable sizes and then seasoned ready for use.

(a)   Produce large end grain sketches to show:
    (i)   A radial sawn plank
    (ii) A tangential sawn plank

(b)   Show the shape that each plank is likely to take up as a result of shrinkage.

(c)   State what is meant by the term 'equilibrium moisture content'.

(d)   Name *two* methods of determining the moisture content of a plank.

(e)   State *four* reasons for seasoning timber.

(f)   Name *two* distortions that can occur during seasoning.

(g)   State the probable causes of the defect.

Typical answer

(a)

(i) Radial cut. Annual rings at 45° or more

(ii) Tangential cut. Annual rings at less than 45°

Figure 527

(b)

(i)

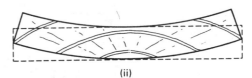

(ii)

Figure 528

(c)   When a piece of timber has a moisture content that is equal to the surrounding atmosphere, it is said to have an equilibrium moisture content.

(d)   (i)   Oven-drying method
    (ii) Electric moisture meter

(e)   (i)   To ensure the moisture content of the timber is below the dry rot safety line of 20 per cent.
    (ii) To ensure that any shrinkage takes place before the timber is used.
    (iii) Using seasoned timber, the finished article will be more reliable and less likely to split or distort.
    (iv) Wet timber will not readily accept glue, paint or polish.

(f)   (i)   Bow
    (ii) Twist

(g)   Distortions can be caused as a result of poor stacking or bad air circulation.

Long-answer questions

This more 'traditional' form of question calls for an extended unguided answer to a particular problem, thus requiring the students to structure their answers. This may consist of either an essay, or a scale drawing, or a geometrical development. Questions requiring this type of answer, especially the essay, are rarely set at this level, preference being given to short-answer or structured questions.

Example

To a scale of 1:10 draw the front elevation and section of an arch centre made from timber which is required to construct a 3 metre span semicircular brick arch. Name all components and suggest suitable sizes.

Typical answer

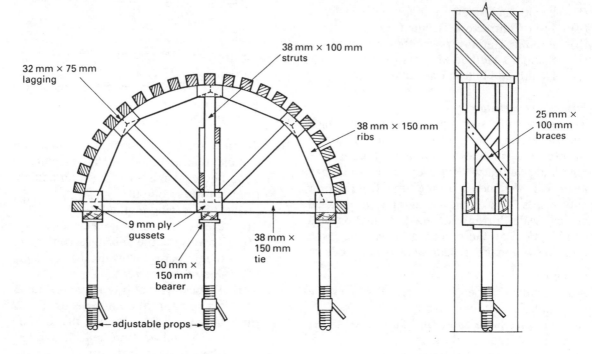

Figure 529

Marking

Completed examination scripts are marked by a team of examiners under the supervision of a chief examiner, who ensures the marks from each member of the team are standardized. At the moderating meeting where the draft paper was discussed an outline solution and marking scheme for each question will have been agreed. A typical question, outline solution and marking scheme is shown in the following example.

Example

Define briefly *each* of the following formwork terms:
(a) Gang mould
(b) Kicker
(c) Ledger
(d) Soldier
(e) Waling

Outline solution	*Possible marks*
(a) *Gang mould* Precast mould to cast more than one unit	2
(b) *Kicker* Concrete upstand to locate form and prevent loss of grout	2
(c) *Ledger* Horizontal timber to carry joists	2
(d) *Soldier* Vertical member to stiffen forms	2
(e) *Waling* Horizontal member to stiffen forms	2
Maximum total	10

Before marking commences the team of examiners will meet to decide on a common approach to marking. During the marking each examiner will have to forward to the chief examiner samples of their marking. From these samples the chief examiner can tell if any particular examiner is marking too strictly or too easily and advise them accordingly.

You should remember that:

1 Marks can only be given for correct information that is relevant to the question.
2 Marks are not taken away for wrong information.
3 Marks are not deducted for poor spelling or ungrammatical expressions.
4 Marks are awarded for each question separately. Care is taken not to let a poor performance or a good performance in one answer reflect in the marks for the rest of your paper. Each answer gets the marks it deserves!
5 A few days after the examination an examiner will receive several batches of papers; one of these will be yours. An impression comes across immediately: is the paper neatly laid out and the sketches well proportioned, or is the paper untidy and the sketches scrappy? One thing is certain: anything you can do to make the examiner's job easier will be appreciated.

Examination preparation

Examination papers are not set with the intent of tricking you. It is not the examiner's fault if you fail to understand or misread a question and give an answer that has not been asked for. The main causes of student failure in examinations are:

1 Lack of preparation
2 Lack of topic knowledge or understanding
3 Bad examination technique

The first two of these causes can be overcome by following a sensible revision programme.

Revision

Revision is an extremely important part of study. Unless facts and information are repe-

ated, used or revised they will quickly be forgotten. Ideally revision should be a continual process, starting from the very beginning of your course, not just at the end of it, although it will, of course, become more concentrated as the examination approaches. Revision is an individual thing; it is impossible to define the 'ideal method'. What suits one person may not be suitable for another.

Revision techniques

As a guide some of the following revision techniques could be incorporated into your personal study programme.

1 Rewrite rough class written notes after each lesson.
2 Underline main or key points in notes, class handouts and textbooks, as remembering these words can bring back to mind the whole topic.
3 Write brief revision notes. These condense a lot of information into a skeleton of a topic that can be recalled at a later date.
4 Read textbooks, magazine articles and technical brochures to supplement your class lectures and notes. Condense this information and add to your revision notes.
5 Answer the self-assessment questions in this book and repeat them periodically; this will show up your weak areas which you should list for more concentrated revision.
6 Research topics on your concentrated revision list.
7 Reread notes and textbooks periodically. This recalls facts and reinforces them in your mind.
8 Mentally ask yourself questions on a particular topic. This can be done anywhere, even on a bus or train when travelling to work. Decide if your answer was suitable: if not add the topic to your concentrated revision list.
9 Read past question papers and attempt timed answers. This is often done in class as a run-up to the examination.
10 In addition, use any technique you have found successful in your previous studies.

Examination technique

As the examination day approaches, anxiety is normally the main problem to be encountered. Much of this can be overcome by the confidence derived from the knowledge that you have studied the course to the full and have undertaken a comprehensive revision programme. However, do not be overconfident; a little anxiety is required to help you do your best. The use of the following checklist will aid you both prior to and during the examination itself.

Examination checklist

1   Arrive at the examination in good time, ensuring that you have everything you are likely to need – examination card or number, pens, pencils, drawing equipment and electronic calculator.

2   Listen carefully to the invigilator's instructions.

3   Read the instructions at the top of the paper carefully.

4   Read through the whole paper. Many students at this stage underline key words in each question. In addition to the subject matter, look for words that indicate the length and precision of the expected answer.

   (i)   Questions or parts of a question that start with 'name', 'list', 'suggest' or 'state' normally require a fairly brief answer of one or two words or a sentence at the most.

   (ii)   Words such as 'define', 'describe' or 'explain' require a longer answer, although these can also be shortened by the inclusion of 'briefly'; for example, 'briefly describe' etc.

   (iii)   'Sketch' or 'find' call for less accurate answers than required from 'draw', 'develop' or 'calculate'.

   (iv)   Look out for questions that contain two indicating words; for example, 'explain with the aid of sketches' etc.

5   Divide up the available time evenly between the number of questions to be answered, allowing say ten minutes reading time at each end of the examination. For example, for a three-hour paper with ten questions to be answered, the time would be divided up as follows:

Reading time at the start   10 minutes
Reading/correction time
at the end   10 minutes
Time for each question
      $(180{-}20)/10 = 16$ minutes

6   Attempt your best answer first as this will give you confidence to tackle the rest of the paper.

7   Attempt the remaining questions in increasing order of difficulty. This gives you more time to think about and plan the harder questions subconsciously while you are completing the easier ones.

8   Keep to your time plan. When you reach the end of the time allocated to each question, stop writing even if you have not finished the answer. Leave a space before starting the next question so that if time permits you may come back and complete the answer later. It is far better to have attempted all the questions even if some of the answers are incomplete than to run out of time and leave out the last four or so questions, which could happen if you spent five or ten minutes longer on each question.

9   If time is short, your final question can be put down in a condensed skeleton form; this will obtain you some marks at least.

10   Read through your paper at the end of the examination. This gives you a chance to spot and correct errors. Also you may have time at this stage to complete any unfinished answers.

11   Finally ensure you have put your name and student examination number on all your answer sheets and drawing paper.

Specimen examination papers

You should now be ready to tackle the following examination papers.

Read the front page of each paper carefully. It will tell you what you need for the examination, and from the information given you can calculate the length of time to be spent on each question.

Each examination is designed to be completed within a three hour period, so before starting make sure that you have this amount of time available.

Good luck!

CITY AND GUILDS OF LONDON INSTITUTE

PAPER NUMBER	EXAMINATION	Sample Paper
585–2–11	**CARPENTRY AND JOINERY** **ADVANCED CRAFT**	**1985 Onwards**

SERIES	PAPER	
	GENERAL CARPENTRY AND JOINERY	**14 00 – 17 00** **3 hours**

YOU SHOULD HAVE THE FOLLOWING FOR THIS EXAMINATION
one answer book
1 sheet A3 drawing paper
drawing instruments
drawing board and tee square
metric scale rule

SAMPLE QUESTIONS FOR EXAMINATIONS FROM MAY–JUNE 1985 ONWARDS

This question paper contains 10 compulsory structured questions to be answered in 3 hours.

ALL questions carry equal marks.

1 (a) State clearly the responsibilities of the employee in respect of The Health and Safety at Work Act.
   (b) List FIVE safety checks which should be made on an independent scaffold before commencing work.
   (c) Give TWO examples of the work done by the Timber Research and Development Association.

2 (a) Sketch a suitable method of supporting 2440 × 1220 × 12 plywood sheeting placed 2440 in height when being used as a security hoarding around a small building site.
   (b) Prepare a list of materials using the information in (a) if the site measures 20 m × 30 m and is completely enclosed.

3 Fig. 1 shows the top portion of a fully glazed semi-circular hardwood external door one metre wide.
   (a) Choosing suitable dimensions for head, stile and rail, sketch the jointing arrangement at X.
   (b) Draw to a scale of 1:1 the section through A – A to show the method of jointing the small curved boss to the straight horizontal rail clearly indicating how the glass is held in position.

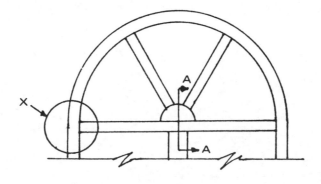

FIG. 1

See next page

4   The octagonal plan of a pyramid turret roof on an architect's drawing indicates the length of each side as 3500 and the rise 6000.

    (a)   To a scale of 1:50
        (i)   develop the true shape of the boarding for one side
        (ii) determine the backing angle of one of the hip rafters.
    (b)   Sketch the jointing arrangement of the rafters at the apex.

5   (a)   Sketch sufficient detail to indicate the method of construction of a one hour fire resistant internal door and frame.
    (b)   List the ironmongery for two such doors hung as a pair.

6   (a)   Sketch and describe a method of improving the sound resisting qualities of an existing solid concrete floor in a multi-storey block of flats.
    (b)   Define with illustrations the difference between air and structure borne sound.

7   (a)   Describe the meaning of the following terms in relation to a structural timber beam
        (i)   compression
        (ii)   tension
        (iii) neutral layer
        (iv) shear stress
        (v)   factor of safety.
    (b)   Determine the reactions for the simply supported beam in Fig. 2.

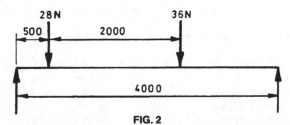

FIG. 2

8   (a)   List and describe briefly FIVE essential items of equipment required in a workshop producing structural laminated timber sections.
    (b)   Name an adhesive suitable for use in the construction of a laminated timber beam which is to be used in an exposed position
    (c)   List and give a brief explanation of FOUR factors that affect the bond between the timber laminates.

9   (a)   To which document would a carpenter refer for information on sizes and grades of timber for floor joists?
    (b)   Name TWO methods of stress grading.
    (c)   Describe ONE method of stress grading.
    (d)   Sketch a typical section through a timber dead shore and explain the reasons for its shape.

10   (a)   Suggest TWO possible structural defects which may give rise to wet rot in timber floor joists.
    (b)   Describe how to recognize wet rot.
    (c)   What remedial treatments can be made for timber subject to wet rot.
    (d)   Name TWO types of preservative which can be used on timber joists.
    (e)   Describe briefly the process of the 'full cell' method of timber impregnation.

CITY AND GUILDS OF LONDON INSTITUTE

PAPER NUMBER	EXAMINATION	
585—2—12	**CARPENTRY AND JOINERY** **ADVANCED CRAFT**	**Sample Paper** **1985 Onwards**
SERIES	PAPER	
	SITE PRACTICE	**14 00 — 17 00** **3 hours**

YOU SHOULD HAVE THE FOLLOWING FOR THIS EXAMINATION
one answer book
1 sheet A3 drawing paper
drawing instruments
drawing board and tee square
metric scale rule

SAMPLE QUESTIONS FOR EXAMINATIONS FROM MAY— JUNE 1985 ONWARDS

This question paper contains 8 structured questions (with a choice of 6 from 8) to be answered in 3 hours.

ALL questions carry equal marks.

1   The level and setting out of formwork to ground beams and column pads is to be checked prior to concreting.
   (a)   List the sequence of operations for setting up a quickset telescopic level ready to take the first reading.
   (b)   Using the following information state the correct staff readings for the top of the formwork.

        TBM   30.500
        Staff reading on TBM   1.250
        Top of ground beam formwork   29.150
        Top of column pad base formwork   28.950.

   (c)   Describe, with the aid of a sketch, how the setting out of the formwork may be checked.

2   Temporary shoring is required during the extensive alteration of a four-storey structurally defective building.
   (a)   Use labelled sketches to show an example of EACH of the following shore systems
      (i)   dead shores
      (ii)   multiple raking shores with rider.
   (b)   State in what circumstances EACH would normally be used.
   (c)   Describe the sequence of operations for the erection of ONE of the systems.
   (d)   List FIVE points to be included in the periodic safety check of erected shoring.

3   Describe, with the aid of sketches, how EACH of the following would be fixed.
   (a)   A newel post to a concrete ground floor.
   (b)   Hardwood strip flooring to concrete floor slab.
   (c)   Hardwood facings to concrete stair treads.
   (d)   Leg of portal frame to foundations.
   (e)   Slot screwing of hardwood skirtings to framed panelling.

4 (a) List FIVE general safety requirements of an on-site woodworking machine shop.

   (b) Sketch the correct position of the bridge guard to a surface planer, when surfacing and edging a piece of 50 mm x 150 mm timber in consecutive operations.

   (c) State ONE advantage and ONE disadvantage for EACH of the following types of power supply
      (i) mains electricity
      (ii) compressed air
      (iii) rechargeable batteries.

   (d) Name FOUR items of protective wear and state a situation requiring the use of EACH when operating either a woodworking machine or powered hand tool or both.

   (e) Sketch a jig that can be used with a portable router for forming recesses for butt hinges.

5 Fig. 1 shows the roof plan of a detached house which is to be constructed using trussed rafters.

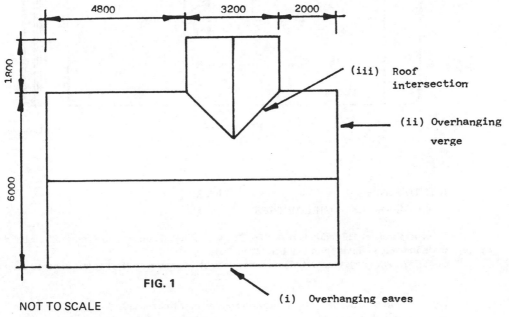

FIG. 1

NOT TO SCALE

ALL DIMENSIONS IN MILLIMETRES

   (a) Sketch the construction details at the
      (i) overhanging closed eaves
      (ii) overhanging verge
      (iii) intersection of the two roof surfaces.

   (b) State the purpose of a cross ventilated roof space.

   (c) Using brief notes and a sketch, show how the trussed rafters may be safely lifted into position with the aid of a crane.

   (d) Explain briefly how the completed roof is given lateral stability.

6   Fig. 2 shows an outline elevation and section of a standard timber frame panel which is to form
     part of a house extension.

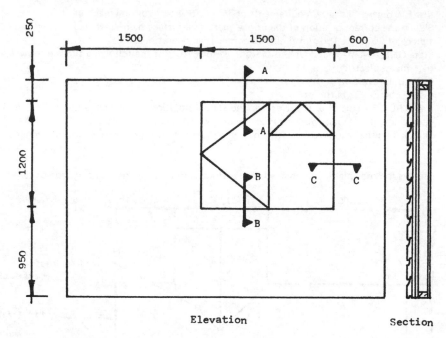

Elevation   Section

NOT TO SCALE   FIG. 2

ALL DIMENSIONS IN MILLIMETRES

(a) Draw to a scale of 1:5 sections A-A, B-B, C-C, indicating all construction and finishing details.
(b) State the precise function of any barriers indicated.
(c) State TWO advantages that a timber frame construction has over other forms of construction.

7   A large office is to be sub-divided by a hardwood glazed partition. Access through the partition is
     provided by a pair of double action doors.
(a) Sketch a suitable helical spring hinge.
(b) Explain how this hinge is adjusted for tension after fitting.
(c) Sketch a section through the door stile and the frame jamb.
(d) Describe, with the aid of a sketch, how the problem of fitting the frame to uneven wall and
     ceiling surfaces may be overcome.

8   (a) Sketch the following timber and plywood formwork arrangements
     (i)   a horizontal section through a form for a 450 mm square column with 25 mm radius corners
     (ii) a knockdown mould for pre-casting four 1500 mm long × 225 mm square lintels in one
           operation.
     (b) List FOUR points of safety concerning the use of release agents.
     (c) Define the term hydrostatic pressure and list THREE factors that affect its development.

CO890/574/2697. S15. © 1983. City and Guilds of London Institute.

Index